Celtic Theology

Celtic Theology

Humanity, World and God in Early Irish Writings

Thomas O'Loughlin

CONTINUUM

London and New York

Continuum
The Tower Building, 11 York Road, London SE1 7NX
370 Lexington Avenue, New York, NY 10017–6503

British Library Cataloguing-in-Publication Data
A catalogue record for this book is available from the British Library.

ISBN 0–8264–4870–4 (hardback)
    0–8264 4871–2 (paperback)

Library of Congress Cataloging-in-Publication Data
O'Loughlin, Thomas.
    Celtic theology: humanity, world, and God in early Irish writings /
    Thomas O'Loughlin.
        p. cm.
    Includes bibliographical references (p.) and index
    ISBN 0-8264-4870-4 (HB) — ISBN 0-8264-487-12 (PB)
        1. Celtic Church—Doctrines. 2. Ireland—Church history—600–1500.
    3. Christian Literature, Latin (Medieval and modern)—Ireland—History
    and criticism. I. Title.
    BR794.O46 2000
    274.15′02—dc21   00–027623

Typeset by YHT Ltd, London
Printed and bound in Great Britain by TJ International Ltd, Padstow, Cornwall

Contents

List of Illustrations

Preface

It is more than a decade since I began to lecture on the material in this book. Then it was to the occasional group of visitors, usually North American, to Ireland who wished to visit an ancient site like Glendalough or Clonmacnoise. At other times I found that I had a lecture 'in hand' in a course on patristics or medieval thought for philosophy or theology undergraduates, and I slipped into the vacant slot an item on Patrick or Eriugena to add the spice of local history. That was before the explosion of the interest in 'Celtic Christianity' when from being a backwater, the people and ideas that are explored here became objects of intense interest for a wide range of people. It is with those in mind who are interested in 'Celtic religion', the 'Celtic Church' and 'Celtic spirituality' that this book took shape. However, it is also my hope that this exploration of parts of the local theology of Ireland in the early Middle Ages will also interest those whose primary concern is history and who wish to be introduced to its religious dimension; and that those whose primary interest lies in theology might uncover a part their discipline's history.

Much of the material in the book first took shape while I taught in the Faculty of Theology in the Milltown Institute, Dublin. As a book it took shape as a M.Div. module for clergy on postgraduate studies in Nashotah House Episcopal Seminary in Wisconsin in 1997. To the students whom I taught in both places I own a debt for forcing me to clarify my thinking and to unravel knots. However, the most important influence on this book have been five successive generations of graduate students on the MA in Celtic Christianity in the University of Wales Lampeter. In the course of my annual text seminar – reading line-by-line the writings of Muirchú, Adomnán, and other texts that figure here – I was forced to develop my own understanding of them, helped at every turn by excellent – if at the time, uncomfortable – questions. I owe all those students a great debt of gratitude. Lampeter is one of the more pleasant universities in which to set about writing a book, and the presence of students engaging with the material of the book made it most pleasant indeed.

However, while one's students are stimulating, this book could not have been written without the help of many others. The generosity of scholars with their time never ceases to amaze me, especially today when one can pester one's friends for help so easily by e-mail. There are scholars/friends in Ireland, Wales, Scotland, England, the US, Canada, France, Germany and Italy who have chatted with me, answered detailed queries, or sent me offprints of their labours. I do not wish to single any out by name, as I would surely omit someone unjustly, but each will recognize my debt in the footnotes and bibliography.

The other group of helpers without whom we could not work are librarians. Here I have to mention names: in Dublin to Fergus O'Donoghue s.j. and Bríd O'Brien of the Jesuit Library in Milltown; to Tom Osterfield in the library of Nashotah House; Helen Davis in the Boole Library, University College Cork; and to the staff of the Main Library here in Lampeter, and especially to Kathy Miles of the Inter-Library Loan Department. They too know how indebted I am for their patient generosity.

Lastly, I want to thank my colleague here in Lampeter, Dr Jonathan Wooding – now Director of the MA in Celtic Christianity – for agreeing to read the completed type-script and for having saved me from more than one blunder. However, what errors and imperfections remain are upon my head. And that errors and false judgements do remain I am in no doubt; if you can offer me a correction it will be welcomed for as I finish this work I hear the words of Marcus Aurelius: 'if anyone shows how I am incorrect in my views, I shall happily change them – for my quest is for truth which has never harmed anyone'.

Lampeter
Centre for the Study of Religion in Celtic Societies
1 January 2000

Abbreviations

BIBLICAL MATERIALS

Gen	Genesis
Ex	Exodus
Lev	Leviticus
Num	Numbers
Dt	Deuteronomy
Jos	Joshua
Jds	Judges
Ruth	Ruth
1 Sam	1 Samuel (*I Regum*)
2 Sam	2 Samuel (*II Regum*)
1 Kgs	1 Kings (*III Regum*)
2 Kgs	2 Kings (*IV Regum*)
1 Chr	1 Chronicles (*I Paralipomenon*)
2 Chr	2 Chronicles (*II Paralipomenon*)
Ezra	Ezra (*I Esdras*)
Neh	Nehemiah (*II Esdras*)
1 Esd	1 Esdras (*III Esdras*)
2 Esd	2 Esdras (*IV Esdras*)
Tob	Tobit
Jth	Judith
Est	Esther
Job	Job
Ps	Psalms
Prov	Proverbs
Qo	Qoheleth (*Ecclesiastes*)
Song	Song of Solomon (*Canticum canticorum*)
Wis	Wisdom of Solomon (*Sapientia*)
Sir	Wisdom of Sirach (*Ecclesiasticus*)
Is	Isaiah
Jer	Jeremiah
Lam	Lamentations
Bar	Baruch
Ez	Ezekiel
Dan	Daniel

Hos	Hosea
Joel	Joel
Amos	Amos
Obad	Obadiah
Jon	Jonah
Mic	Micah
Nah	Nahum
Zeph	Zephaniah
Hag	Haggai
Zech	Zechariah
Mal	Malachi
1 Mac	1 Maccabees
2 Mac	2 Maccabees
3 Mac	3 Maccabees
4 Mac	4 Maccabees
OrMan	Prayer of Manasseh
Mt	Matthew
Mk	Mark
Lk	Luke
Jn	John
Acts	Acts of the Apostles
Rom	Romans
1 Cor	1 Corinthians
2 Cor	2 Corinthians
Gal	Galatians
Eph	Ephesians
Phil	Philippians
Col	Colossians
1 Thess	1 Thessalonians
2 Thess	2 Thessalonians
1 Tim	1 Timothy
2 Tim	2 Timothy
Tit	Titus
Philem	Philemon
Heb	Hebrews
Jas	James
1 Pet	1 Peter
2 Pet	2 Peter
1 Jn	1 John
2 Jn	2 John
3 Jn	3 John
Jude	Jude
Apoc	Apocalypse (Revelation of John the Divine)

ABBREVIATIONS FOR WORKS OF REFERENCE AND JOURNALS

AB	*Anchor Bible*
ABD	*Anchor Bible Dictionary* (D. N. Freedman *et al.* (eds)) (New York 1992)
ABR	*American Benedictine Review*
ACW	*Ancient Christian Writers*
AM	*Annuale Medievale*
AnB	*Analecta Bollandiana*
AS	*Augustinian Studies*
ASE	*Anglo-Saxon England*
BZAW	*Beihefte zur Zeitschrift für alttestamentliche Wissenschaft*
CBQ	*Catholic Biblical Quarterly*
CCHS	*Catholic Commentary on Holy Scripture* (B. Orchard, E. F. Sutcliffe, R. C. Fuller and R. Russell (eds)) (London 1953)
CCSL	*Corpus Christianorum (Series Latina)*
CD	*Ciudad de Dios*
CH	*Church History*
CMCS	*Cambridge Medieval Celtic Studies* (later *Cambrian Medieval Celtic Studies*)
CPL	*Clauis Patrum Latinorum* (A. Gaar and E. Dekkers (eds), 3rd edn) (Steenbrugge 1995)
CQ	*Classical Quarterly*
CS	*Cistercian Studies*
CSEL	*Corpus Scriptorum Ecclesiasticorum Latinorum*
D&L	*Doctrine and Life*
DHGE	*Dictionnaire d'Histoire et de Géographique Ecclésiastiques*
DMA	*Dictionary of the Middle Ages* (New York 1988)
DTC	*Dictionnaire de Théologie Catholique*
EEC	A. Di Berardino (ed.) with amendments by W. H. C. Frend, *Encyclopaedia of the Early Church* (ET: A. Walford, 2 vols, Cambridge 1992) (*Dizionario Patristico e di Antichità Cristiane*)
ERE	*Encyclopaedia of Religion and Ethics*
ET	English translation
FC	*Fathers of the Church*
H&S	A. W. Haddan and W. Stubbs, *Councils and Ecclesiastical Documents relating to Great Britain and Ireland*, 3 vols (Oxford 1869–78)
HBS	*Henry Bradshaw Society*
HDB	*Dictionary of the Bible* (J. Hastings (ed.)) (Edinburgh 1898–1908)
HTR	*Harvard Theological Review*
Hughes	K. Hughes, *The Church in Early Irish Society* (London 1966)
IDB	*Interpreter's Dictionary of the Bible* (Nashville (vols 1–4) 1962; and (supplementary volume) 1976)
IHS	*Irish Historical Studies*

IPJ	*Irish Philosophical Journal*
IR	*Innes Review*
ISR	*Irish Studies Review*
ITQ	*Irish Theological Quarterly*
ITS	*Irish Texts Society*
JAAR	*Journal of American Academy of Religion*
JBC	*Jerome Biblical Commentary* (R. E. Brown, J. A. Fitzmyer and R. E. Murphy) (Englewood Cliffs, NJ, 1968)
JBL	*Journal of Biblical Literature*
JCKAS	*Journal of the County Kildare Archaeological Society*
JE	*Jewish Encyclopaedia* (London 1901)
JEH	*Journal of Ecclesiastical History*
JL	*Jahrbuch für Liturgiewissenschaft*
JML	*Journal of Medieval Latin*
JQR	*Jewish Quarterly Review*
JRS	*Journal of Roman Studies*
JRSAI	*Journal of the Royal Society of Antiquaries of Ireland*
JTS	*Journal of Theological Studies*
JWAG	*Journal of the Walters Art Gallery*
Kenney	J. F. Kenney, *The Sources for the Early History of Ireland: Ecclesiastical: An Introduction and Guide* (New York 1929; and (with addenda by L. Bieler) New York 1966)
KVS	H. J. Frede, *Kirchenschriftsteller: Verzeichnis und Sigel (Vetus Latina: Die Reste der Altlateinischen Bibel 1/1)* (Freiburg 1995)
L&S	M. Lapidge and R. Sharpe, *A Bibliography of Celtic-Latin Literature 400–1200* (Dublin 1985)
LS	*Louvain Studies*
M&H	*Mediaevalia et Humanistica*
MA	*Medium Aevum*
MedS	*Mediaeval Studies*
MonS	*Monastic Studies*
MS	*Milltown Studies*
NB	*New Blackfriars*
NCCHS	*New Catholic Commentary on Holy Scripture* (R. C. Fuller, L. Johnston and C. Kearns (eds)) (London 1969, revised edn 1975)
NCE	*New Catholic Encyclopaedia* (New York 1967)
NJBC	*New Jerome Biblical Commentary* (R. E. Brown, J. A. Fitzmyer and R. E. Murphy) (London 1989)
NPNF	*Nicene and Post-Nicene Fathers*
NS	*The New Scholasticism*
ODCC	*Oxford Dictionary of the Christian Church*
PG	*Patrologia Graeca*
PHCC	*Proceedings of the Harvard Celtic Colloquium*
PIBA	*Proceedings of the Irish Biblical Association*
PL	*Patrologia Latina*
PLS	*Patrologia Latina, Supplementum*
PMLA	*Proceedings of the Modern Language Association*

PRIA	*Proceedings of the Royal Irish Academy*
RA	*Recherches Augustiniennes*
RB	*Revue Bénédictine*
RBib	*Revue Biblique*
RÉA	*Revue des Études Augustiniennes*
RÉL	*Revue des Études Latines*
RLR	*Religious Life Review*
RMA	*Revue du Moyen Age*
RSR	*Revue des Sciences Religieuses*
RTAM	*Recherches de Théologie Ancienne et Médiévale*
RTPM	*Recherches de Théologie et Philosophie Médiévale*
SA	*Seanchas Ardmhacha*
SBET	*Scottish Bulletin of Evangelical Theology*
SC	*Sources Chrétiennes*
SGM	*Scottish Geographical Magazine*
SE	*Sacris Erudiri*
SG	*Studi Gregoriani*
SH	*Studia Hibernica*
SHR	*Scottish Historical Review*
SLH	*Scriptores Latini Hiberniae*
SM	*Studi Medievali*
SP	*Studia Patristica*
StC	*Studia Celtica*
TFT	*Tijdschrift voor filosofie en theologie*
TRSC	*Transactions of the Royal Society of Canada*
TS	*Theological Studies*
TU	*Texte und Untersuchungen*
VC	*Vigiliae Christianae*
VT	*Vetus Testamentum*
ZCP	*Zeitschrift für Celtische Philologie*
ZNW	*Zeitschrift für die neutestamentliche Wissenschaft und die Kunde der Älteren Kirche*
ZSSR	*Zeitschrift der Savigny-Stiftung für Rechtsgeschichte*

In memory of
Maurice and Leonard
*. . . qui ad iustitiam erudiunt multos quasi stellae in perpetuas
aeternitates* (Dan 12:3)

1 Celtic Theology?

CURRENT INTERESTS

A remarkable recent development in Christianity in the English-speaking world has been the growth in interest in everything religious with the qualifier 'Celtic'. It has affected individuals and small groups, it has altered the way parishes have viewed liturgy, it has created a handful of best-sellers – although such books are as often on the 'self-help' as the 'religion' shelves in bookshops.

In this flurry of activity with wild claims being made for the 'Celtic Church' on the one hand, and equally excessive assertions that this is a modern myth, the kernel of truth in the whole discussion is liable to be forgotten entirely. First of all, the Christians of early medieval Ireland were conscious that they received Christianity from the British Christians, British Christians were conscious of their links with the Church in Brittany, while the Irish were conscious that they brought Christianity to the inhabitants of present-day Scotland, and throughout the early medieval period there were exchanges of ideas, books and people between the different peoples and languages of the islands of Britain and Ireland. As such, we should expect a regional flavour to their religion as we expect of Christianity in other regions. Whether we call it 'Celtic Christianity' or 'Christianity in Celtic lands' or 'insular Christianity' will largely be a matter of emphasis, but that the Christian religion took on certain features in its praxis and theology is not in doubt. More importantly for this book is that those Christians produced a sizeable body of theological literature, and this deserves to be studied in its own right as a particular intellectual expression of the inhabitants of these islands. It is an aspect of their intellectual history that deserves attention, but which is not a high priority for attention by many who are engaged in Celtic studies. Equally, those who are interested in the evolution of western Christian theology need to pay closer attention to the theological products of the insular region, for they are fully a cog in the intellectual history of the western church. While the islands may lie off the north-west coast of Europe, peripheral geographically, several of their innovations entered the mainstream of Latin theology. It has been the desire to isolate the kernel of truth within the contemporary Celtic euphoria that gave me the incentive to begin this book, but it was the desire to show the depth of theological reflection in many well-known texts from the first millennium, and how the ideas first found in those documents became accepted commonplaces in whole of the Latin church, that has been my guiding ambition. This is not a book about 'the genius of the Celts' nor a book on the nature of the church or its history in the early Middle Ages in these islands; rather, it wishes to examine some significant theological products of one of those societies, those from Ireland, and present them as part of the tapestry of medieval theology.

Meanwhile 'Celtic' has been working its magic in the larger environment. One has only to glance at 'alternative' bookshops to see that 'Celtic' is big. The words 'druid' and 'pre-Christian' from being words of opprobrium conveying a sense of darkness to Christians, and foul superstition to rationalists, are being used as positive endorsements. 'The wisdom of the druids' seems to cover everything from soil management and meteorology to childcare and psychotherapy. In matters religious there has been, on the one hand, a revival of 'Pagan' as a designation many wish to give themselves; while on the other, many who wish to avoid any religious label seek works belonging to the ill-defined category of 'the new age'. One theme common to all these, and to many of the recent developments among those invoking the name 'Christian', has been their desire 'to rediscover', 'to revive' or 'to re-live' the Celtic 'religious experience'. This blurring of the boundaries between 'new age travellers' and 'Celtic Christianity' bothers many Christians and they seek – often desperately – clear blue water between them. But for others such overlaps are evidence of basic religious instincts that Christianity must take into account. Such debates will continue as long as the present interest, but in the meanwhile each year sees another bumper crops of popular books, Christian, new age or whatever, pro or anti, in the intersection of the sets 'religion' and 'Celtic'.

This popular interest is recent, but the study of the religion of the people of the islands of Britain and Ireland, and of those parts of the continent which spoke Celtic languages, is far from new. Already in the seventeenth century the exiled Irish Franciscans in St Anthony's College in Louvain were busy gathering, preserving and publishing as much material as they could lay their hands on about Ireland, its people, history and religion from the period before 1600. At roughly the same time in Ireland itself, Archbishop James Ussher (1581–1656) was gathering and publishing other materials. His *Britannicarum Ecclesiarum Antiquitates* of 1639, while not using the words 'Celtic Church', can be seen as putting the concept into circulation that in the early medieval period there were distinct churches in these islands, distinct from one another and from Rome.

We sometimes unjustly dismiss these labourers as we know they 'had an agenda' – and in the case of Ussher since he has become the butt of jokes about 'creation in 4004 BC'. It is true that, for the most part, both Catholics and Protestants had a mixture of religious and political motives in their choice of work. The Franciscans saw it as much their duty to preserve the cultural legacy of Gaelic Ireland as to engage in post-Reformation apologetics, while Protestant investigators saw a link between being non-Roman and pro-English: if the country were anciently Protestant then it would seek the English Crown as the defender of that faith against popery. These motives, however, did not undermine the quality of their scholarship, and much of what we know today is built upon their work. Indeed, one of the touching details about these rival groups is that despite their many-layered differences they often communicated with each other, and even more frequently respected each other's scholarly judgement.

Gallarus Oratory, Dingle Peninsula, Co. Kerry. This chapel, shaped like an upturned boat has acted over the centuries as a reminder of earlier Christian times, and still provokes questions about the Christianty of those who built them.

That interest begun in the heat of political and religious revolutions has continued steadily to this day. New disciplines added to the range of materials to hand, while developments in scholarly method transformed our understanding of the past and made earlier researches look naïve and primitive. Today, the resources of historians of various kinds, linguists, theologians and archaeologists are brought to the evidence; in turn these rely on the more specialist disciplines from palaeography (the study of manuscripts) to dendrochronology (dating wooden fragments on the basis of patterns of tree-ring growth); and their results are scrutinized by a large, worldwide academic audience which seeks to relate these specialist studies of early Christian Ireland or Anglo-Saxon England or medieval Wales to a larger picture of European history. However, between the group of scholars who have made Celtic Studies a respected university-driven branch of learning and the large, but more amorphous, body of people interested in 'Celtic Christianity' there is relatively little contact, and often – from both sides – more than a little loathing.

DIVERSE DEMANDS

The piece of wisdom, attributed to Jesus, 'No one can serve two masters; for either he will hate the one and love the other, or he will be devoted to the one and despise the other'[1] stands as a warning to anyone who thinks he or she can interpret one discipline to another, or scholarship to a wider audience – and it is equally a warning to the reader. However, if that warning prevents the attempt to build bridges between different groups with common areas of interest – allowing that they may not have common interests – then human dialogue is doomed. So the warning noted, it is as well to identify the groups involved and their expectations.

The 'Celtic Christians'

The first group, simply by reasons of numbers, are those interested in 'Celtic Christianity' today as a living force inspiring their religious quest. For many historians these are a group to be 'taken out' for the reason that what many 'Celtic Christians' believe was the 'ancient Celtic way' is about as authentic as the material which passes under the name of the 'prayers of Chief Seattle'. Certainly, there is a great deal of imaginary history, pious frauds and just plain bunkum in many of the books and on many courses and retreats that invoke the word 'Celtic'. Just recently a devotee told me – and it was his belief – that 'the Celtic Church was non-authoritarian, non-Roman, evangelical and capable of listening to the rhythms of nature and women'. The list is interesting as its shows the qualities that that person desires within Christianity today – and presumably does not find in many of its contemporary expressions, but at the same time it is almost wholly without any historical justification within the various expressions of Christianity in these islands between the fifth and twelfth centuries. However, it is not the business of the historian to 'take out' someone's religious search and declare it void. It is a fact that this interest is helping many people to discover the Christian message in a new way, it is helping them make sense of the religious landscape in a time when there are no great publicly acclaimed spiritual landmarks, and it is helping very many people to pray.

---

1. Mt 6:24.

Given that fact, anyone who wishes to criticize should do so gently as it is a wise principle in spirituality to 'pray as you can, not as you can't'. Indeed, movements which help people make sense of their lives must be treated according to the maxim 'For he that is not against us is for us.'[2] As someone who believes that humans need rituals in their lives, and that we have a profound need for liturgical drama in times of crisis and transition, I am struck by the way 'Celtic Christianity' has given many people a vehicle to experience liturgy. For some it is attractive because liturgical drama was not part of their religious tradition which focused on the spoken and written word to the exclusion of the other senses as 'Romish' or 'superstitious'. For others its attractiveness lies in a vibrancy not associated with tired formulae in liturgical traditions such as Anglicanism and Catholicism where the dramatic and sensual elements are often reduced to tokens. This current interest is touching genuine religious veins among its followers, and it is worth noting that when a historian goes on the warpath against such religious phenomena he or she does so as a believer or non-believer, and not as a historian *per se*.

But why should contemporary Christians look to these ancient materials which are only accessible through the skills of historians? The answer appears to lie in the nature of Christianity itself. As a religion it sees its basis as a series of events that happened in the past, the 'history of salvation' leading up to the 'Christ-event' which forms the basis of its present, and it must continually recall that past through reading of it (e.g. the gospels) and seeking to remember it through actions such as the Eucharist.[3] This link to the past has had, at least since the late second century and the writings of Irenaeus of Lyons, another significance for Christians: the past is the authenticator of the present. If something has a long history, or can be presented as having a long history, then somehow its value and right to exist within Christianity today is validated. This desire for the past to justify the present needs and desires of Christians takes many forms. After the Reformation both sides sought to justify their positions by appealing to antiquity upon the principle that 'if they were what we are, then we are in the right'. One of Archbishop Ussher's first books (1623) was *A Discourse of the Religion anciently professed by the Irish* which sought to show that his own theology and that of St Patrick were to all intents the same. In a similar vein in the 1860s the flagship of Irish Catholic scholarship, the *Irish Ecclesiastical Record*, had as its motto *Ut Christiani, ita Romani sitis*

---

2. Mk 9:40.
3. Christian groups have fought wars over the exact force of 'remember', but all agree they must do it *now* because they were told *back then* to 'Do this in remembrance of me' (Lk 22:19).

on the basis that it showed St Patrick and themselves as in continuity.[4] Still today many practices are justified, or changes rejected, on the basis of 'ancient practice' and this seems to be an appeal that many expect can resolve disputes without further ado.

Whether or not Christians of whatever variety should or must refer to the past to authenticate their praxis in new situations is a crucial question that faces systematic theologians today – for instance, it is at the heart of the question about ordaining women priests – but it is not my question. The fact is that humans look to the past for identity, roots and a sense of belonging. Christians too wish to belong, but also wish to draw inspiration from the past, and they wish to declare that their approaches and activities are in keeping with the tradition of those who have handed on the faith of Christ. In this quest they have need of the historian and the skills that he or she can bring to the sources upon which they want to draw. Historians are often aggrieved that their work is being put to use by Christians in their search for faith. For the most part historians do not see their work as aimed at providing materials for contemporary Christian practice, and they feel ill-used when questioned about 'Celtic Christianity'; but we, as historians, might console ourselves with the thought that without such living religious interest our discipline would be so much the poorer – we have only to think of the work of the Bollandists and the Maurists.[5] And while historians must point out to believers that history and theology are distinct disciplines,[6] the historian should recognize the fact that, in Marc Bloch's phrase, 'Christianity is a religion of historians'.[7] Equally the believers must respect the work of historians and recognize that it is not the historian's task to make it either attractive or palatable – those who falsify the past deserve to be scorned by all sides – and they should remember the words of Mabillon on the duty of historians:

> If he is honest . . . he must present as certain, things certain; as false, things false; and as doubtful, things doubtful; he must not seek to hide facts that tell for or against either party to an issue. Piety and truth

---

4. This was one of the sayings attributed to Patrick in the Book of Armagh; cf. A. Gwynn, 'The Problem of the *Dicta Patricii*', *SA* 8 (1975–7), 69–80.
5. Cf. M. D. Knowles, *Great Historical Enterprises* (London 1963), chs 1 and 2.
6. Many may wish to take the position of E. H. Carr that they are mutually exclusive: history deals with 'human achievement' not 'divine purpose' which is the realm of theology (*What is History?* (Harmondsworth 1964), pp. 124–5); but whether such clear-cut distinctions can actually be made is an empirical (in Carr's terms, an historical) question that does not admit a clear answer.
7. *The Historian's Craft* (ET: P. Putnam, Manchester, rept 1992), p. 4:

> Christianity is a religion of historians. Other religious systems have been able to found their beliefs and their rites on a mythology nearly outside human time. For sacred books, the Christians have books of history, and their liturgies commemorate, together with episodes from the terrestrial life of a God, the annals of the church and the lives of the saints.

must never be considered as separable, for honest and genuine piety will never come into conflict with truth.[8]

Theologians

Another group who look at the Christianity lived, and the theology written, in these islands in the first millennium are theologians. The nature of some of their sources (the scriptures, conciliar decisions, the works of long-dead writers) and the fact that they deal with ideas and practices that emerged over time mean that theologians have to keep company with historians. But apart from clarifying and contextualizing their sources, theologians use the work of historians in other ways. The most interesting use was described by Karl Rahner as 'the church is always forgetting and always remembering'. The community's past is like a storehouse of precedents and examples of how things could be otherwise. While earlier generations saw the evolution of the church's structures and the development of its teachings as the unfolding manifestation of Providence, many today wish to glory in the accidental: it went this way, but could have gone in any number of other ways. History can illumine the period before one solution or one approach won the field. History can explain the way that institutions grew, the factors that determined their form, and in a curious way reveal to the theologian whether there is an underlying edifice or whether the building is only an excuse for the scaffolding. But this relationship with history should not obscure the difference in disciplines between the historian and the theologian. The theologian wishes to construct a world, to some extent an ideal one, in the present some of whose elements will be of venerable antiquity; the historian wishes to reconstruct a world that is past, and to some extent alien, but which attracts his or her curiosity. This distinction may seem no more than a binary 'not this, but that', but this difference in temporal perspectives is central – when it is blurred we move from history to propaganda: 'morality teaching by example', the fixed processes of Hegelianism or the 'unfolding of God's purposes'. When the historian rejects philosophies of history he or she is left with a sequence of events which cannot be reduced to some grand metaphysical plan – it could all have been different; the same situation confronting the theologian should be seen as one more example of the autonomy and contingency of the created order. Where theologians and historians come together is that they both have to accept what has actually happened as a given, and as the starting point for their reflections.

A more recent use of history, and one more directly relevant to this

---

8. Cited in M. D. Knowles, 'Jean Mabillon', *JEH* 10 (1959), 169 (punctuation slightly altered).

book, has been the growing awareness of how theology is tied to culture/place/time/society. For centuries theology gloried in the notion that it was a universal discourse that affected all peoples and times similarly and that while there was growth, this was the growth of a single unitary body. This body of knowledge was imagined as being unchanging, and alteration was merely growth in detail and explication. This view was often expressed with what was called the 'Vincentian Canon' – that true doctrine was that which was accepted 'by everyone, everywhere, always'[9] – or more picturesquely by a teacher who concluded a class on the doctrine of the Trinity with words to this effect: 'If there is intelligent life on some distant planet, they will accept all of this as the truth!' Having long accepted the difference between western and other Christian theologies, we now take for granted that in every human society there will be variations in the way that Christianity will be made part of the life of that society, and in turn expect that those who write and teach theology will not only have the similarities that every group of scholars have who share a particular culture, but will reflect or react to the values and conditions of their surroundings. This diversity had been given many names such as 'culture sensitive theology' or 'inculturated theology' by those in favour of the process, and less favourable names by those who see it as selling the Christian message, with its intrinsic ecumenism (*oikoumene* as equivalent to 'whole world'), short. I prefer the neutral term of 'local theology' and I take it as a fact that, like it or not, local theologies have existed and do exist today. We might think of local theologies in terms of the call today that an African theology should not be identical to a European, a third-world theology should be distinct in its agenda from that of the rich north; but it is a far more diffuse phenomenon. Wherever there is a group of Christians (ordinary believers, their pastors, some teachers) with a shared language, culture, and social and economic conditions, then a local theology will develop. It will have a shared agenda of questions, shared books and assumptions that are seen as setting the parameters of argument, and a shared style which is the product of their mutual interaction. My favourite example of such a local theology is that which emerged in southern Gaul in the mid-fifth century, centred on Lérins – Eucherius, Cassian, Gennadius, Vincent – whose urbanity and confidence seem to give their works a warm glow, and which sets them unmistakably apart from the North African theology of Augustine.[10] Equally today if one takes down two comparable

---

9. Vincent of Lérins, *Commonitorium* II, 5 (*CCSL* 64, p. 149); cf. my 'Newman, Vincent of Lérins and Development', *ITQ* 58 (1991), 147–66.
10. See H. G. J. Beck, *The Pastoral Care of Souls in South-East France During the Sixth Century* (Rome 1950); and my 'The Symbol Gives Life: Eucherius of Lyons' Formula for Exegesis', in T. Finan and V. Twomey (eds), *Scriptural Interpretation in the Fathers: Letter and Spirit* (Dublin 1995).

theological journals from neighbouring countries and looks at the range of articles over a period, one cannot but notice that there are different drumbeats. Local theologies reflect particular communities' interests, but do not break the world up into isolated cantons, for there is a constant trading of ideas and personnel within Christianity.[11] Examples of such contacts abound: post-war German theology was a major influence on the development of Liberation Theology in South America; books written in America are textbooks in Ireland; Augustine was being read (and quietly corrected) by the Lérins' theologians; the French School of spirituality read the Spanish mystics; and, in the past, language was even less a barrier to sharing ideas. But still the shifts in focus, however subtle, are unmistakable – indeed even in the heyday of rejecting theological variations in the Catholic Church at the beginning of the twentieth century, the Irish priest-novelist Canon Sheehan was able in *Luke Delmege* to appreciate that there was a far greater balance and humanity in the Latin manuals of the French theologians than in the more rigorous works of the Spanish authors from Salamanca. I shall argue that in early Christian Ireland we should expect to find just such a local theology, and that detecting such local variations in a theme is the work of the historian. If theology today wishes to celebrate such local theologies, be it Welsh or Scottish or whatever, then there will be an inevitable, and justifiable, interest in earlier theologies of the same place – and this is a quest where the theologian must call on the historian.

There is one other area where the theologian needs to call on the historian of insular ideas to help fill out the general picture with precision. The insular world (Britain and Ireland in the first millennium) made many distinctive contributions to the life of Latin Christianity as a whole, most particularly in the area of penitential practice and in the systematization of canon law.[12] However, often the material is presented in ways that do not suggest to theologians that there is much material there for them.[13] This means that even specialists in medieval theology feel on uncertain ground when they study 'Celtic material' as if it stood off from 'Frankish material' or 'north-Italian material' in a special category, and then basic blunders occur on the assumption that it is exotic and peripheral. A striking example of theologians and insular historians living in isolation is to be found in Cardinal Stickler's recent defence of clerical celibacy:

---

11. The wide fissures between various groups in the aftermath of the sixteenth-century Reformation are exceptional – and even in this case there were often more cross-denominational influences than were popularly acknowledged.
12. See chapters 3 and 6.
13. For example, several of the texts edited in the series *Scriptores Latini Hiberniae* are clearly the work of scholars whose primary interest is the texts as Irish cultural documents or witnesses to medieval Latin, and who did not interact with the texts as products of theologians or present an *apparatus* which would show their authors as working theologians.

> Of striking significance for a complete understanding of the discipline of celibacy in medieval Europe are the relevant regulations of the Celtic Churches. The Penitential Books, which faithfully reflected the actual life and discipline practised in these particular Churches, asserted the same obligation to continence . . . That these serious obligations were insisted upon and substantially observed in the Celtic Churches, of whose rude customs we find a lively witness in the Penitential Books, is the best proof that celibacy was founded on an old and venerable tradition which no one doubted.[14]

Leaving aside the issue being pleaded, this shows how wide the gulf can be between someone highly skilled in the use of medieval theological sources in general and someone particularly familiar with insular materials. That any particular customs are 'rude' is a matter of taste, but that the penitentials should be seen as somehow 'apart' from the development of western Christian praxis is perverse. Stickler's argument turns on the notion that even 'out there' the practice of celibacy was recognized, therefore it must be a basic issue. In reality, the insular evidence has no value beyond being one more instance of Latin practice, for there was a constant two-way traffic between the islands and the continent. If these penitentials were 'rude', exotic, an isolated spur from the main lines of western development, then how does one explain their subsequent role in bringing about on the continent the changes that eventually led to the 'sacrament of penance'. Regrettably many studies of theology by Celticists fail to locate Latin Christian material from these islands within its larger world; while, in return, many theologians assume it to be quaint and quirky, and so really only of antiquarian interest.

The Historians

What we know of the Christianity of the early medieval period in Britain and Ireland is in large part due to the work of historians whose primary interest was society in general and whose involvement with religious materials was an accidental consequence of the fact that most of our sources for the period can be termed 'ecclesiastical'.[15] However, historians whose primary concern is

---

14. *The Case for Clerical Celibacy* (San Francisco 1995), p. 42; it should be noted that Stickler understands 'Celtic Church' not as a distinct church as one might speak of the Eastern Church as distinct from the Roman Church, but in terms of 'particular churches' and the 'universal church' as these terms are used in modern Roman Catholic canon law – in this usage, here used anachronistically, a particular church is a subsection of the universal church which could be as small as a diocese or as large as a region whose bishops meet together in synods.

15. We see this in the use made of J. F. Kenney's book *The Sources for the Early History of Ireland* (New York 1929) in all work on the period. What every historian has on his or her shelf is the first volume ('ecclesiastical sources') of what was projected as a two-volume work where the second volume was never completed; the fact that so much use is made of the existing volume shows the extent to which 'the sources' and 'the ecclesiastical sources' are coextensive.

political or social history, cannot devote equal care to the history of religious ideas. A good example is the *Vita Patricii* by Muirchú.[16] This has been intensively studied for the incidental information it contains about the geopolitics of the later seventh century, and especially the light it throws on the role of Armagh as a religious centre within the Uí Néill lands. This is valuable work for everyone interested in the text as it established the socio-political context and thus prevents us reading it anhistorically. But Muirchú's book is also a witness to that society's understanding of the theology of conversion and their view of the relationship between 'revealed' and 'natural' truth, and it shows its author as having a distinctive theological voice through his view of liturgy and dramatic theology. These issues cannot be the concern of the political or social historian, but cannot be ignored if we are to have, in Marc Bloch's phrase, a view of 'the mentality' of the time. To fill out his or her picture of early historical societies in the Celtic lands, the historian needs the historian of theology.[17]

It might be added that this need for the historian of theology is equally great if the older category of 'ecclesiastical historian' is used.[18] That group, in their focus on church structures and bishops, monasteries and the like, have traditionally ignored the theological content of the documents, unless they perceived it as somehow deviant. Thus they created an image of 'an island of saints and scholars', but they produced little information on what those scholars studied.[19] This avoidance of the content of theology can be seen in much of the writing of a previous generation of 'church historians' whose books are sometimes still cited. It is a view that there is a gulf between history (changing matters of human concern affected by times and places) and theology (a revelation of divine truths immune to change). In this view, orthodox theology has no history, but heresy, as it is the admixture of the human, has. Thus there can be a history of heresy, but none of 'genuine' theology; and if the historian cannot find any formal heresy (e.g. that favourite culprit 'Pelagianism'), then earlier writers must all have been orthodox, and in that case their theology was roughly the same as what one could find in a

---

16. See chapter 5.
17. See my 'The Latin Sources of Medieval Irish Culture', in K. McCone and K. Simms (eds), *Progress in Medieval Irish Studies* (Maynooth 1996).
18. See my 'Medieval Church History: Beyond apologetics, after development, the awkward memories', *The Way* 38 (1998), 65–76.
19. The pathetic structure of so many lectures on these topics has taken this format: a bald statement of an exotic and extreme holiness linked to great wisdom and learning of the early Irish church; then a presentation of slides of early Irish art in the form of gospel-book illumination and ecclesiastical metalwork – faced with such aesthetic wonders the audience were expected to subscribe to the thesis. It is an intellectual scandal that such sleights of hand have even been perpetrated at conferences organized by theologians: these aesthetic wonders prove their skill in art, not theology!

contemporary manual or catechism. This may seem an extreme presentation but it should be remembered that among non-Catholics this is a view of theology that was first questioned in English in the 1840s, and was still prevalent among Catholics until a generation ago. Moreover, some of the bad habits of the older approach are still with us: only recently at a conference I heard a paper which examined the notions of a *post mortem* otherworld in a poem in Old Irish; the curious factor was that the definitions against which the poem's ideas were assessed were taken from a nearly contemporary Catholic catechism. In such situations the dialogue between other early medievalists and historians of theology is not based on supplying another aspect of a complex reality, but in providing basic directions.

A SERIES OF TRENCHES

A complex dialogue is what is desirable between the many groups who are interested in the whole question of early Celtic society, but this cannot be initiated here. This book's aim is more modest: to alert the various groups to the existence of the others and to show, here and there, the benefits of collaborating in the enterprise of history. Because of this aim of dialogue between different interests it will not attempt to be a synopsis of 'what they thought about in theology', but rather a series of studies which attempt to bring out their theological thinking in a historical context. In the terminology of archaeologists this book is a series of trial trenches, small-scale excavations scattered over the field of study to show the extent of what is there. It does not attempt to cover the whole field, nor to provide a plan of the site. So what were the criteria by which the selection of particular trenches was made?

A feature of many books written on 'Celtic Christianity' has been the 'pick-and-mix' approach. One picks items from here and there, spatially, temporally and linguistically with the effect that one can find virtually anything one wants. So a seventh-century Latin text from Ireland is combined with a ninth-century monastic text in Irish, and then a piece from twelfth-century Scotland is added, and the whole rounded-off by a bit of *Carmina Gadelica* or some modern Irish folklore. This nonchalance with chronology and blithe dismissal of differences in culture and genre is wholly unacceptable. It is not only unacceptable in terms of historical method, but also culturally: it is based on a notion that the people out on the Atlantic fringe are unlike the more sophisticated, fast-witted and fast-moving people at the centre. Out at the edges, people do not change, think creatively, or engage in serious dialogue with intellectual forces! Yet, if one used a similar pick-and-mix approach for the United Kingdom or the continent for a period of just two centuries from 1700–1900, everyone would point out its silliness. To take the theology produced by the

Celtic-speaking peoples in the first millennium seriously, that random cherry-picking must be avoided, and – given the paucity of sources – we must proceed by (1) taking examples where we can define the chronological parameters with care (the longer the time-span dealt with in any trench the greater the likelihood of nonsense); (2) seeking to define the culture as closely as possible; and (3) determining the theological level and genre of each textual witness used.

The Parameter of Place and Culture

In order that the individual trenches can all be seen to be explorations of a single site, I have confined myself in the following ways. First, there are two major families of the Celtic languages designated as 'P' (represented by modern Welsh) and 'Q' (represented by modern Irish) since, when drawing on common roots, each language characteristically uses one of these sounds rather than the other. For example, the word for 'head' in a place-name will be *pen-* in Welsh (e.g. Penarth), but *cenn-*, a 'q' sound, in Irish (e.g. Kenmare). Moreover, we know that these two forms of Celtic were not mutually intelligible in the historical period. So in the early Middle Ages, whatever of Pan-Celtic consciousness today, the two societies of Ireland and Wales saw themselves as distinct. Thus, when we wish to select examples to illustrate their religious sense, we should pick either Irish material (and related materials from the area now called Scotland where a dialect of Irish was used) or Welsh material (and other P-Celtic-speaking societies such as Cornwall and Brittany), but they should not be combined willy-nilly.[20] At the same time, we must remember that Ireland saw itself as having received Christianity from the British (i.e. the Welsh) and there was much interchange of ideas and people; however, given that this book is a history not of churches as social organizations in history but of theology, I have chosen to limit myself to as narrow a band of material as possible. This self-restriction implies that one should concentrate on Irish or Welsh material, and only cite from one to the other when a common source can be seen in both (e.g. when two authors rely on the same text) or else only as illustrative parallels. So if the trenches are to have any hope of illustrating a particular site, they must all be based in one of the distinct peoples of these islands at the time: this, in

---

20. Some would argue (reviving an idea put forward in the nineteenth century) that there is 'a Pan-Celtic religious consciousness' that can be discerned in their religious creations, even if the people themselves were unaware of this distinctive outlook. However, this approach invokes vague theories of 'cultural distinctiveness' which are alien to the mentality of most historians – and to this writer, at least, repugnant as almost racist in their basic assumptions.

effect, demands the choice of Ireland, as the amount of material that has survived is so much greater than from any other Celtic language area.

The Parameter of Language

Bede stated at the beginning of his *Historia* that in Britain there are 'five languages . . . English, British [Welsh], Irish, Pictish, and Latin which through meditation on the revealed law is common use among them all'.[21] Christianity came to these islands from a Latin-speaking culture, and it was through Latin that the peoples of these islands saw themselves sharing a larger Christian culture and, to an extent, the medium (Latin) and the message (Christianity) became one. So while in Ireland we have religious texts in both languages (e.g. the poems of Blathmac in Irish, the hymns from the *Liber hymnorum* in Latin[22]), the material in Latin has a certain priority in that the writers had first to master Latin, and then transfer the ideas and images found there back into their vernacular. Latin was the language which supplied the bulk of their theological ideas, and it was the language in which they believed theology should be done[23] – hence in this book there is a concentration on their writings in that language. The concentration on Latin has other advantages besides. First, Latin was a foreign language to the Irish, and one of the distinctive features about Christianity in Ireland is that it was the first occasion when westerners had to do theology in an acquired scholarly language. Second, since it was always an acquired language it forms a common link between people in different centuries in Ireland from the outset – not until the ninth century would this be a factor on the continent. This special continuity of Latin from the fifth to the ninth centuries somewhat offsets the problems of having to compare texts which occasionally are separated by more than a century. Thus by focusing on Latin texts we can be more certain that our explorations relate to a single body of people held together by many cultural bonds, a common situation, and with common difficulties.

---

21. *Historia ecclesiastica gentis anglorum* I, 1 (p. 16).
22. The *Liber hymnorum* is an eleventh-century manuscript which contains a large selection of hymns and other liturgical material, but of special interest here are the fourteen Hiberno-Latin hymns some of which are, at least, seventh-century in date. See L&S 542–64 and 578–91.
23. Muirchú in his *Vita Patricii* I, 9 makes this clear.

The Parameter of Time

The third factor in ensuring that the various trenches are probes into a single site concerns time. A study which gathers evidence over a long time-range, or seeks to compare two items separated by centuries, cannot reveal the actual situation in the way that one with a well-bounded time-frame can – although by the standards of modern history most medieval time-frames seem impossibly wide. In this book the material ranges from the fifth century to the twelfth and thirteenth centuries; however, the bulk of the material falls within a smaller band, roughly late sixth to late ninth centuries. Moreover, in most chapters the range in an individual trench is narrowed down to a single lifetime. The medieval historian has to grow accustomed to material that is drawn from century after century in chapter after chapter – this is a function of our surviving sources, but we must always seek to keep the range and sequence as tight as possible – hence the order of the chapters is roughly chronological. So the objective is to show up, through a series of investigations, the directions that theology took in Ireland, as seen for the most part through the medium of Latin, over a period of about four hundred years.

So how did I select the topics of examination? Some suggested themselves, insofar as they could not be omitted from any book on this subject. The chapters on Patrick and the penitentials are representative of this group.[24] Then there are those authors whose sheer skill in setting about their tasks assured them of a place, for example Muirchú and Adomnán.[25] Then there was the need to look at materials that are of great significance for understanding both early Irish theology and the contribution of those writers to the larger Latin world. An obvious choice here is the *Collectio canonum hibernensis* which, while well known in Celtic studies and legal history circles, is virtually unknown among theologians – yet it has contributed more than a little to the formation of their discipline.[26] The *lex credendi* cannot be divorced from the *lex orandi* – so liturgy must have a place. The Stowe Missal's distinctive material is an obvious choice, but the selection of the litanies may seem strange.[27] Unlike the other materials these exist in both Latin and the vernacular and are more difficult to date with accuracy. However, they do introduce us directly to the world of medieval liturgy. Lastly, there was the need to follow some themes over a period to show how change took place within the tradition, and to show that theology when used by successive generations within a culture has a particular dynamism.[28] While each topic has been tackled 'on its

---

24. Chapters 2 and 3.
25. Chapters 5 and 4.
26. Chapter 6.
27. Chapters 7 and 8.
28. Chapter 9 on time; and chapter 10 on eschatology.

own', I think that the whole is more than the sum of the parts and, at the very least, has shown that there is plenty of material awaiting further investigation.

It is also useful to explain why some topics are not even touched upon in this book. In most discussion of insular theology there has been a detailed discussion of Pelagius. However, this is only incidentally a topic touching upon theology in Celtic lands, as his theology belongs to the debates of Italy and North Africa in the early fifth century, and is more properly considered – as it is in all general histories of fifth-century Christian thought – in that context. I have not devoted a specific chapter to scriptural exegesis as that topic is addressed incidentally in several chapters,[29] and I have recently examined the academic culture of insular exegesis in the period before 800 in another book.[30] I have avoided discusion of Eriugena, not only as he was someone whose theological contribution was outside the Celtic lands, but also as there are several fine introductions to his thought,[31] scholarly research tools,[32] and the Society for the Promotion of Eriugenian Studies which through its colloquia produces studies and bibliographies for his thought.[33] There is no chapter devoted to any other of the *peregrini* either. This omission of the *peregrini* is necessary as the topics chosen all overlap within the insular region and so can be seen as aspects of a local theology; once one examines the theology of an Irishman working within a different society, his writings (which would be central if this book was a history of the Irish contribution to the continent at the time[34]) become part of that local theology where he wrote. Lastly, there is no discussion of *anamchara* as the praxis within which the notion arose is treated in the chapter on the penitentials.

---

29. For example in ch. 4 which is devoted to an exegete, and in ch. 10 which looks at how specific texts were interpreted.
30. See my *Teachers and Code-Breakers: the Latin Genesis Tradition, 430–800* (Turnhout 1999).
31. For example: J. J. O'Meara, *Eriugena* (Oxford 1988); or D. Moran, *The Philosophy of John Scottus Eriugena: A Study of Idealism in the Middle Ages* (Cambridge 1989).
32. For example, M. Brennan, *A Guide to Eriugenian Studies: A Survey of Publications 1930–1987* (Fribourg and Paris 1989); or G. H. Allard, *Johannis Scoti Eriugenae Periphyseon Indices Generales* (Montréal and Paris 1983).
33. The last collection of papers produced was from the 1995 colloquium: G. Van Riel, C. Steele and J. McEvoy (eds), *Iohannes Scottus Eriugena: The Bible and Hermeneutics* (Leuven 1996).
34. For a fine survey of the topic of the Irish contribution to mainland Europe in the period covered by this book, see M. Richter, *Ireland and her Neighbours in the Seventh Century* (Dublin 1999).

A CELTIC CHURCH?

Before looking at any of the texts that have survived from early Christian Ireland, one awkward issue has to be addressed: was there a form of Christianity in these islands distinctive from that in the rest of the Latin world or, put in more socio-political terms, was there a 'Celtic Church'? It is probably already clear that I belong to that camp of scholars who believe these are misleading notions. Moreover, the 'Celtic Church' notion fails to recognize the most obvious facts: the early medieval writers whom we shall examine all sought that theological ideal that the truth was 'what was held always, every-where, by everyone', and if they had suspected that they were in any way idiosyncratic, they would have been the first to adapt their ideas to that of the larger group. Equally, when we look at where their works have survived, we find that for the most part it is in continental manuscripts, which shows that not only the scholars but their works were received and appreciated without any awareness of deviancy. The acid text is this: did the Christians in the Celtic lands have a markedly different liturgy or system of law?[35] Here the most brief sampling of the evidence shows that the Irish material is no more distinctive than materials from any other part of the Latin world of the time. For example the Stowe Missal contains the Roman Rite and its local additions would not amount to judging it a distinct rite. The best example for legal structures is the *Collectio canonum hibernensis*: it reflects the social situation in Ireland, but it was used throughout Europe and many of its *sententiae* can be followed from collection to collection until they are found in Gratian.

The counter-example of the Easter-dating controversy does not undermine this position. At issue was a very technical piece of maths that only bothered a small number of people for a limited time, and would hardly surface on the horizon of history save that it was a technical matter close to the heart of Bede. In any case, the disagreements were as much among theologians in one culture – Ségéne and Cummian – as between 'the Celts' and 'the others'. We should remember two things. First, that Bede had his own religious and ethnic reasons for recalling the question in the way he did – it was part of his aim to create a Christian Anglo-Saxon identity as an elect people.[36] Second, the matter of dating Easter could not be

---

35. The qualifier 'markedly' is important since no two liturgical books from before the age of print are identical: every manuscript book is a distinct creation and reflects all the variations that have accumulated over decades or even centuries as a copy became the exemplar for the next copy and so on. The same is true of law books – each to an extent represents its user and his court. So regional and local variations were the order of the day; modern notions of uniformity are a function of printing.

36. See C. W. Jones, 'Some Introductory Remarks on Bede's Commentary on Genesis', *SE* 19 (1969), 115–98; and A. A. M. Duncan, 'Bede, Iona, and the Picts', in R. H. C. Davis and J. M. Wallace-Hadrill (eds), *The Writing of History in the Middle Ages* (Oxford 1981).

finally settled by anyone in the early Middle Ages, and therefore –
just as a matter of mathematics – each side could pick holes in the
calculation methods of the other side.[37] Hence the debate is better
evidence of their endurance in learned argument than of their
theology.

If 'the Celtic Church' is a concept that disappears the more one
scrutinizes it, then why has it had so many supporters? This is not
just a question about the history of recent scholarship, but one about
the various groups who have sought to bring 'history' in on their side.
The notion's origin lies within the aftermath of the Reformation:
could someone who rejected Rome (the 'old religion') in the present
still appropriate the past as their own. If the past was *their past*, and
their present involved the very conscious rejection of Rome, then the
past had to be non-Roman as well. This desire to claim the past could
be formalized in many ways; for example, through changing the date
of Rome's corruption until after the period one wished to claim, or
through holding that the bonds with Rome were recent and that in
the earlier period there were no important links. Later, this was
further formalized into 'the branch theory' of the Church whereby
the Church Universal was made up of many branches: Antioch,
Constantinople, Roman, and *inter alia*, the Celtic branch. The effects
of this were two-fold: first, it made the study of the early Irish church
a battleground for sectarian warfare – and generated as much heat
as light in the process. Second, it led to an inordinate interest in
anything that could be considered 'exceptional'. The exceptional
became the guarantee of ecclesial distinctiveness, and after many
generations of noting what was exceptional an impression was
formed among the general public that the 'Celtic' and continental
Churches were as chalk and cheese. Each local difference was not
simply an instance of that variety of Christian expression that
occurred of every diocese in the medieval Latin church, but was a
token of a difference as great as that between Latin Christianity and
the Christians of Ethiopia or Armenia. For many today who seek to
link their Christian faith more closely with their locality, and to
enliven their spirituality and worship with a more expressive liturgy,
but for whom anything that 'smacks of High Church or Romish
practice' sparks an allergic reaction, this image of the 'Celtic Church'
still has great attractiveness.

Another prop of the 'Celtic Church' came from nationalists in
Ireland. If in the present Ireland was to stand alone as a nation, then

---

37. The fundamental assumption was that the Creator had to work with perfect
    numbers – upon that assumption every calculation could be destroyed if the
    calculations were projected far enough into the future. The problem was only
    solved in 1582 by the Jesuit mathematicians working for Pope Gregory XIII. They
    tacitly abandoned the notion that the calculation would result in perfect whole
    numbers by eliminating eleven days from the calendar and then proposing a
    perpetual system of corrective balances.

it must have the antiquity and dignity of a nationhood which had been conquered. To be just an island on the western fringe of Europe was of no avail – that merely was an argument that it should be a rural province ruled by a centre which happened to be in London. For an island 'long a province, to be a nation once again',[38] it was necessary to have a language, an ancient history, and a pride in its individual and distinctive achievements. The notion of 'the island of saints and scholars', of the Irish language as an offshoot from the Indo-European stock just as ancient as Latin or Greek, and of the ancient books as 'the work of angels' (the phrase came from their great enemy: Giraldus Cambrensis[39]) were all ammunition for argument. The church in Ireland was distinctive not in its theology but in its purity, holiness and zeal. While to Anglicans seeking to reclaim a past through the notion of the 'Celtic Church', that church was essentially *non-Roman*; but to the nationalist group it was essentially *distinctive*. Since this distinction was its antiquity, cultural brilliance and zeal, it was a distinctiveness that was very acceptable to Roman Catholics. The important thing for all concerned was that there was a great world-envied Celtic culture long before there were any Anglo-Saxons, Normans or English. In a head-to-head comparison between 'the English Church' and 'the Celtic Church' – then for antiquity, purity and brilliance the Celts won! Such a gloriously distinctive church was another indication that here was an ancient free land that had a right to freedom once again. This may now seem a far-off battle, but it still flares up from time to time. Among scholars it has a residual life in the energy devoted to refuting any suggestion that an insular manuscript with nice pictures (e.g. the Book of Kells) was produced in a Northumbrian rather than an Irish centre. At a popular level it can be found among many Catholics, but Catholics who wish to distance themselves from their church's formal positions – for such people 'the Celtic Church' was not constitutionally distinct, but rather an eco-friendly, Augustine-free zone without formal theology or law.[40]

The third group are those in France, Germany and, more recently, the United States, who see the 'Celtic World' as a romantic alternative to the corruption and decay that was found in the decadent Roman Empire, and then as the noble bearers of civilization to its barbarian successors. In imagery this is the most powerfully coloured of the 'Celtic Church' myths: it reduces the 'fall of Rome', the

---

38. The phrase is taken from Thomas Davis's ballad, 'A Nation once again', which was the de facto anthem of Irish nationalism in the nineteenth century.
39. See C. Bourke, 'The Work of Angels?', *IR* 50 (1999), 76–9.
40. Curiously, at the other end of the religious spectrum, it is still an element in preachers' rhetoric among some conservative Catholics in Ireland – although they usually abandon the imagery more quickly than others on hearing that divorce was commonplace, that clerical celibacy was unknown outside monasteries and that in some instances bishops were seen as liturgical figures without administrative power.

'barbarian invasions' and 'conversion of Europe' down to a simple
narrative of black and white. Finally, a 'saviour' appears in the form
of a band of rugged Irish monks. The theme has all the stuff of
drama, and it is not so long since (in a refined form) it could find
academic supporters.[41] This notion, it could be argued, could be
found as early as Bede's presentation of the Irish missionaries in
Britain as men of simple faith and apostolic courage, but it drew its
attraction for many on the continent from the nineteenth-century
image of the Celts as quaint mystics forgotten by time whose
spiritual energy was great but whose lesser practical skills meant
they would be crushed by their crude neighbours.[42] This theme of a
'church out there' which could send missionaries to help an ailing
continental church had a wide appeal, particularly in France, before
the Second Vatican Council (1962–5); it was favoured in Ireland as a
proof of spiritual and intellectual prowess; and recently it has been
adopted in promoting a strong, positive cultural image abroad with
benefits in terms of tourism and as historical credentials for closer
European links as the EEC became the EC and then the EU. Today,
this image is reserved for ceremonial rhetoric at symbolic events
which draw together Irish and continental politicians. However, as is
the wont of strong narratives, it can still attract the crowds. As
recently as 1995 an American author, Thomas Cahill, retold the
whole myth – without a blush of embarrassment or a nod to
scholarship – and had enormous sales![43]

A common factor linking all these uses of the notion of a 'Celtic
Church' is their emphasis on the distinctness and separation of the
Celtic fringe from a 'mainland'. 'Out there' things are different: times
move more slowly, ideas take fantastic forms, and the learned
activities are not those common to Franks, Italians and Germans, but
of 'a race apart'. In essentials this is just a variant on the myth of
rustic simplicity, and the longing for a simple, worry-free life.
However, this dream has had a pernicious effect on studies of the
early Irish church, for it has turned that study into a search for the
peculiar, the unique and the bizarre: what is common between that
culture and the rest of Christendom becomes invisible, and what
seems jarring becomes the norm. At a learned level, it can be seen in
the practice of continental librarians who, when faced with an
otherwise unattributable and unusual text, use the label 'insular ?' as
an escape hatch. Equally, in the rumbling debate about the extent of

---

41. See the collection of articles edited by H. Daniel-Rops with the title: *The Miracle
of Ireland* (ET: The Earl of Wicklow, Dublin 1959).
42. These nineteenth-century origins in writers such as Ernest Renan have been
sketched by P. Sims-Williams, 'Celtomania and Celtoscepticism', *CMCS* 36
(1998), 1–35.
43. The book's title leaves the potential reader in no doubt about what he or she is
going to be told: *How the Irish Saved Civilization: The Untold Story of Ireland's
Heroic Role from the Fall of Rome to the Rise of Medieval Europe.*

'Irish exegesis' there seems to be an assumption among many scholars that either the products of the early Irish were wholly distinctive or they were non-Irish.[44] And at a popular level, it can be seen in the willingness to believe any story, no matter how far fetched, about the beliefs and practices of early insular monks. What we need is a model that allows for differences, but does not measure difference by the exceptional.

A LOCAL THEOLOGY

In this book the working hypothesis is that the theological and pastoral work of the early Irish church constitutes a 'local theology'. This is a concept which requires some elaboration. First, it is a notion that most who work in the history of theology take, often unwittingly, for granted. Among historians of Christianity in England in the eighteenth and nineteenth centuries it is assumed that there was an 'Oxford' and a 'Cambridge' theology, that each had its *genius loci* and produced divines of differing temperaments and churchmanship. John Henry Newman, for instance, reflected on how his life might have developed differently if, on the day he was sent by his father to university, a chance encounter had not pointed his father toward Oxford rather than Cambridge. In these cases it is largely the result of how people function in the group to which they physically belong, and with whom they share a sense of belonging. This sort of difference can be seen today in the way that particular universities become 'schools of thought'. In the past there were the 'Sorbonne theologians', the 'Tübingen School' and the 'Louvain approach' to Thomism; and still today a gathering of like-minded scholars – while sharing the same belief system with scholars elsewhere – can give a particular place a prominence in advancing one aspect of theology so as to make it distinctive.

A concept of a 'local theology' does not entail that those who share its positions are close geographically or temporally. The Catholic religious orders provide many examples of how a group can have a distinctive view of theology but where distinctiveness is relative to a community of belief, rather than the symptoms of a sectarianism. Thus 'Dominican' and 'Jesuit' theologies were, in the days before teaching clusters, two camps which inducted their own disciples into distinct ways of going about theology, pastoral work and prayer. The awareness of such differences was not confined to those who could follow the distinctions regarding the theologies of actual grace (the 'Thomists' versus the 'Molinists') in the manuals *De gratia* of each order. The local parish priest knew that a mission from the

---

44. See my 'The Latin Sources of Medieval Irish Culture', already cited; and M. M. Gorman, 'A Critique of Bischoff's Theory of Irish Exegesis', *JML* 7 (1997), 178–233.

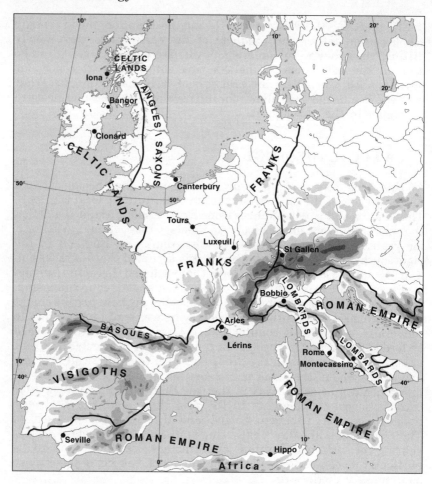

Christian Europe, AD 600

Redemptorists or the Passionists was very different from one preached by Vincentians or Jesuits. The parishioners knew likewise that one's reception 'in the [confession] box' would vary with the confessor's stable. Yet, such differences lived within Catholicism, despite the post-Trent cult of uniformity, the existence of print, and an ever more centralizing canon law.

Second, wherever a group of Christians have cultural experiences in common and share specific pastoral difficulties, a local theology will develop. Again, we take such groupings for granted. The Worker Priest movement in France was largely confined within France as it arose out of the circumstances of the Second World War there and its aftermath. Today, the Episcopal Church in the United States and the Church of England draw apart on issues relative to the place each holds in its respective society. The attractiveness of some theological issues in the First World is in sharp contrast to the lack of interest in poorer countries. Liberation Theology is a vital issue in South America; it is often little more than a curiosity in Europe. In a similar way the theology of early medieval Europe has to be seen not as a continental monolith with a distinctive Celtic rock lying off to one side, but as a patchwork of local theologies which influence one another for good and ill.

The religious interests of Gregory the Great (made pope 590, died 604) in Italy, *c.* 600, with his love of the new Benedictine monasticism on the one hand and his dealings with Constantinople on the other, seem far removed from Visigothic Spain and the works of Isidore of Seville (made bishop *c.* 600, died 630). In some ways the works of Isidore are more reflective of the classical past than of the Visigothic present. Both Spain and Italy seem distant from the dioceses and monasteries in Frankish lands that we meet in the course of Columbanus's life (on the continent from 590–615); and all seem different to the Ireland of St Columba's time (died on Iona 597) and the England upon which St Augustine of Canterbury landed (arrived in Kent 597, died 604/5). Yet, all these people are linked one with another. Isidore used Gregory's works, Columbanus wrote to him, the monasticism of Columba and Columbanus was formed from the same Gaulish materials – mainly Cassian – that produced the Frankish monasteries and which influenced the *Rule* Gregory championed, and within a few years the works of Gregory were being read on Iona and those of Isidore were its basic textbooks. To say that all these expressions of Christianity were merely one, 'western', 'Latin Catholicism' blinds us to the rich diversity of texture; to split them up into 'churches' dismisses the abundant links and their own perception of their unity in Christ. Reality is more complex than either the 'clumpers' or 'splitters' would have it.[45] The notion of 'local theologies' is an attempt to hold links and differences in tension. As such it is 'Celtic' or 'Irish' not because it can be brought into contrast with some other theology imagined as a highly consistent unity, but because its practitioners would have recognized their common links with a particular island, and that in many ways they shared cultural and linguistic experiences which set them apart from their fellow Christians elsewhere in the Latin West.

FURTHER READING

I. Bradley, *Celtic Christianity: Making Myths and Chasing Dreams* (Edinburgh 1999).

---

45. The distinction of 'clumpers' or 'unifiers' and 'splitters' or 'diversifiers' is one used to characterize scholarly tendencies among evolutionary biologists, but, as F. M. Cross has shown in *The Ancient Library of Qumran* (3rd edn, Sheffield 1995), pp. 177–9, it can be used profitably to characterize those who work with the partial remains of long-past religious groups.

W. Davies, 'The Myth of the Celtic Church', in N. Edwards and A. Lane (eds), *The Early Church in Wales and the West: Recent Work in Early Christian Archaeology, History and Place-Names* (London 1992).

K. Hughes, 'The Celtic Church: Is This a Valid Concept?', *CMCS* 1 (1981), 1–20.

D. E. Meek, 'Modern Celtic Christianity', in T. Brown (ed.), *Celticism. Studia Imagologica: Amsterdam Studies on Cultural Identity* 8 (1996), 143–57.

—— 'Surveying the Saints: Reflections on Recent Writings on "Celtic Christianity" ', *SBET* 15 (1997), 50–60.

T. O'Loughlin, 'The Latin Sources of Medieval Irish Culture', in K. McCone and K. Simms (eds), *Progress in Medieval Irish Studies* (Maynooth 1996), pp. 91–105.

M. Richter, *Ireland and her Neighbours in the Seventh Century* (Dublin 1999).

P. Sims-Williams, 'Celtomania and Celtoscepticism', *CMCS* 36 (1998), 1–35.

Throughout this book whenever a text has been catalogued by L&S, the number they assigned to it will be given, as it supplies details of editions and a bibliography up to 1985.

2 Patrick the Missionary

So it would be neither right nor proper to do anything but to tell you all of the many great blessings and grace which the Lord chose to give me in this land of my captivity – St Patrick (*Confessio* 3)

The writings of Patrick – Roman citizen, captive, visionary, bishop, missionary – form the obvious starting point for any study of Christian texts from the Celtic lands. Indeed, this starting point may appear to be almost a cliché, and one that seems tired, pious and even frivolous. Patrick has been so buried by hagiographers, so shamrock-laden by the cultural politics of defining Irish identity that for many he has become an almost mythical figure. Yet the man of flesh and blood can still be glimpsed in the two documents by him which we possess. Of Patrick's dates and background, and of the extent of his labours, we know nothing beyond what he tells us; but we still know more about him than about any other fifth-century British, let alone Irish, person. While the aim of this chapter is to draw attention to certain theological themes in his writings, we must begin by looking at the state of our evidence regarding the man.

KNOWLEDGE OF PATRICK

The traditional picture of Patrick is build up from four sources.

Prosper and Palladius

The first source is just one line. The fifth-century writer Prosper of Aquitaine (*c.* 390–*c.* 463) compiled a *Chronicle* which listed important events in history against the dates of their occurrence. For the period before his own time he simply copied earlier works, but for the period of the second quarter of the fifth century (425–455) he provided contemporary witness. So when for the year 431 he records that: 'Palladius, ordained by Pope Celestine, was sent to the Irish, who are believers in Christ, as their first bishop',[1] this is a contemporary report of a matter about which he has direct knowledge.

This Palladius is a shadowy figure. He is not mentioned in any other insular source until the late seventh century when Muirchú found it necessary to 'write him out' of the history of the conversion of Ireland in order for Patrick to become the sole patron and evangelist.[2] We have only one other piece of information about Palladius, and again Prosper is the source. In his *De gratia Dei et libero arbitrio contra Collatorem* (written in 434) he tells us that Celestine had sent a bishop to the British Church to free it from 'Pelagianism' – Prosper's pet hate – and that he ordained a bishop for the Irish so that 'the barbarian island might be made Christian'.[3] In a study of these passages Thomas Charles-Edwards has argued that these items from Prosper, taken with other references to missionary work beyond the imperial frontiers, point to a Roman mission to Ireland which was still working there twenty years later in the 450s.[4] There are no contemporary references to Patrick's mission, Prosper does not mention Patrick, and Patrick does not mention Palladius: we must therefore assume that both – and possibly others – were working as missionaries among the Irish in the fifth century, and consequently that it was a group of workers (without any known connection between them), rather than a single individual, who should be seen as the 'founders' of Christianity in Ireland.

Patrick's Writings

Our second source is the two works written by Patrick himself. The longer work is his *Confessio* in which he explains before God and his fellow Christians the integrity of his work as a missionary. The second is a *Letter to the Soldiers of Coroticus* delivering a formal sentence of excommunication. Both are complex documents as they are directed at several perceived audiences. At some points they are addressed to God, and the reader is allowed to overhear Patrick's words; at other points he directly addresses the reader, while on occasion he wants his reader to take his words to some others whom

---

1. *Ad Scottos in Christum credentes ordinatur a papa Coelestino Palladius et primus episcopus mittitur* (*PL* 51, 595; *Chronica minora*, vol. 1, p. 473); note that in Kenney, p. 165, no. 40, this quotation is given in a slightly different form. On Prosper, see R. W. Mathisen, 'Prosper of Aquitaine', *DMA* 10, 153–4; and Kenney, op. cit., pp. 164–5 (no. 28).
2. See ch. 5 below.
3. Ch. 21 (*PL* 51, 271).
4. T. Charles-Edwards, 'Palladius, Prosper, and Leo the Great: Mission and Primatial Authority', in D. N. Dumville, *et al.* (eds), *Saint Patrick, AD 493–1993* (Woodbridge 1993), pp. 1–12.

he wishes to address.[5] In the *Confessio* his goal appears to have been a narration of the great works that God has wrought through him, and so is a declaration of praise, while his purpose in the *Letter* is to state what he has bound on earth[6] as Christ's ambassador.[7] At the same time, there are parts of the *Confessio* that directly answer clerical critics (probably in Britain), while parts of the *Letter* assume that the slavers working with Coroticus will actually hear or read his words.

Neither document is much use to us for the historical details of early Irish society or its Christianization in the sense of giving dates, places or the names of rulers, but together they do provide us with insights into Patrick the Christian man of faith. There are, of course, references by Patrick to places, the most famous being Bannaven Taburniae (*Confessio* 1) which he says was the village near his family's home; another is the 'wood of Foclut, near the western sea' (*Confessio* 23). However, we have no idea where these places were, and their location was already a puzzle for people only a couple of centuries after him.

Patrick's dates are a special problem. The traditional date for Patrick's arrival (432) comes from Muirchú and is based solely on Prosper. If Prosper, so Muirchú's logic goes, says a pope sent the *first* bishop to the Irish, then this *must be* correct, hence Patrick must be after that. But, on the other hand, Patrick was for Muirchú the first to convert the Irish, so Palladius has to be taken out of the picture, and Patrick has to begin work as soon as possible after that: hence the date of AD 432. A similar uncertainty applies to his dates of death. There are two traditional ones: 461 and 493. All we can say is that a fifth-century date for Patrick's mission does not clash with any of the evidence.

Hagiography

The third source of the traditional picture is various later 'lives' (*uitae*) of Patrick. There are several medieval *uitae* of Patrick each building on those earlier than it. The earliest life is Muirchú's *Vita Patricii*, from the late seventh century. That *uita*, as we shall see in chapter 5, is a most carefully constructed theological picture of Patrick; its main task is to fulfil the religious need for a hagiograph of its hero. All such *uitae* fit within a precise literary genre which has

---

5. The questions of purpose and audience are gone into in greater detail in the introductions and running commentary in T. O'Loughlin, *Saint Patrick: The Man and His Works* (London 1999).
6. See Mt 16:19 and 18:18.
7. See Eph 6:20.

little in common with our notion of a biography, and their historical worth has to be judged in that light.[8] Muirchú's *uita* is valueless for information about Ireland in the fifth century. In any case, Muirchú was already aware that there was little to go on for the 'facts' of Patrick's life. He wove the 'historical' parts of his *uita* from the reference in Prosper and Patrick's works, and his elaborate fantasy to maintain that Prosper was the first bishop to arrive in Ireland, while Patrick was the first bishop who actually carried out the mission of converting the Irish, deserves to be read simply as an example of literary creativity 'saving all the appearances'.

Annals

The fourth source is references in annals kept, from at least the seventh century, in Irish monasteries. These are the Irish analogues of chronicles, modelled ultimately on Eusebius, which were kept throughout Christendom.[9] While the annals are accurate for the times during which they were being compiled (seventh century and later), for earlier dates they rely on continental chronicles, such as Prosper's, and on other traditions which cannot be verified. Thus the arguments about the date of Patrick's death are futile since we cannot trust the evidence of the annals when they claim to record the fifth century.

This negative appraisal of the size of our evidentiary base was first put forward in an epoch-making essay by D. A. Binchy in 1962.[10] Binchy wrote to show the hollowness in so much that was written about 'the national apostle' by churchmen anxious to employ Patrick in one way or another, and by secular historians anxious to show that Ireland's early history was as rich in detail as that of any part of the Roman empire. But Binchy's essay has had another effect with regard to the study of Patrick. In demolishing a false icon which others were afraid to expose lest they 'offend pious ears', Binchy allowed us to focus on what we actually know about Patrick without distraction. Questions still surface about where Patrick came from, where he went, whether he founded the See of Armagh (there is no

---

8. For the genre, see H. Delehaye, *The Legends of the Saints* (Brussels 1905; ET: London 1962; rept Dublin 1998).
9. For the Irish background to annals, see D. N. Dumville, 'Latin and Irish in the Annals of Ulster, AD 431–1050', in D. Whitelock, R. McKitterick, D. Dumville (eds), *Ireland in Early Medieval Europe* (Cambridge 1982), pp. 320–41; for the background to the genre, see D. Hay, *Annalists and Historians: Western Historiography from the Eighth to the Eighteenth Century* (London 1977), ch. 3.
10. D. A. Binchy, 'Patrick and His Biographers, Ancient and Modern', *SH* 2 (1962), 7–173.

early evidence), or who Coroticus was;[11] they still grab media attention, and are still clutched at by those wanting the security of thinking they know 'the whole story'. However, unless we were to find new *documents* whose content dates from the fifth century and which name Patrick or describe Christianity in Ireland, then we are limited to Patrick's writings. It is sobering to reflect that if Muirchú, in the seventh century, could not determine where Patrick's British home was located, then our speculations have little likelihood of being correct!

A CAPTIVE AND A STRANGER

By the late fourth century the carefully fostered image of 'the immense majesty of Roman peace' was in disarray. On the frontiers of the empire the defences were patchy, the ability of the army to repel and punish raiders was uneven or non-existent, and a movement of peoples was afoot that would transform western Europe and, within a century, lead to the dominance of Germanic warlords in half-Roman dress, such as Theodoric. It was an upheaval such as people had never imagined in their worst dreams. The shock of events such as Alaric sacking Rome in 410 not only symbolically destroyed for many any sense of political security, but also prompted Christian leaders to seek answers as to where the Providence of God could be in all this turmoil. The very different theologies of history by Augustine of Hippo and the Spanish priest Orosius were both formal theological responses to this crisis. But for thousands of people on the frontiers what was happening was not a problem within a vast theory of God's purposes, but the brutal reality of destruction, kidnapping and slavery. Our knowledge of all this is far from complete: raiding parties do not employ scribes to record their work. But we know, for instance, that Christianity first reached the Goths through large groups of Christians taken as slaves.[12] Indeed, the first Christian communities in Ireland were probably such groups. Patrick tells us that they took 'many thousands' (*Confessio* 1) in the raid on which he was captured. His estimate, even allowing for exaggeration, means that there were sizeable groups of Christian slaves in Ireland. Such

---

11. E. A. Thompson ('St. Patrick and Coroticus', *JTS* n.s. 31 (1980), 12–27) pointed out the anomaly that while, since Binchy, most historians had given up futile speculations about Patrick, the old ways had continued apace with regard to Coroticus, but that this was equally a false trail as we have no definite information about Coroticus apart from Patrick. Thompson put forward a fine argument, based solely on Patrick's letter, that Coroticus and his men were British outlaws living in Ireland and engaged in the slave trade with Britons, Picts and Irish.

12. See E. A. Thompson, *The Visigoths in the Time of Ulfila* (Oxford 1966).

groups of slaves, along with a few slavers who may have been Romano-British Christians based in Ireland (as Coroticus seems to have been), and possibly a few people in trading ports, were the believers to whom Palladius was sent. We get another glimpse of this slave-raiding environment from Caesarius, bishop of Arles in Gaul in the mid-sixth century when he sold off church vessels to ransom Christian captives.[13] This practice is already mentioned by Patrick as the Christian practice in Gaul (*Epistola* 14).[14] But we have few other details. With the exception of Patrick, we have no idea how those captives made sense of what was happening to them, or how they explained to themselves why a loving God could let such a fate befall them. Patrick is the one person from that period who lived through a raid and slavery, who managed to escape, and whose own story has survived. This makes his first-hand account of his experience as a slave a document of outstanding importance.

By the fifth century Christian clergy were a major social force within the empire with a clear group identity. And they had secured through canonical legislation a position of authority and control among Christians.[15] It is a measure of that social power that they could assume without difficulty so many functions of the civil magistrates (for example, Augustine in Hippo) in those troubled times. Patrick was very conscious of that social position: he tells us that he was the son of a deacon and the grandson of a priest (*Confessio* 1) and that he belonged to the *decurion* – minor rural gentry – class (*Epistola* 10). These distinctions seem to be still important reference points for Patrick, yet in the world where he lived they in fact mattered little. Patrick was conscious that he was a Roman, a writer of Latin, and the representative of a world-wide religion,[16] yet these facts do not seem to have impressed those with whom he was in contact in Ireland. In both writings Patrick comes across as someone isolated, homesick, and far from those with whom he feels he could easily share the concerns of his heart (see *Confessio* 43), and so we should also read him as someone who had a deep sense of being misunderstood and cut off from his natural companions. This was what it was to be part of the post-Roman world on the far-off frontier.

---

13. See W. Klingshirn, 'Charity and Power: Caesarius of Arles and the Ransoming of Captives in Sub-Roman Gaul', *JRS* 75 (1985) 183–203.
14. See T. Charles-Edwards, 'Palladius, Prosper, and Leo', loc. cit.
15. See S. Laeuchli, *Power and Sexuality: The Emergence of Canon at the Synod of Elvira* (Philadelphia 1972).
16. For this consciousness in Prosper and Pope Leo the Great of Christianity as the religion whose bounds were greater than any human empire as a result of Providence, see T. Charles-Edwards, 'Palladius, Prosper, and Leo', loc. cit.

THE CONVERT

Patrick was not a theologian in the sense of someone whose life task is the formal explication of the Christian faith. But if we see him as someone who had to make sense of the world around him in terms of God's plan of salvation and who saw himself charged to be a teacher of the Christian faith, then his implicit assumptions about that faith, and the way he presented himself, his relations to others and his relationship to God can be seen as his theological position. I shall examine these relationships under four headings: convert, missionary, teacher, and pilgrim.

Patrick's first attempt to make sense of what was happening to him was during his captivity in Ireland from the ages of about sixteen to twenty-two when he says he changed from being someone 'ignorant of God' to someone who prayed incessantly in all weathers and night and day for God's help. As Patrick recalls, it was a time when he fulfilled the cry of the Psalmist: 'O Lord, my God, I call for help by day; I cry out in the night before thee.'[17] What he had to explain was how God could let such an evil thing as being enslaved befall him. His answer is a simple one: he and his folk deserved it as a punishment for their sins.[18] They had no one to blame but themselves, and God in punishing, or letting their sufferings occur, was acting in accord with his own justice. Patrick expressed it succinctly:

> I was taken into captivity in Ireland – at that time I was ignorant of the true God – along with many thousand others. This was our punishment for departing from God, abandoning his commandments, and ignoring our priests who kept on warning us about our salvation. And 'so' the Lord 'poured upon' us 'the heat of his anger'[19] and dispersed us among many peoples right 'out to the very ends of the earth'.[20] (*Confessio* 1)

This passage was written with the hindsight and knowledge of the later bishop/missionary, but probably does record how he thought and felt at the time. The notion of dispersal among the nations as a divine punishment for infidelity is found in many places in the Old Testament, for example Leviticus 26:33; Ezekiel 4:13; or Tobit 13:4–7, and was the explanation offered repeatedly for Israel's defeats by foreign armies and for the deportation to Babylon. It surfaced in the

---

17. Ps. 88:1; this theme of prayer night and day is found elsewhere in the Psalms (Pss 1:2; 19:2; 22:2; 42:3, 8; 77:2) and provided the framework within which Patrick understood his situation.
18. This is the explanation offered by Gildas – another British Christian but probably a little later than Patrick – to explain the sufferings imposed on his Christian fellow countrymen through the invasions of Germanic peoples.
19. Is 42:25.
20. Acts 1:8.

New Testament when the question of suffering was posed to Jesus regarding a man born blind: 'Rabbi, who sinned, this man or his parents?' (Jn 9:2), where the notion that suffering is a direct result of sin was rejected. But despite what Jesus said, the notion that God is now setting about his work of repaying 'sinners' recurs periodically in the history of Christianity: in the fourteenth century many preachers made sense of the Black Death in this way, and even today the idea is heard that AIDS is an act of divine punishment. Formal Christian theology rejects the idea as perverse, but it has deep roots in our religious psyche and part of Patrick shares this position. As a theory it is easy to see its attractiveness – quite apart from the 'precedents' in the Scriptures.[21] The notion can make a disaster somehow comprehensible, it can be imagined as fitting into some mysterious plan; and this seems more satisfying than the thought that one lives in a randomly free universe where 'bad luck' just happens – striking good and bad alike. One's pain is lessened if one has an explanation, any explanation, and the notion that one deserves it leaves the hope intact that 'God is still in charge'. A punitive God seems preferable to a chaos where God appears indifferent to innocent suffering.

God is Just

There are two theological presumptions at work in any use, such as Patrick's, of the notion that suffering is one's just recompense. The first is that disasters are the work of God, who is viewed as the dispenser of justice. This view of God is not one that Christians produce in peaceful reflection nor one that is reached through preaching that is based on the life of Jesus and his words, but one that is forged in the bitter pain of collective suffering. And, when a group – such as those captives with Patrick – invokes this image of God, then it appears to them as a more true and real perception of God than any other. Here was the core of his conversion. He now had *felt* the work of the real God, he realized he must have been a sinner,

---

21. That ill-fortune was a punishment from God for sin is the solution to the problem of theodicy in many of the texts of the Old Testament; thus many who wish to adopt it can rightly claim it can be found 'in the Bible' – and by assuming that 'the Bible' is consistent and inerrant they proceed that if they can find it once, it is 'the Bible's' position and forget that (even if one assumes for dogmatic reasons that the Scriptures have a single author) it is a position rejected by Jesus. The term 'the Bible' must not be used directly with reference to Patrick – it supposes a unified view of the canonical texts which did not emerge until the scholastic period, and which has been reinforced by the practice of having all the Scriptures in a single book – Patrick would never have seen more than a few texts (e.g. the gospels or the epistles) bound together. For the early Middle Ages the correct term to use is 'the Scriptures'.

and so he now knew that he must serve this God who is not to be trifled with.

But was he a great sinner while a youngster? Did he and his people ignore God as he claims? The situation of suffering, now perceived as the situation of punishment, alters the memory of the time prior to the disaster for the worse. The disaster is punishment and it dominates the horizon, therefore the sin causing it must have been equally great. How else, Patrick reasoned, could God have let this awful fate befall them unless they were awful sinners who abandoned God? He too, he reckoned, must have been unacquainted with God, or else he would have been spared the punishment. So when we read Patrick's account of his ignorance of God or his view on the quality of Christianity in Britain we must not imagine these as neutral descriptions or memories, but projections into the past forced on him by his present horrors. He came from a long and respected local clerical family of which he was proud. Yet he claims ignorance of God before arriving in Ireland; but he clearly knew how to pray and knew enough about Christian notions of God's action that he could produce his explanation of his situation. 'Ignorance' was his way of describing his knowledge of God before he felt the divine wrath. He had now, through circumstances he perceived as a punishment, been driven to see the urgency of the demand to follow God. The sense of urgency was derived from a belief that unless he attends to God, he will know his judgement.

God is Close

The second presumption is that God is directly behind every action on earth: good things are his gifts, but equally when bad things happen this is God's will and judgement. This idea that nothing is random and that all is controlled closely by Providence is an aspect of Christianity not emphasized today. We tend to speak of God as withdrawing to give his creation 'room for movement', we allow for chance, and we reject the tendency to trace events back to God as their direct cause as invoking a false image of God as one meting out rewards and punishments like a slave-owner. The notion is still heard after natural disasters when reporters speak of 'Acts of God' – but this is now pompous rhetoric rather than a statement of belief: all this amounts to is that an event has had great devastating power and was not expected. Human freedom and dignity seem to us to demand a non-meddlesome God who cannot be blamed for every rainstorm, every car crash, every person who falls ill, or the mighty horrors of Auschwitz, Rwanda, or some other bloodbath. But this reluctance is at odds with most of our Christian predecessors. Building on Matthew 10:29, and similar texts such as Luke 12:7, Christians have claimed that not a sparrow falls to the ground without God directly willing it, and even the hairs on our heads are counted. To Patrick the presence of God was immediate and ubiquitous not as a theological postulate but in the sense that God is constantly effecting his will in this or that situation. At every point in his life Patrick sees the will of God becoming manifest to him: God is not just another actor in the human drama of suffering, joy, damnation and salvation, but the supreme actor whose power is unlimited, and constantly active.

Many today find the 'closeness of God to the Celtic saints' or their sense of the 'presence of God around them' as attractive, as it seems such a contrast to the modern experience of the 'absence of God'. But we should remember that their sense of God was very often that of a mighty power hovering over every situation. The closeness is the overpowering closeness of the stern, all-seeing master. Prayers that begin 'All powerful, everlasting God' were said with awe and trembling, for his manifestations expressing his justice were at times all too close. But could a society which had been raided for slaves, had suffered a series of social disruptions and had lived with mayhem avoid this sense that there was a powerful force always circling around their lives and making itself felt in terrifying events? Experiencing God as raw power was assumed by Paul (Rom 1:20) as a basic category; equally, in the early twentieth century Rudolf Otto would see the *'mysterium tremendum'* as a key to religious experience, and Patrick gives evidence that he and his family also shared that perspective.

An Individual's Theology

These presumptions that God is punitive and is hovering behind every event are a part of Patrick that is easily ignored since most who look at his beliefs do so from the perspective of admiration.[22] However, to my mind they do not detract from Patrick. No Christian has ever has a perfect theology; each is defective, slanted, limited to a greater or lesser extent as the result of culture, influences from others and the events of life. Patrick's picture of God in his writings is not attractive to us, it is a picture of a stern Omnipotence who demands 'every last penny' (cf. Matthew 5:26). Patrick's sense of his conversion was that God wanted to let him know exactly what was demanded of him. Patrick had been enslaved by the Irish with God's permission, and in Ireland he learned that he must be a slave of God if he were to save himself. Before the 'punishment' he did not know this side of God, but he saw it when brought to his senses: this was the living God who had to be obeyed. When he wished to describe his

---

22. For example, N. D. O'Donoghue, *Aristocracy of Soul: Patrick of Ireland* (London 1987).

life he did it in terms of servitude to the divine will which sentenced him to work in Ireland; and he dared not leave that post, for the ever-living God watched over him, at once caring for him and judging him.

Patrick's view of God was born of the desperate situation in which he and so many of his people found themselves; however, there is something else in his case which sets him apart:

> For it was [God] who 'looked on my lowliness'[23] and had mercy on the ignorance of my youth, who cared for me before I knew him and before I had gained wisdom or could choose good from evil. It was as a father comforts his son that he protected me. So it would be neither right nor proper to do anything but to tell you all of the many great blessings and grace which the Lord chose to give me in this land of my captivity. I tell you these things because this is how we return thanks to God, that after being corrected and having come to an awareness of God, that we glorify and bear witness to his wonderful works in the presence of every nation under heaven. (*Confessio* 2–3)

Seeing suffering as divine justice carries two costs. First, it creates an image that is at odds with so much else in the traditions of Judaism and Christianity. It conflicts with seeing God as unconditional love, forgiveness, 'slow to anger and rich in mercy' (Ps 103:8) and the message of peace proclaimed by Jesus. The second cost is hidden: most people confronted by the image of a punitive God simply abandon any vision of God's love and goodness in despair. If both those who strive to be good and those who ignore every rule are punished, then punishment is the last word and one might as well abandon attempts to avoid it. Any mention of God's loving plan becomes a silly joke: so abandon attempts to make sense of one's situation and grab whatever solace is to be found before the crunch. Such a loss of faith and the rejection of a religion often comes on the heels of punitive theologies. It can be seen across Europe after the Black Death – in Boccaccio's *Decameron* the time before death is spent with amusing stories rather than in penitence – and in the rejection of belief by many today who see Christianity as a message of gloom and penalties. Patrick, forced into that theology by the need to explain his circumstances, did not let it dominate his view. God, for Patrick, is punitive but also comforting, strict but merciful, a master but also a teacher; and all his actions originate in his love and goodness. So he can pick himself up in his captivity and pray; he can labour to make God's word known; and he can offer a confession of praise before he dies (*Confessio* 62). The convert was a man of perseverance who never abandoned hope. God had punished him, but not simply as an act of justice but because he loved him; God had enslaved him, but he would care for him and lead him to glory.

---

23. Lk 1:48.

THE MISSIONARY

People in their actual lives do not have a wholly consistent theological vision: they picture God now in this way, now in that way. Someone may have a sense of Christ as an intimate friend, but the same person might also speak of Jesus as a distant teacher. These inconsistencies can frustrate biographers who take one set of utterances and assert that these portray the individual and represent the 'real' person. Then another picks a different set, challenges the first writer and discovers that the person's 'real' religious views are quite different. The assumption is that individuals sift all their ideas and attitudes about some aspect of Christianity and come to a consistent position in the manner of someone writing a theological textbook. Human beings often utter statements which, though appropriate individually to making sense of a situation, when put coldly side-by-side with other statements, contradict them. This is the case with Patrick. Reflecting on his life, he puts forward the notion of divine punishment to explain his being taken captive. This notion of God is then modified by other experiences and he also sees God as his loving protector. But at the same time he also puts forward a completely different view of his past: *all happened as part of his election by God as a missionary*, for he has a definite place in the whole history of salvation. It could be that the notion of divine punishment held sway in his youth, contributed to his conversion and remained always a part of his thinking; yet as he grew older, with a greater range of experience to reflect upon, a new perception of what God was doing emerged. But both co-existed in his thinking, the newer not replacing the earlier – for both views can be seen at work in the *Confessio*. Patrick operated out of both in the way that most humans live much of their lives with mixed motives and confused objectives, and without any single rationale that can explain their thoughts and actions. This newer self-understanding as a divinely chosen apostle was that of being the final missionary, the one specially prepared in his youth in Ireland to preach where no Christians had yet been, and so to be the one who ushers in the Last Times.

At the Edge of Time and Space

One of the phrases that recurs in Patrick is that he is at 'the very ends of the earth' (*Confessio* 1, 34, 38; *Epistola* 9) or similar expressions. These phrases, which for Patrick locate the position of Ireland, are taken from the New Testament. In Luke 11:31 (= Matthew 12:42) Christ tells of the 'Queen of the South' who came 'from the ends of the earth' to hear Solomon's wisdom. In Acts 1:8 and 13:47, both of which are in Patrick's mind at the opening of the *Confessio*, 'the ends of the earth' are linked to the preaching of the gospel: the Spirit will make the apostles witnesses to Christ in

Jerusalem, the surrounding areas and 'right out to the end of the earth' (Acts 1:8), and thus the apostles are set up as light for the salvation of the nations 'out to the very end of earth' (Acts 13:47). Moreover, the notion that the gospel is heard 'at the ends of the earth' is also found, but with a different focus, in Romans 10:18 which quotes Psalm 19:4: 'Their voice [the heavens' proclamation] goes out through all the earth, and their words to the ends of the world.' So Scripture provides a framework to locate where Patrick finds himself by the will of God. He has been sent to the last place among all the lands, to the furthest-out nation, first by a divine judgement and latterly by a divine commission – or was it all part of the plan?

In Luke/Acts we have the story of the early preaching which presents the message of Jesus spreading through Jerusalem (preaching to Jews); next, through the apostles, to the surrounding areas (also Jews); and then, through the journeys of Paul, reaching 'the nations' (Gentiles) within the Roman Empire. Luke makes clear that this is a three-stage process. This can be represented as a message spreading through three concentric circles. But as Patrick sees it, the limit of the preaching up to his time was the boundary of the Empire in the west, but there were a few places even beyond that. Now he has gone out there to the very end, to the nations that were beyond the reach of everyone until then. He is with the nations that are the furthest west (*Confessio* 39) to carry out this commission to teach the nations (*Confessio* 40 and *Epistola* 1). Indeed, he has gone beyond where people live (*Confessio* 51), right out the shore of the western sea (*Confessio* 23).

Patrick's World

The probability is that Patrick thought the world to be something like this: towards the centre of the great land mass of the earth was the city of Jerusalem, and around it the promised land. Around this were ranged the nations (cf. Ezekiel 5:5), and their lands stretched out to the Ocean. Most of this land mass was held by the Romans, but out on the fringe was, at least, one place outside both the orbit of Rome and, as yet, of Jerusalem: Ireland. This was destined to be the outer limit of preaching. That Patrick was thinking in this structural way about his location is confirmed, possibly, by his addition of the other two 'corners' of the earth, north and south, to his citation of Matthew 8:11: 'I tell you, many will come from east and west, and south and north, and sit at table with Abraham, Isaac and Jacob in the kingdom of heaven' (*Confessio* 39). And the particular people being called, through him, to the banquet is from the extremity of the earth (*Confessio* 38). He presents this as the fulfilment of a prophecy in Jeremiah 16:19; and then returns to the Lukan theme of the gospel spreading from Jerusalem by quoting Acts 13:47. Patrick was someone operating out on the final frontier. From one extreme of the world to the other, people are being summoned to the Lord's banquet: Patrick is one of the last offering invitations to the feast of the Lamb. Through his work the message of the gospel, which originated at the centre and had been carried to the nearby nations by the first apostles as recorded in Acts, was brought out to the very last piece of land.

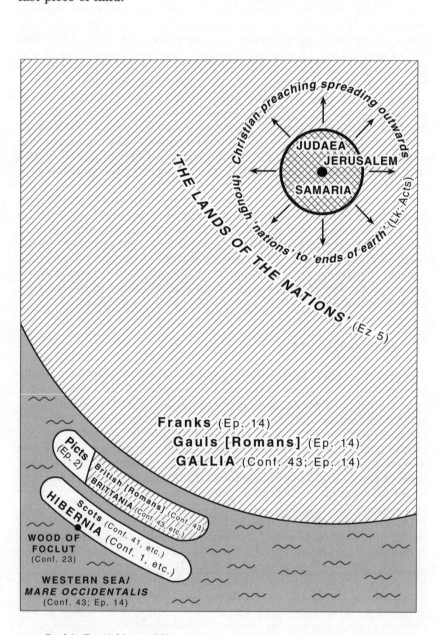

Is this Patrick's world?

The Eschaton

If Patrick imagined his location as being on the edge, the borders, the last place of the lands, he had a similar view of his place in history: he belongs to the last times, and the end is imminent. Indeed, the end will not be delayed very long after the completion of his own work in Ireland. He develops this theme in the central section of the *Confessio* by seeing a direct relationship between the preaching of the gospel and the close of human history.

The theme is announced by Patrick thanking God for the task he has been given in 'the last days'.[24] The basis for his belief that these were the final times was that God has promised that he would 'announce his gospel before all nations before the world's end'. Now, Patrick is the instrument of this proclamation, and with his fellow Irish Christians he bears witness to it, beyond which no one lives (*Confessio* 34). So we presume that since everywhere has now heard the gospel, there is nothing to delay the end, so it is now close at hand!

Having announced repeatedly that he has preached the gospel at the ends of the earth, and how thus a prophecy is fulfilled (*Confessio* 37–39), Patrick turns to the basis of all his work: Christ's command to preach (*Confessio* 40). He strings together three roughly parallel texts: first, Matthew 28:19–20, 'Go therefore and make disciples of all nations, baptizing them in the name of the Father and of the Son and of the Holy Spirit, teaching them to observe all that I have commanded you; and behold, I am with you all days until the consummation'; then Mark 16:15–16, 'Go, therefore, into all the world and preach the gospel to every creature; whoever believes and is baptized will be saved; but whoever does not believe will be condemned'; and finally Matthew 24:14, 'This gospel of the kingdom will be preached throughout the whole world, as a testimony to all nations; and then will come the end.' As Patrick reads these verses they convey a single structure: preaching followed by completion, judgement and the end. Moreover, the second event – the final judgement that marks the end of the age – is the direct consequence of the completion of the task of preaching. Put simply, once everyone has heard the gospel then there will be no further reason to delay the End. Patrick sees this as the plan in the divine mind for the period between the Ascension and the return of Christ in the Last Times (see *Confessio* 35). Moreover, this vast plan for the history of the world is something that addresses and involves him in a particular way. He is the one who is preaching to the very last nation to hear the message. As such Patrick sees himself as the final preacher in a

---

24. This theme will be examined in more detail in ch. 10.

chain going back to the apostles. He has had a unique task given to him, for when he has finished his work in Ireland, then the preaching phase of history is finished. With history complete, the universe enters the next stage in God's agenda: the judgement before the End. And in the very next sentence (*Confessio* 41) Patrick announces the state of history: the gospel has reached Ireland, the outermost place, and those who had only known idols are now 'the prepared people' (Luke 1:17) of the Lord and the children of God. Although Patrick never quotes the verse he seems to have Matthew 10:23, 'When they persecute you in one town, flee to the next; for truly, I say to you, you will not have gone through all the towns of Israel, before the Son of man comes', or something like it, in mind in formulating his theory. There is a fixed amount of time before the End; this is determined by the need to preach everywhere, and it is not as great as the length of time needed to get around all the towns of Israel. In any case, there is no need for more time as the given task of preaching is complete.

THE TEACHER

Patrick's sense of the awful closeness of God is something few Christians today share with him. His sense of being the final missionary, likewise, is something we find difficult to understand. We do not link together scriptural phrases and derive a fixed understanding of where we as individuals stand in the universe of space and time: those with similar specific views of their own religious vocation we view as cranks. Indeed, all our experience of special messengers just prior to the eschaton leads us to adopt a stance of suspicious incredulity: special messengers are either frauds or those who recall for us memories of Jonestown or Waco, Texas. But in Patrick this sense of being a chosen vessel is balanced by his awareness that he must act at all times as a Christian teacher. Today, if a group of Christians were asked to draw up a list of church ministries it is unlikely that many would mention teaching, and even fewer would give it prominence. But in the early centuries of Christianity the teacher, as someone with a vocation and skill, was seen as one of the most dignified of ministers – indeed, being a teacher was seen as the primary occupation of bishops. For Patrick and his contemporaries, to be called as a teacher was to participate in the action of Christ by which Christ made his light known and so made the Father visible. We can see Patrick as a formal teacher of Christianity in two places. The first in the *Confessio* (5) where he uses a creed to summarize his own belief; the other occasion is in the *Epistola* (9) where he sets out the kind of actions that Christians must avoid.

A Confession of Faith

There is not, nor ever was, any other God – there was none before him and there shall not be any after him – besides him who is God the Father unbegotten: without a source, from him everything else takes its beginning. He is, as we say, the one who keeps hold of all things.

And his Son, Jesus Christ, whom we declare to have always existed with the Father. He was with the Father spiritually before the world came into being; begotten of the Father before the beginning of anything in a way that is beyond our speech. And 'through him all things were made',[25] all things visible and invisible. He was made man, and having conquered death was taken back into the heavens to the Father. 'And he has bestowed on him all power above every name in heaven and on earth and under the earth, so that every tongue may confess that our Lord and God is Jesus Christ'. In him we believe, looking forward to his coming in the very near future when he will judge the living and the dead, and 'will repay each according to his works'.

And '[the Father] has plentifully poured upon us the Holy Spirit', the gift and pledge of immortality, who makes those who believe and listen into 'sons of God' the Father 'and fellow heirs with Christ'.

[This is] whom we profess and worship, One God in Trinity of sacred name.

It is easy to see that this is related to the Creed of the Councils of Nicaea (325) and Constantinople (381), and a great deal of effort has been devoted to the question of whether or not Patrick is the first Latin-speaker to witness the use of the Creed of 381 in the West.[26] However, that interest assumes that creeds are legally precise formulae and that such formulae appeared from nowhere at the great early councils. However, creeds with a trinitarian shape had been in use for several centuries throughout the church as guides in preparing candidates for baptism, as part of the liturgy of baptism through which they declared their belief and as convenient summaries of belief to be carried in the memory – their use at the councils as tests for orthodoxy is just one specific development of their use.[27] The creed we find in Patrick is clearly one that he knew by heart and which he must have used on countless occasions in teaching and baptizing in Ireland. That which he preached was the central core of his whole view of God, hence its place at the start of his narrative of God's great works. We should just note two points about this creed. First, at the beginning of his *Confessio* Patrick

---

25. Jn 1:3.
26. For example, L. Bieler, 'The "Creeds" of St Victorinus and St Patrick', *TS* 9 (1948), 121–4; or R. P. C. Hanson, 'Witness from St. Patrick to the Creed of 381', *AnB* 101 (1983), 297–9.
27. See J. N. D. Kelly, *Early Christian Creeds* (London 1950), for an overview.

announces that he wants this document to be a declaration of God's mighty works. Significantly the declaration then begins with this creed. By this Patrick wishes to state, first and foremost, who he believes God is, then the rest of the text tells about what God has done in his creation. The second point is that since this, as a formal creed, was his own creed text in his ministry, it is most likely to have been the creed with which he was brought up, and with which he was familiar from childhood. Thus, this creed is a precious relic of the Romano-British liturgy of the time.

A Moral Checklist

The other teaching text is, like the creed, something that Patrick had ready to hand:

> But it would take too long to describe individual crimes and set out the testimonies from the whole law which deal with such greed. [So here are the basics:]
>
> - avarice is a deadly crime;[28]
> - 'You shall not covet you neighbour's goods';[29]
> - 'You shall not kill';[30]
> - A murderer cannot be with Christ;[31]
> - 'He who hates his brother is a murderer',[32] or
> - 'he who does not love his brother remains in death'.[33]

What he means by 'the testimonies from the whole law' is unclear, but he obviously had some sort of handbook of scriptural quotations which he could call upon to show the evil of murder and other such crimes. He gives to his flock as a teacher (cf. Mark 6:34) a law setting out those actions which were incompatible with faith, and each of these prescriptions he could illustrate and develop from the store of tradition.

His Belonging to the Church

The most significant point about Patrick's theology that emerges from these incidents concerns neither his creed formula nor his use of preaching materials, but that in both cases he did not see it as his

---

28. This is the only item on his list of basic moral rules that is not taken directly from Scripture, but it clearly echoes statements about greed such as Lk 12:15.
29. Ex 20:17. This gathering of crimes is found in Rom 13:9 and is based on the decalogue.
30. Ex 20:13.
31. Cf. 1 Pet 4:15.
32. 1 Jn 3:15.
33. 1 Jn 3:14.

task to invent afresh. Patrick expressed himself as but one member of a community in the words of that community. This view of being a part of a body that is larger than me as an individual, a corporate sense that the body of which I am a member lived before me and will live after me, and that I am but a moment in a stream of tradition, is one we can barely grasp. For us, being but a moment in a tradition, or asserting that the tradition is larger than the individual, seems to destroy our independence, our freedom as individuals, and to invite totalitarianism. But for Patrick, as for Augustine and the great teachers before him,[34] or for umpteen medieval teachers after him,[35] not to belong to a body would mean that one was an isolated singleton, a mere blip in the plan of history. Their sense was of the insignificance of the individual mind. The limitations of an individual's understanding of the mysteries of life could only be overcome by being part of a whole: and of all the bodies to which one might belong there was none more splendid than the Christian church, for the splendour of a body was its head, and the church's head was Christ himself.[36] We read this body imagery in Paul, and in letters ascribed to Paul, as 'body imagery' to provide an analogy for the church in relation to Christ, or even more distantly as a metaphor of the relationship to Christ of the individual (albeit announced via the group). However, for any Christian in the first millennium this is not an image but the ground plan of the organism/organization. All the Pauline texts were read in terms of 1 Cor 12 as the basic text, and it was read on the assumption that complex realities work in similar ways. The human body with all its different bits and parts was one such complex organism; the gathering of the baptized in Christ was another, but far more complex, organism. It was simply a fact of understanding that the smaller (human) body explained the greater (the church); it was a matter of faith that the earthly body could explain the heavenly (the union of the saints in Christ). For Patrick, being a part of this body, i.e. of the 'whole Christ', was not an option: being apart meant the destruction of the meaning of his own life just as an eye without a head is useless. Likewise, as a body, in the church each member had his own precise task and so membership of the body enhanced, rather than diminished, his uniqueness and need for individual action. As a distinct member only he could bring the

34. Cf. T. van Bavel, 'The "Christus Totus" Idea: A Forgotten Aspect of Augustine's Spirituality', in T. Finan and V. Twomey (eds), *Studies in Patristic Christology* (Dublin 1998), pp. 84–94.
35. Cf. T. O'Loughlin, *Teachers and Code-Breakers: The Latin Genesis Tradition, 430–800* (Turnhout 1999).
36. This body language of the interconnection of parts was read in a very realist manner and it is useful to track down these body metaphors in scripture and imagine them in relation to one's own body to see the way they were read.

gospel to certain places at that particular time, and his task had not been, and so could not have been, carried out by Peter, Paul or someone else who had his or her own allotted tasks.

When Patrick wanted to express his deepest beliefs about reality and human action he did so using words of the tradition, and would have been loath to do otherwise. If we were asked about our ultimate beliefs it might seem a cliché, a 'cop-out', or we might fear being labelled 'inauthentic' if we did the same and just recited a learned-by-rote creed – that shows the gap between our religious world and Patrick's. For Patrick faith was seen as the personal appropriation of the tradition, not as an assent to a 'body of doctrines'. It was the act of engrafting oneself into a living human body (the people of the church) whose life-blood was Christ. In using the creed as his most personal thoughts he was appropriating as his own that which was larger than him, and the incident in the *Confessio* is an individual's experience of what the church teaches publicly.

THE PILGRIM

The fourth frame within which we can view Patrick is that of pilgrim. The pilgrim has aspects of the explorer and the holiday-maker, but also something more: as part of a quest for holiness, as part of a desire to know and do the divine will, the pilgrim leaves the familiar and crosses boundaries to where he or she is not-at-home – and for pilgrims in the past this involved personal risk, for to leave one's own place was to leave behind security, recognized rights and legal protection. We see this more radical form of pilgrimage in Gen 12:1, 'Now the Lord said to Abram, "Go from your country and your kindred and your father's house to the land that I will show you." ' Patrick not only left his own country, but went voluntarily outside the empire – a move in his society akin to the way people referred to 'going behind the Iron Curtain' a few decades ago. The country into which he went was not only foreign, but indeed was the homeland of his enemies and, as incidental points in the *Confessio* (e.g. no. 53) make clear, it was a place where he knew that legally and socially he was an outsider.

Reading through the *Confessio* one notes repeatedly Patrick's perception of himself as one who has been sent, of a duty to be done, of a journey to be made, confident that God will provide. Patrick, perhaps naturally for someone whose life involved much movement, saw his life in metaphors of journeys, frontiers and goals to be reached which are off in the distance. In this he seems to have had – as he tells us that he preached at the very ends of the earth – a view that his own life journey was but a moment in the larger journey to spread the word of the Kingdom.

THE SAINT

Patrick has been addressed as a 'saint' since his death. The community in which he lived held him as their leader, and from the time of his death they venerated him as one who had 'gone before' them 'marked with the sign of faith'.[37] In this he is no different to countless other Christian leaders from the first millennium where often all we know of the saint is the name and the day of death – the day seen as the day of birth into the new life of heaven and thus recorded carefully.[38] On the latter point we have the one tradition relating to Patrick independent of his writings: he died on 17 March. Not only is there unanimity in the sources on this point, but in the calendar of St Willibrord (658–739) we find this entry for 17 March: '[The feast] of Saint Patrick, Bishop in Ireland'.[39] However, is there anything in this man's life that Christians today can recognize as exemplary discipleship of Jesus? To set the matter in context we should note that the fact that we are here to ask the question would have surprised Patrick. Part of his energy came from his deeply held belief that the end of the world was nigh, and that his mission was to hasten its coming by bringing about the completion of the church. Equally, the question would have surprised the medieval Christians to whom Patrick's holy status and worthiness was simply a fact – was he not the powerful man of God whose miracles were testimony to his place in heaven and so to his intercessory power?[40]

Perhaps the most striking feature of Patrick's life is his willingness to learn from difficulties, to forget bitterness and to forgive. The people he went to live among were not some foreign, distant group with whom he had not had contact. He went to the very people with whom he had had too much contact, and not by his own choosing. The people he evangelized were those from whom he had escaped. This involved a personal act of forgiving and forgetting their hurts not just to himself but to his family and his people. His escape from Ireland must have been a dangerous and hazardous experience – he imagined it as two hundred miles – and one which, to gain sympathy from his readers, he could have dwelt on in the *Confessio* to show the

---

37. Cf. the Eucharistic Prayer of the Roman liturgy: *qui nos praecesserunt cum signo fidei et dormiunt in somno pacis.*
38. Delehaye, op. cit., saw these two elements (name and feast-day) as the basic pillars in any saint's dossier; from them a whole cult could be elaborated.
39. Paris, B. N. Lat. 10837, fol. 35ᵛ: *s[an]c[t]i Patrici[i] epis[copi] in Scotia.* There is a facsimile and edition by H. A. Wilson for the *HBS.*
40. We should note the antiquity within Christianity of this notion of the attestation of divine election/holiness by works: Mt 7:22; Jn 5:36; 10:25; 14:11–2; Acts 2:22; 2 Cor 12:12; and Gal 3:5.

hardships he had endured, but he passes over the whole incident with just one adverb: *uix* – he escaped 'with difficulty'.[41] Surely one of *the* understatements of all time. He had further difficulties on his route home, but again he put these down to experience and used them as an opportunity to witness to Christ. He was betrayed by a trusted, long-standing friend, but again he forgave and saw the event as training him further in discipleship. Both Christian clergy and Irish leaders objected to his activities yet he did not reply in kind but passed on, forgiving, and learning from the trial. If forgiving others as we wish to be forgiven – especially those who have hurt us as part of a group/nation/culture/religion/denomination – is one of the hardest lessons of Christian discipleship, then Patrick is certainly exemplary. His theological perspective may seem a world away from us, but his example of living and working in culturally complex situations is still relevant.

FURTHER READING

Texts

N. J. D. White (ed.), 'Libri Sancti Patricii; The Latin Writings of St Patrick', *PRIA* 25c (1905), 201–326.
L. Bieler, *Libri Epistolarum Sancti Patricii Episcopi* (Dublin 1952).

Translation

T. O'Loughlin, *Saint Patrick: The Man and His Works* (London 1999).

Bibliography

L&S, 25–6.
T. O'Loughlin, *Saint Patrick: The Man and His Works*, pp. 106–12.

Studies

D. A. Binchy, 'Patrick and His Biographers, Ancient and Modern', *SH* 2 (1962), 7–173.
J. B. Bury, *The Life of St Patrick and his Place in History* (London 1905).

---

41. *Confessio* no. 51.

T. Charles-Edwards, 'Palladius, Prosper, and Leo the Great: Mission and Primatial Authority', in D. N. Dumville, *et al.* (eds), *Saint Patrick, AD 493–1993* (Woodbridge 1993).

R. P. C. Hanson, 'The Mission of St Patrick', in J. Mackey (ed.), *An Introduction to Celtic Christianity* (Edinburgh 1989).

J. F. Kelly, 'The Escape of Saint Patrick from Ireland', *SP* 18 (1985), 41–5.

N. D. O'Donoghue, *Aristocracy of Soul: Patrick of Ireland* (London 1987).

E. A. Thompson, 'St. Patrick and Coroticus', *JTS* n.s. 31 (1980), 12–27.

3 The Penitentials: The Human Dilemma

Real penitence consists in avoiding actions which require penitence; but once these have been committed, in being sorry – St Columbanus[1]

THE ENIGMA OF THE PENITENTIALS

Almost universally, the penitentials of the early Irish church have in recent times received a bad press. Many would still side with this judgement from 1896:

> The penitential literature is in truth a deplorable feature of the mediaeval Church. Evil deeds, the imagination of which may perhaps have dimly floated through our minds in our darkest moments, are here tabulated and reduced to system. It is hard to see how anyone could busy himself with such literature and not be the worst for it.[2]

Insular scholars have examined them as curious items in the growth of legislation, for example Kathleen Hughes who found that '[t]hey are certainly not very congenial reading'.[3] Historians of canon law treat them as inferior to formal canonical collections and tend to see them as collections of 'rude customs'.[4] Historians of penance in the western church also look at them, but usually only as a background to developments that led to the discussions found in such writers as Peter Abailard (1079–1142) of the nature of the 'sacrament' – and in the process the penitentials are lost from sight, for they are seen as merely a 'practical' development with little theological significance.

---

1. *Paenitentiale*, A 1 (L. Bieler (ed.), *The Irish Penitentials* (Dublin 1975), p. 96; J. T. McNeill and H. M. Gamer, *Medieval Handbooks of Penance* (New York 1938), p. 250).
2. C. Plummer's edition of Bede's *Historia ecclesiastica gentis anglorum*, vol. 1, pp. clvii–clviii.
3. K. Hughes, *Early Christian Ireland: Introduction to the Sources* (Cambridge 1972), p. 84.
4. A. M. Stickler, *The Case for Clerical Celibacy* (San Francisco 1995), p. 42.

The penitentials are presented simply as a stage in the growth which flowered in the twelfth-century understanding of 'the Sacrament of Penance'.[5] Indeed, the most recent book-length study devoted to them focuses on demonstrating that despite their appearances, they can be fitted into a modern Catholic theology of penance – but the notion that they might have their own theology was not examined.[6] In general, Catholic writers have subsumed them into the history of the 'sacrament', while Protestant scholars have seen them as the beginnings of the false trails of private auricular confession and indulgences.[7] For both, their importance is as stepping stones. Recent years have seen renewed interest from medievalists viewing the penitentials as a source for social history and popular religion, but while these studies have concentrated on the contents of these documents, they are not interested directly in theology.[8] In most popular books on 'Celtic Christianity' the penitentials hardly get a mention: their emphasis on humans as sinful creatures and the need for bodily mortification and their implicit strict sexual code[9] are not perceived as agreeable with a 'body-friendly' religion of 'original blessing'.

In stark contrast to this general avoidance of the penitentials is the fact that they are the most distinctive feature of the insular churches. They provide the one case where Irish and Welsh clergy were highly innovative, and actually shaped western Christian practice and theology. More importantly, they provide evidence that those clerics were prepared to grapple with theological basics.

A PASTORAL IMPASSE[10]

By the middle of the fifth century – around the time that we assume that Christianity began to make major advances within Irish society

---

5. E.g. B. Poschmann, *Penance and the Anointing of the Sick* (ET: F. Courtney, London 1963), pp. 122–38; or, more recently, K. B. Osborne, *Reconciliation and Justification: The Sacrament and its Theology* (New York 1990), pp. 84–9.
6. H. Connolly, *The Irish Penitentials and their Significance for the Sacrament of Penance Today* (Dublin 1995).
7. E.g. F. W. H. Wasserschleben, *Die Bussordnungen der abendländischen Kirche nebst einer rechtgeschichtlichen Einleitung* (Halle 1851).
8. See for example A. J. Frantzen, 'The Significance of the Frankish Penitentials', *JEH* 30 (1979), 409–21; P. J. Payer, 'The Humanism of the Penitentials and the Continuity of the Penitential Tradition', *MedS* 46 (1984), 340–54; F. G. Clancy, 'The Irish Penitentials', *MS* 21 (1988), 87–109; D. Billy, 'The Penitentials and "The Making of Moral Theology" ', *LS* 14 (1989), 143–51.
9. For a detailed study of sexual topics in the penitentials, see P. J. Payer, *Sex and the Penitentials: The Development of a Sexual Code 550–1150* (Toronto 1984).
10. For greater detail on the problems of public penance, see T. O'Loughlin, 'Penitentials and Pastoral Care' in G. R. Evans (ed.), *A History of Pastoral Care* (London 2000); and idem, 'A Woman's Plight and the Western Fathers', in L. J. Kreitzer (ed.), *Scribblings in the Sand: Interpretations of the Adulterous Woman (John 7: 53–8:11)*, forthcoming.

– a major impasse had arisen within the pastoral life of the western church regarding sins committed by Christians ('sins committed after baptism') in the course of their lives. While 'small' sins were accepted as being purged by the normal life of prayer and penitence (as one prays in the *Our Father*: 'forgive us our sins as we forgive'), the major sins were seen as being so serious that they needed a far more drastic remedy. This was to be a rigorous, drawn-out official programme of penance (usually referred to as 'public penance'). This process was referred to as 'a plank after shipwreck' and a 'second laborious baptism', and its most signal feature was not that it was public, but that it was a once-off second chance: so while the sins were repeatable, penance was not. It was reserved for three sins in particular – murder, apostasy and fornication – as these were seen as the great sins mentioned in Acts 15:29.[11] Since, by the fifth century, Christianity was no longer persecuted, apostasy was not a problem. Equally murder[12] was a crime in the eyes of the state, and so if someone was known to be guilty of murder then the censure of the church was not the most pressing form of punishment to be feared. The pressing problem, at a pastoral level, arose with fornication. In this case, human nature broke through and overrode noble intentions, and effectively turned the system on its head. If baptismal grace could only be restored once through penance – and the loss of that grace was seen as being sentenced to outer darkness – then prudence demanded that one keep one's options as open as possible.[13] So instead of penance being a chance to restore baptism through suffering, why not postpone baptism until late in life, sow one's wild oats, and then have all one's sins removed without penitential discipline! It made perfect practical sense, but destroyed the whole structure of Christian discipleship: the daily effort to continue following Christ and seeking to grow more perfect day-by-day. Augustine – whose own parents had delayed his baptism for this

---

11. Acts says 'from what is offered to idols, from strangled blood, and from fornication'; the first element was interpreted to cover reversion to paganism and idolatry, the second to cover bloodshed, and the third to cover a range of sexual sins.

12. By the fifth century, Christians had developed a distinction between lawful homicide (e.g. by judges and executioners) and murder. A Christian could lawfully take life if it was to maintain the coercive force of the civil law. See Ambrose, *Epistula 50* (*ad Studium*), 1–2 where he assumes this as a basic Christian position on the basis of Rom 13:4. There are several numerations in use for Ambrose's letters. I am following that of the most recent critical edition (*CSEL* 82/2 (Vienna 1990)). This particular letter is found on pp. 56–9. In older editions, based on the seventeenth-century Maurist edition, this is *Epistola 25*; in the ET in the *FC* series this is *Letter 90*, pp. 492–4.

13. This is still common sense: if you have only one life-line, keep it until the last possible moment!

reason – railed against the habit and fought fire with fire: you may delay, but what if the child dies as an infant, what of a sudden death? Augustine argued that the only way to be sure of heaven was to be baptized as soon as possible – delay was more risky than the prospect of penance! While the vision of 'a mass of the damned' scared people away from delaying baptism, it did not remove the basic problem with penance.

Not only was public penance 'once off', it created other problems. It skewed the notion of discipleship from the life-long struggle to grow more like Christ (*metanoia*) toward one where the 'little' sins and overcoming 'little' evil habits receded from the consciousness of people through an emphasis on the 'great' sins. Thus holiness seemed to consist in avoiding shipwreck after baptism, rather than in steering one's course after Christ. Another consequence of the practice, and one directly related to the once-off character of penance, was that sins were viewed by analogy with crimes in the state's law. A sin was an event which took place at a given moment which carried a penalty in God's justice; penance was getting off that penalty through forgiveness asked for through penance. The notion that one had to look at the sinner rather than the sin was one which Augustine embraced in preaching,[14] but it was not one that had any effect in practice: the church dealt with those who had committed a sin within the same mind-set that the city's count dealt with criminals. In using such a model the personal dimension of sin was lost. On the one hand, it forgets that sinful actions are located within a human being, the sins being the fruits of a disorder within life; and on the other, it tends to emphasize sin as a case of breaking a rule, rather than as a disruption in a relationship with the Living God. Sin disrupts relationships on earth and with Christ, and it flows from an internal disorder in someone who is trying to 'be perfect as the heavenly Father is perfect' (Mt 5:48). Above all, and here was the great problem of public penance, penance must fit within a life of discipleship: it must start with baptism, and must reflect the belief that Christ is the healer, the one who frees people of burdens and the one who goes after sinners to carry them home with rejoicing (cf. Lk 15:4–10).

It seems strange that these basic notions about sin and forgiveness could be appreciated in theory by someone like Augustine, but have had so little impact in his own pastoral practice.[15] The problem was that anyone who sought a way around the problem, or suggested that forgiveness should be more widely available within the church, was seen as 'going soft on sin', and cheapening discipleship, for in the 'old

---

14. E.g. in *Tractatus in Ioannis euangelium* XXXIII, 7.
15. See F. van der Meer, *Augustine the Bishop* (London 1961), pp. 384–7.

days' the *confessores* had chosen death in the arena rather than apostasy! In effect, the church had too great a corporate, and long-standing, psychological commitment to the *status quo* to have the ability to cast off from the whole débâcle. When bishops like the admirably practical pastor Caesarius of Arles practically dumped the system as causing more spiritual problems than it solved, he was accused of almost heretical leniency.[16] Such calls for a return to the 'old' ways, seen as a kind of 'gold standard', would appear for another three hundred years as synods looked back to earlier synods and repeated calls made first in North Africa in the early fifth century; by mouthing these pieties they hoped to show that they were no less tough on sin than their predecessors – the notion that bishops in the past could simply have been on the wrong track was, of course, not an option they considered. By contrast, it meant that the way out of the impasse would most likely occur where there was not a long-standing involvement with (as opposed to a knowledge of) the system of public penance: the Celtic lands were just such a place.

THE ORIGINS OF THE PENITENTIALS

Exactly when and where the first penitential was written we cannot say. We know from Patrick's *Epistola ad milites Corotici*[17] that Patrick publicly condemned Coroticus and his men as guilty of the capital sins of apostasy and shedding blood,[18] and they are excluded for not submitting to penance – clearly he was thinking in terms of public penance. We then enter a dark period until we meet the fully developed *Penitential of Finnian* (usually dated to the late sixth century[19]). It was probably written in Clonard, the great monastery founded by Finnian. Here we have a deliberately short handbook for pastoral use in dealing with the sins of repentant Christians.[20] We should note that the penitentials were intended for dealing with people who had sinned, not with the abstract problems (the sins) nor with a marked-off category of people ('the sinners'). The fifty or more situations envisaged as requiring penance cover the whole range of sins, and it assumes that the one judging the required penance – and there is no hint as to his status in terms of Holy Orders – will meet

---

16. See H. G. J. Beck, *The Pastoral Care of Souls in South-East France During the Sixth Century* (Rome 1950), pp. 187–222, especially 216–22.
17. This aspect of Patrick's writing is dealt with in the running notes to my translation of this letter in *St Patrick: The Man and His Works* (London 1999).
18. *Epistola* 2.
19. See L&S, no. 598 for this date; for information on Finnian (possibly a British cleric who went to Ireland) see D. N. Dumville, 'Gildas and Uinniau', in M. Lapidge and D. Dumville (eds), *Gildas: New Approaches* (Woodbridge 1984).
20. The text is in L. Bieler (ed.), *Penitentials*, pp. 74–95.

people from the whole of society, lay, monastic, clerical, men and women. To each crime it prescribes a specific 'penitential remedy'[21] of a fixed quantity of prayer, fasting and alms. However, for such an elaborate document (it presupposes major shifts in how sin and penance are viewed and dealt with in the church) to make its appearance, a series of crucial developments must have taken place – yet we have only a few indirect glimpses in surviving documents.

We can isolate four major factors that can help explain this shift in theology and practice. The first, and probably most important, factor was the growth of monasticism in the west, and particularly in Ireland where the whole church came to possess certain administrative features that are monastic in origin. By the mid-fifth century, about the time that Christianity was spreading in Ireland, sin in the life of Christians was a concern in the Latin Church in two virtually discrete spheres. In the dioceses the question was one of restoring someone after a lapse from baptismal regeneration through a once-off severe public penance. Meanwhile, in the expanding monasteries, sin was being seen as what hindered perfection; the overcoming of sin was, therefore, an integral part of conversion and discipleship based on the command *paenitentiam agite* ('Do penance!'),[22] and so perfection involved a life of penitence. Within monasticism, the overcoming of sin was not a problem generated in a criminal moment, but something that came from a weakness inherent in the person and which was overcome by the therapy of a specific lifestyle.

No writings were of greater importance in forming the insular view of monasticism than those of John Cassian – indeed when today commentators see links between 'Celtic' and 'Eastern' monasticism, what they really see is Cassian's influence. John Cassian in his series of works on monasticism addressed in detail the question of what impeded the perfect life. In cataloguing the sins of monks his aim was not primarily a code of crimes, but an analysis of the nature of the afflictions of the soul by analogy with a physician's knowledge of bodily diseases. And if sin is a disease then the overcoming of sins must be understood medicinally and, adapting a medical basic principle of 'contraries are healed by contraries', he propounded a model of penance as a set a remedies congruent with a set of maladies. Just as a bodily disease such as fever is healed by applying cold, so the damage of a spiritual disease such as gluttony is repaired

---

21. Cf. the conclusion of the penitential; it is worth our remembering that *remedium* belongs first and foremost to the language of medicine.
22. Mt 4:17; however, this command was not read as an isolated text but as part of a biblical mosaic of texts which used *paenitentia* in the Vulgate: Jesus is in line with the command of John the Baptist (Mt 3:2) and the prophets (e.g. Ezek 18:30); it fits into the larger scheme of his mission as saviour (e.g. Lk 5:32; 13:3; 15:7); and this theme was continued in the Church: e.g. Peter preaching in Acts 2:38.

by fasting.[23] Although often underestimated, Cassian more than anyone else deserves the credit for the sophistication of the post-patristic theology of sin. By studying sin as that part of the ongoing life of the monk which had to be examined and removed as an ailment, he shifted the view of penance in several significant ways. First, it was not punishment but medicine: penance was to make good damage done and so was a reparation and repayment rather than the cost of being saved after disaster. Second, there was a new emphasis on the individual, since sin was a sickness needing diagnosis rather than a crime needing prosecution. This put a value on spiritual self-knowledge in place of the need for public declaration within the Church; equally the one who announced the nature of sins was not necessarily the bishop acting as a judge in the forum, but rather the one who had the care of the souls of the monks, and his decisions were those of physician or trainer with the patient or trainee. Third, since it was designed to deal with the range of sins that afflicted the monk's life it was by nature a sliding scale capable of dealing with minor as well as major diseases, and so it was an ongoing life-long process. Thus the question of repeating penance ceased to be of importance, and the distinction between those who needed formal penance and those who did not disappeared. Cassian's work became widely available from the middle of the fifth century, yet on the Continent the major development he inspired in relation to sin was the reformulation from his work of the list of Eight Principal Vices by Gregory the Great,[24] which in turn influenced later penitentials. In a society such as Ireland's where increasingly the external form of the church was monastic, his widespread use is not surprising, nor that every sin was viewed by analogy with the sins hampering the growth of holiness within a monastery.

The second factor in the developments that led to the penitentials also has an eastern source: the route around the problem of public penance which Greek theology called 'the baptism of tears'.[25] Building on a series of biblical images of repentance, a number of fourth-century writers, most notably Gregory Nazianzen, had stressed that the essential element in forgiveness after baptism was that the sinners were truly sad for their sins. This sadness was expressed in their tearfulness day-after-day and night-after-night at

23. For an account of Cassian's monastic vision see C. Stewart, *Cassian the Monk* (Oxford 1998), especially pp. 62–84. For the medical theory underlying Cassian's approach, see J. T. McNeill, 'Medicine for Sin as Prescribed in the Penitentials', *CH* 1 (1932), 14–26.
24. On Gregory and penance, see C. Straw, *Gregory the Great: Perfection in Imperfection* (Berkeley 1988), pp. 213–35.
25. T. O'Loughlin and H. Conrad-O'Briain, 'The "baptism of tears" in early Anglo-Saxon sources', *ASE* 22 (1993), 65–83.

the thought of their offences. If sinners were truly sorry, then the pain of that sadness and the waters of those tears would wash away sins as surely as the waters of baptism had done. So a key to penance was contrition, compunction and tearfulness. We are not sure how widespread this theme became in the west in the fifth and sixth centuries, but we know that one of Gregory Nazianzen's homilies on the theme was translated by Rufinus; we see the notion of compunction appear as part of the penitential thought of Cassian and Caesarius of Arles; and later again we know that Isidore of Seville was familiar with the notion from Rufinus. When the two themes of penance as medicine and as contrition were combined in a pastoral context, the result is a theology of sin and forgiveness like that underlying our penitentials.

Old Irish law is a third factor in the development of the penitentials. While the law texts that survive are not only later than the penitentials, and indeed show the influence of Latin canon law, it does appear that a central native feature is that crimes, from the smallest trespass by an animal to homicide, can be punished by the payment of a fine between the two parties involved.[26] In this system a crime is an offence committed against a person and his or her family group. In this, Irish law resembles other northern non-Roman (e.g. Germanic) legal systems. The offence is made good by the payment of an honour price by the guilty party or by the guilty party's family. That fine varies with the nature of the offence, and in a society of complex social ranks it also varied with the status of the one offended, and the status of the offender. If this aspect of native law was already present in the fifth/sixth centuries, then an extension of it to the religious realm – where a sin is an offence against God's dignity which carries a price if the offence is to be removed – would explain how the monastic notion of ascetic reparation could so easily be extended to the whole society as a way of understanding and overcoming sin. Each offence has a particular price and when that is paid in penance, then the harmony between the parties is restored; moreover, the price should vary with the status and culpability of the offender, and we see this in the incipient casuistry of the penitentials. Moreover, the hesitation to abandon public penance was in large part a product of a culture of

---

26. The essential introduction is F. Kelly, *A Guide to Early Irish Law* (Dublin 1988); on the relationship between native law and canon law, see L. Breatnach, 'Canon Law and Secular Law in Early Ireland: The Significance of *Bretha Nemed*', *Peritia* 3 (1984), 439–59; for a window into the society reflected in early Irish law tracts, see F. Kelly, *Early Irish Farming* (Dublin 1997) in conjunction with T. P. Oakley, 'The Penitentials as Sources for Medieval History', *Speculum* 15 (1940), 210–23; for the *status quaestionis* of early Irish law, cf. L. Breatnach, 'Law', in K. McCone and K. Simms (eds), *Progress in Medieval Irish Studies* (Maynooth 1996), pp. 107–21.

Roman law – for all notions of divine justice are formed by analogy with human systems of justice[27] – and any leniency was equivalent to letting someone 'get away' with a crime. Irish society with a legal process with different expectations of what constituted the penalty of a crime was free of the psychological barriers that held Christians within the empire enthralled. Irish law saw penalties as reparations of damage done, not as punishments to inflict suffering on the criminal; and within that framework the penitentials were merely an extension of their basic legal attitude into the realm of the sacred. As public penance reflected the legal culture of its origins, so did the penitentials; as Roman justice and law became the basis for a conception of divine justice and law, so too Irish law furnished a model for the dealings of God with the sinner.

The fourth factor is also cultural. Christianity came to Ireland with its history in tow. But while the receiving culture worked hard to adopt that new Christian history and to fit its own past into the Christian framework of world history, the adopted past was far more easily shed by the culture than by those on the continent whose past it was without an effort of identification. Public penance was hoary with age and sacred in the memory of those who could identify closely with the tales of persecution which had occurred in their own cities; to abandon it was a breaking of faith with the past. But as with any potent cultural memory, outside the group which strongly identified with that past, the memory rapidly lost its binding force: the new people could experiment without being limited by the past – for it was only 'their' past by adoption and at second hand.

THE PENITENTIAL OF FINNIAN

The best way to appreciate the theology of the penitentials is to read them, one at a time, as a guide to an actual person engaged in dealing with someone's sins. They are not treatises on the nature of forgiveness, nor homilies. Their starting point is that someone has done something which transgresses God's law. Now they seek a remedy which will remove the offence which stands between the sinner and his or her Creator. It is at this point that the sinner's guide enters the scene with his penitential in hand. And we can only extract its implicit theology of sin and redemption when we locate the text in such a specific and isolated pastoral moment.

---

27. Indeed, the major danger in all theories of divine forgiveness is that divine and human justice are seen univocally, i.e. as grades on a single scale.

The first assumption within the text is that whatever sin the individual has committed, there is an appropriate remedy. This sounds trite, but actually contains a profound theological truth: there is no distance from the Path of Righteousness that cannot be crossed, and there are no limits to the extent of the divine mercy as expressed through the ministry of the Church. The presumption in making the list covering so many aspects of human action is that there is a solution to the problem, there is a remedy. In a system which relied heavily on a supposed analogy between spiritual and physical health, penance as medicine, the administrator of penance as a healer, this initial confidence must have been of psychological benefit to the penitent, conveying trust in God's mercy and removing the sense of hopeless dejection.

The more explicit notions underlying the penitentials can be seen in its first statement:

> If anyone has sinned in his heart through thought, and then at once has repented, let him strike his breast, and ask God for pardon, and make satisfaction, and thus he will become well (*sanus*).[28] (no. 1)

For Finnian sin is always an internal matter between the conscience of the individual and God who is offended. This offence between persons is where sin is located, not in the external criminal act. This shift marks a crucial development in western theology: the distinction between a crime (the evil act) and sin (the evil intention of the actor). Corresponding to this shift to the subject, the crucial element in reconciliation is what later would be termed 'contrition' – the subject's awareness of the nature of his or her intention and his or her rejection of it. So the first step in returning is sorrow towards God for the offence: manifested in the gesture of striking the breast and so immediately accepting responsibility and expressing regret. Then comes the next stage which is the petition to God for pardon, and then comes the actual payment of the fine which satisfies the demands of justice between the offender and the One offended. The basis of the possibility of being able to repay the offence with a fixed penance – the most obvious part of the whole system of penitentials – is that the offender is already sorry. And that this sadness for sin is central is made even more clear later in the text where it speaks of 'weeping and crying for sin both day and night' (no. 29) and of the necessity for 'compunction' (no. 31). The text stands in the tradition of Cassian's emphasis on compunction and conversion of heart, and combines that with the notion of 'the baptism of tears'.

Finnian saw reconciliation as a process rather than as a single

---

28. Finnian claims that his work draws from the Scriptures; while there are few direct quotations, right through the text there are echoes and allusions to Scripture as here: for *et sanus sit*, cf. Jn 5:6–14 and Lk 8:36.

momentary act: it is a regime of medicine and exercise which leads to a restored and stronger Christian, rather than a prison sentence where the convict is suddenly free ('let out') having being purged. Public penance imagined a Christian who 'shipwrecked' (the patristic image) himself in an action that was seen without connection to the rest of life; then mercy restores life after a period of suffering. Finnian conceived the actual crime as 'the presenting problem' showing an underlying weakness; penance for the crime is believed to be an antidote to that underlying weakness – for the penance is the opposite of the deep-seated malaise, and the working assumption is that 'opposites heal opposites'.[29] Finnian is obviously drawing on the medical imagery which Cassian had intended for monks and extending it to the sins of the whole of Christian society. However, he does not theorize about this, and so it is worth quoting the *Penitential* of Columbanus where the theology of sin as sickness needing various remedies is made explicit:

> A variety of offences makes for a variety of penances. And as physicians have to make a variety of medicines [for different ailments], so spiritual doctors (*spiritales medici*) must have different cures for the different wounds, ailments, pains, weaknesses of the soul. But since few know all the correct treatments to cure and bring back the soul to complete health, these are a few [instructions] for that purpose gathered from the tradition of the elders . . .[30]

The task of overcoming sin is the continual presence of penitence in Christian life, and Finnian is aware that as one departs so one must seek at once to return. On the practical level this process expresses itself in the sequence of sin, then sorrow, then penance, and then health. In that the starting point of the return to God after sin is sorrow for sin and petition for mercy, we have here the first inkling of later debates about the essence of forgiveness: is it the moment of contrite internal conversion or the moment of sacerdotal absolution or some combination of these?[31] And in the very act of noting a sequence beginning with the sense of contrition, Finnian is assuming a complexity in the process that allows one to see foreshadowings of later scholastic distinctions such as the 'Two Debts' (the *reatus culpae* which is for the offence to God, and the *reatus poenae* which repays the penalty imposed by God as the just reward of sin); and the

---

29. The medical maxim *contraria contrariis sanantur* can be translated literally as 'contraries by contraries are healed'; however, it is wrong to translate it only in this way as if *contraria* is to be read in terms of logical 'contraries' – what is intended is any form of opposition.
30. [Prologue] B, p. 96.
31. For a convenient summary see K. B. Osborne, *Reconciliation and Justification: The Sacrament and its Theology* (New York 1990), pp. 106–8.

debates about the *processus iustificationis* ('the sequence of justification').

The penances that Finnian laid down in his *Penitential* vary not
only with the rank and status of the offender, but also with the
offender's intention and state of mind, and with the speed of his or
her sorrow for his or her offences. All this reflects a genuine
awareness built up in actual practice that 'situations alter cases'.
Such a casuistry, while abstracted and generalized in a manual,
indicates that Finnian's expertise was not limited to the Scriptures –
which he invokes as his authority – but based in actual pastoral care.
And while in common with most church documents of the period
there is a great deal of emphasis on sexual sins and a tendency to see
women as the source of such sins,[32] the most consistent image is that
of caring. There are references to health, to curing sins as if they
were ailments and to remedies; moreover, Finnian sees his own work
in producing the manual as paternal work of caring for his children.
In several places the text says that the sinner must 'ask pardon or
help of God' (e.g. nos 1, 2, 5, 29) or that they have access to 'the mercy
of God' (e.g. nos 8, 12, 22, 29); or it mentions the heart as the place of
the offence between the sinner and God (e.g. nos 3, 6, 17, 45), and so
it produces an image of God as One who is always ready to forgive
and who with help and mercy is standing close to the situations in
which people find themselves.

Reading Finnian's penitential is a sobering experience for
theologians. He assumes that Christians will sin after baptism and
that they will not be perfect disciples, but will fall short of Christ's
measure in all sorts of ways. But equally he believes that there are
remedies – many of them stiff and demanding – which can lead the
person towards his or her goal. This sturdy realism assumes that
Christian life is the dynamic of following, a movement rather than a
state, a pilgrimage rather than an achievement. While patristic
theologians could not stop looking backwards in their views of
penance, analysing how a perfection once given in baptism had been
lost, Finnian starts with the facts of imperfect discipleship and asks
how it can be repaired, improved and hastened towards its purpose,
so that those who come to him 'can reign with Christ in the life to
come, with the holy Abraham, Isaac, Jacob, Job, Noah, and all the
saints' (no. 46). Finnian concluded his work with a statement of
humility that reveals his view of his work as a healer:

> Here, beloved brothers, are a few things on the remedies of penance . . .
> taken from Scripture and from the decisions of learned men . . . there
> are still other remedies and other kinds [of illness] that need to be
> cured but my need for brevity, my situation, and my lack of skill

---

32. See Payer, *Sex and the Penitentials*; and chapter 6, below.

prevented me from noting them here. But if a diligent student of the divine readings should find them, or bring forth better things, then we shall agree with and follow them also. (Epilogue)

Just such a man was Cummean who wrote a penitential sometime during the seventh century.

THE PENITENTIAL OF CUMMEAN[33]

This work is interesting not for the penances it prescribes nor for the range of people whose failings it covers – in these it stands close to Finnian – but, first, for the depth of pastoral concern; and, second, for its careful explication of the notion of Christian forgiveness. Most of its contents is formally arranged using Cassian's eightfold scheme of vices,[34] seen as the sources of sinfulness in all Christians, the differences being the way they manifest themselves in different ways of life. Moreover, reading the prescriptions about greed (Part III) or drunkenness (Part I) one has the impression that this document was forged in real experience rather than looking outwards from the cloister.

If Cassian's works provided most of the architecture of this penitential, his view of sin as an ailment needing therapy introduces it: it is medicine for the health/salvation (*medicinae salutaris*) of souls, and they are to be seen as 'remedies for wounds:

> Here begins the prologue regarding the saving medicine of souls:
> Before we begin to tell you, my dearest brother, of the decisions of the fathers who went before us regarding how the wounds [of sin] are to repaired, let me summarize for you the sources of all these medicines [i.e. ways of having sins forgiven]. (Incipit, and no. 1)

In addition, it provided a detailed explanation of the principle of 'contraries healed by contraries' as the basis of Christian hope:

> [The fathers] also laid down the principle that the eight sources of evil habits that are central to human [spiritual] health are healed by the eight remedies, their opposites. For indeed it is an old proverb which

---

33. L&S, no. 601; for text: Bieler (ed.), *Penitentials*, pp. 108–34.
34. Cf. *Institutiones* 5, 1 and *Collationes* 5, 18: gluttony, fornication, greed, anger, dejection, sloth, vainglory, pride. This scheme can be found in many places in early medieval Latin writing on penance, but rarely is it so consciously employed as a guide in actual practice. On the theme in the penitentials, cf. T. P. Oakley, 'Cultural Affiliations of Early Ireland in the Penitentials', *Speculum* 8 (1933), 489–500; and on its larger context, cf. U. Voll, 'Sins, Capital', in the *NCE*, vol. 13, pp. 253–4.

states that 'contraries are healed by contraries'. So for the person who committed unlawful actions without measure,[35] it is lawful that he ought to restrain himself (*cohercere se*) from lawful things.[36] (no. 15)

Healing the deep problems from which flow particular crimes is the purpose of penance. It is achieved when a correct balance has been achieved in the person and the person's actions. And the means of administering the remedy is not a punishing administered from without, nor a medicine 'shoved down the throat' of the sick person, but when *he or she restrains him- or herself* from lawful things and so brings about the balance needed for the Christian life. The penitent going to the person with the penitential is not going to a healer in the sense of someone with charismatic powers, and certainly not to someone who doles out correct punishments: rather they are going to someone with diagnostic skills, through their acquaintance with Christian wisdom, as to what are the sources causing these presenting problems. The administrator of the penitential is neither a guru nor a wonder-worker, but a spiritual General Practitioner. This GP, through having learned from the previous experience of those dealing with sick souls, then prescribes a course of therapy which will bring balance and measure into an unbalanced and unstable person. But the sick persons themselves must take on the therapy, and assume responsibility for their own fitness regime; they cannot be healed from outside, nor can they be made whole or healthy as a result of the direct actions by their physician.

In contrast to later sacramental theories of penance, the operator of the penitential does not act *in persona Christi*, actually forgiving. Cummean, or anyone using his penitential, acts as someone who is a member of the tradition of spiritual diagnosticians (here lies the full implication of all the references to the fathers in these texts), who directs a route by which healing – and so forgiveness – can come about. In the relationship between the sick Christian and Christ, Cummean is not an intermediary who either 'binds' or 'looses' (cf. Mt 16:19 or 18:18) but an expert consultant who assesses problems and offers solutions.

Cummean repeatedly draws attention to the fact that his work is based on the decisions of the elders, those greater than him who have gone before him. However, apart from Cassian and those who gave advice in monasteries, he was part of a new system that broke radically with the practice of penance in the church at the time of the fathers in whose tradition Cummean claims to belong. So was he aware of his novelty, and if so are his references to the fathers simply

---

35. There is a play on words here: *inlicita licenter commisit* (literally: he who committed the illicit with licence).

36. There is a second play on words in the second part of the sentence: *a licitis licit* (literally: it is lawful from lawful things).

a smoke screen for that novelty? The answer to the first question is, almost certainly, yes, he knew the novelty of the Irish system; and my basis for saying so is that his first act was to lay out a theology of forgiveness which deliberately by-passed the patristic impasse – this I shall examine in a moment. Was it a smoke screen? The answer here is complex. One of the features of early Christian writers – until the universities – was their corporate sense: they only functioned as teachers/theologians 'in Christ' and as individuals they were just members of a body conceived of in a most literal way, of which Christ was the head. The imagery went back to Paul, but it drew on an even older notion of corporate personality within Israel,[37] and it fitted well with the same medical theory from which they drew 'contraries heal contraries'.[38] This sense of belonging meant that they feared innovation as the equivalent of self-amputation from the body of Christ. On the other hand, they knew they needed to evolve new procedures and get better solutions to problems. Thus we have one of the great enigmas of post-patristic pre-scholastic theology – the period roughly between Vincent of Lérins (died before 450) and Anselm of Canterbury (*c.* 1033–1109) – when writers stressed that they were not saying anything new; yet the fact that they were writing new books indicated that they were saying something not said previously.[39] Hence, their love of quotations and excerpts[40] – but quotations in new contexts could establish a very different theology![41]

So how did Cummean create a theological context which while being in line with the fathers, allowed him to depart so far from their practice? His solution (the most original element in the whole work) was to set the treatment of the baptized person who had committed sins within a much larger framework of divine forgiveness. In broadening the debate, Cummean set the patristic impasse in proper focus and so allowed a solution to emerge. Patristic writers had driven themselves into a cul-de-sac by simply contrasting two forms of divine forgiveness (that granted in baptism, and a second form – penance – which was only a repair-measure after the resulting

---

37. I have gone into this sense of tradition in detail in 'Individual Anonymity and Collective Identity: the Enigma of Early Medieval Latin Theologians', *RTPM* 64 (1997), 291–314.
38. See R. M. Grant, 'Paul, Galen, and Origen', *JTS* ns 34 (1983), 533–6.
39. See T. O'Loughlin, *Teachers and Code-Breakers: The Latin Genesis Tradition, 430–800* (Turnhout 1999), especially ch. 9.
40. Compare T. O'Loughlin, 'Christ as the focus of Genesis Exegesis in Isidore of Seville', in T. Finan and V. Twomey (eds), *Studies in Patristic Christology* (Dublin 1998).
41. See T. O'Loughlin, 'Tradition and Exegesis in the Eighth Century: The Use of Patristic Sources in Early Medieval Scriptural Commentaries', in T. O'Loughlin (ed.), *The Scriptures and Early Medieval Ireland* (Turnhout 1999), pp. 217–39.

forgiveness of baptism had broken down) while acknowledging the truth that God's mercy is infinite, even if this could not be accessed within the church. Considered in this way, the notion of baptism limited the debate about everything else; so the first task for Cummean was to set even baptism in a context of divine activity towards humanity. The remission of sins is shown by Cummean to take place in twelve distinct ways which are *not presented as limiting one another*, but all of which are supported by a proof-text from Scripture.

The first is baptism with water, and by placing it first Cummean is being true to the place given it in the tradition. Second, the individual's disposition (*affectus*) of love as in the case of the woman who loved much and so had much forgiven her (Lk 7:47). By putting this second, Cummean established the priority of the intention of the penitent as a key to forgiveness in general. The third mode of penitence is almsgiving, and so the activity of charity toward the poor which is such a part of Christian holiness is also a part of the Christian's overcoming sin – thus he integrated the twin activities of discipleship and forgiveness to an extent the patristic authors never did. Fourth is the presence of tears – again linking forgiveness to the attitude of sorrow within the individual's conscience. The fifth is the acknowledgement of crimes (*criminum confessio*). This is, in effect, the practice of penance as known among the fathers – now it has been downgraded and made just one mode of forgiveness in the midst of a group of ways towards reconciliation. The sixth is 'affliction of heart and body' (*cordis et corporis*) – penitential exercises; but note that those of the body follow after those of the heart. Again, Cummean places greater emphasis on the intention of the penitent in the process of forgiveness than on the external penitential actions. The seventh mode makes even clearer that growth in discipleship and the overcoming of sin are identical, and that forgiveness is a process rather than an event: 'The seventh is amendment of one's ways, which is the renunciation of vices.' This explicit identification shifts the moment of full forgiveness from the moment after baptism at the beginning of the Christian life to its very end. Christians in life are not those who have fallen from a perfection granted at baptism, but those who began a life of discipleship and who continue to grow toward the fullness of Christ during their lives.[42] The eighth mode is 'the intercession of the saints' which is explicitly linked to the prayer and anointing by the Church, for he quotes James 5:14–16. In Cummean's mind, baptism, the activity of penance, spiritual and

---

42. This shift in the theology of baptism does not appear to have been noticed by theologians at the time, but it would become a major cause of contention during the Reformation. What is significant is that the shift from the earlier position had occurred so early.

physical healing, and the anointing of the sick are all inextricably linked as places, modes or 'sacraments' wherein the individual encounters the mercy of God in Christ in the midst of his people. Later, this unity would be split up into boxes: the 'Sacrament of Baptism'; the 'Sacrament of Penance'. Then the 'Sacrament of the Sick' ('Extreme Unction') moved aside in western theology with the notion of healing left in a spiritual siding, while debate arose as to how that Sacrament differed from the Sacrament of Penance in extent of forgiving sins, which of them was more important, how did they delimit one another, who could administer which and when, and were they all 'real' sacraments (i.e. did they have a proper and distinct object which involved the use of spiritual power in a legally accountable way).[43] The unified way that Cummean presents them could easily be presented as a case where they had not yet 'developed' in the consciousness of the theological community so as to reveal their distinctiveness,[44] yet this is no more than hallowing what subsequently happened. Cummean's unity seems preferable as it reflects an awareness that the divine mercy is itself manifold and when parcelled out it is, to an extent, denied. The ninth, tenth and eleventh modes are variants on the theme that if the penitent is him- or herself forgiving to others, then God too will be forgiving with that person. So the ninth mode is 'mercy and faith', for 'the merciful shall obtain mercy' (Mt 5:7); the tenth is that one who helps another to convert from sin will himself be helped by God (again an appeal is made to James – Jas 5:20), and the eleventh is that one who offers forgiveness to another will have the offer of forgiveness from God (Lk 6:37). In these three cases Cummean again integrates the ongoing demands of the Christian life – and especially its demands towards others – and the need for repentance and forgiveness from God. In his thought there is an underlying analogy – probably based in part on 'forgive us our trespasses as we forgive those who trespass against us' in the *Our Father* – between humans being forgiving in their daily lives, and the reception by humans of divine forgiveness. The twelfth mode is that of martyrdom based on Christ's reply to the repentant thief on the cross (Lk 23:42). Here Cummean inserts the traditional 'baptism of blood' within his scheme.[45]

---

43. It is always worth remembering that the definition of sacrament which identified the seven of western Catholic worship was originally derived from canon lawyers anxious to set out rights and responsibilities (cf. S. G. Kuttner, *Harmony from Dissonance: An Interpretation of Medieval Canon Law* (Latrobe 1960)); the 'theological' definitions (over which there were so many disputes at the Reformation) emerged subsequently to justify theologically what had emerged *de facto* in the Latin church's praxis as set out by the lawyers.

44. In traditional defences of the origins of the seven sacraments system found in western Catholic theology, such arguments from 'development' have been much to the fore in the late nineteenth and twentieth centuries.

45. This list of the means of forgiveness, each supported by scriptural testimonies, does not appear to have any parallels in medieval theology.

Through this synoptic presentation of the Christian life as the interaction of the mercy of God and human effort Cummean situated his actual prescriptions, and justified theologically the whole practice of the penitentials. In effect, he had made the whole of life penitential, but did so by focusing penance on the redeeming love of God: human beings thus existed within the drama of God's love, received by them as mercy.

THE PENITENTIALS: A MIXED LEGACY

The negative contributions of the penitentials to the development of western praxis and theology of penance are well known. They led to an increasingly individualistic understanding of sin: the notion of sinfulness as a list of 'black marks' that could be bought off by a mechanistic application of spiritual payments. This practice eventually contributed to the growth of indulgences, and so to an approach to forgiveness that made the whole process liable to abuse and misunderstanding. Equally, there has been criticism of the penitentials as fostering an unhealthy introspection, and that they have contributed to guilt complexes especially in relation to sexuality. However, it is unfair to the creative and brave theologians and pastors who pioneered this solution to a problem that had dogged Christianity since the second century (the problem is first found in Hermas's *Shepherd*) to blame them for later corruptions and abuses. Men like Finnian, Cummean and the other Irish theologians who produced penitentials are not responsible for what happened later, and deserve to have their texts judged on their intrinsic merits as Christian religious documents.

The first step is to note just how radically the praxis of the penitentials broke with that of the patristic period. We can tabulate this change thus:

Patristic notions of penance within the church	Assumptions underlying the penitentials
Once-off unrepeatable event, that must be seen as extraordinary	A repeatable action, seen as part of ordinary Christian discipline
The sin which necessitates penance is a major one, seen as a crime which wilfully breaches the law	It covers the range of human weakness, seen as the presenting problems of a deeper sickness.
Penitential acts are presented as punitive suffering keyed to the criminal act.	Penitential acts are seen as therapy keyed to the patient and the illness.

There is a distinction between the penitence demanded as part of the decision of discipleship and penance to recover the baptismal condition	Penance and discipleship are integrated as aspects of ongoing Christian growth to 'the fullness of Christ' at the end of life.
Recovery after the event of penance is a static condition of the soul, focused on the moment of the beginning of Christian life in baptism.	Recovery is a life-long process, focused on the destination of the Christian life when the individual is called into paradise.

In short, the penitentials turned the praxis and preaching of public penance on its head.

A second step in surveying the penitentials is to note the speed with which this new understanding developed. Patrick (probably mid-fifth century) assumed the praxis of public penance, hence he stands near the beginning of the process; while by Finnian's time (probably mid-sixth century) it was complete, both practically and theoretically. And, we have no reason to suppose that Finnian was the first to compile a penitential, but simply that his is the oldest that has survived. Such a shift in theology in what can be little more than a century is amazing for any period of Christian history apart from the twentieth century. It is all the more amazing that it took place in a country where Christianity was still finding its feet. That period is one which is dark to historians, but on the basis of what emerged we should be slow to assume that growth in Irish theology only began in the late sixth and early seventh centuries: that dark period after Patrick must be seen as one of vigorous intellectual growth in the young church.

The penitentials were pastorally effective and helped to develop a deeper understanding of the process of life in Christian discipleship. They shifted the emphasis from crime to therapy, from evil nature to illness, from judge to physician, from recovering a lost purity to becoming whole, and from life as a sequence of snap-shots to one of process: the cumulative effect of this was a shift to the individual's intentions and conscience. In this, they highlighted for the west the notion of contrition in the restoration of the harmony destroyed by sin. Contrition as a movement towards God, manifested in a new willingness to tackle the deep problems of one's soul, became the key to God's mercy. And in this emphasis on contrition as central to penance, the penitentials are the harbingers of all later theologies of penance in the west.

FURTHER READING

Texts/Translations

L. Bieler ed., *The Irish Penitentials* (Dublin 1975).
J. T. McNeill and H. M. Gamer, *Medieval Handbooks of Penance* (New York 1938), pts I, II, III, IV and VIII.

Bibliography

H. Connolly, *The Irish Penitentials and their Significance for the Sacrament of Penance Today* (Dublin 1995), pp. 237–46.
L&S, nos 598, 601, 614 and 640.

Studies

D. Billy, 'The Penitentials and "The Making of Moral Theology" ', *Louvain Studies* 14 (1989), 143–51.
Connolly, op. cit.
K. Hughes, *Early Christian Ireland: Introduction to the Sources* (Cambridge 1972), chs 2 and 3.
Kenney, pp. 235–50.
J. T. McNeill, 'Medicine for Sin as Prescribed in the Penitentials', *CH* 1 (1932), 14–26.
McNeill and Gamer, op. cit., with texts.
T. O'Loughlin, 'Penitentials and Pastoral Care', in G. R. Evans (ed.), *A History of Pastoral Care* (London 2000), pp. 93–111.
—— and H. Conrad-O'Briain, 'The "baptism of tears" in early Anglo-Saxon sources', *ASE* 22 (1993), 65–83.
K. B. Osborne, *Reconciliation and Justification: The Sacrament and its Theology* (New York 1990), pp. 84–94
P. J. Payer, 'The Humanism of the Penitentials and the Continuity of the Penitential Tradition', *MedS* 46 (1984), 340–54.
—— *Sex and the Penitentials: The Development of a Sexual Code 550–1150* (Toronto 1984).

4 Adomnán: A Theologian at Work

On hearing of 'theology' we usually think first of a discipline, a body of knowledge, an academic skill and discourse that exists 'out there'. As such, it is the Christian religious equivalent to geometry: just as a student learns about the different parts of triangles and circles and becomes proficient in answering questions regarding them, so the theologian is the one who has learned about scripture and Christology and so on. In a sense this is a true analogy, as one factor distinguishing the theologian from someone reflecting on religion is that he or she is aware of the past and present discourse of others interested in religious questions, and is anxious to make a contribution to the discourse. So theology is always a community activity, and – whether the individual likes it or not – an activity within a tradition. However, in another way theology is poles apart from geometry. Many people can read theology books, and indeed write them, but the creative theologian is above all someone who is grappling with his or her own religious questions and passions. There is a personal and passionate element in areas like theology and philosophy that is not present in those sciences which emphasize the repetition of experiments as their proof-mark. Thus the history of theology is punctuated by great religious figures whose personal quests, engagements with the world, their individual make-up – and indeed hang-ups – have shaped what they have done and written. These, in turn, raised the questions to be answered, and laid out the directions to be taken, for generations after them. We have only to think of the lives of Augustine, Aquinas and Luther to note how their personal questions inspired their works and moved theology in one way rather than another. Theology is activity: one does it, one theologizes, and the way one does theology says much about the theologian. So, for the historian to have an overview of a theology we have to situate the works within the life, and be attuned to noting the impact of the life in the works. Theology, therefore, can be seen as the results of the searches of individuals – aware of the community of Christians and giving weight to the results of others' searches – for understanding. The individual who searched and the account of the searching are interdependent.[1]

If you accept that one *does* theology, then a proper appreciation of any text requires that we know about the life of its author. And here lies the great difficulty for understanding the theology produced in early Christian Ireland: a great many of the texts are anonymous[2] while the supposed authorship of other texts is a result of modern conjecture, and many more texts are named but we have almost no biography of their authors (even dates often being only scholarly conjectures). So we have the situation that the only writers for whom we can set their works within their lives are Columbanus, Adomnán and Eriugena. But since Adomnán engaged in a range of pursuits – exegesis, law, hagiography, in addition to being the busy abbot of Iona – he is especially interesting.

SEVERAL PEOPLE?

From the way Adomnán is presented in many books and articles one could think that there are several Adomnáns, and description depends upon whom and when you ask. Probably the oldest basis of his fame in Ireland, and one which receives great attention among historians of Irish institutions and from Celtic-language specialists today, is as the law-maker at the Synod of Birr who was responsible for the proclamation of the *Cáin Adomnáin* – his 'law of the innocents' for the protection of women and children in war. There is also the Adomnán who is the author of the *Vita Columbae* where interest, naturally, tends to focus on Columba. Then there is the Adomnán who is simply the scribe recording a few facts as related by a bishop named Arculf about Palestine in the *De locis sanctis*; this Adomnán is only a incidental figure mentioned in footnotes to studies devoted to early Christian Ireland or the history of geography. Then there are the aspects of Adomnán that are almost completely ignored: Adomnán the abbot; Adomnán the monastic teacher; Adomnán the illustrious theologian; and Adomnán the saint. We can pick out a few of these points here.

---

1. See T. O'Loughlin, 'Newman and *Doing* Theology', *NB* 76 (1995), 92–8.
2. Many of the scriptural commentaries, homilies and legal texts are wholly anonymous; many others are pseudonymous (i.e. are attributed to great figures such as Augustine) which is *de facto* the equivalent of anonymity for the historian. Moreover, names such as 'Pseudo-Isidore' and 'Augustinus Hibernicus' while convenient among scholars to distinguish one nameless writer from another, also tend to cloud the fact that we know so little about the individuals who produced these works.

LEGISLATOR

The Law of the Innocents

In a commentary to the *Félire Oengusso*, possibly written in the ninth century, we read:

> These are the four laws (*cána*) of Ireland:
> Patrick's law, not to kill the clergy;
> and Adomnán's law, not to kill women;
> Dáire's law, not to kill cattle;
> and the law of Sunday, not to transgress thereon.[3]

This is Adomnán as the dominant figure at Birr in 697. The *Annals of Ulster* state that 'Adomnán travelled to Ireland and gave the Law of the Innocents to its people.' There, in the presence of ninety-one guarantors (including Muirchú the hagiographer of Patrick) he sought to change the conventions of warfare: women were no longer to be combatants, they were to be excluded from capital punishment, the mutilation of women and rape in warfare were to be considered serious crimes.[4] The *Cáin Adomnáin* is a monument to his dedication and desire to be at the service of those who most needed protection and gives us that warm feeling for the man that we have for humanitarians who work to limit injustice. We want to expect that sort of witness from powerful church leaders, but often opposing the forces of power and wealth is too daunting, and many churchmen become chaplains to the executioners. Adomnán at Birr does not disappoint us: he is a courageous figure. From his Christian view of warfare he supplemented native law in a radical way. We also sense that a task's size will not put him off; this we will see again in the task he undertook in *De locis sanctis*.

However, propounding a 'Law' is not what we think of as the work of an abbot – to us the monastery is the place of retreat from the world and its cares. For Adomnán, our notion of the monastery more belonged to those who left the monastery for a hermitage such as Cormac;[5] the life of the monk, by contrast, was one of dedication to God and to his service in a community set in the midst of the larger community of the Church. In the monastery he daily heard in the Psalms that God's law was a gift to his people, and that to proclaim it was a holy task; and with those texts ringing in his ears we can

---

3. See Kenney, p. 237.
4. See Kenney, pp. 245–6 (no. 81). The most comprehensive accounts are in M. Ní Dhonnchadha, 'The Guarantor List of *Cáin Adomnáin*, 697', *Peritia* 1 (1982), 178–215; and idem, 'The *Lex Innocentium*: Adomnán's Law for Women, Clerics and Youths, 697 AD', in M. O'Dowd and S. Wichert (eds), *Chattel, Servant or Citizen: Women's Status in Church, State and Society* (Belfast 1995), pp. 58–69.
5. *Vita Columbae* 1, 6.

imagine him setting out for Birr. 'The just man's . . . delight is in the law of the Lord, and on his law he meditates day and night' (Ps 1:2) or 'The law of the Lord is perfect, reviving the soul; . . . making wise the simple' (Ps 19:7) or 'Open my eyes, that I may behold wondrous things out of your law' (Ps 119:18). Today Scripture scholars point out that when the early Jewish translators chose the Greek word *nomos* to render the Hebrew *torah*, they opened the way to the notion of 'laws' and legalities that goes with *nomos* (or its Latin equivalent *lex*) and which is more impersonal than the sense it had originally.[6] Yes, but it was in this impersonal way that Adomnán and most Christians until recent centuries understood it, and so they used the Scriptures as a quarry of laws and guides for their societies.[7] At Birr, Adomnán was engaging in a task wholly in line with his role as the leader of a monastery wishing to serve God by carrying out what God asked of them in relation to the wider community: just as they sent out missions to the Picts, or provided education and counsel, so they had to proclaim God's law within the society. And in proclaiming the *Cáin* other passages from the Scriptures would have come to mind: 'the father of orphans and protecting judge of widows, such is God in his holy place' (Ps 68:5); or the Gospel's warning about those who engage in the rituals of religion but make war on defenceless women: 'Those who devour widows' houses and for a pretence make long prayers, they will receive a longer punishment' (Mk 12:40). To secure the passage of a law that defended widows – i.e. women who were defenceless – was to announce God's will as Isaiah the prophet had done: 'Listen to me, my people, and give ear to me, my nation; for a law will go forth from me, and my justice for a light to the peoples' (Is 51:4).

Hostage Mediator

Another aspect of Adomnán's concern for the larger society is his trips to England – he refers to it as *Saxonia*[8] – at least one of these was on behalf of hostages. What we know of this is built up from several sources. He himself tells us that he made two trips to England and visited King Aldfrith of Northumbria, a friend of Iona, 'and that on both our first visit (which was after Ecfrith's battle) and

---

6. Cf. R. Murray, 'Hebrew Bible, Jewish Scriptures, Christian Old Testament', *The Month* 259 (1998), 468–74 at 474, n. 11.
7. On the differences between the way that medieval and modern Christians use Scripture, cf. L. T. Johnston, 'Imagining the World Scripture Imagines', *Modern Theology* 14 (1998), 165–80; and T. O'Loughlin, 'Christ and the Scriptures: the Chasm between Modern and Pre-modern Exegesis', *The Month* 259 (1998), 475–85.
8. *Vita Columbae* 2, 46.

on our second visit two years later' he was 'protected from a raging plague affecting those around him through the intercession of Columba'.[9] Aldfrith was his friend and was connected with Ireland in many ways – indeed he has a place in Irish tradition as a man of learning.[10] It is likely that the future king stayed on Iona with Adomnán, for Bede says (as he does of Adomnán also) that Aldfrith 'was a man most learned in the Scriptures'[11] and Adomnán refers to him as 'our [the community's] friend'. We know that King Ecfrith of Northumbria was killed at the battle of Nechtanesmere in May 685, so Adomnán's trip was shortly after that date. From the Irish annals we learn that the purpose of his visit on the first occasion was 'to lead sixty captives back to Ireland' that had been taken 'the previous year from Mag-Breg', but they date it to 686.[12] The annals date the second visit, naturally enough, as 688 and say that then also he brought back captives.[13] Let us leave aside the purpose of the second trip and concentrate on the first. That there were captives in Ecfrith's kingdom in 685/6 is very likely, for we know that he had led a ruthless attack on Brega, 'sparing' as Bede says 'neither churches nor monasteries'[14] in 684. Indeed, Bede sees his death in battle the following year as a divine punishment.[15] If Ecfrith had now been succeeded by a man noted for learning and holiness, and Adomnán's friend, then the scene would be just right for Adomnán to go and negotiate a return of captives.

Again we applaud this 'humanitarian' work. We know from modern accounts by former hostages that their plight can be desperate, and we often admire church-people who act as intermediaries between political factions. This negotiator function was one that had been performed by church leaders in western Europe since the break-up of the Roman Empire, as we saw already with St Patrick.[16] Adomnán fits into this pattern, but we miss part of his vision of the Christian universe when we see it as only humanitarianism. In the *Vita Columbae* Adomnán says that Columba's

---

9. *Vita Columbae* 2, 46.
10. The best convenient account is in R. Sharpe's translation of the *Vita Columbae*, pp. 350–2; and for more detail see C. Ireland, 'Aldfrith of Northumbria and the Learning of a *Sapiens*', in K. A. Klar, E. E. Sweetser and C. Thomas (eds), *A Celtic Florilegium* (Lawrence MA 1996), pp. 63–77.
11. *Historia ecclesiastica gentis anglorum* 4, 26.
12. See the *Annals of Tigernach* and the *Annals of the Four Masters*, cf. A. O. Anderson, *Early Sources of Scottish History: AD 500–1286* (Edinburgh 1922/ Stamford 1990), p. 196.
13. Ibid., p. 199.
14. *Historia ecclesiastica gentis anglorum* 4, 26.
15. See Sharpe, op. cit. where he presents all the known historical details in a well-focused passage.
16. See ch. 2 above; and W. Klingshirn, 'Charity and Power: Caesarius of Arles and the Ransoming of Captives in Sub-Roman Gaul', *JRS* 75 (1985), 183–203.

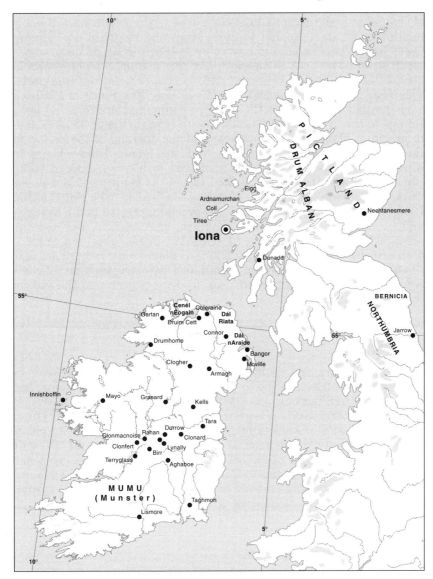

Iona and its connections

monasteries stretch across northern Britain over the lands of the Irish in Britain and of the Picts, and that this area is under Columba's protection.[17] This means that Adomnán, as the successor

---

17. *Vita Columbae* 2, 46; Sharpe questions whether Adomnán's boundaries represent the political situation at the time (Sharpe, op. cit., p. 349), but my concern is how Adomnán saw his own role in this area, not whether his geopolitical description can be trusted.

of Columba, is the senior Christian leader in the whole area. It is his mission to act as a prophet to those kings and rulers in proclaiming God's law. When he goes to any ruler in that region, or those which touch upon it, he goes as one with a divine mandate, as he shows in book I of the *Vita* that Columba had, to be a prophet to those parts. The basic text that inspired this activity was 'The Spirit of the Lord God is upon me, because the Lord has anointed me to bring good tidings to the afflicted; he has sent me to bind up the brokenhearted, to proclaim liberty to the captives, and the opening of the prison to those who are bound' (Is 61:1). And this going before kings to intercede for captives was a central part of his own task of being Christ's minister to all who looked to him as leader and abbot, for Christ had made his own the statement in Isaiah: 'The Spirit of the Lord is upon me . . . to preach . . . to proclaim release to the captives and . . . to set at liberty those who are oppressed, to proclaim the acceptable year of the Lord' (Lk 4:18–19). When king and abbot – both scripture scholars – met in 686 they would have recognized that freeing captives was part of Adomnán's primary task as Christ's representative, his apostolic witness, in those parts out at the ends of the earth (see Acts 1:8).[18]

Canons

Adomnán at Birr and on his trips to King Aldfrith can be seen as bringing God's law into the larger society of kings and nations, but there is another aspect to law: law as the work of a pastor. A strange set of regulations survives known as the *Canones Adomnani*.[19] Often they are ignored in studies of Adomnán or a doubt is raised about their authenticity,[20] but there is no basis for such a doubt. They fit neatly into a pattern of canonical writing from the period which seeks to adapt Old Testament law to Christian situations. And, when found in manuscripts either as a body of twenty canons or quoted singly in other canonical collections, they are always linked to him by name.

---

18. For the significance of this, and related scriptural texts, for Adomnán, cf. T. O'Loughlin, 'The View from Iona: Adomnán's Mental Maps', *Peritia* 10 (1996), 98–122; and idem, 'Living in the Ocean', in C. Bourke (ed.), *Studies in the Cult of Saint Columba* (Dublin 1997), pp. 11–23.
19. See L. Bieler (ed.), *The Irish Penitentials* (Dublin 1975), pp. 176–81.
20. For example, H. Connolly (*The Irish Penitentials and their Significance for the Sacrament of Penance Today* (Dublin 1995), p. 35) states: 'There is no substantial evidence, however, to link these canons with Adamnan, and scholars are of the opinion that their attribution to him is entirely legendary.' However, this author does not give any reason as to why there is a doubt over the attribution, nor does he cite scholarly opinions by name, and he ignored the fact that there is no doubt in the manuscripts about attribution, so his 'entirely legendary' is somewhat overstating the case.

Perhaps the reason for hesitation in linking them to Adomnán is simply that they are not very attractive in content. One deals with the remarriage of a man whose wife has become a prostitute (he cannot remarry while the wife lives), and one deals with handling stolen goods, or, more precisely, with cattle taken in a raid (Christians are not to accept stolen beasts as trade or gifts). However, the other eighteen out of the twenty canons are concerned with what can be eaten in unusual circumstances and 'health' issues, mainly dealing with when and when not it is lawful to eat carrion. That such food was unclean was a theme found widely in the Old Testament,[21] yet in the Gospel it is said that Christ 'declared all foods clean' (Mk 7:19). So why these laws? The answer probably lies in a complex of reasons. The first is in the fact that there is a hesitation in many societies about eating carrion. Second, the instruction to Peter to 'kill and eat' (Acts 10:13 and 11:7) – seen as the basis for abrogating the Old Law about clean and unclean foods – covered the killing of animals for food, but not carrion; and anyway the dead flesh is not declared unclean in these *canones*, but rules are given as to when it can be eaten and when it should be avoided. Third, the whole question was part of the concern of canonists at the time both in the insular world and further afield.[22] And fourth, in many medieval laws about food our clear distinction between 'health regulations' and 'moral rules' does not exist. In setting out these rules Adomnán is answering what were real questions from those who looked to him for guidance; he is making sense of God's law which he finds in the Old Testament and which could not be simply ignored; and in many cases he is simply applying common sense to situations that cropped up in his communities. A good example is canon 1:

> Sea animals found dead on the shore, and where we do not know how they died, can be eaten in good faith; but may not be eaten if they are putrid.

Again in the ninth canon we see the forerunner of modern hygiene regulations:

> A well in which a carcass (whether human, dog or other animal) is found is to be emptied, all the mud is to be taken out, and then the well will be clean.

A simple rule, but one that many people until relatively recently never thought about and thus suffered the consequences through the spread of disease. Such rules were for the good of the community in small things, just as the law of the Synod of Birr was for its good in major events. These simple rules tell us as much about Adomnán the

---

21. For example: Lev 11:18; Deut 14:17; or Ezek 4:14.
22. There are regulations of a similar nature in the *Collectio canonum hibernensis* 54, especially ch. 14 (pp. 215–19).

legislator, to whom many looked for answers and judgments, as the other documents connected with him.

Easter Dating

Lastly, we know from Bede that Adomnán was concerned about another law: that regulating the date of Easter, and that Iona should use the same calculation for the feast as the rest of the Church. He realized while visiting Northumbria that Iona was aberrant in this matter – probably while on a third visit only a couple of years before his death – and then he tried to bring Ireland and Iona 'back into catholic unity' (*ad unitatem reduxit catholicam*) through the 'universal observance' (*catholicam . . . obseruantiam*) of the date of Easter.[23] Bede tells us that while he had much success in Ireland, Iona itself – to Adomnán's regret – refused to use the more modern calculations. To us this might seem only a matter of a liturgical detail and, in any case, the calculations among both parties were flawed. When we do try to understand it we are apt to see it as church politics: like two modern denominations each holding for its particular tradition. This question of the Easter date is complex, not only in its technicalities,[24] but also in its significance for people at the time. What was at stake was the harmony between human and divine law. God had created the universe in an orderly and numbered way; everywhere its order was a testimony to the ideas in mind of God as he created, and to see these patterns in the material creation was to see beyond matter into the divine purposes. The crucial text for the seventh and eighth centuries, as it had been for Augustine, was 'You have arranged all things in measure, number, and weight' (Wis 11:20).[25] Moreover, this law within the universe had been put there by God from the beginning so that people could measure the passage of time and celebrate at the right time: 'And God said, "Let there be lights in the firmament of the heavens to separate the day from the night; and let them be for signs and for seasons and for days and years" ' (Gen 1:14).[26] Moreover, the moment for the Passover had been given by God to his people (Lev 23) and it was to be calculated with the celestial reckoner. So fixing any festival, much less the central festival of Easter,[27] was not just a matter of ecclesiastical

---

23. *Historia ecclesiastica* 5, 15.
24. See D. Ó Cróinín and M. Walsh (eds), *Cummian's Letter De controversia paschali and the De ratione computandi* (Toronto 1988).
25. This verse is often cited using Vulgate numbering: 11:21; for its significance for insular scholars in this period, cf. T. O'Loughlin, 'The Mysticism of Number in the Medieval Period before Eriugena', in J. J. Cleary (ed.), *The Perennial Tradition of Neoplatonism* (Leuven 1997), pp. 397–416.
26. See ch. 9 below.
27. On its centrality in the perception of people in the first millennium see the next chapter and its role in Muirchú's dramatic presentation of the conversion of Ireland.

decision, but of tuning in to the law in the universe around one. Christ had suffered at the time of the Passover; that was when the divinely chosen 'Hour had come' (Mk 14:41; Jn 12:23; etc.), and it was this key moment in the whole history of the universe that they wanted to relive at Easter. The Word had been there when the ordered universe was created (Jn 1:3); he had waited for the right moment to enter his creation as a man (Wis 18:14–15; Gal 4:4; and Jn 7:8); and then came the moment of his victory, 'his hour', over the powers of death (cf. Lk 22:53). Getting the arithmetic right was a matter of the basic law of the creation and the divine plan. Many in Ireland might accept a change on the authority of the learned Adomnán as a way of being more in line with the basic clock of the universe; but for his own monks, to whom he was a more familiar figure, this was too serious a matter to change just on the basis of what he had seen among 'the Saxons'. Bede records that before the next Easter (in 705), Adomnán had died; so it appears he was a legislator to the very end as 'the blessed man who ponders God's law day and night' (Ps 1:1–3).

THE SCHOLAR

We see Adomnán as a theologian and scholar in his two books: the *Vita Columbae* and the *De locis sanctis*, but particularly in the latter. This statement will surprise many, for they know, indeed love, the *Vita* but dismiss the other as curious medieval lore about faraway places and the sort of book that is only of interest to antiquarians. The most recent book looking at Adomnán as a saint is an example of this. It refers to the *De locis sanctis* only incidentally, cites no literature about it, and has this as its meagre praise: 'Adomnán's book on the Holy Places deserves to be better known, if only because it is the oldest book to have been written in Scotland whose text has survived'![28] Yet, the *De locis sanctis* was copied extensively throughout medieval Europe, was excerpted, translated and used as a basis for other works.[29] Likewise, it was solely on the basis of the *De locis sanctis* that Adomnán, virtually alone among early Irish writers, gained the medieval honour of being known as an 'illustrious teacher' (cf. Sir 44), namely one who had 'instructed many in wisdom' and so deserved 'to shine like the stars' (Dan 12:3). Adomnán was so known down to the sixteenth century.[30] The basic fact is this: we may

---

28. A. Macquarrie, *The Saints of Scotland: Essays in Scottish Church History AD 450–1093* (Edinburgh 1997), p. 162.
29. For a preliminary study of the extent of its use, see T. O'Loughlin, 'The Diffusion of Adomnán's *De locis sanctis* in the Medieval Period', in Ériu *Proceedings of the 1997 Derry Conference on Columba*, forthcoming.
30. See T. O'Loughlin, 'Adomnán the Illustrious', *IR* 46 (1995), 1–14.

value the *Vita* for what it tells us about Iona and say that it is a far better document than most medieval saints' lives,[31] but it is only a saint's life nonetheless. This is not to devalue hagiography, but to set it in the context of medieval learning. Each community was interested in the great saints of the whole Church and in their own local saints, and very many people wrote saints' lives, but in the case of the regional saints only people with special interest paid much attention to their cults or lives. This explains the paucity of copies of the *Vita* in manuscript: outside those places where Columba was a popular saint, his life contained little of interest. *De locis sanctis*, on the other hand, deals with places mentioned in the Scriptures and with specific problems relating to them. Its subject was of interest and concern to every teacher of Scripture in the Latin world at that time.

Adomnán wrote his two books with different audiences in mind. The *Vita* has the people connected with his own monasteries as its primary audience; it tells of their founder and origins, their heavenly intercessor and role model. Its secondary audience is those whom Adomnán might be able to interest in Columba. An example of how he wants to promote Columba's cult to those who know little about him can be seen in the stories about how during a worldwide plague those territories watched over by Columba were spared.[32] The message to his own monks is to be imitators of Columba in the way he imitated Christ (cf. 1 Cor 11:1), and to those who do not yet invoke the help and protection of Columba that they should do so, for he is one chosen as a prophet through whom God reveals himself, one through whom God manifests his power miraculously and one whom God points out as holy through special events.[33] It is a book to be read in public to anyone who will listen, it is for reading in the liturgy at the time around Columba's feast and it is a good story. The primary audience of *De locis sanctis* is the teacher seeking to make sense of certain problems in the Scriptures and it assumes an existing knowledge of those problems. This teacher could be anywhere in the Latin church, for it supposes a familiarity not only with the Scriptures, but with the great western theologians, especially Jerome and Augustine, upon whose work Adomnán builds. While often dismissed, wrongly, as little more than the travel accounts of a certain pilgrim, the 'gallic bishop Arculf', with a few extra details from what Adomnán knew from books, it is in fact a complex work solving textual contradictions by appealing to geographical knowledge. But it has as well a good storyline, as the various solutions are strung together by being linked to successive moments on Arculf's

---

31. See, for example, the comments by K. Hughes, *Early Christian Ireland: Introduction to the Sources* (Cambridge 1972), p. 224.
32. *Vita Columbae* 2, 46.
33. *Vita Columbae*, second preface, 3b.

journey; this indicates its secondary audience who can find material there which will help them imagine the world of Jesus and the places they heard named every day in the liturgy. For instance, in the Psalms alone, which were at the heart of monastic prayer, Jerusalem/Zion is mentioned fifty-seven times and the monks were expected to draw a symbolic message from these references.[34] Without the book one's image might be no more than that of a city and a hill; but after reading it – one-third of which is devoted to Jerusalem – one 'feels' one knows the city, or rather one has a mental picture of the city as mentioned in the Scriptures.

The specific purpose of *De locis sanctis* was to supply a much-needed work of reference in scriptural exegesis and to resolve 'problems' that arise in the scriptures.[35] Augustine had stated that among the tools needed by Christian scholars to resolve the 'knots' in the Scriptures was a book on the geography of Palestine.[36] Augustine showed how such knowledge could assist the reader, and expressed the desire that such a work would soon appear. Adomnán produced his book to meet this need. This desire also decided what should be included: the extent to which certain things/places were described, and what questions were put to Arculf, his visitor on Iona who had been in Palestine.[37] Here are just ten examples of the kinds of problem that Augustine had in mind and which Adomnán addressed:

1. How information about Jerusalem provides detail to answer questions about the city posed by the scriptures.[38]

---

34. On this method of reading the Scriptures, and the symbolic significance of Jerusalem, see T. O'Loughlin, 'The Symbol gives Life: Eucherius of Lyons' Formula for Exegesis', in T. Finan and V. Twomey (eds), *Scriptural Interpretation in the Fathers: Letter and Spirit* (Dublin 1995), pp. 221–52.

35. See T. O'Loughlin, 'The Exegetical Purpose of Adomnán's *De Locis Sanctis*', *CMCS* 24 (1992), 37–53.

36. I am thinking in particular of the problems which Augustine, among others, called '*aenigmates*' (cf. *De doctrina christiana* 2 and 3) which has a technical meaning in the LXX of a problem which is an apparent contradiction, or at least something like a riddle (cf. 1 Kgs 10:1: '. . . and [the Queen of Sheba] came to test him with tricky questions (*in enigmatibus)*'; and cf. 2 Chr 9:1). For the origins of the notion, cf. S. Brock, 'The Queen of Sheba's Questions to Solomon: A Syriac Version', *Le Muséon* 92 (1979), 331–45 at 332; and on the place of such material in medieval exegesis see G. R. Evans, *The Logic and Language of the Bible: The Earlier Middle Ages* (Cambridge 1984), chs 9 and 10.

37. While most writing on *De locis sanctis* has concentrated on it as a work (or curiosity) of early medieval geography or as an item of pilgrim literature, there have been some mentions of it as a work relating to exegesis: D. A. Bullough, 'Columba, Adomnán, and the Achievement of Iona', *SHR* 43 (1964), 111–30; 44 (1965), 17–33 at 121–5; J. F. Kelly, 'Hiberno-Latin Exegesis and Exegetes', *AM* 22 (1981), 46–60 at 49; and 'A Catalogue of Early Medieval Hiberno-Latin Biblical Commentaries (II)', *Traditio* 45 (1989–90), 393–434 at 393; and R. D. Ray's assessment of the purpose of Bede's *De locis sanctis* in 'What do we know about Bede's Commentaries?' *RTAM* 49 (1982), 5–20 at 5–6.

38. See *De locis sanctis* 1, i.

2. How 'facts' explain the *aenigmates* which arise from the use of different nouns[39] – assuming that they cannot be synonyms.[40]
3. How places explain obscure texts and show their fuller prophetic sense.[41]
4. How geography shows that the scriptural text contains all truth.[42]
5. How geography can help harmonize the gospels. Adomnán even improves on Augustine's already famous attempt to harmonize the movement of Jesus between the first Palm Sunday and Good Friday.[43]
6. How resolving conflicting texts about David's tomb has an unspoken importance in relation to Christ's resurrection.[44]
7. How Adomnán uses authorities and claims to certainty in an attempt to overcome a real contradiction in the scriptural evidence (Rachel's tomb) and so preserve a notion of literal inerrancy.[45]
8. Teasing out references to places in the Fathers which were considered significant. Thus Adomnán has a long description of Hebron, while Arculf describes it as being in ruins.[46]
9. A description of salt in Sicily which fulfils a need, expressed by Augustine, for books on minerals mentioned in the Scriptures.[47]
10. By assuming that the 'transfiguration' took place on Mount Tabor Adomnán combined what was mentioned in the Scriptures with 'common knowledge' about them.[48]

These examples illustrate the kinds of problem with which Adomnán was grappling. However, they also show that any assumptions about the 'dictation' of *De locis sanctis* or its status as a pilgrim's account are very wide of the mark. The text shows Adomnán as a most

---

39. See *De locis sanctis* 1, 2, 9 and 10.
40. Behind this is the notion that every word in the scriptures has a specific meaning and profundity. So, for example, scripture must be translated word-for-word, while differences in words are not to be ignored as merely verbal, cf. W. Schwartz, 'The Meaning of *Fidus interpres* in Medieval Translation', *JTS* 45 (1944), 73–8.
41. See *De locis sanctis* 1, 2, 13.
42. See *De locis sanctis* 1, 9.
43. See *De locis sanctis* 1, 25; for a detailed examination of this piece of exegesis, see T. O'Loughlin, '*Res, tempus, locus, persona*: Adomnán's exegetical method', *IR* 48 (1997), 95–111; and idem, 'Adomnán's *De Locis Sanctis*: A Textual Emendation and an Additional Source Identification', *Ériu* 48 (1997), 37–40.
44. See *De locis sanctis* 2, 4.
45. See *De locis sanctis* 2, 7.
46. See *De locis sanctis* 2, 8–10. The text is the result of piecing together the information that could be gleaned from the Scriptures, specifically the Vulg.; cf. my 'Adam's Burial at Hebron: Some Aspects of its Significance in the Latin Tradition', *PIBA* 15 (1992), 66–88.
47. See *De locis sanctis* 2, 17, 3 – 18, 6.
48. See *De locis sanctis* 2, 27.

competent and searching scriptural scholar,[49] keenly attuned to textual problems, and ingenious in his solutions.

This contrasts with the picture that is often presented of Adomnán as little more than a note-taker and that all the information came from a bishop named Arculf. So despite Bede's description of Adomnán as 'a man most learned in the Scriptures',[50] many focus on Arculf rather than on the book's author. The whole question of Arculf is complex. On the one hand, Augustine states that geographical information for solving scriptural problems has to be gathered by direct observation: clearly Arculf is presented by Adomnán as this ideal witness, and without him the book would have had little authority. However, against this, when we actually note what information is put into the mouth of Arculf, we see that it is precious little indeed, and this information seems to be details about candles and shrines and the like.[51] Moreover, the information concerning the Arabs after the conquest of Palestine which seems to be most 'up-to-date' – and is often treated as reportage – is very confused and full of errors.[52] Then when we look at some of the information that Bede records about Arculf we are left in an even bigger quandary: Bede says he was returning home to Gaul, was shipwrecked and, having been washed up ashore, was able to make his way to Iona.[53] What a strange route! In any case, the information that receives careful attention in the book is based on studies of the books already in Iona's library. So we can say that while this shadowy figure of Arculf provided Adomnán an occasion to write the *De locis sanctis*, it is wholly Adomnán's book, the fruit of many years of study and reflection.

The *De locis sanctis* reveals the intellectual life of Iona in the late seventh century: it is a place of study, questioning, teaching and books. Some of the great books of the Latin fathers, some books of poetry, manuals of instruction and encyclopaedic works were in use there. It was a library as well-stocked as most in the Latin west at the time. In the *De locis sanctis* alone we have evidence for seventeen books that we know with certainty were there, and indications for five more, and further research will reveal others.[54] When new

---

49. This was Bede's judgement in the *Historia ecclesiastica*, see above; and, through Bede, it became the widespread medieval opinion of Adomnán, see 'Adomnán the Illustrious'.

50. *Historia ecclesiastica* 5, 15; and in the colophon to his own *De locis sanctis* which is an abridgement of Adomnán.

51. Cf. T. O'Loughlin, 'Adomnán and Arculf: The Case of an Expert Witness', *JML* 7 (1997), 127–46.

52. Cf. T. O'Loughlin, 'Palestine in the aftermath of the Arab conquest: the earliest Latin account', in R. N. Swanson (ed.), *Studies in Church History*, forthcoming.

53. See 'The View from Iona: Adomnán's Mental Maps'.

54. See T. O'Loughlin, 'The Library of Iona in the Late Seventh Century: The Evidence from Adomnán's *De Locis Sanctis*', *Ériu* 45 (1994), 33–52; and 'Adomnán's *De Locis Sanctis*: A Textual Emendation and an Additional Source Identification'.

studies of the other works produced on Iona are carried out, our knowledge of the library may increase even further.

The *De locis sanctis* also gives us an insight into Iona's religious life. The work begins by Adomnán carrying out the command of the Psalmist that the walls of Jerusalem should be surveyed and its towers and ramparts counted.[55] It ends with a fearful description of the island of Vulcano, a few miles north of Sicily, thundering, blazing and smoking. Is this range of events significant? We cannot answer with certainty for Adomnán, yet the implication of what he had described could easily be drawn by anyone who was reading the same books Adomnán was using for his information. The Jerusalem that he describes is not only the city in Palestine but the wondrous city that was a motif in Christian belief and a forerunner of heavenly life. In the last centuries before Christ, Jerusalem as 'Zion' had become a central symbol in Jewish messianic hopes about the Last Days.[56] Christianity took over this symbolism and saw it as a symbol of the Church in the final times and of the life to come. Christians were waiting for the New Jerusalem which the Apocalypse depicted as coming down from heaven enveloped in angels. This theme was developed by many of the Latin fathers but nowhere more significantly for Adomnán than by Augustine. Among his reflections on Jerusalem is this: 'On apostolic authority it becomes clear to us that the earthly city [of Jerusalem] points not only to itself, but also points to another city, the heavenly one of which it is the image and which it serves' (*De ciuitate Dei* 15, 2). So every reference to the earthly city is also a statement about the one to come. Thus Adomnán sees this city through the optic of the powerful image from Genesis: 'this place is nothing other than the house of God and the gate of heaven (*porta caeli*)' (Gen 28:17).

Mons Vulcanus, which gave its name to the little island of Vulcano on which it is situated and which gave us our word 'volcano', is for Adomnán far more than a geographical wonder. In the Latin fathers two strands of tradition came together in this place. First, in classical mythology this place was the abode and smithy of Vulcan the god of fire and the entrance to the underworld. Second, for Jews and Christians the place of the damned was the smoking, sulphurous fire of Gehenna; and, since Tertullian, volcanoes had been presented as a means by which God punished sinners.[57] This identification of a volcano in the region of Sicily with 'the gates of hell (*portae inferi*)'[58] was to be found in two books in Adomnán's library. Isidore in his *De*

---

55. Ps 48:12–14.
56. This will be examined in more detail in ch. 10 below.
57. *De penitentia* 12; and cf. M. Richard, 'Enfer', *DTC* 5, cols 47–49.
58. Mt 16:18; and for a special study of Adomnán's description of the 'Gates of Hell' see T. O'Loughlin, ' "The Gates of Hell": From Metaphor to Fact', *MS* 38 (1996), 98–114.

natura rerum had confused this mountain with Mount Etna but was
clear that it was a pointer to Gehenna (*ad exemplum Gehennae*) and
that 'there the bodies of the damned would be crucified without
end'.[59] Gregory the Great identified the mountain correctly and
reported a vision of the devils conducting the soul of a wicked king
down to hell through it;[60] and this account was followed by Adomnán.

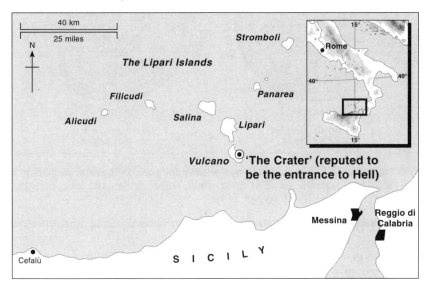

The Lipari Islands

Thus Adomnán has framed his book with these two images: it opens
with a description of the gates of heaven and closes with a description
of the gates of hell. Arculf is presented as walking and sailing
between Jerusalem and Sicily on a trip the reader is not expected to
take; but he is also travelling between the portals of two destinations
of a more real journey upon which all the book's readers are making
their way. The work's initial audience would have been more than
aware that they would end their journeys either in the city above or
the fire beneath; here they found depictions of each, and it was to
assist them in their travelling that Adomnán wrote his book.

---

59. *De natura rerum* 47, 4.
60. *Dialogi* 4, 31, 2–4.

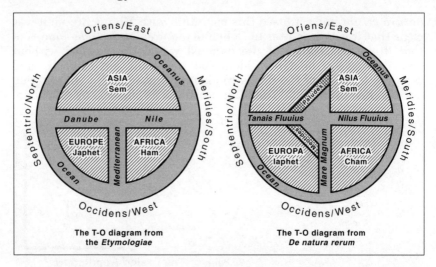

The T-O diagram from
the *Etymologiae*

The T-O diagram from
De natura rerum

Isidorean T-O Diagrams. It was with maps such as these, from Isidore's writings (known as T-O diagrams), that Adomnán imagined the position of the lands on the globe.

A BUSY MAN

Trying to get an insight into the deepest motivations of someone alive today, whom we know directly, is one of the most difficult tasks we can undertake: every human is an individual, to some extent mysterious, and we do a person an injustice when we think we have him or her fully described and put in little boxes. A biography of someone whom we have never met, but about whom we have vast quantities of public and private records – for example, Napoleon – is even more difficult. But perhaps hardest of all is where the person lived over a millennium ago and all we have are a few formal documents that were not intended as autobiographical, and where many of the dates and details are deductions or shrewd guesses. Such is the case with Adomnán. I have tried to build up two vignettes of the man and his labours by looking at what he produced against a background of the Christian Scriptures which we know he held dear and believed and upon which he based his life. But the results are no more than two thumb-nail sketches out of the many that could be produced even on the slim evidence we do have. However, the last word should come from Adomnán himself, and is one of the very few statements in his works where he speaks of himself. This request is the final lines of *De locis sanctis*:

> I have written down these things [about the Holy Places] in what I admit is a poor style, but I have done so in the face of daily labour coming at me from all sides: the amount of ecclesiastical concerns seems overwhelming. So I wish that you who read of these places not neglect to pray for me, the sinner who wrote this, to Christ the judge of the ages.

FURTHER READING

Texts/Translations

D. Meehan with L. Bieler (eds), *Adamnan's De locis sanctis* (Dublin 1958).

A. O. Anderson and M. O. Anderson (eds and trans), *Adomnan's Life of Columba* (Edinburgh 1961, 2nd edn Oxford 1991).

R. Sharpe (trans), *Adomnán of Iona: Life of St Columba* (Harmondsworth 1995).

K. Meyer (ed. and trans), *Cáin Adomnáin: An Old-Irish Treatise on the Law of Adamnan* (Oxford 1905).

G. Márkus (trans), *Adomnán's 'Law of the Innocents': Cáin Adomnáin* (Glasgow, 1997).

L. Bieler (ed.), *The Irish Penitentials* (Dublin 1975), pp. 176–81.

Bibliography

L&S, nos 304, 305 and 609.

Studies

D. A. Bullough, 'Columba, Adomnán, and the Achievement of Iona', *SHR* 43 (1964), 111–30 and 44 (1965), 17–33.

T. O. Clancy and G. Márkus, *Iona: The Earliest Poetry of a Celtic Monastery* (Edinburgh 1995).

M. Herbert, *Iona, Kells and Derry: the History and Hagiography of the Monastic* familia *of Columba* (Oxford 1988).

Kenney, pp. 245–6, 283–7 and 428–33.

M. Ní Dhonnchadha, 'The *Lex Innocentium*: Adomnán's Law for Women, Clerics and Youths, 697 AD', in M. O'Dowd and S. Wichert (eds), *Chattel, Servant or Citizen: Women's Status in Church, State and Society* (Belfast 1995), pp. 58–69.

——'The Guarantor List of *Cáin Adomnáin*, 697', *Peritia* 1 (1982), 178–215.

T. O'Loughlin, 'The Exegetical Purpose of Adomnán's *De Locis Sanctis*', *CMCS* 24 (1992), 37–53.

——'Adam's Burial at Hebron: Some Aspects of its Significance in the Latin Tradition', *PIBA* 15 (1992), 66–88.

——'The Library of Iona in the Late Seventh Century: The Evidence from Adomnán's *De Locis Sanctis*', *Ériu* 45 (1994), 33–52.

——'The Latin Version of the Scriptures in use on Iona', *Peritia* 8 (1994), 18–26.

——'Adomnán the Illustrious', *IR* 46 (1995), 1–14.

——'The View from Iona: Adomnán's Mental Maps', *Peritia* 10 (1996), 98–122.

——'Adomnán and *mira rotunditas*', *Ériu* 47 (1996), 95–9.

——' "The Gates of Hell": From Metaphor to Fact', *MS* 38 (1996), 98–114.

——'Living in the Ocean', in C. Bourke (ed.), *Studies in the Cult of Saint Columba* (Dublin 1997), pp. 11–23.

——'*Res, tempus, locus, persona*: Adomnán's exegetical method', *IR* 48 (1997), 95–111.

——'Adomnán's *De Locis Sanctis*: A Textual Emendation and an Additional Source Identification', *Ériu* 48 (1997), 37–40.

——'Adomnán and Arculf: The Case of an Expert Witness', *JML* 7 (1997), 127–46.

J. Ryan, 'The *Cáin Adomnáin*', in D. A. Binchy (ed.), *Studies in Early Irish Law* (Dublin 1936), pp. 269–76.

5   Muirchú: Dramatist or Theologian?

> *Of this night Scripture says:*
> *'The night will be as clear as day:*
> *It will become my light, my joy'*
> (The Exultet)[1]

THE ECLIPSE OF MUIRCHÚ

Muirchú: the man

Muirchú,[2] author of the most famous of the *vitae* of Patrick,[3] is one of the more elusive writers of early Christian Ireland.[4] Apart from what we can learn from the *vita*, we have only one item of contemporary

---

1. *The Roman Missal* (rite of 1970), p. 199. Finding where Scripture says this can prove difficult because the Latin liturgy uses two verses (in inverted order) from the Psalms following the Old Greek (the Septuagint) translation rather than the wording found in the Hebrew. In Latin the phrase is: *Et nox sicut dies inluminabitur* (Ps 138:12), *Et nox inluminatio mea in deliciis meis* (Ps 138:11). To see how it reads in contemporary translations, cf. Ps 139:11–12. On the background to the whole of this hymn, commonly known as 'the *Exultet*', see L. Duchesne, *Christian Worship: Its Origins and Evolution* (ET: M. L. McClure, 5th edn London 1923), p. 255; and P. Verbraken, 'Une "Laus cerei" africaine', *RB* 70 (1960), 301–12.
2. The name means 'sea hound'.
3. At the beginning of any writing involving a saint's life it is worth recalling that the intentions of the hagiographer are not those of the historian or biographer – yet they do have overlapping concerns. The aim of the hagiographer is to communicate with his audience in such a way that they are moved to identify themselves in various ways with the saint, and thus to become imitations of the saint (i.e. become one with the saint in their here and now, rather than some sort of moral imitation). A parallel is the gospel genre where the intention of the evangelist is to elicit identification with the risen Christ, and it is in support of that aim that we learn of the biography of Jesus. The best introduction to the genre of hagiography is still H. Delehaye, *The Legends of the Saints* (Brussels 1905; ET: London 1962; rept Dublin 1998).
4. L&S, no. 303; Kenney, no. 128, pp. 331–4; and the introduction by L. Bieler to his edition, pp. 1–35.

information about him: he was present at the Synod of Birr in 697 as one of the guarantors to the *Cáin Adomnáin*.[5] This indicates that at the end of the seventh century he was an important Irish churchman.

His tribal name *moccu Machthéni* has been taken to indicate that he belonged to the Túath Mochtaine whose lands were in the Mag Machae ('the plain of Armagh'), an area roughly south of Armagh. Because of this, since Kenney, scholars have linked him to Armagh – by the seventh century the traditional church of Patrick – as one of its clerics. This seems a most reasonable inference as he clearly identifies his hero with Armagh, and such identification makes most sense if he were an Armagh cleric writing for an Armagh audience about their patron saint.

From the *vita* we learn that Muirchú considered himself to be following in the footsteps of Cogitosus who earlier in the century had written a *vita* for Brigid.[6] He refers to him as his 'father', which is best understood in terms of discipleship.[7] Muirchú also tells us that he composed the work at the request of 'Aed, Bishop of the city of Sléibte' (Sleaty)[8] and he dedicated the work to Aed.[9] We know little of Aed except that he placed his diocese under the protection of Patrick (i.e. Armagh) during the time that Ségéne was bishop (661–88). We know also that Aed was, along with Muirchú, one of the guarantors at the Synod of Birr, but had already relinquished office by 692 (for in that year his successor as bishop died) in favour of an anchoritic life, and in all likelihood he died in 700.[10] So the *vita* was certainly composed prior to 700, and some scholars see its purpose, in part, as fostering the assimilation of Sleaty within the jurisdiction of Armagh and so place it before 688 (as we know that the incorporation had taken place by that date).

Our only other piece of information is from a later date: the *Félire Oengusso* mentions a 'Murchon' as having a feast day on 8 June.[11] It is possible that this is our Muirchú, but the identification is not certain.[12] And this raises other problems because later comments in

5. See M. Ní Dhonnchadha, 'The Guarantor List of *Cáin Adomnáin*, 697', *Peritia* 1 (1982), 196; and see ch. 4 above.
6. Prologue 2, p. 62.
7. See T. O'Loughlin, 'Master and Pupil: Christian Perspectives', in *The Encyclopedia of Monasticism*, forthcoming.
8. This is the present parish of Sleaty; the village is on the River Barrow, in Co. Laois, about 3 km north-west of Carlow Town. This information is found after the list of chapters (p. 66).
9. Prologue 1 (p. 62).
10. See M. Ní Dhonnchadha, loc. cit., p. 192.
11. Stokes's edition, p. 139.
12. Kenney, p. 332, note 129, notes the difficulties; but M. Ní Dhonnchadha, loc. cit., p. 196, makes the identification without comment.

the *Félire* say that his church (*Cell Murchon*) was among the Uí Ailella which can be identified with Kilmorgan in Co. Sligo[13] or with another group near Wicklow.[14] In favour of the last suggestion is that it would put Muirchú into the same region as Sleaty. However, all these arguments – including those which see the *vita* as somehow connected with a reforming programme of *romanitas* being spearheaded by Adomnán and those at Birr in favour of a 'Roman dating' of Easter[15] – are built on only a slim base of solid evidence.

Perceptions of Muirchú

So we have a *vita* from the later seventh century by an important and well-connected churchman, written in the context of Armagh's growth as the heir to the legacy of Patrick, and so the focus of devotion to Patrick at that time. As a piece of hagiography it should be read as providing an insight into how those people saw their great patron, and through their perception of Patrick we should be able to see how they interpreted their own past as a people (a *gens*) who had become a Christian people through the ministry of Patrick.[16] The *vita* can therefore be read as providing information about its author's sense of his Christian identity. Moreover, since this story involves a history of conversion, we can use the *vita* as a window on to Muirchú's theology of mission, his understanding of the relationship between Christian and non-Christian religions and his view of the availability of religious truth. So, following Delehaye's dictum that a *vita* tells us more about the time of its composition than about the time of the saint it narrates, we can use the *vita* to assess its author's views on several theological questions which cannot but emerge in the course of writing such a text, especially about a missionary bishop, and as evidence for assessing his skill, or otherwise, as a theologian.[17] It is this approach that will be adopted here.

---

13. Cf. M. Ní Dhonnchadha, loc. cit., p. 196; the town is about 3 km south of Ballymote.
14. So argued John Colgan in the seventeenth century; see Kenney, p. 332.
15. See ch. 4 above on Adomnán and the Easter dating question; the theory that the *vita* is part of a larger ecclesiastical scheme was first hinted at by Kenney (p. 333 and note 137), and further advanced by L. Bieler in 'The Celtic Hagiographer', *SP* 5 (1962), 241–65, although by the time of his edition, Bieler described it as 'Guesswork [that] would provide a very plausible background [for] Muirchú's *Vita*' (p. 1).
16. A similar question has been explored by J. F. Nagy in *Conversing with Angels and Ancients* (Dublin 1997); on the perception by people in Ireland in the seventh century of themselves as a distinct *gens*, cf. M. Richter, *Ireland and her Neighbours in the Seventh Century* (Dublin 1999).
17. In ch.1, above, we noted that when we use the title 'theologian' we mean someone involved in reflection upon the Christian religion in such a way that he or she produces written documents which allow us to see his or her theological suppositions; we do not mean 'theologian' in the sense of a description of a particular type of academic.

It is worth noting that while this approach may seem uncontroversial – we have similar studies of works by Bede[18] – it is one that has attracted very little attention from those who study the 'dossier'[19] of Patrick.[20] Until a generation ago, the approach to hagiography from the Celtic lands was out of phase with that of historians elsewhere. Historians on the continent had long before adopted the methodological principles pioneered by the Bollandists,[21] and in particular Delehaye, and had come to see hagiography as a valuable resource for understanding the *mentalité* of the societies that produced the *vitae*.[22] Celticists, however, conscious that they were dealing with precious national icons, followed another path. On the one hand they adopted a positivism with regard to the miraculous – this was simply excised as the product of medieval gullibility. On the other, faced with so meagre a quantity of evidence for the earliest period (if *vitae* were considered primarily witnesses to the concerns of later times), they adopted a policy of 'maximalism'. If an item *could* be historically true, provided that there was no positive evidence against it, then it was accepted as a fact. This approach found some of its most ardent supporters just before its demise. Writing in 1961, James Carney took issue in his book *The Problem of St. Patrick* with the then recently advanced notion that the fifth century was either 'lost' or 'dark', and advanced the argument that the proof lay in the details known about the life of Patrick who, he claimed, arrived in Ireland on Holy Thursday (thus reading Muirchú's Paschal drama, minus its miraculous element, as an historical fact), 5 April 456. He went on to note that Tírechán (another late seventh-century writer on Patrick) mentioned that Patrick arrived at dawn. Carney, to his credit, recognized that this latter detail could not be verified, but said it was 'a likely enough touch'.[23] The method was simple: something is mentioned by an ancient source; it could be correct, so why not accept it in the absence of a counter-indicator. The ploy was satisfying to historians in giving them a fairly full narrative, while avoiding the social opprobrium attached to attacking sacred texts with critical tools.

18. For example: C. W. Jones, 'Some Introductory Remarks on Bede's Commentary on Genesis', *SE* 19 (1969), 115–98; or W. D. McCready, *Miracles and the Venerable Bede* (Toronto 1994).
19. This technical term, introduced by the Bollandists, describes the collection of documents (*vitae*, charters, lists of dedications, etc.) which belong to a particular saint's cult, and which collectively testify to how he or she was perceived by those who fostered the cult of that saint.
20. There is a preliminary survey in T. O'Loughlin, 'St Patrick and an Irish Theology', *D&L* 44 (1994), 153–9.
21. See M. D. Knowles, *Great Historical Enterprises* (London 1963), ch. 1.
22. See M. Bloch, *The Historian's Craft* (ET: P. Putnam, Manchester, rept 1992), pp. 58, 68–9, 102 and 108.
23. J. Carney, *The Problem of St. Patrick* (Dublin 1961), pp. 24 and 95; for a debunking of this, see D. A. Binchy, 'Patrick and His Biographers, Ancient and Modern', *SH* 2 (1962), 39.

This cosy world fell under a single salvo of deadly fire: the 1962 article of D. A. Binchy, 'Patrick and His Biographers, Ancient and Modern'.[24] Although this is seen as inaugurating a new era in Patrician studies and studies of the fifth century, it also brought Irish hagiographical studies into line with those of the continent. In his approach to hagiography Binchy was anything but revolutionary.[25] In essence he simply applied the lessons of Delehaye consistently to Muirchú and Tírechán. In the aftermath of Binchy's attack many scholars were quick to take up the newly respectable approach and Muirchú and Tírechán ceased to be sources of the fifth century. They were now texts in a Bollandist 'dossier' of the saint and, again following Delehaye's principles, they were sources for the time of their composition, the seventh century.[26]

However, *vitae* stripped of their value to tell us anything – except by accident – about the period they claim to narrate, now came to be seen as propaganda building the fictitious history of Armagh in the seventh century as the centre of ecclesiastical power belonging to the Uí Néill dynasty, then growing as a political force in the northern half of Ireland. The bolstering of Armagh, through Patrick, was just another dimension of their political ambitions and territorial expansion. The pieces fitted so well together chronologically (just at the time of Uí Néill expansion we get *vitae*, the *vitae* mention Armagh) and there are so many other links (Aed places his see under Armagh, Muirchú writes at his request, Muirchú may have been from Armagh) that coincidence seemed to be ruled out as an explanation. Moreover, so much of the Patrician/Armagh dossier survived in books coming from Armagh (the Book of Armagh[27]) – even if a century later than the composition of some of its Patrician texts – that hagiography appeared to be little more than the pursuit of politics by other means. In the process, the religious motivations found behind *vitae* all over the Christian world were given relatively little attention – and some recent scholarship simply ignored the fact that hagiography was an important element in pre-modern Christian literature. In such a climate, the notion that some *vitae* might contain a sophisticated theological vision is all but ignored.

However, while I do not wish to deny that there is a political

---

24. *SH* 2 (1962), 7–173.
25. See the introduction by T. O'Loughlin to the 1998 re-print of H. Delehaye, *The Legends of the Saints*.
26. Already in the article 'The Celtic Hagiographer' Ludwig Bieler had adopted that approach, albeit with too great an emphasis on making 'Celtic' hagiography 'distinctive'; in later articles he read Muirchú in a far more 'Bollandist' manner: e.g. 'Muirchú's Life of Patrick as a work of literature', *MA* 43 (1974), 219–33; 'Hagiography and Romance in Medieval Ireland', *M&H* 6 (1975), 13–24; 'Ancient Hagiography and the Lives of St Patrick', in F. Paolo and M. Barrera (eds), *Forma Futuri: Studi in onore del Cardinale Michele Pellegrino* (Turin 1975), pp. 650–5.
27. See R. Sharpe, 'Palaeographical Considerations in the Study of the Patrician Documents in the Book of Armagh', *Scriptorium* 36 (1983), 3–28.

dimension to the Patrician dossier which could have furthered the growth of the religious centre of the Uí Néill (and discovering this is a laudable use of *vitae* by historians of dynastic politics in seventh-century Ireland), to see in that political use the rationale for the creation of the *vita* is to ignore the complexity of human activity and motivation, especially when it involves an explicitly religious dimension. First, the cult of the saints is found throughout the Christian world and the Irish examples conform to the genre as it is found elsewhere at the time. Second, in writers such as Muirchú we have a careful use of theological motifs, usually in the form of deliberate scriptural echoes,[28] which are explicable in terms of a religious rationale but are redundant as propaganda. This was insightfully recognized recently by Edel Bhreathnach in an article on Tara as '*caput Scotorum*' ('capital of the Irish' – a phrase from Muirchú). Her examination of Muirchú – she assumes her readership approach Muirchú's work primarily as a deliberate buttress to Uí Néill expansion and their claims to the kingship of Tara – led her to this conclusion:

> Muirchú's *Life of Patrick* represents Lóegaire, like Conaire Mór in *Togail Bruidne Da Derga*, as a king doomed as his *gessa* are transgressed. He could not triumph over Patrick. Muirchú consistently portrays Lóegaire in an unfavourable light, and his depiction of the king of Tara does not reflect that of a propagandist on behalf of the Uí Néill but rather of an ecclesiastic championing Patrick and, in particular, Christianity.[29]

Here, my working assumption shall be that a churchman like Muirchú, who filled his work with echoes of conversion/deliverance events from the Scriptures, would have the relationship of Christianity to paganism at the forefront of his mind when he wrote, and that other concerns would have been secondary and incidental.

A PERFORMANCE THEOLOGY

There are many ways of doing theology. The systematic exposition of some part of Christian doctrine usually comes to mind in the first instance, as this is a form we are familiar with as a means of conveying a religious message. It is then presented as a sermon or a lecture, a book on some topic or as a teaching manual with a title such as 'A theology of redemption' or 'New perspectives on missiology'. Another common form of theology today is the commen-

---

28. These have been identified in the apparatus to my translation of Muirchú in O. Davies with T. O'Loughlin (eds), *Celtic Spirituality* (Mahwah NJ 1999); for a similar case, albeit somewhat later in time, see the use of scripture by Rhygyfarch in his *Vita Dauidis*, see T. O'Loughlin, 'Rhygyfarch's *Vita Dauidis*: An Apparatus biblicus', *StC* 32 (1998), 179–88.
29. E. Bhreathnach, 'Temoria: Caput Scotorum?' *Ériu* 47 (1996), 67–88 at 73.

Significant Places for Muirchú's *Vita Patricii*

tary on some classic text, be it considered part of the Scriptures or by some recognized genius of the tradition. By way of the commentary a deeper understanding is, it's to be hoped, granted to those who read the key text; and theology is somehow advanced by bringing an earlier text into contact with the methods and concerns of the day. This mode of theology expresses itself in the homily explaining some point in the Scriptures, in the line-by-line commentary, in the overview of a thinker's work or as a key to understanding that work. This book that you are reading now is theology in this mode. It aims to set a text (Muirchú) in its context, enable you to have a deeper appreciation of it and, through the interaction of you with that text (having been assisted by this book), to allow you to develop you own theological understanding and position. However, there is another major approach to theology which, despite being widespread in earlier times, is rarely used today: theology through narrative. In this mode one tells a story that claims to recall the facts of the workings of God in creation, and this story is the basis of belief which can later be formalized as a system or explored through a commentary. This is the form that much of the theology in the Old Testament takes – for instance both accounts (Gen 1–2:4 and Gen 2:4–4:26) of the creation are portrayed as historical tales. Equally, the gospels convey their message by way of a narrative of events, and one is to learn the Christian mystery through interpreting the significance of these events. And all these accounts contain far more than we would expect a television camera to be able to record.

Today, these narratives are problematic as we make very clear distinction between history (an account of what 'really' happened), theological interpretation (what an event means in relation to the revelation of God) and stories that are just good stories: fiction where imagination is unfettered. Our disquiet can be seen in the fundamentalists' rage that 'it must be true [in our terms]' or in the need we have to say that Gen 1 should be read as poetry or that the gospel miracles should be read as reflections and metaphors. Likewise, those religious writers who have used story narratives to do theology in recent decades have made it clear that they see the story as fictional and have not made it seem like history: C. S. Lewis in the 'Screwtape' books is a fine example. However, these distinctions that we make were not the concern of early medieval writers or readers: the story of Patrick was the splendid narrative of the mighty work of God as he called his servant, and then sent him to proclaim the gospel and how he 'went forth and preached everywhere, while the Lord worked with [him] and confirmed the message by the signs that attended it' (Mk 16:20).[30] This was the core of the Patrick story, and it was this that had to be clearly conveyed by Muirchú if he were to fulfil his task. All the details – what we might call 'the history' – were then only the local colours which gave a particular shape to the key 'event' which was the coming of Christianity into Ireland. The nearest parallel today is the historical film when a fictional form is used to join many disparate events and convey the story of a period – often with a great deal of accuracy – in a visual way in a slot of less than 180 minutes. Characters have to be combined and suitable characters to carry the story forward created; and there has to be some thread of continuity so that one does not 'lose the plot'.

Muirchú not only wrote a story, he also conceived his tale as a series of dramatic scenes: each scene is a carefully constructed dramatic set-piece which captures the whole story in a single act that

---

30. This is cited by Muirchú (*Vita*, bk 1, ch. 22) as the ultimate explanation of Patrick's activity.

is narrated in a matter of minutes. There are many cases similar to this in the Scriptures (for example Moses on Mount Sinai (Ex 19) or Elijah confronting the priests of Baal (1 Kgs 18) or Jesus at Cana (Jn 2)), but Muirchú probably thought of his drama as echoing those events while itself being a synecdoche for the whole conversion of the island. Synecdoche was defined by Isidore of Seville as 'a manner of thought by which a whole is understood from a part, or a part is understood through understanding a whole'.[31] And it was a manner of thinking that was very familiar to anyone who read Scripture in the Latin world at the time, as it was a favourite tool in exegesis: given any single action of Jesus such as healing a blind man (e.g. Mk 10:46–52), by synecdoche the interpreter could move from this single event to the general conclusion: Christ gives light to the eyes of all humanity – the single moment is to be seen as a part, a token, a sacrament of the whole Christian story. Just so, Muirchú presents a sequence of acts each of which can be understood, by synecdoche, to portray the whole 'event' of Patrick and the conversion of the Irish. However, one act takes precedence and forms the centrepiece of the whole performance: the events of Easter night at Tara – in this we have the message of Patrick's life as understood by Muirchú in a nutshell.

THE *DRAMATIS PERSONAE*

The events at Tara are at the centre of Muirchú's work. Everything before the encounter with the summit of pagan power – the account of Patrick's childhood, the events leading up to his setting out and the account of his arrival in Ireland – comes together to put Patrick at the centre of the action, in the centre of the country, at the centre of the Christian year and of the religious year of the pagans, all within a few days of his arrival in Ireland. Then within a few hours the clash of religions has taken place, the evil ones are put to flight, the country has had its Passover/paschal event by which it moved from being a seeker for the Lord to being baptized, and so the mission has succeeded. Everything that happens after that night can be seen as mopping up, and as more specific instances of the conversion process that has already taken place for the people as a whole. At the beginning of the drama the Irish are a *gens* (a nation) in the sense of the pagan *gentes* (gentiles/nations) to whom the apostles are sent: 'Go teach all nations (*gentes*)' (Mt 28:19); by the following evening they are a *gens electa* in the sense of 1 Pet 2:9: 'you are a chosen race, a royal priesthood, a holy nation, God's own people, that you may

---

31. *Etymologiae* I, xxxvii, 13.

declare the wonderful deeds of him who called you out of darkness into his marvellous light'.

But to appreciate the drama of Ireland's night of deliverance and baptism we must know its characters. Patrick we are expected to know: not only is he our – i.e. the audience's – saint and intercessor, the one whose relics among us bring us his protection. He is one of the apostles: chosen, prepared and sent to bring the gospel 'to the ends of the earth'; Muirchú in this portrayal of Patrick is true to his source, Patrick's own *Confessio*.[32] But lest his readers fail to appreciate that to understand Patrick we must see Patrick in the light of the scriptural characters he resembles, Muirchú states that Patrick is like Moses (who was the revealer of the Law, and a fore-type of Christ and the gospel), like Jonah (who was the preacher of repentance and so a fore-type of Christ and the gospel) and like John the Baptist (who announces the Christ and initiates the preaching of the gospel).[33] With Patrick are his companions, but they are really little more than an entourage and a group of liturgical assistants. Christ was about to come to Ireland, he would have just one herald and champion.

Opposite Patrick is an array of people who vary in power, wisdom, moral virtue and the desire for the truth/good/God – for all three of these desires are seen by Muirchú as aspects of a single human longing. He introduces 'the opposition' even before he tells of Patrick's arrival in Ireland, so that we will know, once we meet them again in the story, exactly what Patrick is up against.

First, there is the king:

> At that time there was a mighty and fierce pagan king in those parts. This was the Emperor of the Barbarians, who reigned at Tara which was then the capital of the kingdom of the Irish. This king was Lóegaire, son of Níall, whose family rule almost the whole island.[34]

The king is no less than an emperor! Here we see a tendency of Muirchú to describe his own ancestors in terms of the literary pictures of ancient courts derived, principally, from the Scriptures. Lóegaire is not a local chieftain or petty ruler, he is the Irish example of the dazzling displays of royal might that threaten Moses, and Daniel, and the *magi* at Herod's court – he not only has the same titles as these literary potentates, but has a similar court full of *magi*, scholars, philosophers; packed with bureaucrats – even satraps straight from Persia,[35] and with a great standing army – like Pharaoh's army in Ex 14:6–7 – on call at a moment's notice for a rapid cavalry deployment. This tendency to dramatically 'play up' his ancestors in terms of his most prestigious authority – Scripture –

---

32. See ch. 2 above.
33. *Vita*, bk 1, ch. 2.
34. *Vita*, bk 1, ch. 9.
35. Muirchú's language is based on Est 9:3 and Dan 3:2–3 and 27.

reveals some interesting aspects of Muirchú. First, he does not equate civilization with Christianity. The meeting of the two cultures is a meeting of equals – there is as much glory in Ireland as in any of the courts which the Word of God has previously encountered. Second, the 'conversion' is precisely that: a turning based on choice. It is not a case of Christianity walking into a void – into a place where God is not, where religion is not, culture is not – nor into a place where the Spirit has not been at work. Thirdly, and in a most complex manner, it shows a sense of inferiority, for Muirchú does not try to project backwards the actual Tara he knew, but in order to make his own ancestors seem mighty he has to make them mighty like those he knows from his Christian reading. Indeed, the initial audience, knowing the realities of the seventh century, may have felt that there had been a great fall in status and pomp since the arrival of Christianity, for no real Uí Néill ruler could compare with the biblical splendour of Lóegaire! For Muirchú the two forces about to duel on Easter Night are worthy adversaries, and what will sway the balance between them is the matter of revealed truth alone.

Lóegaire was not alone:

> He had with him seers and *magi* and augurs and spell-casters and those skilled in every one of the evil arts. They were able to know and predict everything, according to the pagan idolatrous custom, before it occurred. Two of these were preferred by the king above the rest: Lothrock and Lucet Máel.

These combine the prophetic skills of biblical *magi* as found in Dan 2:12–24 and 27 with those of the religious advisers of King Herod in Mt 2:4 and those of the High Priest who can prophesy *ex officio* even when the truth he prophesies is desired for evil purposes as in Jn 11:51.

Since truth, as the gift of the Spirit, knows no boundaries they can discover the providential plan of God for history, as such they are the unwitting instruments of an unknown God (cf. Acts 17:23), and so, knowing that there is another and greater truth than that which they serve, they can be culpable when they do not accept it when it makes its advent to them through Patrick (cf. Rom 1:20).

So Muirchú presents them with the exact religious knowledge they need for their meeting with Patrick, and they were even aware that the appointed time was fast approaching:

> With their magical skill this pair often declared that they could see another way of life about to come to Ireland from outside. It would be like a kingdom, it would come from far away across the seas, and it would bring an unknown and annoying teaching with it. This teaching would be given out by a handful, yet be received by many, and held in honour by all. It would overthrow kingdoms, kill the kings who resisted it, seduce the crowds, destroy all their gods, caste out their own skills and works, and this kingdom would have no end. They also pointed to the man who would bring this new way of life and persuade people [to accept it]. They prophesied in words that made up a kind of poem which

was often recited in those days, and especially in the two or three years just before Patrick's coming. Because of their 'language's peculiar idiom'[36] the poem's meaning is not very clear, but here it is:

One with shaven head will come here with his curled-headed stick.
He will sing foul things from his home with perforated head.
From his table in the front part of his house his whole family will reply
   to him: 'Let it be! Let it be!'[37]

The meeting is not just one of religion with another, Muirchú wants to characterize the relationship between them. It is like the distinction between shadow and reality, between anticipation and achievement, part and whole, un-named and named, incomplete and complete, and, most importantly, between a past 'age' of the world – the age of the Law of Nature – and the final age of the Christ and the gospel:

When all these things happen,[38] our kingdom – which is pagan – shall not stand.[39]

For, as Muirchú explains:

With the advent of Patrick came the destruction of the cult of the idols, and everything was filled with the universal faith of Christ.

THE DRAMA

Muirchú presupposes in his audience that they will understand the significance of the scene into which he has compressed the conversion of Ireland, and in addition that they will pick up the clues from the images he uses within the scene, to other biblical duels between life and death.[40]

Time, Stage set, Backdrop

The key image is that of the liturgy of the Paschal Vigil. This is not

---

36. This phrase is taken from Jerome's *Prologue to the Book of Job* (these were a standard part of the biblical apparatus in scriptural codices in Muirchú's time).
37. This phrase (*Fiat, fiat*) is found in this form in Jth 10:9; 13:26; and 15:12 and, more importantly, in the more used Latin version (that based on the Septuagint) of the Psalms (40:14; 71:19; 88:53; 105:48); it renders the phrase 'Amen, Amen.'
38. Cf. Mt 24:33.
39. Muirchú, whose native language was Irish and for whom Latin was a learned language, engages in a literary conceit here in telling his audience that *their* language is a foreign one, and *our* language (in this case Latin) can express this more clearly. To wish to identify himself with Latin to this extent may indicate that he sees this as the Christian language or the language of light and sophistication.
40. I take the metaphor from the Easter Morning sequence *Victimae paschali*; although it was written in the eleventh century it uses the same range of liturgical images as Muirchú.

immediately obvious today because that Vigil disappeared from the Roman Rite into a vestigial form in the later Middle Ages and was lost sight of by western Christians until the work of the liturgical reformers in the early twentieth century. It was restored to the Roman Rite in 1955, but even now, half a century later, it still is only on the periphery of Catholic consciousness, and is usually celebrated in such a trite manner that it is little more than an Easter variant on Christmas 'Midnight Mass'. Among Reformed churches it is beginning to make a re-appearance, but again it is not part of that lifeblood of liturgy: festival activity that is long-experienced and expected from deep within the memory.

The Easter Vigil was the central moment of the whole liturgical year – it towered above the other ritual gatherings at Easter, and dwarfed other festivals such as Christmas.[41] Unless we reckon with this uniqueness – not part of modern Christian experience – we do not understand the power of Muirchú's scene. As a unique liturgical event it can be traced back to the time of Hippolytus (c. 170–c. 236) in the late second century, if not further.[42] By Muirchú's time it had developed an elaborate ritual based on fire and light, along with a complex set of readings which, claiming to be a history of humanity down to the time of Christ, laid layer on layer of meaning onto the Vigil's central focus.[43] The basic symbolism is that there is a wholly new fire, struck from flint (*e silice*), which is the new beginning ushered in by Christ's resurrection. This new beginning marks the beginning of a new age/era in which Christ is the Lord of History. The flame comes within a completely darkened church building and then spreads first to the great Paschal Candle and then 'to all believers' standing around. Light and life, Christ, have triumphed and the victory is proclaimed in the dark territory that was formerly controlled by the great enemy. The best guide to the various meanings is the fourth/fifth-century hymn that is sung to proclaim the new light, the *Exultet*, and Muirchú supposes that just as Patrick is portrayed lighting the new fire in the darkened enemy territory, so one of his company (for the *Exultet* is not sung by the celebrant but by a deacon) would have gone on to sing it. More importantly, Muirchú's audience know that this is the background sound of the Vigil and its phrases would have been ringing in their ears as they heard the story in much the same way that when we think of a football final we can

---

41. A vast amount has been written about the history of this Vigil in the patristic and early medieval periods; however, if this area is unfamiliar the works that I would recommend are: 1. the text and rubrics of the rite as used today in the Roman Rite – its structure and content copies the early medieval rite to a remarkable extent; 2. A. J. McGregor, *Fire and Light in the Western Triduum: Their Use at Tenebrae and at the Paschal Vigil* (Collegeville MN 1992); and 3. G. Dix, *The Shape of the Liturgy* (London 1945), pp. 325–30.
42. Dix, op. cit., p. 325.
43. Cf. M. Avery, 'The Beneventan Lections for the Vigil of Easter and the Ambrosian Chant Banned by Pope Stephen IX at Montecassino', *SG* 1 (1947), 433–58.

hear the anthems that are sung as background.

Four themes in particular are woven together in the vigil. First, it is the night of the Pasch/the Passover and the image of the chosen people of God being delivered from slavery in Egypt. They leave through the Red Sea, and are pursued by Pharaoh in chariots which with their charioteers are then destroyed in the confusion of the sea closing over them – thus the mighty hand of God, delivering his people from slavery, is made manifest. Second, it is the night that Christ's victory enters a darkened world having overcome death and evil: the focus is that now Christ victoriously 'stands up' in our world. Third, it is the night of baptism – not only was it the night for people to be baptized, it was the recollection of moving from being a non-Christian to being a Christian. And fourth, it was the night when Christ 'broke down the gates of death' and rising 'triumphant from the grave' (the *Exultet*) brought with him all those righteous ones who had lived good lives according to the Law of Nature and now could be brought out of 'the waiting room' (*limbus patrum*) into heaven now that the gates of paradise were re-opened.

Two other images are also expected by Muirchú to be common knowledge, one relating to the Vigil, the other not. Muirchú makes a special point that Lóegaire had called for a festival of idolatry at Tara 'in the same way that King Nebuchadnezzar (*Nabuchodonosor Rex*) of Babylon had done'.[44] This might appear to be just one more of the Old Testament parallels which abound in Muirchú and to which he likes to draw attention, but it is also something more. The reference is to the story of Shadrach, Meshach and Abednego in the fiery furnace (Dan 3:1–24[45]). This was not only a good story of a clash between the servants of God in a foreign land of idolatry, the background story to one of the most used prayers (the *Benedicite*), but also one of the readings prescribed for use during the Easter Vigil – since the phrase 'Nebuchadnezzar the king' (*Nabuchodonosor Rex*) occurs twelve times in the reading, the pericope was often simply known as '*Nabuchodonosor Rex*'. Muirchú needed only that tail word to remind any in his audience that Dan 3:1–24 was the pattern for his story of Patrick.

Within the Easter Vigil the meaning of the text was that in the clash between truth and falsehood, Christ versus the powers of this world, the righteous cannot be held in death. Thus the three faithful servants of God who could walk in the fiery furnace were an antetype of Christ whom the tomb and the Prince of this World[46] cannot hold

---

44. Patrick's actual words are '*ad Nabuchodonosor Regem*' (*Vita*, bk 1, ch. 14); I have restored it to the nominative simply for clarity.

45. There is a problem in numeration in this section of many printed Bibles in that they insert the Song of the Three Young Men (the *Benedicite*) between verse 23 and verse 24: Muirchú's text, and that read in the liturgy, ran straight through from vv. 1 to 24. See below, p. 148.

46. Cf. Jn 12:31; 14:30; and 16:11.

prisoner. Muirchú, by contrast, read the whole story more literally in that it supplies a clash between the liturgy of the servant of God and the demands of an idolatrous emperor, detail by detail.

DANIEL 3:1–24	MUIRCHÚ
Nebuchadnezzar the king, emperor of Babylon	Lóegaire the king, emperor of the barbarians
built a gold statue for his pagan liturgy	lights a fire for his 'great festival of idolatry'
in the plain of Dura	in the plain of Brega
He calls an assembly of his satraps, magistrates, judges, leaders, rulers, prefects, and all the princes of the people	He call an assembly of his kings, satraps, leaders, princes, nobles of the people
The king's command is made known: all must partake in the liturgy; those who break the law must be cast into the furnace	The king issues an edict: all must follow the king in his fire-lighting liturgy or face death
the group of satraps, *et al.*, gather around him	the group of magicians, *et al.*, gather around him
the young men break the law and follow the liturgy and law of the living God	Patrick breaks the law and follows the liturgy and law of the living God
the breach is reported to the king	the king sees the breach
religious experts report on the meaning of the breach, greeting the king: *Rex, in aeternum uiue!*	religious experts report on the meaning of the breach, greeting the king: *Rex, in aeternum uiue!*
	MUIRCHÚ NOW INTRODUCED AN ELEMENT BASED ON HEROD IN MT 2, AND PHARAOH IN EX 14
The king summons the young men	the king goes out to Patrick[47]

---

47. That the king goes to Patrick is not a case of Muirchú presenting the king as less than Patrick, and so going to him; rather it is a consequence of wishing the king to bring out his chariots on the night of the Pasch (the Passover), so that they can be vanquished as were Pharaoh's on the night of the first Pasch.

after the audience, the king in anger orders punishments	after the audience, the king in anger orders punishments
the youths are cast into the furnace	they attack Patrick
and remain unharmed and escape	Patrick cannot be harmed and escapes
the king recognizes the true God.	THIS COMES LATER, IN THE SECOND SCENE.

The parallels are not perfect, for there are several Old Testament storylines being interwoven, but the general parallel is clear, and the explicit reference to the Daniel passage, along with the quotations from it, make it certain that for Muirchú the event of Ireland's conversion is to be seen as an act of deliverance typologically in line with that of the Young Men in the furnace and that of Christ breaking forth from the tomb (the *Exultet*).

The other theme Muirchú explicitly echoes concerns another court: that of Herod in Mt 2; and again there is not only a similarity of structure in the way that he arranges the details, but the exact words of Mt 2 are used by him to describe the scene.

Mt 2:1–6	Muirchú
King Herod hears of the event	King Lóegaire hears of the event
he is troubled and with him all Jerusalem	he is troubled and with him all Tara
he calls his chief priests and scribes	he calls his elders
who know the truth	who know the truth
and cite a prophecy to confirm this.	and have already cited a prophecy to to confirm this.

Herod is the king whose reign is surpassed by Christ, so for Muirchú the arrival of Christ through Patrick marks the end of the old kingdom of idolatry personified in Lóegaire. Both knew through the wisdom available at their courts, given to them by the Spirit, that they should go and worship; but both sought to frustrate the truth with power. This is a key message for Muirchú in his desire to echo these biblical courts. All four kings (Pharaoh, Nabuchodonosor, Herod, Lóegaire) are wicked, and they seek to use their laws and powers to oppose the revelation of God. But rather than succeed in this aim, their opposition becomes an occasion for God's power to be revealed among the Gentiles: the Egyptians, the Babylonians, the *magi* and the Irish. God is working his salvation in the midst of the nations (see Ps 73:12[48]), and Patrick is his apostle and sacrament.

Scene One: Easter Night

The first scene is the confrontation on the night itself: a single night sees the deliverance of the People of God from slavery and death, and their enlightenment and baptism. This is the night of the great contest, the great clash of good and evil, truth and falsehood, light and dark, life and death, Christ and Satan, and the old Age and the new Age, of Patrick and Lóegaire. It is also the moment of revealing: the revealing of Christ's message in Ireland in a public way as light, in the same manner that the Easter Vigil is the revelation of Christ as 'the light of the nations'. The 'stage set' that Muirchú wants us to imagine is one of darkness with a single fire, Patrick's, glowing at its centre and making everything in the world around it appear as shadows.

In the *Exultet* it states that the light from the Easter Candle eventually becomes so great that 'the night becomes as clear as day'. This happens, literally, in Muirchú's account, for now, while it is still night-time, a darkness suddenly comes down around the place where Patrick is in order to create confusion in which Lóegaire's chariots are destroyed. The king's chariots and horsemen are crushed on the first Irish Pasch as were the King of Egypt's on the night of the very first Passover. The scene closes with Patrick and his companions escaping miraculously from the clutches of the king.

Scene Two: Easter Morning

Muirchú presents the second scene in the drama of Ireland's conversion/baptism taking place on Easter day – which is the day hours after the Passover/Pasch/deliverance.[49] This time is liturgically strange, for it occurs during the same day as the Vigil, yet the actual moment of Passover/resurrection is past. Hence, it has an emphasis on the fact of the victory that has been won – and this is reflected in the scene offered us by Muirchú. The day becomes a

---

48. This reading is based on the Vulgate; Muirchú draws attention to this psalm in the context of the contest at Tara: 'There in the great plain of Brega, as the Psalmist says, he "crushed the head of the dragon" [Ps 73:14].'

49. The word used by Muirchú is *Pascha* which for convenience has to be translated as 'Easter'; however, in Latin the same word is used for the Christian feast as is used for the Passover in both Old and New Testaments and therefore it calls up a wealth of biblical imagery (as is the case with Muirchú) which 'Easter' does not.

series of contests which show up the superiority of adherence to the living God, the grandeur of his power, his care of his saints, and that Patrick fulfils all the requirements of the disciple/apostle.

Once again, the proof in scriptural fashion is revealed in an assembly:

> [19] The next day, which [for us] was the Day of the Passover [Easter Day], was for the pagans the day of their greatest festival; and many kings, princes, and wise men had gathered with Lóegaire for a feast.[50] While they were eating and drinking in the palace of Tara,[51] some speaking about what had happened, others turning it over in their minds, Patrick with only five companions appeared among them having come in through 'closed doors' in the way we read about Christ.[52]

Patrick now shares the nature of the risen Christ – he can move through locked doors, and so is the one who is the perfect apostle proclaiming the resurrection:

> He went there to proclaim and demonstrate the holy faith in Tara in the presence of all nations.[53]

Those who receive him, receive Christ who sent him (cf. Lk 10:16), and so are numbered among the saints:

> As he entered the dining hall of Tara only one out of the whole group stood to salute his arrival. This was Dubthach maccu Lugir, the greatest of the poets. . . . When Dubthach stood to honour St Patrick, the saint blessed him and he was the first who believed in God on that day,[54] 'and it was reckoned to him as righteousness'.[55]

The scene then develops:

> Seeing Patrick, the pagans asked him to eat with them so that they could test him later. And he, 'knowing all that was going to happen',[56] accepted their invitation.

Patrick in proclaiming the risen Christ shares in the protection promised to preachers in Mk 16:17–18:

---

50. The phrase 'kings and princes' is found on several occasions in the scriptures: e.g. Jer 44:17, Dan 9:6, Neh 9:32; and often there is the sense that they are gathered to witness a divine action: e.g. Is 19:11, 49:7, or Ps 76:12. This seems to be the motive here: they are assembled for their own purposes, yet God uses this for his own and their gathering provides a suitable audience for his mighty deeds through Patrick.
51. The imagery is drawn from the description of King Belshazzar's feast in Dan 5.
52. Cf. Jn 20:19–29.
53. Muirchú combines the notion of testifying to all peoples (Mt 24:14 and *Confessio* 3) with that of bearing witness before hostile authorities (Lk 21:12).
54. This notion of believing on the day of hearing the word is modelled on the accounts of large numbers being converted in Acts 2:41 on the first day of preaching (Pentecost).
55. Gen 15:6; and cf. Ps 105:31; 1 Mac 2:52; Rom 4:3, 9, 22; Gal 3:6; and Jas 2:23.
56. Jn 18:4.

[20] 'While they were' all 'eating',[57] one of the wise men, called Lucet Máel, despite having taken part in the nocturnal conflict when his colleague perished, still wanted to challenge Patrick. His first move was to slip something into Patrick's cup from a flask he had with him.[58] Those around him watched to see what Patrick would do. When St Patrick recognized what kind of test this was he blessed his cup. Its contents now became like ice. Then he turned it upside down and only the drop added by the wise man fell out. Blessing it again the contents returned to their natural liquid form, 'and they were all amazed'.[59]

We are now given a series of classic miracles (*signa*) by Muirchú modelled on those which distinguish the living God from the gods of the nations in 1 Kgs 18. Here is a specimen:

After the cup test the wise man said: 'Let us perform signs in this great field.'[60] So Patrick asked him which kind they should perform. The wise man said: 'Let us call down snow upon the earth.' But Patrick said: 'I do not wish to do anything which is contrary to the will of God.'[61] So the wise man said: 'I will bring it upon the earth for all to see.' Then sending forth magical spells he covered the whole field with snow. It reached the height of a man's belt in depth, and all saw it 'and were amazed'.[62] Then the saint said: 'Behold we have all seen this, now get rid of it!' The wise man replied: 'I am unable to get rid of it until the same time tomorrow.' So the saint declared: 'You are capable of doing ill, but not of doing good. This is not the case with me.' Then as he cast his blessing around the field the snow disappeared. Without rain or mist or wind it went in a moment. 'The crowd' applauded and 'were amazed',[63] and 'it touched their hearts'.[64]

---

57. Mt 26:26.
58. This constitutes a particular kind of test for Muirchú: the saint in accordance with Mk 16:18 cannot be injured by any deadly thing in his drink; and note the incident of Paul with the viper in Acts 28:1–6. Hence I depart from Bieler's text, but with two of the manuscripts, in reading 'After the cup test (*poculum*)' rather than 'After a little while (*paululum*)'. Note that Muirchú sees it as a *kind* of test (*hoc probationis genus*).
59. Mk 1:27.
60. Muirchú's notion of a miracle (*signum*) becomes clear here. He combines the New Testament notion of a miracle as that which produces 'amazement' (*stupor*), e.g. at Lk 5:26, in the Synoptics with that found in Jn, e.g. Jn 2:18, where the miracle is a 'sign' (*signum*); in both cases it is the recognition of the event that reveals the person who instigates it. The miraculous is testimony to the power that is present; this can be seen in the number of occasions when there is a connection between seeing 'signs and wonders' (*signa et prodigia*) and belief in some way or other (Mt 24:24; Mk 13:22; Jn 4:48; Acts 4:30; 5:12; 14:3; 15:12; Rom 15:19; 2 Cor 12:12; 2 Thess 2:9; and Heb 2:4).
61. This might seem to be an unusual humility given what Patrick had already done; however, allowing that it may be a dramatic refusal to encourage the wise man to do what he cannot undo – and so showing *a fortiori* the relative power of Patrick – it should be noted that sending snow has specific links in the tradition with the will of God; cf. Job 37:6; 38:22; and Sir 43:14.
62. Mk 1:27.
63. Mt 9:33.
64. Acts 2:37.

Muirchú sets out a series of similar tests, and in each the faith of Patrick is shown to have more power and so to be more true, and he is the one vindicated from on high. Finally, Patrick, having proclaimed the faith, must point out that a moment of decision has arrived:

> The king 'was greatly infuriated'[65] with Patrick over the death of his wise man and would have killed him except he was prevented by God. At Patrick's bidding and by his word the anger of God came down upon that blasphemous people,[66] and many of them perished.[67] Then St Patrick spoke thus to the king: 'Unless you now believe, you shall quickly die, for the anger of God has come down upon your head.'[68] And the king feared greatly and his heart was in turmoil,[69] and with him that of the whole city.[70]

And as the foreign kings had finally recognized the God of Israel, so now the king of Tara must recognize that the Word has now reached his kingdom, believe, and be baptized:

> [21] So King Lóegaire gathered his elders and whole senate and said: 'It is better that I believe, than that I die.'[71] So, on the counsel of his fellows, he believed on that day and turned to the eternal Lord God; and in that place many others believed.[72] And Patrick told the king: 'Because you have resisted my teaching and have put obstacles in my way, although the day of your reign shall be prolonged, none of your descendants shall ever be king.'[73]
>
> [22] So then St Patrick, according to the precept of the Lord Jesus, 'went off teaching all the nations and baptizing them in the name of the Father and of the Son and of the Holy Spirit'.[74] He 'went out' from Tara 'and proclaimed the good news everywhere, while the Lord worked with him and confirmed the message by the signs that accompanied it'.[75]

THE CORE OF MUIRCHÚ'S VISION

Muirchú's *vita* is one of the more skilfully crafted pieces of theology expressed as history in the form of drama/liturgy that have come down to us from the Middle Ages. Where did he get the idea for this manner of presenting the process of his people's entry to the people of God? The only source that could have given him a parallel use of

---

65. Mt 2:16; again the king is being modelled on Herod.
66. Rom 1:18.
67. Cf. 1 Mac 13:49.
68. Cf. Jn 8:24; and Ps 7:17.
69. Cf. 1 Sam 28:5.
70. The phrase is modelled on Mt 2:3, but its language follows Mt 21:10.
71. Cf. Jonah 4:8.
72. Cf. Jn 7:31; 8:30; 12:42; and Acts 17:12.
73. Cf. Jer 33:26.
74. Mt 28:19.
75. Mk 16:20.

scriptural scenery would have been the *Dialogues* of Gregory the Great and his use of the Old Testament to bring out the power of Benedict,[76] and we know that this work was being read on Iona at the time Muirchú was writing.[77] But such parallels only take us part of the way toward explaining his creativity. Muirchú had a few uncertain traditions about Patrick, but he had one theological certainty: the changing of a people from being not-the-people-of-God to being part of Christ was the drama of the Paschal Mystery; the Paschal Mystery was entered through the drama of liturgy, so the story of his people was the story of the Easter Night. From his perspective as theologian/churchman could he have provided a more fitting origin story – a people reborn in the great event of Christian rebirth – for his people's faith?

Muirchú was a theologian who displayed his theology using the skills of the dramatist. He believed that the Word had encountered the people waiting for him in the drama of the Incarnation, and now that people encountered the Word in the drama of the liturgy. Patrick's day of preaching/conversion/believing/baptism, the Pasch of the Irish, was just another instance in the divine pattern. This story was for Muirchú more true than history:[78] it revealed not just the visible deeds of flesh and blood, but the work of God through Patrick seen with the eyes of faith.[79] Patrick had proclaimed to the Irish the *Exultet* – Christ is risen; they in response had joined with 'Christians everywhere' and were now 'washed clean of sin and freed from all defilement, restored to grace to grow together in holiness' (the *Exultet*).

---

76. See P. Cusack, *An Interpretation of the Second Dialogue of Gregory the Great: Hagiography and St. Benedict* (Lampeter 1993), *passim*; a full study of the use of Scripture in the development of seventh-century Irish hagiography – using the methods developed by Cusack for Gregory – is long overdue.
77. See T. O'Loughlin, 'The Library of Iona in the Late Seventh Century: The Evidence from Adomnán's *De Locis Sanctis*', *Ériu* 45 (1994), 33–52.
78. For an insightful comparison with the drama of Christ's passion – another event presented within the time-span of a day – see M. Ramsey, *The Narratives of the Passion* (London 1962).
79. I have touched upon Muirchú's views of the relationship between the pagan and Christian religions as responses to God, and the inherent theology of the liturgy found in the *vita*; however, I do not want to consider them here as they both would require much space to treat adequately, and it is better to leave them than to sketch them inadequately.

FURTHER READING

Texts

Muirchú, *Vita Patricii*.

Bibliography

L&S, no. 303.

Studies

E. Bhreathnach, 'Temoria: Caput Scotorum?' *Ériu* 47 (1996), 67–88.

L. Bieler, 'Muirchu's Life of Patrick as a work of literature', *MA* 43 (1974), 219–33.

——'Ancient Hagiography and the Lives of St Patrick', in F. Paolo and M. Barrera (eds), *Forma Futuri: Studi in onore del Cardinale Michele Pellegrino* (Turin 1975), pp. 650–5.

Kenney, no. 128, pp. 331–4.

A. J. McGregor, *Fire and Light in the Western Triduum: Their Use at Tenebrae and at the Paschal Vigil* (Collegeville MN 1992).

R. Sharpe, 'Palaeographical Considerations in the Study of the Patrician Documents in the Book of Armagh', *Scriptorium* 36 (1983), 3–28.

6 The *Collectio canonum hibernensis*: Marriage and Sexuality

We have seen in examining the penitentials and Adomnán that law was a central concern of Celtic theologians, but by far the greatest legal endeavour of theologian-lawyers – the forerunners of the later 'canonists' – was the *Collectio canonum hibernensis* ('the Irish collection of canons'). It is justly held to be one of the greatest monuments to Christian learning in these islands, for two reasons. Primarily, as it was one of the first works, if not the very first, which systematically arranged Christian law under topic headings. And even if its compilers had seen a similar arrangement – and that is only a possibility – they still had to forge much of the taxonomy themselves as they had to systematize Christian legal demands in a society other than the one in which many of those demands had taken shape. Secondly, the usefulness of this collection, both practically and in developing jurisprudence, soon became obvious across Latin Europe. From the surviving manuscripts we know that within decades of its compilation it was being used in Anglo-Saxon dioceses, in teaching law in Köln, and in judging cases in Cambrai. From its Irish origins at the end of the seventh century – it seems to belong to the milieu that produced the Synod of Birr and men like Adomnán and Muirchú – it exercised a crucial influence in the development of the canon law of the Latin church.[1] And so along with the penitentials it is one of the two major contributions from Celtic lands to the rest of Latin Christianity. What follows is a case study to introduce the *Collectio*.

CONSTANT CONCERNS

The history of Christian theology repeatedly displays two striking features: first, the amount of concern that is devoted to sexual

---

1. For an introduction to this influence see R. E. Reynolds, 'Unity and Diversity in Carolingian Canon Law Collections: The Case of the *Collectio Hibernensis* and Its Derivatives', in U.-R. Blumenthal (ed.), *Carolingian Essays: Andrew W. Mellon Lectures in Early Christian Studies* (Washington 1983), pp. 99–135.

morality and the regulation of marriage; and second, that Christian positions on these matters find their primary expression in legislation. The Synod of Elvira (Spain 309), one of the earliest councils whose laws are extant, provides a good example: 45 per cent of its legislation deals with sexuality and marriage.[2] An interest in legislation relating to marriage and sexual morality seems always close to the centre of the moral concern of leaders in the Church.[3] Early Christian Ireland was no exception to this overall pattern, and indeed its bishops, abbots and canon lawyers were to make two contributions in this field that would have a long-range impact on the Latin church. The first, as we saw in chapter 3, was the penitentials. The second, the subject of this chapter, was through the creation of the first handbook of canonical precedents arranged systematically around topics: this was the *Collectio canonum hibernensis* produced in Ireland around the beginning of the eighth century.[4] This development might seem of little importance – no more than a convenience for those looking up the Christian position on something – but nothing could be further from the truth. In taking a mass of laws, rules and judgments from different places and times, and giving them organization under named offences, in broader classes of problem, and then arranging the laws in order of importance, this work not only helped create canonical jurisprudence, but ensured that canon law would be the leading edge of theological development. The *Collectio* was made in Ireland, yet its fame lay abroad: our manuscripts show it in use in Anglo-Saxon England, in France and Germany, in central Europe and down through Italy.

Despite its enormous influence the *Collectio* is not well known to those whose primary interest is theology.[5] Histories of canon law often concentrate on a later period,[6] and it is ignored in histories of Christian thinking about marriage.[7] This is surprising when we recall that a generation or two ago, few would have suggested that studying the canon law of Gratian would alter how we view the

---

2. See S. Laeuchli, *Power and Sexuality: The Emergence of Canon Law at the Synod of Elvira* (Philadelphia 1972), p. 12.
3. See U. Ranke-Heinemann, *Eunuchs for the Kingdom of Heaven* (ET: P. Heinegg, Harmondsworth 1990).
4. H. Wasserschleben (ed.), *Die irische Kanonensammlung*; for the background see K. Hughes, *Early Christian Ireland: Introduction to the Sources* (Cambridge 1972), pp. 65–95.
5. The criticism by James Muldoon of historians of philosophy regarding the history of canon law ('Medieval Canon Law and the Formation of International Law', *ZSSR* 112 (1995), 64–82) is equally applicable to historians of theology.
6. E.g. J. A. Brundage, *Medieval Canon Law* (London 1995); however, this is changing: see R. Somerville and B. C. Brasington, *Prefaces to Canon Law Books in Latin Christianity: Selected Translations 500–700* (New Haven, Conn. 1998); but for detailed comment one has to rely on older works such as P. Fournier and G. Le Bras, *Histoire des collections canoniques en Occident depuis les fausses décrétales jusqu'au Décret de Gratien* (2 vols, Paris 1931–32).
7. E.g. T. Mackin, *The Marital Sacrament* (New York 1989).

sacramental theology of the thirteenth century; yet today, due to the work of such scholars as Kuttner, we see that this is of primary importance to understanding of such writers as Aquinas.[8] The only group who have examined it in detail are early Irish historians for the light it can throw on that society and its institutions.[9] So here I want to examine it as a document of importance for the history of theology as such: thus my interest is neither in its sources and origins nor in what it can tell us of early Irish society, but rather the view of sexuality and marriage it projected to its many users in the Latin church who used it not because it was Irish, but because it was one of the best expositions of the law of Christ to which they had access. It is no exaggeration to say that it is one of the first pan-Latin church manuals of moral theology; indeed, if the *Collectio* were combined with a few lines of running commentary, one would have exactly such a manual.

THE *COLLECTIO*

Over the years the *Collectio* has been the subject of many controversies, but two early judgements have stood the test of time: first, it is one of the earliest, if not the earliest, of the systematic collections; and, second, it stands as a source to many other collections up to the time of Gratian. Indeed, its impact can be traced lineally from its earliest uses in the eighth century through to Gratian, on into the *Corpus iuris canonici*, and even the *Codex* of 1917.[10] Thus, it is an appropriate place in which to observe the development of any aspect of theology that was amenable to law.

The most important development that is directly witnessed in the *Collectio* is that it is a systematic collection, and it is the significance of this for the Latin understanding of marriage and sexuality that is my central concern. In the period before the *Collectio*, there had been several widely used collections of legal texts but the organizing principle was chronological.[11] They contained all the available decrees of early synods but arranged them sequentially. In them one finds all the canons of the council of Nicaea, then those of

---

8. Cf. S. G. Kuttner, *Harmony from Dissonance: An Interpretation of Medieval Canon Law* (Latrobe 1960).
9. For example, see such studies as D. Ó Corráin, 'Irish Law and Canon Law' in P. Ní Chatháin and M. Richter (eds), *Irland und Europa: Die Kirche im Frühmittelalter* (Stuttgart 1984), pp. 157–66; D. Ó Corráin, L. Breatnach and A. Breen, 'The Laws of the Irish', *Peritia* 3 (1984), 382–438; L. Breatnach, 'Canon Law and Secular Law in Early Ireland: The Significance of *Bretha Nemed*', *Peritia* 3 (1984), 439–59; and F. Kelly, *A Guide to Early Irish Law* (Dublin 1988), pp. 233–4.
10. That is the Canon Law that governed the Latin Catholic Church until 1984.
11. The *Dionysiana* (cf. J. Rambaud-Buhot in *NCE* 4, 876) and the *Isidoriana* (cf. G. Martínez Díez in *NCE* 7, 1) being the most famous.

Chalcedon, then of another, until finally the canons of the latest nearby synod. The laws were recorded and available, but the format was unwieldy and reference to a particular decision presupposes that one could at least remember at which council it was decreed. Another difficulty in such collections was the problem of disagreements between texts that came from different places and times. One could cite a Greek synod of the fourth century whose law on a topic someone claimed to follow, while the law from a Latin council in Gaul in the sixth century was exactly the opposite: how could one reconcile these laws and relate them to one another? The solution was to arrange all the authorities: the decisions of councils (canons), the decisions of popes (decretals), the opinions of illustrious writers (extracts from Jerome, Augustine or Isidore), prescriptions and precedents from the Old and New Laws (the Scriptures were par excellence *law*, and also the greatest repository of laws and precedents); and a few other items that had a bearing on law (local legal traditions), in a such a way that they could be found under the crimes or concerns they dealt with. This achievement constitutes the originality of the *Collectio*.

The *Collectio* is divided into 67 books:[12] each of them can be viewed as a major topic division. Thus, there is a book dealing with law relating to bishops, another that is concerned with kings, another with theft, and so on. Each book is further divided into 'headings' (*capitula*) which correspond to particular legal problems of prescribing or prohibiting.[13] For example, in the book (XXV) on laws relating to the state (*De regno*) there is a heading declaring that church property should be free from tax. Each of these headings is then supported by a range of actual legal decisions (the *sententiae*) which show what the law is.[14] These *sententiae* are, on the whole, arranged in order of precedence: first the great source of law: the Scriptures; then

12. This number varies in the manuscripts and will only be cleared up when a new edition makes clear the question of different recensions; here I simply follow Wasserschleben.

13. Many early systematic canon law collections are referred to by the word *capitula*, e.g. the *Collectio in CCCIX Capitula* (cf. J. J. Ryan, 'Observations on pre-Gratian canonical collections: Some recent work and present problems', *Congrès de Droit Canonique Médiéval, Louvain et Bruxelles: 22–26 Juillet*, esp. 91–3); however, I wish to avoid the usual English rendering 'chapter', as it stresses the form of the collection, i.e. in chapters, without making sufficiently clear why this is important: 309 *capitula* means that the sources of a judgment (i.e. the laws) are provided to cover a possible 309 legal situations. Hence, I translate *capitulum* as 'heading' and suggest it be understood as, for the most part, a single issue which can be legally disputed.

14. The word *sententia* is to be understood not in its grammatical sense, but in its logical and forensic meaning where it stands for a proposition – note the phrase still used in court proceedings: 'The sentence of the court is . . .'. Each *sententia* in the *Collectio*, whether it is a single line or a full chapter from scripture, is to be taken as a single proposition asserting or denying the proposition contained in the heading.

conciliar and papal decisions; then the opinions of church writers; then other materials. Each of these categories is further divided hierarchically: from within the Scriptures the foremost authority is Christ (the gospels), then Paul, then the great law-givers of the Old Testament (David and Solomon: as recorded in writings ascribed to them or in Kings), then the Books of the Law (the Pentateuch), then the prophets, then other books. With church decisions, the canons of councils outweigh papal judgments.[15] Among church writers, Augustine and Jerome, and to a lesser extent Ambrose, have special prominence. While there are plenty of exceptions to these organizing principles in the *Collectio*, they are sufficiently attested to show that there is a hierarchical logic at work throughout. Now to our question: what views of sexuality and marriage emerge within this system?

VIRGINITY AS THE CRITERION OF MARRIAGE

While there are references to marriage and sexuality throughout the *Collectio*, two books deal with the topic directly: Book XLV: 'Questions concerning women' and Book XLVI: 'On marriage'. Here the order of the books is a key indicator of the mind of the compiler: sexuality is a matter concerning women and can be examined independently of, and before, marriage. When, however, we examine the order of topics in Bk 45 another agenda becomes visible. The whole area of sexuality and marriage is opened by an unambiguous statement to the effect that virginity is the highest perfection and is the state against which all subsequent statements should be read. The book begins with this heading: 'that virginity is to be praised in either sex'. Since virginity is the prior and more perfect reality, any other state, be it marriage or widowhood, is secondary and 'lower down' in the hierarchy of human activity.

The support for this position is presented as coming from Jerome to whom is credited this statement:[16]

> Jerome [said]: Virginity is the beauty of the church, the flower of modesty, the path of life, the guardian of sobriety, the patroness of innocence, the darling of justice, she who eradicates vices, she is the conqueror of lust. [The virgin] is strong in abstinence, firm in humility, sincere in charity, is solid in prayer, careful in vigils, eager in fasts, victorious in life, [and] the company of the angels [Mt 22:30]. For virginity follows the Lamb wherever he goes [Apoc 14:4] and remains always in the mind of the Creator. It is something greater than all

---

15. Included in this category is the pseudo-Clementine literature: laws derived from those writings attributed to Pope Clement (bishop of Rome at the end of the first century); for an introduction to this material, see 'Clementine Literature' in the *ODCC*.

16. In fact, this is a paraphrase of many things said by Jerome in favour of virginity; and while, as it stands in the *Collectio*, it cannot be said to come from his pen, I doubt if he would object that the compiler had misrepresented him.

other things, so great that our Lord would not dare to command, saying: 'Not everyone can receive this word, but to whom it is given' [Mt 19:11] by my Father.[17]

The message is clear: nice people are virgins; problems flow from sexuality. This may seem a stark position, but it is supported by other headings in these books and is nowhere more clearly seen than in the reasoning with which the next book, on marriage, opens. The first heading is: 'in praise of marriage', but the supporting sentence shows that marriage is not really to be praised at all, except insofar as it enables virginity to stand out as excellent. Again Jerome is quoted:

> Jerome: If there was no marriage, there could be no virginity: for as the earth is populated by marriage [cf. Gen 1:28], so heaven is by virginity.

The form this statement has in the *Collectio* (*ex matrimonio terra repletur, ex uirginitate uero coelum*) is just one variant of this well-known *dictum* of Jerome. In its more usual form, '*nuptiae terram replent, uirginitas autem paradisum*',[18] this statement remained at the heart of church thinking on sexuality throughout the Middle Ages.[19] So does the *Collectio* have any importance apart from showing the influence of Jerome?

That the writings of a group of Latin theologians, principally Jerome and Augustine, at the turn of the fourth/fifth century had a profound effect on the western Church's views of sexuality and marriage hardly needs to be stressed.[20] Jerome's view that any sexual activity was inferior, earthly and transient in comparison with what was noble, valuable, superior and holy has been seen as a key element in forming the cult of virginity and celibacy in the Latin church.[21] The attitude of Augustine to sexuality, while less extreme than Jerome's,[22] was none the less at one with his in seeing a direct connection between human disorder (his notion of a Fall and of Original Sin) and human sexuality.

For Augustine, sexuality was filled with danger. Indeed, the source of the disorder in humanity, Original Sin, was transmitted in the act of generation itself, and he noted that sexuality did not exist in paradise: it is after the expulsion that Adam 'knew Eve his wife' (Gen 3:24–4:1). Likewise, he believed that a particular reading of Paul

---

17. Note that this is a misapplication of Mt 19:11.
18. Jerome, *Aduersus Iouinianum* 1, 16 (*PL* 23, 246): 'marriage fills the earth, *but virginity* fills paradise' (note the force of the 'but' which builds on the acknowledged disparity between the earth and paradise, to set up a similar disparity between marriage and virginity).
19. Cf. C. Brooke, *The Medieval Idea of Marriage* (Oxford 1989), ch. 3 gives an account of this phrase in the context of its later use in the twelfth century.
20. This is a recurring theme in Mackin, op. cit. ch. 6.
21. Brooke, op. cit., ch. 3.
22. This can be seen by contrasting Augustine's *De ciuitate Dei* 15, 16–17 on abstinence and sexuality in the first age with Jerome's views on the same period in *Epistola XXII*, 19.

established the true value of sexuality: continence is best, but lawful marriage is to be preferred to burning with desire and fornication (1 Cor 7). Thus marriage was a *remedium concupiscentiae* (an antidote to desire) and sexuality was saved from the sinfulness of wanton passion by the possibility that it could result in procreation. So while Augustine's pessimism about human moral abilities reached it depths when he came to consider sexual desire,[23] he always recognized that marriage was part of the world he believed came from God and as such the dangers of sexuality had to be held in tension with whatever were the goods of marriage.[24] Based on his own experience, and, as many argue, due also to never fully shaking off the sexual attitudes of the Manichees, he considered lust a constant distraction from the things of God and that it had systematically reduced the scope of freedom.[25] It was therefore something that had to be reined in and vigorously controlled. However, he did recognize that the rejection of the flesh that formed part of Greek philosophical culture (such notions as that of a human person being imprisoned in flesh by the sexuality of its parents, and the explicit rejection of sexuality that formed a central part of Manichee belief) could not be squared with the divine command to reproduce that was found in Gen 1, nor with the legislation that upheld and approved of marriage in the Old Testament in general, nor with the implications for sexuality that followed from belief in the incarnation of Christ. Here is the complexity of his position: marriage is to be upheld as good, but the onus of proof is on the person who wants to so uphold it. In other words, given its acknowledged dangers, it seemed more obvious that marriage was to be rejected in favour of complete celibacy as the ideal if only fallen humanity could reach this; yet, such a conclusion must allow that marriage had goods in itself as it is part of the divine order and its absolute rejection is out of the question.[26]

Augustine never drew the various stands of his thought on sexuality into a coherent statement: his comments are scattered throughout his voluminous writings. For example, the dangers of sexuality are stressed in his autobiographical writings, the links with Original Sin in his writings on that topic, the rejection of the Manichee position elsewhere, and the links between sexuality and the divine command to procreate in his commentaries on Genesis.

---

23. See E. H. Pagels, *Adam, Eve, and the Serpent* (London 1988), pp. 98–126.
24. This theme of a tension in the creation between its intrinsic goodness and its distracting attractions, is one that surfaces in many ways in Augustine's thought: see T. O'Loughlin, 'Knowing God and Knowing the Cosmos: Augustine's Legacy of Tension', *IPJ* 6 (1989), 27–58.
25. See E. H. Pagels, ' "Freedom from Necessity": Philosophic and Personal Dimensions of Christian Conversion', in G. A. Robbins (ed.), *Genesis 1–3 in the History of Exegesis: Intrigue in the Garden* (Lewiston NY 1988), pp. 69–97.
26. This synopsis is based on a variety of his writings, but the *De bono coniugali* deserves special mention.

The nearest he came to an overview was in the *De bono coniugali*, but
even here he did not give a complete picture, as his starting point was
the defence of marriage from complete rejection. Thus he wanted to
emphasize what he saw as 'the goods' (*bona*) (i.e. the morally good
results) which 'saved' marriage: it provided a remedy for lust,[27] a
means of procreation,[28] and means of mutual assistance and support
for the spouses.[29] His legacy of tension – on the one hand being
deeply suspicious of all sexuality while on the other wishing to defend
marriage – meant that the great authority of the Latin church was
enigmatic for the generations after him who sought clear positions,
expressed with *breuitas*, and in a form that could easily be appealed
to and handed on as a convenient package. In the age of manuals
when short encyclopaedic statements would be central to theology –
the sort of teaching exemplified in the writings of Isidore of Seville[30]
– Augustine would be less than clear-cut: for at one moment he could
be quoted in favour of a position, but a moment later as against it.[31]

Jerome, unlike Augustine, had never addressed marriage directly.
Apart from his exegetical works, much of his writing was devoted to a
bitter style of controversy whereby he attacked the person whose
ideas he perceived to be inimical to his own position; and no position
attracted his attention more than what he saw as a challenge to the

---

27. Augustine believed that he could trace these aspects to the Scriptures and so
    contributed to establishing a series of scriptural texts as standard proofs for the
    theology of marriage that came in his wake; for example, that marriage was a
    remedy for lust was seen to follow from 1 Cor 7:9 ('for it is better to marry than to
    burn [with desire]'); and other places in the New Testament such as Col 3:5; Gal
    5:24; and 1 Jn 2:16.
28. See what were understood as the divine commands to procreate in the Old
    Testament, all of which were seen as repeating the primordial command to
    procreate: Gen 1:28.
29. Compare the creation of Eve as a fit helper in Gen 2:18; for references to the use
    of this verse in Augustine and the tradition after him, see T. O'Loughlin, 'Adam's
    Rib and the Equality of the Sexes: Some Medieval Exegesis of Gn 2:21–22', *ITQ*
    59 (1993), 44–54.
30. An example of this process with regard to marriage can be seen in the different
    ways that Augustine (in the *De ciuitate Dei* 16) and Isidore (in the *In Genesim* 20;
    and using Augustine as his main source) react to the marriage of the old man
    Abraham to Keturah with whom he has more children (Gen 25). The basic
    problem is this: since Abraham was very old, the justification of marriage as a
    remedium concupiscentiae was ruled out in Augustine's view. Moreover, since
    Abraham had already offspring who would 'number as many as the stars of
    heaven' (Gen 22:17 and Heb 11:12), the purpose of procreation (*bonum prolis*)
    could not justify it; so how can the marriage to, and sexual intercourse with,
    Keturah be justified? The shifting explanations illustrate the changes in the
    Latin understanding of marriage, and indeed theology, in the period.
31. In the most comprehensive survey of the history of the theology of marriage
    (Mackin, op. cit.) this period when the manuals began to make an impact on
    theology only receives a passing reference (p. 232); while in the more recent
    treatment of the history of marriage, devoted explicitly to this period (P. L.
    Reynolds, *Marriage in the Western Church: The Christianization of Marriage
    During the Patristic and Early Medieval Periods* (Leiden 1994)) these works are
    not even mentioned.

superiority of virginity as the most perfect form of the Christian life: be it the virginity of the mother of Jesus, or the virginity practised as an asceticism in the church. Three works in particular, the *Aduersus Iouinianum*, the *Aduersus Heluidium de Mariae uirginitate perpetua* and his *Epistola XXII ad Eustochium*, brought his views on virginity to a frenzied summit. In these he repeatedly used rhetorical tools of contrast and *reductio ad absurdum* to compare sexuality-in-marriage with the perfect state of virginity. His reasoning works like this: assume virginity and marriage as opposites – the proof being that they mutually exclude each other – and then contrast them. Next, set out other sets of oppositions such as: spirit/flesh; before/after the Fall; this world/the world to come; earth/heaven; temporal (i.e. transient)/eternal; the perfect/the imperfect; the perishable/the imperishable; and the list can be continued. For each individual opposition, he could rely on scriptural texts; thus he believed that his premises were not only sound, but based in the very word of God[32] and indeed that such reasoning could be found in Scripture itself.[33] We can appreciate this more easily by imagining these oppositions arrayed horizontally and vertically:

VIRGINITY/SPIRIT/PARADISE/NEXT WORLD/HEAVEN/ETERNITY/ETC.

MARRIAGE/FLESH/FALLEN STATE/THIS WORLD/EARTH/TIME/ETC.

Marriage and virginity now each amalgamate with the other characteristics, qualities and states on their respective levels. The universe is divided into two mutually excluding tiers whose fundamental relationship is that of superiority–inferiority.[34] That a similar relationship exists between virginity and marriage is a direct and necessary consequence. Indeed, in *Epistola XXII* his reasoning leads him to this conclusion: virginity is the true natural state for mankind, (legitimate) sexuality (namely marriage) is a result of sin.[35] Marriage was the poorer and profane state of those who were the less than perfect followers of Christ – and those who entertained

---

32. The distinction, with a sense of opposition, of spirit/flesh can be found on 12 occasions in Paul alone: Rom 8:4; 8:5; 8:6; 8:9; 8:13; 1 Cor 5:5; Gal 3:3; 4:29; 5:16; 5:17; 6:8; and Phil 3:3 – and similar texts can easily be found in support of the other oppositions.

33. 1 Cor 15 is a notable example of such reasoning and several of the pairs mentioned above can be found in this one chapter.

34. I have examined this notion of a two-tier universe, which is not to be confused, at least theoretically, with a Gnostic-Manichaean dualism, in 'The Symbol gives Life: Eucherius of Lyons' Formula for Exegesis', in T. Finan and V. Twomey (eds), *Scriptural Interpretation in the Fathers: Letter and Spirit* (Dublin 1995).

35. *Ep. XXII*, 19. The purpose of this section of the letter is to show that sexuality with all its inherent sordidness began after and as a result of the sin in paradise; his tone can be seen in the opening words of paragraph 20 (170): 'I praise marriage, I praise wedlock, for they produce virgins for me.' In paragraph 19 Jerome uses Mt 19:11 as a text supporting celibacy/virginity: on this misapplication, see note 50 below.

a criticism of this found themselves by the force of Jerome's logic grouped with the worst of heretics. Jerome's theological method is often no more than guilt by association given a vague respectability by his stylistic elegance, and added weight by his authority as a translator; but anyone, such as the compiler of the *Collectio*, taking Jerome as his starting point for a theology of marriage takes an extreme as his measure.

Again unlike Augustine, Jerome did not find pagan views on the evils of marriage and the Greek virginity cults repulsive.[36] And, on occasion, he used these as witnesses to the superiority of virginity as a basic religious truth known to all. Augustine, knowing how the pagan virginity cults would play into the hands of the Manichees, carefully avoided reference to them; but Jerome, either unaware or unmindful of the dangers, proudly re-used the myth of Iphigenia as a proof of the power of a virgin's prayers. If Agamemnon, in the Homeric legend, believed the soothsayer Calchas that only the smell of the blood of a virgin would calm the anger of Artemis and allow his ships to sail and so slaughtered his own virgin daughter, what doubt should there be that the prayers of a Christian virgin are more pleasing to God?[37]

While Jerome, even less than Augustine, produced no systematic position on virginity, his stance was far easier to encapsulate; and so he probably had a greater impact on later generations. He did this in two ways. First, his thought was to be found in a few short works, all of which were important for other reasons apart from the views on virginity – both Helvidius and Jovinian were seen as attacking the Virgin Mary and, thereby, the person of Christ. So they were studied in connection with the virgin birth, the perpetual virginity of Mary, and as a source of apologetic on such matters as references to 'the brothers of Jesus' in the gospels (e.g. Mt 12:46).[38] Likewise, *Epistola XXII* was read as a general attack on anyone wanting to 'water down' the purity of the gospels by reading pagan authors, or to rely on the arguments of rhetoric rather than the simple divinely revealed truths of the scriptures.[39] Second, his writings contained memorable

---

36. The use of pagan literature to provide examples of virginity raises some complex questions about Jerome: first, he must have known from his reading and his contacts with Jewish scholars, that these were radically at variance with the Old Testament position, yet when he uses them he never points to any difficulty; second, in many places in his writings, and most famously in *Ep. XXII*, he objects to the corrupting influence of pagan literature on Christians, yet when these sexual fantasies suit his purpose he uses them without hesitation.

37. *Aduersus Iouinianum* 1, 41 (*PL* 23, 270); in this passage he draws on a wide range of literary texts and accounts of cults which involve virginity or sexual abstinence.

38. For an analysis of the importance of these works of Jerome, see J. McHugh, *The Mother of Jesus in the New Testament* (London 1975), pp. 200–54.

39. The irony of Jerome the rhetorician, even allowing for his own self-doubts in *Ep. XXII*, attacking rhetoric as a perverter of religious truth does not seem to have attracted much attention from his medieval readers.

phrases (e.g. *nuptiae terram replent . . .*) which in an age of manuals and *florilegia* had an oracular quality, and were eminently suited to a *collectio* like ours as authoritative declarations.

THE *COLLECTIO* AS A MANUAL

The purpose of the *Collectio* was to provide a clear and simple way to ascertain the true and correct position on the topics it covered. Its key contribution to the evolving tradition was that it focused on particular points of the Christian tradition and made these the values against which other opinions could be evaluated. It took complex arguments and positions out of their historical and narrative contexts in the Scriptures and church writers and treated them as absolute and timeless propositions. In the process Christian thinking on sexuality and marriage became a series of simple slogans presented as admitting of clear and distinct answers. Ambiguity and dispute were no longer necessary.

We can observe this simplicity from the very start of the *Collectio*'s treatment of sexuality. If you want the basic Christian position and the *Collectio* is your reference work then virginity is the perfect Christian reality, while marriage is the tolerated transient, carnal and inferior alternative. The lower status of marriage in the mind of the compilers can be seen in several ways. First, in the order of the books: questions on women (all concerning virgins) come before those on marriage. Second, in the opening heading of Bk 45, virginity is praised *simpliciter* and seen as the superior contrast to its absence. Marriage is not even named but has to be inferred. And third, in the opening of Bk 46, marriage is worthy of praise, but this can only be assessed by reference to its superior, and named, alternative: virginity.

One of the characteristics of many works from the seventh and early eighth centuries was the desire for convenient, didactic summaries. Inevitably this meant the production of simplified reworkings of earlier material as sets of propositions. These created the impression that once one had the summary one had adequately explored an issue. If these reworkings were formed around questions, then answers were a matter of simple deduction from the supplied summary.[40] This process can be seen in science/natural philosophy in works such as the *De natura rerum* of Isidore,[41] in manuals to solve complexities in Scripture such as the *Antikeimenon* of Julian of Toledo,[42] in exegetical manuals which reduced commentary to

---

40. I have examined this phenomenon in detail in *Teachers and Code-Breakers: The Latin Genesis Tradition, 430–800* (Turnhout 1999), pp. 273–295.
41. See my ' "The Waters above the Heavens": Isidore and the Latin Tradition', *MS* 36 (1995), 104–17.
42. See my 'Julian of Toledo's *Antikeimenon* and the Development of Latin Exegesis', *PIBA* 16 (1993), 80–98.

individual questions and answers,[43] and in law/church organization works like the *Collectio*. Moreover, this notion of 'propositions' was explicitly in the mind of the compilers in that under each heading are arranged the actual opinions, a series of *sententiae*, supporting the law: namely a statement resulting from an act of decision/judgement which either affirms or denies; and so is either true or false.[44] The overall effect of the *Collectio* is to create/reinforce the impression that knowledge could be conveyed in sequences of staccato snippets and that the arguments of earlier writers could be expressed as single points, perhaps even one-liners, which possess an unquestionable validity. Because of this transformation of religious writing into series of true propositions we must view the *Collectio*, and works similar in format, as marking a new phase in the history of thought. For the same reason we cannot simply treat it as merely repeating earlier opinion. Materially, there might be little that was original in the *Collectio*, but formally (the manual as a medium of thought) it was completely new. As such, 'the medium was the message'; the *Collectio* refocused patristic material and provided the context for its later use. The *Collectio* as a systematic work therefore marks a new departure regarding social-legal-moral thought both in method and in the way its contents were perceived. I shall illustrate this in three ways.

ILLUSTRATION 1: THE LISTS OF HEADINGS

A glance at the list of topics discussed in Bk 45 shows how all problems concerning women are focused around the primary binary opposition of virginity (the superior state) and sexual involvement with men (the inferior state).

The titles are:

1. That virginity is to be praised in either sex.
2. The danger of pride arising from continence.

---

43. See T. O'Loughlin, 'Biblical Contradictions in the *Periphyseon* and the Development of Eriugena's Method', in G. Van Riel, C. Steele and J. McEvoy (eds), *Iohannes Scottus Eriugena: The Bible and Hermeneutics* (Leuven 1996), pp. 103–26.

44. It might be argued that this requires a formal organon and that my point begs the question until the existence of such an organon, and evidence of its use, has been established. This is a valid objection, but one which does not deter me from positing a formal reasoning structure to be inherent in the *Collectio*. My basis for doing this is threefold: (1) within bks 1 and 2 of Isidore's *Etymologiae* (a work widely used in the *Collectio*) we find all the elements for a simple propositional organon (e.g. the definition of logic at I, ii, 1); (2) in other works from this period we see such a propositional organon in operation, cf. my observations on simple organa in the articles cited in notes 41, 42 and 43; (3) the failure to posit such an organon in the minds of the compilers would be self-defeating: no one could set out to systematize as the *Collectio* does, without an organon.

3. On the morals of virgins who have become pregnant.
4. On women who have abortions.
5. The penance for those who have abortions.
6. On the origins [of the state] of widowhood
7. Regarding the true widows
8. That the church ought to support virgins who are weak.
9. Regarding young widows.
10. On the name *palliata* [veiled one].
11. The age at which virgins should be veiled.
12. On the two kinds of veiled women [virgins and penitents].
13. On the honour due to veiled religious women.
14. How the two kinds of religious women [virgins and penitents] ought to live.
15. Regarding women who are bad penitents.
16. On the lifestyle of young women.
17. That [the virginity of] nuns cannot be tainted by the use of oppressive force [i.e. rape].
18. That women are not to teach men.
19. That women are to be silent in church.
20. That women of any kind ought not receive any male or priestly office.

Of these twenty headings, thirteen are concerned solely with what we would today term 'nuns' (i.e. virgins, widows and penitents). And of those six headings not applicable only to nuns (headings 4, 5, 16, 18, 19, 20), *none* is exclusively concerned with women other than nuns: two concern abortion and three are general prohibitions on what women may do within the church. One other (heading 16) concerns young women (*adulescentulae*) and it is possible that this is some other form of religious life, for it states that if a young woman is separated from her family, she is to live an enclosed life under the authority of a priest. Women's questions other than those concerning nuns, wives (i.e. Bk 46), avoiding abortion and roles forbidden to them in the church, do not arise. This is nowhere better illustrated than in the case of rape: it is only mentioned twice in the *Collectio*. On the first occasion the *Collectio* repeats the ancient opinion that in the case of a virgin who is raped the resulting sexual activity does not deprive her, insofar as she was not consenting, of the status of virgin either spiritually or canonically (Bk 45, 17; and repeated in Bk 46, 21).[45] And second, that rape does not break the marriage bond, that is, it does not constitute an act of adultery, for although she has had sexual intercourse with someone other than her husband, this action was not an act of will on her part (Bk 46, 7).

---

45. The text of this heading (46, 21) as it stands in the *Collectio* (Wasserschleben, p. 191) does not make sense: see the appendix to T. O'Loughlin, 'Marriage and Sexuality in the *Hibernensis*', Peritia 11 (1997), 205–6.

ILLUSTRATION 2: THE USE OF SCRIPTURE

A characteristic of the manuals is the careful quarrying of the
Scriptures for statements that can be made to act as certain
propositions, and the *Collectio* is no exception. Of the 58 headings
in Bks 45 and 46, eight are simply prescriptions or precedents taken
from the Scriptures where the relevant texts are cited in full.[46] Bk
45, 19 is a good example of this process. The compiler knows the text
of 1 Cor 14:34–5, and from this formulates his rule: 'That women are
to be silent in church'. He then cites the text in full as the basis for his
law. Here we have an existing legal demand, and a source of law
which is used to validate these demands.[47] The compiler's approach
is not that of someone interested in the problems of the Corinthian
church and looking, perhaps, for the lessons of history, but of
someone who can sever his source at any point and extract those
universally valid rules of behaviour which are demanded by his own
legislative situation. Under other headings in these books, where
Scripture is not the sole source, one or more of the *sententiae* are
taken from it.[48] And, this number rises steeply if scriptural
quotations and allusions within other authorities are counted.

This process of excerpting verses from Scripture as the basis of a
canonical rule often fixes the significance of these verses for the
tradition and constitutes a particular exegesis of the text. So in a
sense we could say that the *Collectio* creates its own Bible. Here are
two examples of the process. The issue in Bk 46, 28 is that a
prostitute does not have her own husband. And for this they adduce a
scriptural text: Jn 4, which may seem strange as there is no mention
of prostitutes in the passage. The text reads:

> Christ in John's Gospel says: ' "Call your husband" [. . .]. The woman
> replied [. . .]: "I have no husband"; Jesus said [. . .]: "You have spoken
> well [. . .], for you have had five husbands and who you have now is
> not your husband." ' (Jn 4:16–18)

The compilers have taken three verses trimmed of every excess word,
from the long pericope dealing with the woman of Samaria at Jacob's
well. The purpose of the text in John is to stress the necessity of faith
in the Messiah – whose identity is proven by his knowledge of the
woman's previous husbands. Linked with this, John has a sub-text of
Jesus supplanting the Old Law. What attracts the compilers is the

---

46. In Bk 45, headings 6 and 19; in Bk 46, 22 (two *sententiae* from Scripture); 23; 24;
    26; 34; 37.
47. A parallel example, this time using the Old Testament, should illustrate the
    consistency of the method. Bk 46, 34: 'The husband of an intact wife is not to go to
    war. The Law says: "And what man is there that has betrothed a wife and has not
    taken her? Let him go back to his house, lest he die in the battle and another man
    take her." [Deut 20:7].'
48. In Bk 45, 7 and 18; in Bk 46, 4, 6, 7 (two quotations), 8 (two quotations), 27, 28
    and 30.

single idea that the woman had husbands, and now lives with another who is not her husband. Who could such a woman be? For the compilers there is no doubt: she must be a prostitute – and so this text can stand behind the law. What is perhaps more significant is that this identification of the woman as a prostitute becomes an unconscious element in the tradition. Needless to remark, the text of John does not mention anything like this: the woman is presented as a most insightful person (4:19 and 25); nor is she reproved in any way by Christ over the matter of her present partner; and she was apparently in good standing in her city, for when she tells them whom she had met, they go out to see Jesus for themselves (4:26). The use of the text in the *Collectio* affects our picture of the original setting and, like so many of the women mentioned in the gospels – e.g. Mary Magdalene,[49] she is now presented as a prostitute.

The issue in Bk 46, 35 is 'That a man is not to take the marriage bed of his dead brother' and the second *sententia* reads:

> The Romans say: A surviving brother must not take the marriage bed of a dead brother, as the Lord says: 'they have become one flesh' [Mt 19:5], therefore your brother's wife is your sister.

The intent of the law is clear: widows shall not marry their brothers-in-law; but the scriptural citation begs many questions. The Law of Moses states that 'If brothers dwell together, and one of them dies and has no son, the wife of the dead shall not be married outside the family to a stranger; her husband's brother shall go in to her, and take her as his wife, and perform the duty of a husband's brother to her' (Dt 25:5). No one in the eighth century could claim ignorance of this, as it is repeated in the Synoptic Tradition (Mk 12:19; Mt 22:24; Lk 20:28), for it is the legal basis of one of the challenges made to Jesus by the Sadducees on the subject of who, in the resurrection, will be the husband of a woman who was married sequentially to seven brothers. Jesus is presented as perceiving this as a conundrum intended to discredit the notion of resurrection, and replies: 'they neither marry nor are given in marriage' (Mt 22:30). The compilers, however, have to give an answer for now, before the resurrection, and completely ignore Deuteronomy in favour of a carefully edited proof-text along with a deduction to fix its meaning in the legal context. The phrase 'they have become one flesh' is used by Jesus in Mt 19:5 quoting Gen 2:24 to give a basis in the Law for his teaching on divorce. However, here it is treated as the Lord's word only, and used to make a completely different point about in-law marriages. The gloss that is added on, 'therefore your brother's wife is your sister', shows the exact mind of the legislator. It is not that a woman cannot marry her brother-in-law because the marriage bond survives death, for this would contradict the notion that second marriages are not

---

49. See C. Ricci, *Mary Magdalene and Many Others* (ET: P. Burns, London 1994), pp. 148–50.

forbidden (cf. Bk 46, 13), but that the relationship established between this man (i.e. the brother-in-law) and woman survives the death of her husband; therefore, in such a marriage a brother would be marrying his sister.

This case illustrates an important point about the use of Scripture in the *Collectio*. The compilers, no doubt, believed that they were merely giving systematic expression to the law (conceived of as an objective reality apart from them) as they 'found it' in their sources: for example, Scripture. In point of fact, they selected and edited Scripture to fit their actual canonical situation; and read as fragments, with explicit authority (. . . *dicente Domino* . . .), this use of Scripture seems to work successfully in that one assumes when one hears it that the scriptural text does support the particular case.[50] The *Collectio* is, therefore, a valuable source for observing the emergence of fixed meanings for scriptural verses (independent of context) as proof-texts for canonical/moral positions.

ILLUSTRATION 3: THE USE OF CHURCH WRITERS

One of the most intriguing headings in Bk 46 concerns the possibility of a woman having sex outside marriage yet not being guilty of adultery. Heading 7 reads:

> It is asked if there is any occasion when a woman can have intercourse with a man who is not her husband, while her husband is alive, without it being a crime. There are three such occasions.

> [a] First, if she is coerced into intercourse with another, this does not break a marriage bond.
> [b] Second, if it is brought about by someone to avoid an evil such as what Sarah did lest Abraham be killed by the wicked king [Gen 12:11–20]. Augustine says: 'Or as happened recently when a rich man demanded a gold coin from a man who had no money to give. Now a certain rich young man said to the wife of the man who owed the money that if she would have intercourse with him, he would give her the money. Now she, knowing that she had not power over her own body [1 Cor 7:4], spoke to her husband about this. The husband gave thanks, permitted her to do this, considering that where there was no desire, it was not adultery.'
> [c] Third, if she be sterile, just as it is read in Genesis that Abraham and Jacob took their maids as wives [Gen 16:1–7; 29:21–35].

We have already looked at the case of rape (*sententia* [a]); and the Old Testament precedents from 'the age of the patriarchs' are not

---

50. U. Ranke-Heinemann has explored a similar case of misapplication regarding the text Mt 19:11 which refers to marriage and remarriage, but which has been taken as a proof-text for virginity/celibacy since the time of Jerome. (See *Eunuchs for the Kingdom*, pp. 32–3, and elsewhere in that book.)

surprising (*sententiae* [b] and [c]). But the quotation from Augustine in [b] is most surprising. In effect, a man can make use of his wife to help resolve his financial difficulties by prostitution. This will not constitute adultery since she does not take part lustily in this activity, but only out of a sense of duty to her impoverished husband. But Augustine may reply that he has been quoted out of context.

An 'Indecent Proposal'

The origin of this strange precedent is in Augustine's commentary on the Sermon on the Mount.[51] He is commenting on the text of Mt 5:32: 'But I say to you that every one who divorces his wife, except on the ground of unchastity, makes her an adulteress; and whoever marries a divorced woman commits adultery.' There the question arises, since in the case of a man marrying a divorced woman there is adultery, is the same true of a woman marrying a divorced man? This leads to a second question: are there cases where a husband, with his wife's permission, has intercourse with another woman and yet he is not guilty of fornication? Augustine at once points to the Old Testament where examples of this could be found, but unlike the *Collectio* he does not actually cite a specific case. In any event he dismisses such cases as being of help with the question, for that behaviour belonged to an earlier age of human history and so is no longer relevant.[52] He then cites Paul: 'For the wife does not rule over her own body, but the husband does; likewise the husband does not rule over his own body, but the wife does' (1 Cor 7:4). Could this mean that a husband, if he had his wife's permission, might have extra-marital intercourse without blame? Augustine answers with certainty: 'This is not what the text means, for if it had this meaning it would follow that a wife could do likewise, with her husband's permission, but this is rejected by every moral sense.' Then having stated his main position he noted that some cases might emerge where the matter was not so clear-cut. He tells the story of the woman whose husband was in great danger, possibly even to his life, unless he could pay a large debt by a specific day. His wife knew that she could get this amount by a single act of prostitution, but had to have her action approved by her husband on the basis of 1 Cor 7:4.[53] Finally (after a comedy of twists and turns) the debt is settled, the husband is spared and they all live happily ever after. Augustine comments: 'I shall not take a position of judgement in this case: let each judge it as he will: for it is not taken from the Scriptures. But we note that the idea of permitted

---

51. *De sermone Domini in monte* 1, 50.
52. A similar argument can be found in *De bono coniugali* 15, 17.
53. In effect, Augustine presents the woman as testing the extreme, but possible, interpretation of the text of Paul.

fornication is less offensive to the senses when presented in a situation like this.'[54]

As the case is excerpted in the *Collectio*, Augustine's ambiguity is removed and a definite judgment is given. This, when combined with the citation of Old Testament examples without Augustine's comment on their relevance, gives the whole a direction very much at variance with its originator. Augustine merely suspended condemnation in a specific case, the *Collectio* generalized it to establish a permission. Here we see the compilers' brilliance in legal innovation – all the while protesting, and perhaps genuinely believing, that they were no more than the loyal disciples of their favourite church authorities: Jerome and Augustine. One can but wonder what these fathers would have made of their eighth-century disciples and the opinions these disciples were attributing to them.

It is too early in the process of analysing the theology of the *Collectio* to try to draw general conclusions. Research on the links between authors, such as Jerome, and the *Collectio*, its use of Scripture, its use of conciliar legislation and its systematics is still in its infancy. This is just a curtain-raiser on Bks 45 and 46, and if it demonstrates anything with assurance it is that the theological underpinning of the *Collectio* is a large field awaiting investigation. However, on the basis even of the little evidence presented here, we can answer the basic question posed at the outset of this chapter: it is clear that we cannot consider the *Collectio* as simply a collection of earlier opinions; and that it is certainly evidence of a significant change in the West's understanding of (1) sexuality and marriage, and (2) how such moral questions should be approached theoretically. Moreover, certain popular presentations of the theology that came from the Celtic lands which present it as 'female-friendly,' 'feelings-friendly', 'affective' and 'an Augustine-free zone' are somewhat wide of the mark!

FURTHER READING

Texts/Translations

H. Wasserschleben (ed.), *Die irische Kanonensammlung* (2nd edn, Leipzig 1885).

T. O'Loughlin (trans.), *The Field-Day Anthology of Irish Writing*, vol. 4.

R. Somerville and B. C. Brasington, *Prefaces to Canon Law Books in Latin Christianity: Selected Translations 500–700* (New Haven, Conn. 1998).

---

54. It does not need to be said that all these cases are meaningful only within a male-centred and male-dominated world-view.

Bibliography

L&S, 612 and 613.

Studies

L. Bieler, 'Hibernensis Collectio', *NCE* 6, 1095.

L. Breatnach, 'Canon Law and Secular Law in Early Ireland: The Significance of *Bretha Nemed*', *Peritia* 3 (1984), 439–59.

L. Breatnach, 'Law', in K. McCone and K. Simms (eds), *Progress in Medieval Irish Studies* (Maynooth 1996), pp. 107–21.

T. Charles-Edwards, 'The Construction of the *Hibernensis*', *Peritia* 12 (1998), 209–37.

K. Hughes, *Early Christian Ireland: Introduction to the Sources* (Cambridge 1972), chs 2 and, especially, 3.

Kenney, pp. 235–50.

S. G. Kuttner, *Harmony from Dissonance: An Interpretation of Medieval Canon Law* (Latrobe 1960).

D. Ó Corráin, 'Irish Law and Canon Law', in P. Ní Chatháin and M. Richter (eds), *Irland und Europa: Die Kirche im Frühmittelalter* (Stuttgart 1984), pp. 157–66.

D. Ó Corráin, L. Breatnach and A. Breen, 'The Laws of the Irish', *Peritia* 3 (1984), 382–438.

7 The Stowe Missal: The Eucharist as Refreshment

In the liturgy on earth we get a foretaste of that heavenly liturgy which is celebrated in the Holy City of Jerusalem towards which we are making our way as pilgrims: there Christ sits at the right hand of God, Minister of the holy of holies and of the true tabernacle. With all the members of the heavenly host we sing a hymn of glory to the Lord; and while we venerate the memory of the saints we hope for a share in their communion; and we await with longing the Saviour, our Lord Jesus Christ, until he who is our life shall appear and we too shall appear with him in glory. (Vatican II)[1]

A CLASH OF PERSPECTIVES

This description of the Christian liturgy was written more than a millennium after the founding of the monastery of Tallaght (now a suburb of Dublin) in 774 by St Maelruain, but it captures in a few sentences the early medieval attitude to worship. If we wish to understand any liturgical text – and our focus here is a small missal (sacramentary), most probably produced in Tallaght around 800 – then we need that sense of the liturgy as a dynamic encounter crossing several thresholds. It is on earth, but that place on earth is also part of heaven; it is now, but that time also strains forward to the end; it is in the world of action, but also in the new Jerusalem after the judgement; it recalls the saints, but also wishes to join them; it is our worshipping activity and ministry, but more truly the ministry of Christ, and it only occurs among us as we live in Christ.

---

1. *Sacrosanctum concilium* (4 December 1963), no. 8. The text is a chain of New Testament images of the heavenly liturgy: Col 3:1–4; Phil 3:20; Heb 8:2; and Apoc 21:2. See ch. 10 below, where the significance of several of these images in early Christian Ireland is explored.

This attitude to liturgy as a dynamic event, the threshold between here/now and our destiny, disappeared in the West sometime between the eleventh and thirteenth centuries. It was replaced by a notion of liturgy as a means of supplying whatever was needed in order to gain sanctifying grace and ultimately salvation.

For many today the later medieval idea of the liturgy (expressed as 'going to church' for particular ceremonies rather than being understood as taking part in a collective ongoing celebration of faith called 'the liturgy') as a way of collecting 'grace' has been replaced by an even more individualistic understanding of worship. We often imagine liturgy as centred on our needs to express or reaffirm our personal faith and commitment – thus we submit liturgy to a test calibrated on our needs: if that 'helped me' then it was a good experience and one which I shall try again; if not, I shall ignore it as wasting my time. Whether or not that attitude is correct is not my concern, but we should recognize that attitude in ourselves or we colonize the Stowe Missal by imposing our mind-set upon it. For the people for whom this missal was produced the liturgy was something greater than them or their needs, it was something personal – as it belongs to Jesus Christ – but external to them: their task was to enter into it and be absorbed within it. They had entered Christ and the communion of saints in baptism; each act of liturgy was a chance to re-enter and be absorbed more completely into this whole Christ, head and members. For the individual this process of being absorbed was not viewed as one of the destruction of the self – the notion of being absorbed is frightening to us – but of its fulfilment: there the creature was reunited with the Creator and with the source of its own unending life. These views of liturgy and life are alien to us, but if we try to operate out of them while reading the few texts from the Stowe Missal which are not a standard part of the Roman rite we see in detail the religious perspective of that monastery. In short, to understand this early medieval text we have to imagine liturgy as a dance which we join for a time, rather than as a 'service' fulfilling a command, or as an activity we engage in to bring us benefits.

THE MONASTERY AND THE BOOK

The Stowe Missal (so named as it once belonged in the collection of manuscripts owned by the Marquis of Buckingham of Stowe House, Buckinghamshire when it first came to scholarly notice[2]) is the oldest

---

2. It is now in the Royal Irish Academy in Dublin, MS D.II.3; and see L&S, 521 and 537. For an account of what we know of its history as a manuscript, see G. F. Warner's introduction to his edition, pp. vii–viii; T. F. O'Rahilly, 'The History of the Stowe Missal', *Ériu* 10 (1926), 95–109; and J. Ryan, 'The Mass in the Early Irish Church', *Studies* 50 (1961), 371–84 (Ryan's article although dated in some respects is still, probably, the best introduction to the Stowe Missal's content and liturgical relations).

such book from the early Irish church that has survived intact. It is a small book consisting of 67 leaves of coarse parchment, each measuring 140 mm × 105 mm. It shows signs of much use in that it has been soiled and darkened with wear, and there have been additions, glosses and other bits and pieces, to it. We know that it came from a monastic setting as the Eucharistic Prayer has a place to mention the name 'of our abbot [and] bishop'.[3] We link it with Tallaght and date it to the late eighth/early ninth centuries for several reasons, but the most telling is that in a litany of saints to be invoked at the Eucharist there is a mention of St Maelruain who died in 792, but none of his successor Eochaid/Echaidh who from his death in 811/12 was also regarded as a saint.[4]

Tallaght, along with the monastery of Finglas (now also a suburb of Dublin), was in the eighth century the driving force in a new 'reform' movement within Irish monasticism whose adherents used the name Céli Dé ('the clients of God') and whose stated aim was to 'restore' monastic practice to the rigour of the earliest times, 'purify' it of distractions and set a new standard of holiness. That the missal comes from close to the centre of this movement, and close to the time of greatest zeal, makes it all the more fascinating. I have placed the words 'reform', 'restore' and 'purify' in inverted commas as that was their own rhetoric, but we should recognize that it was a commonplace within medieval Christianity, and especially monasticism, to justify doing anything new on the basis that the present order of things had degenerated from the original level of excellence. The theory being that you were not 'innovating' (often equated with heresy), but simply 'returning' to something 'more ancient'.[5] For us, the essential point is that Stowe represents the energy of a young community with a clear image of itself as leaders and exemplars of the monastic life.

We imagine liturgical books as impressive altar tomes and as having a rigidly fixed text. Both assumptions are products of the late fifteenth and sixteenth centuries owing not a little to the nature of printing and the fears of the Reformation period. Then it suited all sides to promote uniformity, and their desires were made possible through the new technology. In the earlier period missals had no definite shape as books and their form depended on the particular conditions of when and where they were commissioned and the availability of resources. As to their contents there was a similar variability, not just because no two manuscript books have ever the exact same text, but because the nature of their production allowed

3. . . *et abbate nostro* N *episcopo* . . . (fol. 24r; Warner edition, p. 10).
4. See Warner's introduction to his edition, pp. xxxii–xxxiii.
5. See G. B. Ladner, *The Idea of Reform: Its Impact on Christian Thought and Action in the Age of the Fathers* (Cambridge MA 1959).

for variations and additions to be made with minimal difficulty. Then when that missal was used as an exemplar for another book, all its accretions would be transmitted to the new book as its basic text. We have a fine example of this process of accretions made during use in the Stowe Missal.

Stowe's basic text is that of the Roman rite; for example, it has labelled the Eucharistic Prayer 'the Canon of Pope Gelasius', and it shows several post-seventh-century Roman developments such as a *Gloria*. It also shows some similarities with the rite in use in Milan, such as the text for the breaking of the bread which we will examine below. Equally there is evidence of contact with Spain (the inclusion of the Nicene Creed) and other Irish liturgical books such as the prayers during the administration of communion (which we shall also examine), and one or two details that are not found elsewhere. While tracing these influences can make an interesting detective tale, attempts to show how these influences came together are doomed: one could only know this if we had hundreds of surviving missals which could show the points where various elements fused. Suffice to say that we have only a handful of surviving books and they all show some similarities and some differences with one another – and any time users of these books found something in another missal which was considered useful, e.g. a prayer, it was simply copied into their own missal.

As it stands the basic missal was added to on many occasions over what was probably a lengthy period. First came the basic missal and we do not know the name of its scribe or scribes. It then passed to someone called Moél Caích who added extra leaves, made additions of both prayers and instructions, filled up blank spaces with other bits appropriate to a missal, and even erased and rewrote part of the original text. Sometimes, poor Moél Caích is criticized for doing this as if he were some sort of vandal – but he did not labour with liturgical archaeologists in mind, but as a priest (we know he was a priest as in one case he copies a text without its rubrics so we can assume he knew them by practice) for whom this was a working tool in his service of God. Later, it passed to someone who wanted to have with him in the same book the rite of baptism and that for visiting the sick. Later again, someone added an explanation of the Eucharist in Irish – no doubt for the convenience of having homily material to hand. At some stage someone added three spells in Irish on the final leaf; and someone at some stage – and it may have been very early in its life – bound with it a (defective) text of St John's Gospel. Again, this addition of Jn was determined by the convenience of having a gospel text to hand. These various additions made it all the more valuable to a busy priest as a useful 'package'.[6] What is significant is

---

6. The details of all these parts can be found in the Warner edition (pp. viii–ix); the Old Irish homily text can be found on pp. 40–2; the latter was originally edited by W. Stokes and J. Strachan, *Thesaurus Palaeohibernicus* (2 vols, Cambridge 1901–3), vol. 2, pp. 252–5.

that, taken as a 'pastoral package', it gives us an insight into the actual working life of a monk-priest where the practical problems of serving the people were paramount – so we should look at Stowe less as a monument to the ancient liturgy, than as a testimony to pastoral labour focused on the Eucharist.

THE SHAPE OF THE LITURGY

Trying to imagine what a celebration of the Eucharist actually looked like is always a difficult task as the imagination is apt to use what is most or least attractive. However, there are a few pointers that help set the scene. We know that a monastery was not just the band of monks who sought to keep the religious rule of the monastery. Rather we have to think of it as a large group of people – a village in fact – which had a group of monks at its core, but which also included many who were socially and legally identified with the monastery, who farmed its land, carried on their trades in the service of the community and had their religious needs met by the monks. Often these were relatives of the founder or the descendants of those who had offered the saint their land, and so they had rights within the monastery often to the extent of supplying a lay abbot of the monastery. In this general practice the Céli Dé appear to have been no different to any other groups of monks. So the priest who used this missal may not have just been saying Mass for his fellow monks but someone who may also have had to celebrate for the local people – men, women and children – who were part of the extended monastic family. These lay people who were linked to the monastery were called *manaig*; and sometimes there were smaller churches to meet their needs some distance from the centre of the monastery.[7] By a curious coincidence there is a place less than a mile west of the centre of Tallaght called Kilnamanagh ('church of the *manaig*'), which was just such a church built (although there are no remains today) so as to serve a group belonging to the monastery and farming there. It is not unreasonable to imagine that at some point the Stowe Missal was brought by someone to that very place for Mass. But if we think in these terms we should forget about great solemn monastic buildings such as were then being built in Charlemagne's lands, and think of a small building more on the size of the Gallarus Oratory in Co. Kerry (see p. 3) or St Kevin's Kitchen in Glendalough. It was probably

---

7. See K. Hughes, *Early Christian Ireland: Introduction to the Sources* (Cambridge 1972), pp. 93–4 where she draws attention to the *manaig* linked to the Céli Dé monasteries such as Tallaght.

St Kevin's Kitchen, Glendalough, Co. Wicklow. It is in small buildings like this one that we can imagine them celebrating the Eucharist with a missal like Stowe.

poorly lit and cold and draughty in winter; and a muddy area around the entrance would also fit. The congregation was probably quite small – guessing numbers using the question 'how many would fit?' in conjunction with surviving buildings is a fraught business, but there seems little evidence that the whole community (women, men, children) would be more than a hundred in all. It seems clear that everyone would have known the others by name and that the assembly would include everyone in the locality except the sick and those tending animals. As to vestments and the like, they were probably quite shabby as we hear of splendid vestments being brought back from Rome – by inference, the local products may have left much to be desired. In *vitae* we hear of the wondrous vestments of the saints, e.g. Muirchú mentions Patrick's chasuble,[8] and so we know that the normal eucharistic vestments of the Latin rite were taken for granted. However, the liturgy, from the standpoint of ceremonial, probably had a strong rustic feel – and smell – to it. Early medieval liturgy had high theological ideals, but seems to have had low standards ceremonially.

There is, however, one area where we are on much firmer ground regarding liturgical practicalities: altar plate. Some of the greatest

---

8. Bk 1, ch. 20; the chasuble is the outer vestment for the celebrant of the Eucharist.

artistic treasures that have survived from Celtic Christian Ireland are vessels for celebrating the Eucharist. The Ardagh Chalice (discovered by accident in the nineteenth century) is the most famous, but the Derrynaflan Hoard (a chalice [see the picture on the cover of this book], a paten, a strainer and a large bronze bowl) discovered in 1980[9] is even more interesting as it comes from a monastery important in the later eighth and ninth centuries which was part of the Céli Dé movement.[10] Much has been written about this hoard as its components are magnificent works of art,[11] and in their beauty and richness they are a mute witness to the centrality of the Eucharist in the faith-lives of these monasteries. However, such vessels as these famous ones were always exceptional. These are items of the highest craftsmanship in decoration and were made either as offerings to the monastery or as prestige items used either only occasionally or not at all. Michael Ryan has written:

> It is questionable whether [the Ardagh Chalice] was ever watertight and therefore properly usable for the solemnities of the eucharist. The Derrynaflan Chalice, on the other hand, almost certainly was water-proof, and it could have been employed in a practical way in the liturgy.[12]

However, these exceptional items do show us the form that the more humble vessels in everyday use would have taken.

First, let us take the paten. A modern paten or paten/ciborium is rarely more than 18–20 cm in diameter (many older items still in use are even smaller, e.g. 14–15 cm) because they suppose only a token breaking of the bread, the actual wafers for 'giving communion' being pre-cut. While this pre-cutting destroys the original symbolic force of the Eucharist as presented in Paul, the Didache and Acts,[13] it

---

9. Derrynaflan is near Cashel, Co. Tipperary (see map on p. 140).
10. From the time of the discovery scholars have treated the Stowe Missal and the Derrynaflan Hoard as mutually illuminating; see P. Ní Chatháin, 'The Liturgical Background of the Derrynaflan Altar Service', *JRSAI* 110 (1980), 127–48.
11. Much of the research has been done by Dr Michael Ryan, and any of his many publications on Derrynaflan and early Irish metalwork will throw light on the topic. A particularly good place to start is with his 'The Derrynaflan Hoard and Early Irish Art', *Speculum* 72 (1997), 995–1017.
12. *Speculum* 72 (1997), 1006. Indeed, in an earlier article Dr Ryan pointed out that there was some wear on the handles of the chalice ('The Derrynaflan and other early Irish eucharistic chalices: some speculations', in P. Ní Chatháin and M. Richter (eds), *Irland und Europa: Die Kirche im Frühmittelalter*, (Stuttgart 1984), p. 136) – this would be consistent with handing it back and forth in the liturgy.
13. See É. Nodet and J. Taylor, *The Origins of Christianity: An Exploration* (Collegeville, MN 1998) for the most comprehensive modern account of the origins of the Eucharist; see E. J. Kilmartin, *The Eucharist in the West: History and Theology* (Collegeville, MN 1998) for a detailed account of the changes in theology that separate the modern period from the period of the Stowe Missal.

worries few priests today as they operate using the more recent theology of the Eucharist as 'getting something precious'. By contrast the Derrynaflan paten is a good-sized dinner plate, *c.* 36 cm in diameter. This measurement, along with other evidence, shows us that they were still using a single bread, a loaf, at the Eucharist and then breaking it symbolically as part of the actual celebration. In the Irish homily in the Stowe Missal we find that it was broken symbolically into five, seven, eight, nine, eleven, twelve and thirteen pieces and each manner of breaking was to remind people of different aspects of their belief, and interestingly it was to show the links between that group and the communion of saints. All these breakings taken together allowed the loaf to be broken into 65 pieces which it says is the number for Christmas, Easter and Pentecost. So here we have a possible number for the expected congregation at the Eucharist on the great feasts. The size of the Derrynaflan paten thus allows us to see that they still had a practical appreciation of the symbolism of the 'one loaf' broken into pieces to establish unity among all the partakers of that one loaf (cf. 1 Cor 10:17) and to see that reading the chants for the actual breaking of the bread in terms of symbolic eucharistic theology is not wishful thinking.

Turning to the chalice we find that its shape is eminently suited to the practical problems of having 'one cup' that can provide communion to a sizeable number of people. It does so without the inconvenience often found today where the chalice resembles a stem glass. The handles allowed it to be easily given by a minister to the communicant, and then taken back without spillage. Doing rough calculations on the basis of the cup's diameter of *c.* 21 cm and the bowl's depth of *c.* 11 cm it is clear that if filled it would hold approximately 1.5 litres of wine – though probably it would not have been filled closer than 2 cm below the rim because of the risk of it spilling through slopping around in the bowl.[14] So we can imagine a chalice the size of a medium-sized mixing bowl, with handles to enable it to be easily moved during the liturgy and administered with

---

14. In many studies of early Irish chalices (e.g. L. S. Gogan, *The Ardagh Chalice* (Dublin 1932), p. 44; M. Ryan (ed.), *The Derrynaflan Hoard I* (Dublin 1983), p. 15) there is reference to the description of the chalice 'blessed with the Lord's own hand on the night before he suffered' in Adomnán's *De locis sanctis* I, vii. There it is stated that that chalice held one 'Gaulish pint' (*sextarius Gallicus*); and several writers try to extrapolate from that reference information relevant to the surviving vessels. However, apart from the problems of using *De locis sanctis* in this manner as evidence (cf. my 'Adomnán and Arculf: The Case of an Expert Witness,' *JML* 7 (1997), 127–46) there is still the problem of knowing what amount is equal to a 'Gaulish pint' in our measures. In the *Penitential of Cummean* II, 3 we have a reference to a 'Roman pint' (*sextarius Romanus*), but again we have no way of knowing the exact quantities involved, or of how a 'Gaulish' and 'Roman pint' differed.

ease, and capable of holding just under two modern bottles of wine. A simple experiment shows that such an amount of liquid – about a bottle and a half of wine – provides, on average, about 75 mouthfuls. This number fits well with the figure for the number of fractions of the loaf – let us assume that the chalice was never fully filled and that there was also some left over to be consumed in slightly greater quantity by either the celebrant, other minister or some of the congregation – and so may indicate the size of the group. More importantly, it shows that the New Testament symbolism based on one cup indicating union between partakers (1 Cor 10:16–21; Mk 14:23; and Lk 22:17) was still part of their celebration. In turn, this provides a vantage point for interpreting the communion chant found in Stowe, while the length of time it would take 65 people to drink from one cup would account for the length of the chants provided. Given modern practice where the chalice is barely sipped, assuming a mouthful of the same amount one might take in drinking coffee might seem strange. However, we should remember that modern notions of the chalice as exceptional, fears about drinking from one cup, and worries that there would not be enough in the chalice for everyone if one took more than a sip are precisely that: modern notions, fears and worries. Before the arrival of practices and attitudes that (1) led to the withdrawal of the chalice from the congregation, (2) reduced the significance of the wine in relation to the bread (exemplified in the now near universal identification of 'the Host' – i.e. the Victim – with the form of bread[15]), (3) placed less emphasis on the symbolism of eating and drinking as opposed to 'getting communion', and (4) considered that somehow wine is an 'extra', it was taken for granted that 'drink' (*bibite*) meant precisely that and not 'sip'. Moreover, if sipping was the norm, it would be hard to understand the penalty of six slaps imposed by the *Rule of Columbanus* for those who damage a chalice with their teeth![16]

THE COMMUNION OF SAINTS

We can now look in more detail at three items taken from the missal which are not standard parts of the Latin liturgy. None of the pieces

---

15. It is interesting to note how many conservative Catholic theologians who react swiftly to any linguistic twist that might be taken to imply a theological impropriety fail to note that the phrase 'elevation of the Host' when used in conjunction with that of 'elevation of the chalice' is tantamount to saying that the consecrated cup does not contain the Victim. Those who react to every twist in wording with the fear of heresy should be more on their guard!

16. The *Regula coenobialis* IV, p. 148 (see L&S 642); I am indebted to Dr Michael Ryan for drawing this to my attention.

is unique to Stowe, and their liturgical links to other places have been studied in detail by those seeking to outline Stowe's place in relation to the evolution of the western liturgy; here, however, the focus will be slightly different.[17] Whatever the origins and links of these various pieces, we know that they were part of the liturgy that was celebrated in a Céli Dé community in the early ninth century. So rather than study the prayers as links in a chain, let us see what they tell us about how these people, who actually used them, looked at the Eucharist – for it was one of that group who chose to copy them into this working missal. From this perspective the question of whether they are 'Irish' or not, or 'Celtic' or not, is irrelevant: wherever they came from or whoever wrote them, we know that they reflect the thoughts about the Eucharist of a group of monks in Ireland in the early Middle Ages who had a sense that they were the spiritual shock troops in their society.

The first feature, somewhat strange to modern Christians, is that the Eucharist begins with a litany. This is not in itself unusual, for the litany fulfils the role of what would now be called the Rite of Penance and, as we shall see in the next chapter, litanies are intimately connected with the theme of penitence in Christian worship; indeed the *Kyrie* ('Lord have mercy') in contemporary rites is a direct survival of such litanies. The basic inspiration of the rite is that the Christians gathered for the Lord's meal became aware of their unworthiness to approach the divine table, and so like the tax-collector in the parable they stood 'far off, not lifting their eyes to heaven' but beating their breasts 'saying "God, be merciful to me a sinner!" ' (Lk 18:13). Here is the basic text:

We have sinned, O Lord. We have sinned.
Spare us from our sins. Save us!
You guided Noah over the waves of the flood. Hear us.
You called back Jonah from the abyss with a word: deliver us.
You stretched out your hand to Peter as he sank: help us O Christ.
O Son of God you showed the wonderful works of the Lord to our
    ancestors, be merciful to us in our times: put forth your hand from on
    high and deliver us.
Christ hear us! [Christ graciously hear us].[18]

---

17. The links between Stowe and the liturgical documents was first pursued in detail
    by F. E. Warren, *The Liturgy and Ritual of the Celtic Church* (2nd edn
    Woodbridge 1987); it was later taken up by E. Bishop, 'The Litany of the Saints in
    the Stowe Missal', *Liturgica Historica* (Oxford 1918), pp. 137–64; and more
    recent studies have been noted by P. Ní Chatháin in her 1980 article.
18. The litany only has the invocations for the celebrant (e.g. *Ora pro nobis* is not
    given after each saint's name) and these have to be supplied from the standard
    responses to these invocations in other litanies – the omission of the responses
    shows that this was in common use and that the celebrant could count on his
    congregation knowing them.

Christ hear us! [Christ graciously hear us].
Christ hear us! [Christ graciously hear us].
Lord have mercy.[19]
Saint Mary, [Pray for us]; St Peter, [. . .]; St Paul, [. . .]; St Andrew,
[. . .]; St James, [. . .]; St Bartholomew, [. . .]; St Thomas, [. . .]; St
Matthew, [. . .]; St James, [. . .]; St Thaddeus, [. . .]; St Matthias,
[. . .]; St Mark, [. . .]; St Luke, [. . .].
O [all] you saints, Pray for us.[20]
Be merciful to us, Spare us.
O Lord be merciful to us, Deliver us O Lord.
From every evil, Deliver us O Lord.
Through your cross, Deliver us O Lord.
Sinners, we ask you to hear us.[21]
O Son of God, we ask you to hear us.
That you might give us peace, we ask you to hear us.
Lamb of God who takes away the sins of the world, have mercy on us.
Christ, hear us [Christ graciously hear us].
Christ, hear us [Christ graciously hear us].
Christ, hear us [Christ graciously hear us].

That is as much as we find in the original hand that wrote this book.
It is a very standard shortened litany of the saints. The choice of
saints included by name is significant, for it is a mixture of apostles
and evangelists, along with Mary, and this in all likelihood was
intended as a recollection of the gathering of the apostles at the Last
Supper. That it is not one of the established lists of the apostles, and
the inclusion of Mary, does not take from this fact. First, the
confusion over the list of the twelve, already found in the New
Testament, has always been present, along with the inclusion of Paul
and the evangelists with that list. Equally, the inclusion of Mary is
explicable as due not only to the habit of not omitting her from any
list of saints, but also to the image of the gathering in 'the upper
room' (Acts 1:14) after the Ascension.[22] The key point is that these
are the intimate ones around the Lord's table – those whom he called
'friends' (Jn 15:15) – and so they are the company to which the
congregation at the Eucharist aspire to belong. Seeking to gather at

19. We must assume that at this point the *Kyrie* was said in the normal way: *Kyrie
    eleison* × 3; *Christe eleison* × 3; *Kyrie eleison* × 3.
20. This response is included for the very good reason that the prayer is expressed in
    the plural number: *orate pro nobis*; since this shift from the repetition of *ora* to
    orate is when litanies in Latin lose their rhythm, it is usual now – and from the
    evidence here, then also – for the celebrant to sound out: *OraTE pro nobis* – hence
    its inclusion as a reminder.
21. The last lines of the litany as it originally appeared in the missal have been
    destroyed, but we can reconstruct them through the repetition of the conclusion
    of the litany by Moél Caích.
22. When a fuller study of this missal is carried out, a comparison of this list of saints
    with the names in Acts 1:14 and the list of the apostles ('The *Communicantes*') in
    the Roman Canon (Eucharistic Prayer I) should prove very interesting.

the Lord's table they ask for the intercession of those already there, and indeed those who were the first to be called to that table.

However, Moél Caích sought to have even more intercessors before the throne of God and extended the number of saints mentioned in the litany with these:

> St Steven, [pray for us]; St Martin, [. . .]; St Jerome, [. . .]; St Augustine, [. . .]; St Gregory, [. . .]; St Hilary, [. . .]; St Patrick, [. . .]; St Ailbe [of Emly, . . .]; St Finnian [of Clonard, . . .]; St Finnian [of Moville, . . .]; St Ciaran [of Clonmacnoise, . . .]; St Ciaran [of Saiger, . . .]; St Brendan [of Birr, . . .]; St Brendan [of Clonfert, . . .]; St Columba [of Iona, . . .]; St Columba [of Terryglass, . . .]; St Comgall [of Bangor, . . .]; St Cainnech [of Aghaboe, . . .]; St Findbarr [of Cork, . . .]; St Nessan, [. . .]; St Fachtnae, [. . .]; St Lugaid, [. . .]; St Lachtain, [. . .]; St Ruadán, [. . .]; St Carthach, [. . .]; St Kevin, [. . .]; St Mochonne, [. . .]; St Brigit, [. . .]; St Ita, [. . .]; St Scetha, [. . .] St Sínech, [. . .]; St Samthann, [. . .].

That he should include 'the greats' of the western church is not surprising: the cult of Martin was ubiquitous, Steven as first martyr likewise, and in a monastery the great writing saints Jerome, Augustine, Hilary and the monk-doctor Gregory would have been the saints held in the greatest honour for their wisdom and holiness.[23] The inclusion of the Irish saints brings out other aspects of his thinking. First, all the major saints are mentioned: Patrick, Brigit and Columba. These are the intercessors that we should expect, for they had elaborate and widespread cults and their lives are among the great literary products of the seventh century.[24] But Moél Caích does not want to forget any saint, so he has two saints named Columba, Ciaran, Brendan and Finnian. This is a list that sought to be inclusive! In the process he established a spiritual link with every important monastic founder in Ireland, and so at the beginning of the liturgy this litany stated before God the credentials of Tallaght: an Irish monastery in the tradition of monasticism of all these founders who had already proven their holiness.

A litany is a declaration that the group gathered imagines itself not just made up of those in the building, but of the communion of saints. This is the notion of liturgy as venerating 'the memory of the saints' and hoping 'for a share in their communion'. Present on a Sunday morning, the group's identity is not primarily that of being the

23. For the cult of Martin in Ireland, see M. Richter, *Ireland and her Neighbours in the Seventh Century* (Dublin 1999), pp. 225–31; for that of Gregory, see ibid., pp. 219–20; for the others, see my 'The List of Illustrious Writers in the Pseudo-Bedan *Collectanea*', in H. Conrad O'Briain, A. M. D'Arcy and J. Scattergood (eds.), *Text and Gloss* (Dublin 1999), pp. 34–48.
24. See chapters 4 and 5 above.

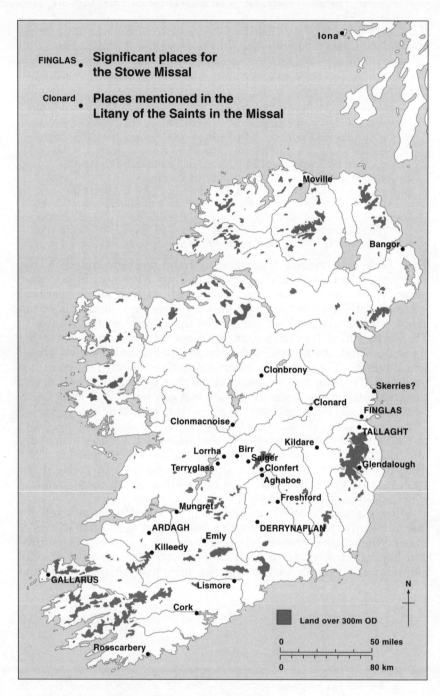

Significant Places for the Stowe Missal

Christians on one part of the monastery lands at Tallaght who have to assemble as they need the services of a priest and 'the church'; their identity is rather that of a small group within the whole communion which Christ had established. The group wanted to be part of a larger communion, share in its benefits and gain the presence and support of its stronger members to balance its unworthiness before 'the table of the Lamb' (Apoc 19:9). And lest its intentions to belong to that communion were not clear, it voiced its desire for the assistance of its saintly brothers and sisters by name. With regard to the apostles and Mary, their foundational place within the community of faith was a basic revealed fact (Apoc 21:14). Any community gathered for the Eucharist wanted to be gathered in their presence. But at a local level, they wanted the saints who were part of their own experience: those who had once been part of monastic communities in Ireland, and therefore should have a special interest in them as close relatives. Equally, these were the actual intercessors whom those they knew in their everyday lives were seeking to follow and be in communion with; these were the saints whose power they had heard of not just in books, but from stories from just 'down the road', and it would be in their company that they would rise again 'in the resurrection at the last day' (Jn 11:24). The litany with its urgent plea for mercy after sin is an expression of ecclesial communion linking now and the future, here with heaven. For our practical purposes how many were gathered for the Eucharist in Tallaght in the early ninth century is a matter of detective work in lieu of counting heads; but from the theological perspective of the participants, it was a far more complex matter.[25]

SHARING THE ONE LOAF

One of the keys to understanding early medieval eucharistic theology is to note that it is less concerned with the notion of Christ's presence as a static fact – the theology of the Blessed Sacrament – than with the notion that it is Christ who is the one who is sharing the meal and breaking the loaf which is his body. It is then having a share in that broken loaf that established comm-union with him. This is the sense found in Paul: 'Is not the loaf of bread which we break a participation in the body of Christ?' (1 Cor 10:16). We see this theology explicitly in a little sequence of verses from Scripture that were strung together to form a devotional chant for use at the actual moment of breaking up the loaf (the 'fraction'). As we have seen when looking at the Derrynaflan paten along with the information contained in the Stowe homily, this involved breaking a single loaf into as many as sixty-five pieces for communion and arranging them on the paten in symbolic arrangements – and so it took time. Because such long periods when the priest is doing something can become distractions, today we usually cover them with a hymn; it is probably that practical need, coupled with the need to explicate the significance of the fraction and heighten the solemnity attached to the repetition of one of the Lord's actions, that led to this:

> They knew it was the Lord, Alleluia;
> In the breaking up of the loaf, Alleluia [Lk 24:35].
> The loaf we break is the body of Jesus Christ, our Lord, Alleluia;
> The chalice we bless is the blood of Jesus Christ, our Lord, Alleluia [1 Cor 10:16–17];
> For the remission of sins, Alleluia [Mt 26:28].
> Lord, let your mercy rest upon us, Alleluia;
> Who put all our confidence in you, Alleluia [Ps 33:22].
> They knew it was the Lord, Alleluia;
> In the breaking up of the loaf, Alleluia [Lk 24:35].
>
> O Lord, we believe that in this breaking of your body and pouring out of your blood we become your redeemed people;
> We confess that in taking the gifts of this pledge here, we lay hold in hope of enjoying its true fruits in the heavenly places.[26]

The breaking and sharing brings about the union between their table, the table of the Last Supper and the table at Emmaus. The quotation from Paul is linked with the line from Matthew's account of the Last Supper which was a fixed part of the Institution Narrative in order to express the specific purpose of the communion and to declare it a sacrifice by which the final communion of Christ's people is established; and a consciousness was expressed that the action in which they were taking part there and then had a future dimension. They now shared in a pledge which strengthened them in faith and hope for the future, but it was in the future that the real communion would be established, in the future the real joys would be enjoyed, it would be then that the Communion of Saints – the gathering of the redeemed – would truly exist.[27] This also captures the eschatological dimension of the Eucharist as presented by Paul: 'When you eat this loaf and drink this cup, you proclaim the Lord's death until he comes' (1 Cor 11:26). The Eucharist strains forward, it reminds people of the transitional status of the present, it is a waiting 'until he comes'. The liturgy may be the most sacred part of the week, yet it is only a token of the reality to come.

---

26. We have no instructions in the missal as to how this prayer was to be used. The first lines were by the first scribe, the material from the Ps quotation onwards is by Moél Caích over an erasure. However, as it stands the prayer would only cover a small amount of the time the fraction would take, so it could be that it was repeated until the task was completed (there are analogues in the Roman rite); or that the whole of Ps 33 was used, and Moél Caích only wrote out the last line as a cue.

27. See ch. 10 below.

IN COMMUNION WITH THE LORD

The distribution of the Body and Blood of the Lord is now seen as a consequence of the most sacred moment of the consecration and so is referred to simply as 'taking communion'. However, when the presence of Christ is viewed dynamically rather than statically the actual eating and drinking of what the Lord wants to give as his body and blood becomes the high point of the whole celebration. Everything up to that point of eating and drinking is part of making ready for the actual meal. The meal then properly begins when the piece of the broken loaf is given to be eaten, and the blessed chalice is handed to the participant to be drunk from; and it is with that perspective in mind that we should look at this chant (wholly in Moél Caích's hand) for use while the people are eating and drinking at the Lord's table. This process probably took quite a time, moving, eating, drinking, and then the tidying up and cleaning of the vessels – so this sequence of antiphons and psalms was probably long enough to cover the length of time even the largest congregation would need, as well as providing a time for reflection after people had received a portion of the loaf and cup – while it could easily be curtailed if the group was smaller.

My peace I give you, Alleluia;
My peace I leave you [Alleluia] [Jn 14:27].
Those who love your law have great peace, Alleluia;
They do not stumble, Alleluia [Ps 119:165].
[Bless] the king of heaven[28] [who comes] with peace, Alleluia;
Full of the odour of life [cf. 2 Cor 2:16], Alleluia.
O sing him a new song, Alleluia [Ps 33:2];
Come, all his saints, Alleluia.
Come, eat of my bread, Alleluia;
And drink of the wine I have mixed for you, Alleluia [Prov 9:5].
Ps 23 is recited.

He who eats my body,[29] Alleluia;
And drinks my blood, Alleluia;
Abides in me and I in him, Alleluia [Jn 6:56].
Ps 24 is recited.

This is the living bread which comes down from heaven, Alleluia [Jn 6:50];
He who eats of it shall live for ever, Alleluia [Jn 6:51].
Ps 25 is recited.

The Lord fed them with bread from heaven, Alleluia;
Men ate the bread of angels, Alleluia [Ps 78:24–5].
Ps 43 is recited.

---

28. Compare Dan 4:34.
29. Note that Jn 6:56 reads *carnem* (flesh), our text reads *corpus* (body).

Eat, O friends, Alleluia;
And drink deeply, O beloved ones, Alleluia [Song 5:1].
This is the sacred body of our Lord, [Alleluia];
The blood of our Saviour, Alleluia;
Feast, all of you, on it for eternal life, Alleluia.
Let my lips declare your praise, Alleluia;
Because you teach me your commands, Alleluia [Ps 119:171–2].
I will bless the Lord at all times, Alleluia;
His praise always on my lips, Alleluia [Ps 34:1].
Taste and see, Alleluia;
How sweet is the Lord, Alleluia [Ps 34:8].
Where I am, Alleluia;
There shall my servant be, Alleluia [Jn 12:26].
Let the children come to me, Alleluia;
And do not stop them, Alleluia;
For to such belongs the Kingdom of heaven, Alleluia [Mt 19:14].
Repent, Alleluia;
For the Kingdom of heaven is at hand, Alleluia [Mt 3:2].
The Kingdom of heaven has suffered violence, Alleluia;
And violent men have taken it by force, Alleluia [Mt 11:12].
Come O blessed of my Father, inherit the kingdom, Alleluia;
Prepared for you before the foundation of the world, Alleluia [Mt
    25:34];
Glory be to the Father, [and to the Son, and to the Holy Spirit];
Come O blessed of my Father, inherit the kingdom;
As it was in the beginning, [is now, and ever shall be, world without
    end];
Come O blessed of my Father, Amen, Alleluia.

The emphasis is upon union with Christ which is established in the
eating and drinking. Sharing in this activity is sharing in the Lord's
gifts, and in this way the participants are being grafted into the body
of the Lord. Drawing together the eating/drinking images in
combination with the texts from John's gospel not only interprets
the actual Eucharistic meal in terms of Jn 6, but shows that it is not
'taking communion' that is of interest, but being brought into
communion with Christ, joining him in body and blood, becoming one
with him through eating and drinking the food which he has
prepared: his body and blood.

COMMUNITY — COMMUNION

The common theme running through these texts is that of
communion: communion with one another, communion with the first
Christ-ian meals, communion with the whole Church on earth and in
heaven, communion with Christ, and the final future communion of
'the whole Christ'. This understanding was wholly realist in its
structures – their gathering was not just some recollection of a past
event; the saints were called to be with them there, they were eating

and drinking the Lord's body and blood there, they were being united with him there – but it was also incomplete as yet.

However, in its realism it avoids 'the realism of things' that came to the forefront in a later period when interest in the eucharistic presence became static and questions took the form of 'what is this I hold in my hands?' or 'what is that which is in the tabernacle?' Then the question of presence had been reduced to one that is primarily one of analysing substances analogous to asking 'what sort of stuff is that?' Such questions came to a dark dominance over the whole of the Christian religion with the Reformation and its aftermath, when the meal of unity became the acid-test for divisional allegiances: 'we are for real presence' or 'we only acknowledge a symbolic presence' or 'we are for transubstantiation' or 'we only accept consubstantiation'. In the process the importance of the actual images of one loaf broken at the ceremony, one cup drunk, and actually eating and drinking were virtually forgotten. If the current interest in early medieval theology has anything to teach modern Christians it is that every group needs to deepen and develop its eucharistic theology remembering that the Lord's meal is a mystery. And, at the same time restoring the basic symbols of one loaf and one cup: token-sized breads, pre-cut wafers, sips from little chalices or thimbles with individual portions are all pointers to bad theology rather than to the Lord.

FURTHER READING

Edition

G. F. Warner (ed.), *The Stowe Missal* (London 1906, 1915; rept 1989).

Bibliography

L&S, 521 and 537.

Studies

E. J. Kilmartin, *The Eucharist in the West: History and Theology* (Collegeville, MN 1998).

P. Ní Chatháin, 'The Liturgical Background of the Derrynaflan Altar Service', *JRSAI* 110 (1980), 127–48.

É. Nodet and J. Taylor, *The Origins of Christianity: An Exploration* (Collegeville, MN 1998).

J. Ryan, 'The Mass in the Early Irish Church', *Studies* 50 (1961), 371–84.

M. Ryan, 'The Derrynaflan Hoard and Early Irish Art', *Speculum* 72 (1997), 995–1017.

—— (ed.), *The Derrynaflan Hoard I: A Preliminary Account* (Dublin 1983).

F. E. Warren, *The Liturgy and Ritual of the Celtic Church* (2nd edn Woodbridge 1987), pp. 198–268.

8 The Litanies: Petition, Procession, Protection

Surprisingly, given their simple format, litanies are among the more complex elements that have been, and are, used in the Christian liturgy. The format is that of a series of statements read by a minister, all very similar in form, which can be easily recognized as related to one another (e.g. a list of saints), each followed by the same response from the congregation. They have regularity and monotony in-built almost as a guiding principle, and they have the effect today of making us very conscious of their length. However, allowing for their unpopularity today – the phrase 'a long litany' means a boring list – we should note that they have a definite place in worship, and can reveal an elaborate theology of salvation and redemption/ forgiveness, of the church and of how people speak of God. It is to point out some of these aspects of the content and use of the litanies surviving from the early Irish church that is the purpose of this chapter. But first we should set them in context with a broad introduction to this form.

LITANIES IN THE LITURGY

The earliest litanies with which Christians are familiar come from the psalms.[1] In Ps 136 we have a series of praises of God for his actions in the life of the people of Israel, and after each there is the refrain: 'for his mercy endures for ever'. The whole litany is neatly framed by the phrase 'O give thanks to the Lord' in the first three verses and again in the final verse. A similar litany, where the works of God in the creation are recalled, can be found in Dan 3:52–90 which has this form:

---

1. See L. Sabourin, *The Psalms: Their Origin and Meaning* (New York 1974), pp. 40, 190–2.

Bless the Lord all rain and dew! [*petition*]
Sing praise to him and highly exalt him for ever [*response*].
(Dan 3:64)[2]

And this section of Daniel would become a much-used text in Christian liturgy, as an element in the Office and standing alone as a hymn of thanksgiving called the *Benedicite* (or sometimes 'the *Canticum Trium Puerorum*' (Song of the Three Boys)).[3] We know from surviving Jewish liturgies that the litany form was widespread in prayers of blessing, and so must have been in use in Christian liturgy from the beginning, although it is not until the fourth century AD that we have any positive evidence for their use.[4] That intrepid woman Egeria, writing about the liturgy in Jerusalem in the early fifth century, tells of how the deacons at the evening office mention the names of many people who are to be remembered in prayer 'and the many children standing about answer: *Kyrie eleison* or as we say: "Lord have mercy" '.[5] And from soon after that we have references to them in the liturgy in Constantinople, and in the West where the *Kyrie* and *Agnus Dei* were developing as litanical elements in the Eucharist. This *Kyrie* was a much longer prayer of intercession which named many needs and took place toward the end of the Liturgy of the Word. It survived in its early form as the complex intercessions of the Good Friday liturgy with its petitions, prayers, standings and kneelings; but in the normal Eucharist it was soon shortened and moved to a place near the rite's opening. Only in 1970 did this intercessory litany (petition with repetition of 'Lord hear us' and its response) become common again in the Roman rite as the 'Prayer of the Faithful'.

PROCESSION AND PENITENCE

While intercession, asking for something, is at the core of litanical prayer, as this form developed two other elements were always present. First was the notion of procession: an organized march to ask for divine favour for a particular place and its inhabitants; and the second was a notion of penitence: asking God to pardon sins and

---

2. This part of Daniel is omitted from many printed bibles; however, it is present in the LXX and Vg and was well known, indeed loved, by those with whom we are concerned in this book (on its popularity among Irish Christians in the early Middle Ages, see Kenney, pp. 646, 708, 713, 717, 719 and 721). Moreover, in some bibles the verse numbering varies for this part of Daniel. For an account of the problems associated with this piece of biblical text, see C. A. Moore, *Daniel, Esther and Jeremiah: The Additions* (New York 1977), pp. 39–76 (see above p. 100).

3. See ch. 5 above.

4. A. Baumstark, *Comparative Liturgy* (London 1958), pp. 74–80.

5. See G. E. Gingras, *Egeria: Diary of a Pilgrimage* (New York 1993), p. 90 (i.e. ch. 24 of her account).

to avert his punishments. The idea of the procession asking for divine protection belonged to pagan Roman religion where on 25 April each year there was a festival known as the *Robigalia*. This was a procession around corn fields to pray that pestilence would not destroy the crop. When this desire to ask protection for the coming harvest was brought within the sphere of Christian prayer it took the form of a litanical series of petitions which were chanted out and replied to while the procession took place. Until recently this procession on 25 April, St Mark's Day, was still marked in liturgical books with the title 'the Greater Litanies'. Around the same time of the year fell Ascension Thursday, and the Monday to Wednesday of that week were days of special intercession ('the Rogation Days' from *rogatio* = an entreaty) and on these days too there were processions and litanies (known, by contrast, as 'the Lesser Litanies').[6] As the procession moved around the fields, the litany called on God for mercy, asked that he would not punish his people's sins by sending evil, disease and pestilence on them, their livestock or their crops, and called on the angels and saints to become their protectors.

The actual text used in particular places and times is a matter of conjecture; by its nature, the litany is a form into which extra names of saints or specific urgent petitions could be added,[7] while others could drop out. However, the basic shape is what today we call the 'Litany of the Saints'[8] which in a much-shortened form is still occasionally used in the Roman rite[9] and in altered forms in some Reformation liturgies.[10] While its exact content varied, six elements became standard in this great litany, and when we note them we see that several of these elements reappear in the Irish litanies of which it was the ultimate inspiration. The litany began with repetition of *Kyrie* and *Christe eleison* and a call made directly to God to have mercy. The second element was a list of saints where the response was 'pray for us'. The third and fourth sections are less easily distinguished as they both have the same response 'Deliver us, O Lord', but we must note that the petitions fall into two very different types. The third part is a list of nasty events from which people wished to be spared such as 'From every sin', 'From your anger', 'From disease, famine and war'. Here the notions of penitence and intercession are most clearly seen. In the fourth section the notion was that because Christ had performed great merciful acts for the sake of humanity, such as dying on the cross, by calling these to mind

---

6. This survived in parts of England in the custom of 'Beating the Parish Bounds' at Rogationtide.
7. We have an example of this process in the Stowe Missal; see ch. 7.
8. It can be found in Latin in many places (the *Liber Usualis* and most editions of the *Rituale Romanum*) and was translated in most older (pre-1970) Catholic prayerbooks.
9. It is used in the baptism rite at the Easter Vigil, and at Ordinations.
10. See W. Jardine Grisbrooke, 'Litany', in J. G. Davies (ed.), *A New Dictionary of Liturgy and Worship* (London 1986), pp. 305–7.

Cross Pillar, Gallarus, Dingle Peninsula, Co. Kerry. Stones similar to this are found throughout Ireland. We should imagine them as marker points (*stationes*) in outdoor liturgies such as processions through the fields to invoke divine protection.

the people were asking to be delivered from the sin and suffering. So the prayer is 'By the mystery of your incarnation' and the reply 'Deliver us, O Lord'. Here the recollection of the incarnation in prayer is an expression of the Christian's desire to be part of that divine activity and thus to share in its fruit. Each event in Christ's life from the annunciation to the sending of the Spirit is seen as an action by which he brings his salvation/deliverance to his people: therefore, in the logic of the litany, it should be recalled, for its result – salvation – is what the petitioners desire. In order to distinguish these two parts of the litany they are sometimes referred to as the 'deprecations' and 'obsecrations' respectively. The fifth section is the intercessions in the form 'that we might be saved', 'that the church might grow' and the like, and the response is 'We ask you to hear us'. This part of the litany is the one many are most familiar with as it formed the pattern for the revised Prayer of the Faithful in the 1970 Roman Rite and in the newer liturgies of other churches. The sixth and last section is a return to the opening theme of a direct call on God for mercy using the text 'Lamb of God you take away the sins of the world' and finishing off with *Kyrie eleison*.

PRAYER AND MOVEMENT

When we examine medieval litanies we must remember that this is a form of prayer that was not only very common but, since a ceremony like the Greater Litanies was one of the memorable days in the whole year, of high prominence. A litany was as familiar an element in their prayer as was the rosary – another prayer where repetition provides room for meditation – for generations of Catholics in recent centuries. Likewise, we must remember that while we think of liturgy as tied to a building, and requiring minimal movement once one is in one's pew, this again is a relatively recent development. Most Christians down the centuries, including all those in Celtic lands, had a far wider view of what constituted liturgical prayer, and in addition to words, movement was paramount. The actual act of walking was a sanctifying activity; the act of walking in a group, processing, was a liturgical act of devotion of the first order. There were pilgrimage processions, processions each year to holy wells, the processions prescribed in the Missal (e.g. on the Rogation Days), processions with relics and – in later centuries – with the Blessed Sacrament, and processions with bodies to the place of burial. To be a Christian was to engage in this corporate prayer of movement.

We get several glimpses of these processions. Bede recalls the scene of Augustine of Canterbury approaching King Ethelbert in Kent shortly after their arrival: 'The monks [walking in procession presumably] . . . moved towards the king with a silver cross as their standard and with a banner with the image of our Lord and Saviour painted upon it, and they offered a prayer to God by singing a litany for their own salvation and that of those for whose sake they had come [to England].'[11] We can easily picture the scene by reference to processions that are still held in a few places today. For Bede, movement in procession, with the chanting of litanies, was part of the normal activity of Christians at prayer. Likewise, when disaster threatened, the procession and its accompanying chants became a primary way of asking for divine help. While in the western church the great flagellant processions associated with the Black Death (1347–9) have perhaps seared themselves on the memory – there are echoes of them still in processions of penitents in Spain – this massive movement was just the extreme form of small processions that took place every year in every parish. The processions of the Greater and Lesser Litanies were pleas for protection, and whenever

---

11. Bede, *Historia ecclesiastica gentis anglorum* 1, 25.

sickness of humans or beasts or crops – and, as would still be understood in nineteenth-century Ireland, diseases of animals or crops were terrifying as they brought famine – threatened, then processions with litanies became a first line of defence. The Irish Annals record that the relics of the saints were taken around in procession at times of natural disasters. The *Annals of Tigernach* record that an outbreak of smallpox in 742–3 was followed by a circuit with saints' relics. Similar circuits are recorded in years of drought and in years of cattle disease.[12] We have to imagine these circuits in this way: faced with calamity, the people sought to invoke protection and this was done by an elaborate procession where not only was one's patron saint invoked by name in the area that was under his or her protection, but his or her power was called down by, literally, dragging the saint on to the scene through what he or she had left behind (*reliquiae* = relics) on earth. In this plea for protection we see the basic form of the litany-procession, and the texts we have, and others like them, were probably composed with such events and uses in mind.[13]

USE OF LITANIES: THEN AND NOW

Rare situations – such as the pilgrimage centre of Lourdes – apart, procession is not a part of modern Christian worship. In the average parish even the short processions on Palm Sunday and at the Easter Vigil are usually little more than token affairs, and many wonder if there is much point to walking around in this formal manner. This is an attitude that separates us from the people who wrote these texts. For us, prayer is something done with words; movement is just something added on for dramatic effect. To them the action of processing *was* the prayer; by actually walking one was entering into the mystery, and the words were an addition giving focus and expression to the act of processing. Equally, modern prayer places a high value on accurately reflecting the inner thoughts and feelings of the one who is praying, and so sees a certain perfection in spontaneous prayer utterances which exist just for a moment – it is as if a thought has just caught words and in an instant flown away. Prayer formulae, the 'Our Father' excepted, and repetitious prayers are not to our taste, and are seen as boring and somehow less 'authentic' when compared with shared reflections. In this situation, the litany – formulaic and repetitious by nature – has few admirers. The verses seem trite and distant, the response little more than a

---

12. See K. Hughes, *The Church in Early Irish Society* (London 1966), p. 168.
13. The belief that a saint could protect 'his' area from plague is witnessed to by Adomnán in his *Vita Columbae* 2, 46 where he records that on his visit to Northumbria in 686–7 he noticed that while plague affected the whole land, those areas under the protection of Columba were spared. See ch. 4 above.

parroted slogan. However, these litanies do remind us of certain aspects of prayer that we may not sufficiently attend to. Processions have the effect of making us feel part of a group, of giving us a corporate identity, and such processions have to be bonded together by music or words: the litany does this. This is a phenomenon of human behaviour quite apart from Christian liturgy; it can be seen in the way marching with cadence-calls is used in armies to bond units together and give a sense of united purpose. While that sense of suppressing the individual in the group is not compatible with Christianity – it recalls the repetitive bleating of the sheep in Orwell's *Animal Farm* – we do need to recall that we participate in liturgy not as a collection of individuals, but as members of the whole Christ. Likewise, litanies and procession involve time and root us in a place; we not only use our heads and voices, but we become part of the praying body with our whole body. So too with repetition, when linked with movement it can calm the mind and free us to simply pray with a minimal amount of distraction from thinking about the very task of praying. In the verses also, each closely allied to those before and after it, we get the sense that no words can ever capture our thoughts in prayer. Each image piled on those before it conveys a sense that God is always greater, no matter how much we say. We have a beautiful, and carefully crafted, example of this phenomenon in the Irish 'Litany of the Trinity'.

Today, we have a curious situation regarding litanical prayer. While at a conscious level we have problems with the notion of repetition, the chants from Taizé do not lack admirers. Likewise, many who would never think of processions as part of their praying are pointing to the need to pray with the whole body. And, while church processions have almost entirely disappeared from our streets, the 'march' organized by a pressure group for this or that cause is seen as a key method of making one's voice heard and of consciousness raising, and in this secular form the litany has been re-invented in the chant of questions: 'What do we want?', 'When do we want it?', . . .

GOD'S VENGEANCE

The fact that litanies remind us of some aspects of prayer that could usefully be recalled is one thing, but we must not romanticize the past, for aspects of their underlying theology are seriously defective and should be rejected. Early litanies, and the processions that they accompanied, were deliberately penitential within a particular view of God as punitive. They asked God either to protect them from harm in the near future or deliver them from a present threat, but in both cases the assumption was that God is seeking vengeance. Penitence was not sorrow for the offence of one's sins, but a plea for mercy that the deserved penalty would not be carried out. God when appeased by penance might act with mercy. Thus a sinful people are, or may be, punished by pestilence or plague or famine, and these prayers seek to avert this threat. Whether the actual punishing is direct (God sends a plague on the land as he did in Egypt[14]) or indirect (God permits something to happen), the belief was that the bad things happen as God's retribution, and beneath this is an even more simplistic notion that if one was good then nothing nasty would happen.[15]

The litanies and processions during the smallpox plague of 742–3 were undoubtedly a genuine cry for help from the midst of affliction, but they probably were motivated by the belief that the smallpox was a chastisement by God. It is in this light that we have to read petitions such as 'Be merciful to us', and 'From your anger'. While such notions of God as a retributive and punitive figure have by no means disappeared from popular perceptions, they have been abandoned in modern Church teaching and theology, and this makes several of the petitions in these early Irish litanies not only hard for us to grasp but indeed to sound very strange. Appeasing an angry God with prayer is seen by most Christians today as unworthy of the dignity of God and untrue to his loving kindness, yet it was with this exact notion of penitential atonement that most of these litanies were composed and used. However, that said, some of the Irish litanies do rise far above this punitive notion of God's justice. As we see below, in the 'Litany of the Saviour' Christ is called upon to act in accordance with the love which he is as the Second Person, in accord with the love which he has as the creator, and as merciful love itself. But whether its understanding that the Son's love/mercy/salvation are really nothing other than his own nature was shared by those who used it is another matter.

THE TEXTS

Charles Plummer edited thirteen texts in 1925, all of them in the Irish language and of various dates from the early period to the late Middle Ages. The later ones are identified by the presence of theological ideas that only appeared after the thirteenth century. The earlier are often dated linguistically in terms of the evolution of the Irish language from what is called 'Old Irish' to 'Middle Irish'.[16] The texts themselves are referred to as if they had little merit as religious works, and one point, stressed by Plummer, is found in

---

14. Ex 8:2; 9:3; 11:1; 12:13; and 32:35.
15. See ch. 2 above, where this aspect of Patrick's early spirituality is considered.
16. See the arguments of Sarah Sandelin ('The Date and Provenance of the "Litany of Irish Saints – II" (The Irish Litany of Pilgrim Saints)', *PRIA* 75c (1975), 251–62) where she argues that the date of *c.* 800 given to a particular text by Kathleen Hughes ('On an Irish Litany of Pilgrim Saints compiled *c.* 800', *AnB* 77 (1959), 305–31) is too early for the language involved and should be *c.* 900.

almost everything written since: they were not part of the Church's liturgy and were purely for private devotion. All these statements need qualification.

The notion that there is an 'official liturgy' where one finds 'the genuine' belief of the church and which is formally sanctioned by authority as its 'public worship' is one that belongs to the post-Reformation period where it was a distinction used in argument to reject those elements of the liturgical legacy which could be claimed to imply false belief or superstition. For Catholics, if there were a large category of 'private devotion', then many attacks could be sustained without fear that one's opponents had exposed a weakness; alternatively, for Protestants, many items could be abandoned without the charge that this rejection of the legacy constituted a break with the 'true' tradition. Devotion was seen as less than the liturgy in dignity, belonging to the populace, and inherently open to abuse and superstition. These litanies with their emphasis on doing penance after confession, fulsome praises of the Virgin Mary, and the realism of many of the statements about Jesus (for example: 'For the sake of your own body and blood offered on all the holy altars in the Christian churches of the world'[17]) were best explained as a 'deviation' from the tradition in favour of popular sentimentality. However, no such division between 'public' and 'private' and 'liturgy' and 'devotion' existed in earlier times. All organized prayer was liturgy. If, for example, your community were making a great procession this impinged as much as, if not more than, the need to be present at the Sunday Eucharist. Liturgy, the concerns of combative theologians aside, is official and public if it involves the community, is accepted by them as important and is supported by their priests and used by them when that community assembles. All the litanies that we have suggest that they were used within such community assemblies. Moreover, the very form of a litany suggests community worship, for it is an interchange between the one who calls out the petitions and a group who reply with variants on 'pray for us', 'deliver us', 'hear us'; and they normally assume procession rather than being stationary.[18]

---

17. C. Plummer, *Irish Litanies: Text and Translation* (London 1925), pp. 42–3.
18. C. Plummer, op. cit., p. xv wrote: 'it must be premised that they are all the products of private devotion. There is no hint that they were ever used, or intended to be used, in the public service of the Church, for which most of them are quite unsuited. This is illustrated by the fact that in eight of the thirteen pieces here given the petitions are couched in the first person singular . . .'. But he noted that the last point was 'in itself not quite conclusive' as a Mozarab litany used this form. In fact, the whole premise is faulty as it assumes that litanies if used, were used without movement, that they were not a normal part of people's experience, and that 'public service of the Church' was carefully isolated from a variety of forms in the way that the highly centralized liturgies – both Reformed and Catholic – of the sixteenth century were insulated from encroachment, and could be so protected by the uniformity that was a by-product of the age of printing.

It is also clear from their composition that these litanies were put together not by some vague popular imagination, but by people who knew the great Latin litanies, and understood the technical forms of deprecation, obsecration and supplication since these forms are correctly utilized in them. These are not untutored documents but localized and vernacular versions of the litanies in use throughout the western church. Not only are many of the particular petitions that are common in Latin found here simply in translation, but when we have otherwise unknown petitions we see that they are perfectly adapted to Latin litanical forms. Thus we can say that these were composed by those intimately familiar with the liturgy, who knew that there were a great variety of litanical prayers already in use in the church, and whose desire was for materials that could be used in the vernacular and take account of their specific liturgical needs. Some may have originated with a local priest and the text spread more widely and survived almost by accident; others may have been composed with the liturgy of a monastic community in mind and become widely known through its use by members of that community and through the general influence of that house. In any case, all that we have is but a fraction of the number of such liturgies that were composed and used in Ireland over a period of several centuries.

We have to envisage a situation where almost every priest adapted, added to, occasionally shortened,[19] these prayers. Sometimes bits from several were combined, sometimes two or three were used in sequence when a particularly long period of prayer was needed; while at other times something was produced for a particular situation and may have been promptly forgotten. That this was the pattern of use can be verified by the way the texts which do survive (which, all things being equal, we can assume are typical of a much larger body of material now lost for ever) are found in the manuscripts. In no two cases have we exactly the same text – ignoring ordinary textual variants – for while one manuscript has several more petitions than the rest, another omits a couple, while yet another has a petition unique to it. Indeed, while Plummer counted thirteen litanies, since then Kathleen Hughes has shown that one of these is actually two separate litanies.[20] What Plummer called 'Litany of Irish Saints – II' is made up of the 'Litany of Pilgrim Saints' (Hughes's title), which is 49 invocations of various groups of

---

19. It is of the nature of liturgy that it tends to gather more and more bits, each new element being simply stuck on the existing 'lump'. When liturgy is shortened this is usually the result of elements falling out by accident, rather than the result of deliberate editing.
20. K. Hughes, 'On an Irish Litany of Pilgrim Saints compiled *c*. 800'.

saints who had left home – gone on pilgrimage – to form religious communities in various places, together with a litany invoking saints in specific numerical quantities (e.g. 'the seven holy bishops of Finglas'), intended as a prayer against boils, jaundice and plague.[21] But these must have been combined by someone at an early date, for they are found in this way in the four manuscripts in which they survive, are never found separately, and indeed are found in the four manuscripts immediately after 'Litany of Irish Saints – I'.[22]

READING THE TEXTS WITHIN PATTERNS OF USE

The great value of these vernacular prayers for the historian of theology is the fluidity in text and form allied with that lack of polish that comes from actual use with a congregation, as it shows us how prayer actually took place. In this situation we should not expect wholly unified texts and we should expect variations in practice that surprise us: when liturgical texts are thought of as finished products we expect textual and doctrinal consistency; but when we study texts as used in actual liturgies, then a messy trail in the evidence is proof of how groups prayed in particular places and times.

We can see this phenomenon of use 'distorting' texts in many ways, but I shall take just two examples. The 'Litany of Pilgrim Saints' was dated by Hughes in 1959 to around AD 800 and she produced good evidence to support her case. In 1975 Sanderlin, basing her argument on the presence of Middle Irish in the litany, argued that it dated from AD 900; but she still had to explain the archaic elements. Her explanation was that the monk (she did not explain why she assumed it was a monk) was an antiquary with a particular liking for obsolete language, for 'only in this way can the apparent anachronisms in the material be explained'.[23] Even if the notion of an antiquarian-minded cleric (remembering that since this is vernacular material and so written with an actual pastoral situation in mind)

---

21. Hughes described it as a 'charm' (loc. cit., p. 306), but this is unfair as we do not know the mind of either its composer or any of its users; by the same token, any prayer for a particular need or for particular situations – or eucharistic texts for Masses for such situations – could be categorized as superstition. This notion that there is a clear divide between prayer (an acceptable activity) and charms and superstitions (an unacceptable activity) is, of course, of recent origin; and a distinction that is not only value-laden, but also has a definite intellectual agenda: see J. Z. Smith, *Divine Drudgery: On the Comparison of Early Christianities and the Religions of Antiquity* (London 1990).
22. Plummer, op. cit., p. xx.
23. loc. cit., p. 257.

were not somewhat hard to imagine, this argument fails to understand the basic way that liturgy changes in actual use. The forerunner of our surviving text was composed *c.* 800 or even earlier, and, as time passed, bits were added, bits were silently updated in language, and over the course of a hundred years of recitation and copying from one priest's book to another the text came to the state it is in today. That some bits were not updated is not surprising, for the liturgy is conservative of its forms and often retains archaisms of language next to contemporary expressions. Thus while we can date the specific forms which we possess (and we know these are often much older than our oldest manuscript) by the most recent element, this may not be the date of the litany. And we must note that the content of each litany can be much older than even the oldest language recorded in the surviving examples. The 'distortion' of these texts is due to use which gradually expanded and updated them. Indeed, in the case of the 'Litany of Pilgrim Saints' this phenomenon of expansion provides evidence for its extensive use between the plausible date for the archaic elements (*c.* 800) and the date of the newer material (*c.* 900).

Another example of 'distortion' is the linking of the second part of the 'Litany of the Irish Saints – II' to the 'Litany of Pilgrim Saints'. This second litany has the instruction, at its end, that it is to be said over water to be used against boils, jaundice and plague.[24] Dismissing this as a 'charm' fails to understand the role of blessed water in Catholic liturgy. Today, for the average Catholic 'Holy Water' is a familiar symbol into which fingers are dipped or with which people or things are sprinkled, and most assume – including most of the clergy who 'bless' it – that all such water is the same. However, the present Latin rite knows of several 'kinds' of such water[25] and has an even wider range of blessing formulae[26] recalling different moments of the history of salvation depending on the liturgical context in which the water will be used. Moreover, still today the custom exists of having Holy Water in the home, and until recently many had the custom of sprinkling this just before bedtime to invoke protection during the hours of darkness – a practice which had its formal expression in a similar sprinkling in monasteries after

---

24. Plummer, op. cit., p. 74.
25. There is (1) 'ordinary' Holy Water for stoops; (2) the water blessed at baptisms outside Eastertide; (3) the water blessed in the most solemn way on Easter night for baptisms that night and during the Easter season; (4) the water for the Sunday *Asperges*; and (5) the water blessed for the Easter form of the *Asperges*, the '*Vidi Aquam*'.
26. The 1971 Rite of Baptism contains a suite of blessing prayers from a consecratory prayer that recalls the whole history of salvation as baptismal (and which is one of the glories of the new rite) to a simple prayer that says little more than that this is the water that in a moment will be used for baptizing.

compline where the final prayer begged that the Lord would 'drive far away all the snares of the enemy' and 'send his angels to stand guard'.[27] Again until recently people wanted 'Easter Water' – holy water blessed at the vigil – as something to keep in their homes, and sought water from particular wells for particular ailments,[28] and, of course, there is the special water that comes from Lourdes and Knock which was considered a way of invoking a special healing power. It is as an earlier expression of this attitude to holy things that we have to think of the holy water for curing boils and jaundice. At some point there was either a well or some priest which/who 'had a cure' for these ailments. In this healing ritual a specially blessed water was the sign-medium of grace; and in this blessing there was, perhaps as its principal element, this litany in a manner analogous to the role the Litany of the Saints still plays in the blessing of the baptismal water at the Easter Vigil. At a later date someone detached this liturgy of the 'Seven Holy Bishops' from this blessing of water to incorporate it with the litany recalling the pilgrim saints, and then only by chance did the rubric at the end survive to show us a glimpse of its earlier life.

All of these texts could so easily be dismissed as either banal and idiosyncratic, or as superstitious and ignorant; yet in fact what we have are vernacular simplified forms of the liturgy which can help us reconstruct the pastoral situation of the early medieval period and which bring the structure of the faith – so different to contemporary Christianity – up close to us.

HOW IS SALVATION RECALLED

When 'Christology' is used only for the formal discussion of the questions of who and what Jesus is/was, we ignore the fact that in every community of Christians, in each generation, there is a prevailing view about how one should speak of Jesus and how his importance and relationship to us be described. In this sense Christology is the whole portrait of Jesus conveyed in the liturgy and how the life, ministry, destiny and person of Jesus are seen as significant for the praying group. All the litanies refer to Jesus in one way or another and so each to a greater or lesser extent portrays him, but here I want to look at this in just one of them: the 'Litany of the Saviour'.

---

27. The prayer (*Visita quaesumus*) is still used in the Roman breviary as the collect for the Night Prayer of Solemnities not falling on a Sunday.
28. I remember hearing (early 1970s) of a practice of using water from 'Father Moore's Well' in Rathbride, Co. Kildare as a cure for eye-problems (cf. W. Fitzgerald, 'Father Moore's Well at Rathbride, County Kildare', *JCKAS* 7 (1912–1914), 329–32; and P. Jackson, 'The Holy Wells of Co. Kildare', *JCKAS* 16 (1979–1980), 133–61).

This is a classic example of a litany in that it is a request for mercy from those suffering the results of sin. It begins with five direct pleas for mercy, and then continues with fifteen obsecrations, all in the correct litanical form.[29] As found in the manuscripts it does not have a response, but it is clear from its style and content that the opening five petitions should be replied to with 'Have mercy on us' and the rest with 'Free us, O Lord'.[30] It is followed by a penitential prayer of considerable merit but this was not originally part of the litany and became attached at some point in its use. We know this as the prayer fits with the litany neither narratively nor theologically. The litany's interest is in the condition of sinful and suffering humanity, and it is humankind and not the individual Christian for which it prays and whose state of alienation is addressed – in this it resembles the great Latin Litany of the Saints. In the prayer the focus is on the individual's fight with his or her personal sinfulness which is the result of discrete sinful acts for which that person must be penitent and anxious to make amends, and have a personal desire for holiness of life. The litany reflects a community aware of its need of redemption and calling on the Redeemer by invoking every aspect of his existence that the praying group will stand with the saints on the Last Day.

The litany opens with the twin images of Christ as the physician and the one who pities the broken-hearted, thus emphasizing the divine goodness as condescension.[31] A contrast is then struck with two petitions that emphasize the divine goodness as majesty: fountain of true purity and knowledge and the giver of every treasure. The extent of his mercy is to the whole of humanity and it is found in every moment of human history from the beginning of the creation until the end of time. Although not spelled out as such, this is the same notion as that of the Christ (i.e. the incarnate redeemer) who is the Alpha and Omega whose mercy enwraps the whole of time.[32] This mercy is a direct consequence of his affection for the creation. The imagery is not that of a distant wrathful judge whose violence is averted by pleading, but of God as close and loving who is now having his mercy recalled so that it will be shown to the particular praying group. The litany supposes that mercy can be

---

29. It is found in Plummer, op. cit., pp. 21–2; but as laid out on p. 21 it appears to have only eighteen elements; items 2 and 5 as found there should each be broken into two elements.

30. In Latin litanies – and our text is very close to them verbally – the response to the obsecrations of which here we have variants is always *Libera nos, Domine*; while to the opening petitions the response is *Miserere nobis*.

31. In his edition Plummer did not attempt to look at the sources of these petitions in either Scripture or the tradition of the liturgy. However, a great many elements in these litanies do have such roots (e.g. on Christ as physician, see Mk 2:17, and cf. Mt 9:12; 'pitier of hearts' is based on Is 61:1) but these cannot be explored here.

32. Apoc 21:6 and 22:13, and note how this imagery is used in the liturgy such as in the blessing of the Paschal Candle at the Easter Vigil.

invoked by this community because of the nature of the three divine persons: 'by the heavenly Father, by the holy Spirit, and by your own divinity'; and the point of access to the divinity of Christ, and thus to the other persons, is the classic one of western theology: 'by your humanity which grew in unity of person with your divinity'. The main body of the litany is made up of echoes of the Nicene Creed's summary of the Christ-event, and this presents the humanity of Jesus as where humans encounter God's mercy; this encounter then becomes the encounter with the divinity of the Son, and through the Son they know and call upon the Father and Spirit. This litany lacks any notion of the divine processions (the Son and Spirit coming from the Father, the Father sending the Son) and is extremely Christocentric in that it thinks of the work of Christ as *his* loving, *his* coming, *his* announcing of *himself* and *his* mercy. This Christocentrism continues in its interest in Christ's sacramental humanity as our opening into his divinity but is, to an extent, balanced by seeing the Word made flesh as opening onto the Father and the Spirit.

If the presentation of the Saviour's work is typically western in its Christocentrism, so too is its understanding of the rationale for the saving work: to repair the damage done by sin. The human race, identified as the descendants of Adam, have been taken captive by the devil and are being ruled by him. The effect of this is that humanity cannot escape from the lower parts of the creation into heaven. (They are held outside heaven in 'the darkness of the lower places (*dorchataid ifirn*)'.[33]) But by his coming as a man, the Saviour has not only shown his compassion, but can draw men from Hades, liberate them from the devil's power and gather his people to himself in heaven. The picture is one of Christ as the one whose love for his people compels him to go into battle with the devil and thus liberate the captives. Thus Christ is thought of in terms of light as in Mt 4:16 ('the people who sat in darkness have seen a great light, and . . . on those . . . in the . . . shadow of death light has dawned') and, recalling the prophecy of Is 61:1 (echoed in this litany), Christ has come to bind up the broken-hearted, to proclaim liberty to the captives in prison.[34] The litany is a prayer for Christ to come, bind the evil gaoler and free the creatures he loves.

The series of obsecrations is ordered not only by the sequence of time (creation, incarnation, death, resurrection, judgement) as it has to be, but in conscious imitation of the sequence in the Creed. Having begun with the divine Son, the litany moves on to his coming down from heaven 'for us men and our salvation' ('by your coming in humility from the heavenly places . . . to help . . . and rescue'). At this point there is an explicit reminiscence of two other under-

---

33. This is the *limbus patrum*, the waiting place, the tomb of Adam.
34. This is linked to Christ in Lk 4:18.

standings of the incarnation which the compiler would have known from St Paul. First, that of Christ emptying himself for us (Phil 2:7 – humbly coming in the form of a servant) and, second, of salvation as being 'delivered . . . from the dominion of darkness' (Col 1:13). It is significant that both these additional images which expand the invocation of the incarnation as a cause of our salvation are taken from the great Pauline canticles used in the liturgy: these phrases just flowed into the language of this litany as they were so much part of the prayer of the compiler, while the substitution of the 'devil' for 'darkness' makes it real and personal, and accords with the normal way that the 'dominion of darkness' was glossed, 'that is, the dominion of the devil'.

The Creed's mention of the Virgin Mary received a more developed treatment here: 'by your conception in the womb of the Virgin Mary'. This becomes the source of an even more complex prayer: 'by the loving mother from whom you did receive humanity', where Christ is invited to free his people not only on the basis of his divine love and his shared humanity with them, but also in terms of his recollection of the love that Mary has for him as his mother. This, to modern ears, sounds like tortuous reasoning and muddled theology, but here we confront the foreignness of the past and its ways of religious thinking. We consider the hallmark of rational theology to be a clear causal sequence whose refinement is seen in needing as few premises and images as possible. We seek to use the least number of ideas – and we frown on 'overdoing it' – and want a justification for each additional item presented as touching on belief. So, for example, if we could describe the Saviour's work without any reference to a role for Mary, then that would be all the better; and if one must mention Mary then only insofar as is strictly necessary. However, this principle of theological parsimony was unknown before the four-teenth century, and is alien to liturgy where language is extended far beyond the limits of theological debate. In this litany the reasoning works something like this. All the following propositions are true: the Word loves humanity, the Word shares humanity with us through Mary, Mary loved her Son as his mother. That being so, one can call for mercy in terms of any combination of these basic facts which brings out a threefold bond between the Saviour and ourselves. Being loved by his mother – our fellow creature – should recall to him love for us, just as sharing our humanity from her should recall that love, and just as his own divine nature calls him to have mercy on the creation. The next petition, 'by your birth from her without opening the womb', reflects the notion of the miraculous birth that developed as a result of the growth of belief in the 'virginity in birth' (*uirginitas in partu*) of Mary.[35]

---

35. See D. Ryan, 'Perpetual Virginity', in K. McNamara (ed.), *Mother of the Redeemer* (Dublin 1959), pp. 104–34.

The litany follows the sequence of the Creed: cross, burial, resurrection, ascension, being seated in glory, coming again at the end as judge. The event of the burial is expanded to take in the 'descent into hell' (conflating the Nicene with an element from the 'Apostles' Creed') which was liturgically celebrated on Holy Saturday as the 'harrowing of hell' and about which Adomnán (in *De locis sanctis* 2, 9–10), among others, had expressed such practical interest.[36] There Christ frees 'the just ones of the first five ages' (i.e. those who deserved eternal life from the time before Christ) from the depths (*ifirn*) and brings them with him.[37] This technical precision in describing the 'limbo of the fathers' and the ages of the world shows that this litany is a carefully constructed, theologically conscious product.

We see a similar subtlety in the way the litany presents the divine activity in saving humankind. While the need for salvation is presented in terms of imprisonment, the final liberation is not presented as being plucked from damnation at the divine whim, but as a gathering together of his people in accordance with the deepest impulses of Christ's loving nature. Because of who he is he frees his people from slavery, he comes on earth and takes on humanity for their sake, he goes down into the depths to gather his people (the just ones) who are waiting there for him, and his apostles and disciples are gathered around him in heaven. The final judgement is closely modelled on that scene in Mt 25:31–46 where Christ gathers his people (Mt 25:32) so that the 'just' go 'into eternal life' (Mt 25:46) while the wicked are told: 'Depart from me, you cursed, into the eternal fire prepared for the devil and his angels' (Mt 25:41).[38] Salvation is an act of harvesting and gathering; damnation is a scattering into darkness and confusion.

CONCLUSION

The 'Litany of the Saviour', far from being a curiosity of popular religiosity, is a liturgical document exhibiting a thorough grasp of the demands of this form of collective worship. Moreover, its structure and content shows it to be a text that was put together by someone who was more than theologically competent, even if some of his assumptions are alien to us. The little details such as freeing those waiting 'from the five ages' in hell, the phrases of the Pauline hymns, the Matthaean imagery of the last judgement, and the numerous

---

36. See T. O'Loughlin, 'Adam's Burial at Hebron: Some Aspects of its Significance in the Latin Tradition', *PIBA* 15 (1992), 66–88.
37. See T. O'Loughlin, ' "The Gates of Hell": From Metaphor to Fact', *MS* 38 (1996), 98–114.
38. Note that the text of the litany reflects a conflation of this text with Lk 16:23 in the phrase 'sorrows and torments'.

other scriptural echoes indicate an author who knew the tradition intimately and could interweave it flawlessly into his own work to produce this little gem of liturgy.

The study of these Irish litanies has barely begun; apart from the Plummer edition, there are the articles by Hughes and Sandelin, another by Edmund Bishop on the litany in the Stowe Missal,[39] and references in surveys. However, there is much work to be done. More work on Christology could be done by examining the 'Litany of Jesus – I' and the 'Litany of Jesus – II', and combining it with the 'Litany of the Trinity'. New and interesting light could be thrown on several questions relating to their views of forgiveness and the nature of redemption by studying the 'Litany of Confession' and the 'Litany of the Virgin and All Saints', while some new insights into their understanding of the relationship between Christianity and other religions, the extent of the community of the Church, and the nature of the communion of saints could be gained by an examination of the 'Litany of Jesus – I' and the 'Litany of Irish Saints – I'. Equally, the 'Litany of the Trinity' with its careful use of negative language could be used to assess the quality of the understanding in a liturgical setting of the value of human language when referring to God. Indeed, it is surprising that this litany along with the opening chapter of the *De ordine creaturarum* has not been brought into the numerous discussions of Eriugena's apophatic theology. Of course, in all these discussions the question of dating will be crucial, and for this we must await work from those who are specialists in language.

While this chapter has stressed the role of the community of the Church in the use and tradition of these litanies, and their place in a history of Irish theology, they also provide important evidence for the nature of the piety of the people. They record the actual praises that were sung at umpteen events, along with their pleas for protection. These pleas, in turn, show the links that were made between one's state of holiness and the health of the individual, family, livestock. A good example is the prose 'Litany of the Virgin Mary' which is a litany of praise containing a wealth of patristic and medieval Marian imagery. It well stands comparison with the most famous of the Marian litanies, the 'Litany of Loreto', in use in the western church over the past few centuries.[40] To observe prayer made for protection and deliverance we have a fine example in the 'Litany of the Virgin [Saints]' which prays for immediate needs in a way which is formally based on the great Litany of the Saints of the western church, but whose content is wholly local. Finally there are prayers which share many characteristics with litanies, but which are only related to the genre in a tenuous way. For example the 'Litany of St Michael' and the 'Litany of [the] Creation' both employ the notions of protection

---

39. E. Bishop, 'The Litany of the Saints in the Stowe Missal', *Liturgica Historica* (Oxford 1918), pp. 137–64.
40. See C. H. Bagley, 'Litany of Loreto', *NCE*, 8, pp. 790–1.

and repetition, but could be viewed more as private, individual prayers than as texts for use with a group – the latter was only named a 'litany' by Plummer. Indeed, this 'Litany of the Creation' sounds so strange that it could easily be mistaken as 'a faint echo of ancient nature worship'.[41] However, a simpler explanation is that it is a prayer of adjuration, calling on all creation to witness a cry of help to God and a command to the demons to depart. A good starting point would be to compare it with the uses made of the *Benedicite*. Taken together as a collection, these texts reveal the sense of a people's dependence on what they termed 'God's mercy', which they sought in processions and blessings, and through placing themselves under the protection of their saintly patrons.

FURTHER READING

Text with Translation

C. Plummer (ed.), *Irish Litanies: Text and Translation* (London 1925).

Studies

A. Baumstark, *Comparative Liturgy* (London 1958).
E. Bishop, 'The Litany of the Saints in the Stowe Missal', *Liturgica Historica* (Oxford 1918).
E. J. Gratsch, 'Litany, Liturgical use of', *NCE* 8, pp. 789–90.
K. Hughes, 'On an Irish Litany of Pilgrim Saints compiled *c.* 800', *AnB* 77 (1959), 305–31.
W. Jardine Grisbrooke, 'Litany', in J. G. Davies (ed.), *A New Dictionary of Liturgy and Worship* (London 1986).
Kenney, pp. 723, 728 (no. 586), 730 (nos 592, 593).
J. H. Maude, 'Litany', *ERE* 8, pp. 78–81.
S. Sandelin, 'The Date and Provenance of the "Litany of Irish Saints – II" (The Irish Litany of Pilgrim Saints)', *PRIA* 75c (1975), 251–62.

---

41. Plummer, op. cit., p. xxiv.

9   The Cycles of Prayer

And he came to Nazareth, where he had been brought up; and he went
to the synagogue, as his custom was, on the Sabbath day – Lk 4:16

A CRISIS OF PERCEPTIONS

For most people today, even those who consider themselves
'practising' Christians, the idea that time is inherently linked to
religion is a foreign concept. There are a few residual echoes of the
earlier sense that time is marked off into units within a calendar that
is a testimony to the work of God, but these are no more than quaint
echoes. We still work in weeks (units of seven days) but they end in
the weekend, not in the Sabbath; and they do not begin with the
Lord's Day (Sunday) but on Monday. We still have a great party for
Christmas, but Easter is just a long weekend. We still know the odd
saint's day: St Patrick's Day (17 March) is a big national festival in
Ireland, but St David's (1 March) in Wales, St George's (23 April) in
England and St Andrew's (30 November) in Scotland are very muted
occasions. The 'collective' memorial days – 4 July in the USA, 14 July
in France – are decidedly secular events. For more than a
millennium 11 November was, literally, a red letter day as the feast
of St Martin of Tours, the elaborate saint's-day liturgy of whose cult
dwarfed that of other saints; [1] but today it is the memorial of the end
of World War One. A few names, such as 'Hilary', hang on in labels
used in some legal and academic calendars, but for most users they
are no more than professional jargon.

We measure time in raw quantities – and are often paid or
punished in relation to these quantities – and we use events simply
as convenient markers for 'before' and 'after'. We long for our
'breaks'; we know what happened before and after our holidays; and
we know what demands are made 'on our time'. We have diaries,

---

1. Still today in the Liturgy of the Hours of the Roman Rite this feast has a full
   proper office – the only saint apart from Mary, John the Baptist and the apostles
   – to be so celebrated.

organizers and time-management courses all of which show how central an appreciation of time is to our lives. If religion does figure in this schedule, it is seen as 'taking time out' for reflection, and radically shifting our gaze from this time-pressured existence to another where time is not that important. Indeed, it has become a cliché in religious writing to see spirituality as stepping out of a keen, ever-present awareness of time, and to describe prayer using phrases such as 'wasting time with God'. While such notions may be useful today for those preaching the importance of prayer and reflection, they represent a radical break with the past. For the people whose religious texts we have been examining, time was at the heart of Christianity: to be a believer was to fit oneself ever more precisely into an externally determined schedule. Just as today a worker in a time-sensitive occupation is expected to fit his or her whole time around the schedule of the organization, and indeed is expected to surrender his or her own control of that time, so medieval Christians were expected to merge their time not only with the ineluctable cycles of the weather and agriculture, but also with those of religion. Moreover, the more one sought Christian perfection, the more one was expected not to have a personal schedule at all.

Today, one of the most romantic symbols of the early Irish church are the Round Towers located on the sites of monasteries. But few who visit those places remarking on their 'stillness' or 'peacefulness' reckon with the role of these structures as belfries and the need to regulate the work, rest and prayer within the monastic community with a bell. They lived, as we shall see shortly, with a time-discipline that would today be found only in the most regulated and time-pressured groups. Time was viewed as the background to an unfolding programme running from the moment of the creation, the Alpha, to the moment of the final consummation, the Omega,[2] and the Christian's task was to know that Christ as saviour was the key to this programme, and then to fall into place with it so that the time-pattern of his or her own life was nowhere out of harmony with the divine metronome.

DISTINCTIONS IN OUR PERCEPTIONS OF TIME

If we are to enter into the foreign world of early Irish texts regarding time, then we need to begin by noting some of the complexities involved in the way that we experience time. While our attitudes to time vary greatly, many of the complexities seem to be common to both that early culture and our own.

---

2. Cf. Apoc 1:8; 21:6; and 22:13 – this theme will receive further attention in ch. 10.

Surviving Round Towers and Sundials

Days, Months, Years[3]

The first quality of time is that we experience it in distinct, but interrelated, 'blocks'. We have various 'clocks' running in our lives. Some sequences belong to the day, others to the week, others to

3. For an introduction to the origins of weeks, months and years as units of human time within the history of Christianity, the best work is J. Finegan, *Handbook of Biblical Chronology* (rev. edn, Peabody MA 1998), pp. 6–18.

months; and several are annual. For the shortest interval, the day, we usually have a fairly fixed notion of what it will hold, what has to be done at various hours and the tasks that cannot be left undone: from rising and getting ready for the day, to commuting, to the daily routine of work; for example, the post arrives at a certain time. Or we have the routine of getting children to school or setting about domestic tasks. Then in the evening there is a period of our own time, and finally the day ends. Some tasks need to be done each day, and if they are omitted then they leave their troubles for tomorrow. The monk had an equally full day with a cycle of offices – periods of prayer in common built around the psalms. Fixed times of work, collective meal times and the daily gathering for the Eucharist. These times spread over the full twenty-four hours were well-nigh invariable – day in, day out – and to omit any of them was to fall down on the task one had vowed to take on and accomplish for the whole of one's life. For each day, set out by holy rule, there was a routine, the *horarium*, and the day was the basic unit of time.

Equally, there are tasks we perform on a weekly routine. We have hobbies and interests which occupy our weekends; we know what 'Friday night' and 'Monday morning' mean; we know the bin day, pay day, the day of the weekly seminar. The week was the first long unit in the monastic life. It began with the Day of the Lord; the other days were measured from that, and it ended with the Sabbath. The cycle of prayer using hymns and psalms was usually regulated – as we shall note in the case of Iona – on a weekly basis.

For us today the month is a crucial unit of time. Most of us are paid by the month, and bills, mortgages and credit cards operate on a monthly routine. Meetings are scheduled for fixed days in the month; we have end-of-month reports and jobs that must be finished 'before the end of the month'. The month's importance as a unit of time in the monastery was both the obvious need of locating oneself by date within the year (e.g. this is the first of October) – thus it was the organizing principle with martyrologies and calendars – and the practical one of providing dates for the Moon's phases,[4] and with this came the larger question of Easter dating. There were periods which were larger than a week which had their own character: periods of forty penitential days, the period of Lent, the fifty-day period after Easter. We find constant references to these longer sessions in saints' lives and monastic documents – we shall shortly note this in the *Nauigatio sancti Brendani* – which show they had a significance we do not give to any such periods.

Lastly, there is the largest unit in regular use for routines: the year. We have the AGM, the end of the Tax Year, the date for renewing this licence or that insurance policy. There are the winter

---

4. It should be remembered that, in the countryside until the advent of car lights, travel after dusk was dependent on the phase of the Moon. The statement of Gen 1:16 that it was 'a lesser light to rule the night' was simply a matter of fact.

sales, the spring terms, the holiday season, the 'silly season', and rounds of other activities such as the series of football matches leading up to the Cup Final. There are annual reports and reviews, new timetables, budgets, and a sequence of bank-holidays, birthdays and anniversaries. For Christians during the Middle Ages the year was a microcosm of the whole of faith: a sequence of sacred periods that recalled the key moments in the mystery of Christ; the markers of time – Christmas, Lent, Easter – came round annually, but the whole cycle of celebrations – the saints of each day – also came round annually. To see the liturgy, to know its moods, to know its heroes and heroines required participation for a year. The cycle of prayer of each day (beginning with matins and closing with compline) fitted within the cycle of prayer of the week (beginning with Sunday and ending with the Sabbath), and that in turn fitted within the cycle of the liturgical year with its great feasts, its periods of penance, its times of rejoicing and its diligent recollection of the members of the church who had preceded them: some they could now invoke for their help, while for others' rest they had still to pray.

As with us, so with the medievals; their lives were full of allotted tasks to be done at a certain moment of the day, in the week, in the year. Each time slot was filled with the appropriate response to that moment by which God was served and worshipped, and the holiness of their lives as a community increased: if it is evening, it is time for vespers; if Friday, then it's abstinence from meat; and if it is 23 September, then we must recall the great abbot Adomnán of Iona through whom 'noble Jesus has granted the last liberation of the women of the Gaels'.[5] These units of days, months and years had been given to them by God, as time-markers to be observed in their service of him, at the very beginning of creation. God had even set the courses of the heavenly bodies so that they would be a clock to these periods: 'God said "Let there be lights in the firmament of the heavens to separate the day from the night; and let them be for signs and for times and for days and years" ' (Gen 1:14). Arranging life in these periods was no more than carrying out the basic programming of existence.

Ordinary and Festal Time

Another distinction we need to keep in mind if we want to appreciate attitudes to time is that while the clock moves on minute-by-minute, not all time is experienced in the same way: there is the ordinary 'everyday' time of work and getting on with life, and then there are special times when we celebrate, feel that somehow we are at a special moment, and often abandon our normal concerns and worries,

---

5. *Félire Oengusso* for 23 September (p. 196); cf. Kenney, pp. 479–81.

splurge and 'let our hair down'. The first is the norm – I call it *ordinary time*; the other is the exception, the 'high days and holydays', the special occasions which form fixed times in our lives in that we look forward to them, recall them later and use them to fix the time location of other events as 'before' or 'after' them – I refer to it as *festal time*.[6] Festal times may be a day (Christmas Day) or a season (the long weekend, holidays); they may be recurring (our birthday) or once-off (a wedding or funeral, or a visit from some VIP); what is characteristic is the sense that this is not normal, we are literally *en fête*, and usually the period is preceded by preparation; often the best (or special) clothes have come out, and there is a suspension of many normal social relationships: either there is a deliberate formality or a deliberate camaraderie. This distinction is built up for us from our earliest years through birthday presents and looking with awe at the magic of Christmas decorations, but is only incidentally religious – indeed, in some religious traditions (e.g. Catholicism) where such distinctions have played an important role in the past, today there is a 'flattening-out' of liturgical variation between ordinary and festal times.[7]

By contrast in the medieval monastery those distinctions were rigidly defined and scrupulously observed, precisely because the distinction between ordinary and festal time was seen as a response to the action of God in history. Festivals not only stood out from ordinary time but were the turning points of the year. The feasts themselves varied in content (Christmas/Easter), in dignity (a feast of Mary/a feast of another saint) and in spiritual significance (from

---

6. A distinction based on the Greek words *chronos* (the flow of time) and *kairos* (a point in time) is sometimes employed by liturgists to separate the significant event from the ordinary run of time; however, I wish to avoid those words since using them as the sole distinction in our attitudes to time fails to show up the complexity of human attitudes. It is sometimes asserted that these Greek words carry specific meanings in the New Testament (e.g. *kairos* at Gal 6:10 and 1 Cor 5:14); however, the usage there is *not* precise (e.g. *chronos* is used at Gal 4:4 where, if there was an intentional precision, Paul would have had to use *kairos*; and cf. 'times and seasons' (*chronous é kairous*) at Acts 1:7).

7. For example, on Christmas morning the liturgy is usually similar in external shape to that of an ordinary Sunday save for a Christmas Tree in the sanctuary and some special games for children. This should be contrasted with the distinction between Low Mass (a priest and a server, no music, few candles, dull vestments, and the legal requirement that it last no more than 1/48 of a day's length) and High Mass (priest, deacon, subdeacon, other major ministers, many servers, incense, music, many candles and splendid vestments, and a most elaborate – and lengthy – choreography). The effect of laudable attempts to remove encrusted pomposity has been a uniform ordinariness, which when it failed to meet our sense of occasion – a basic emotional response to festal time – has produced in the case of Christmas (for Christmas is the last moment where there is a substantial interface between the religious year and our sense of festival) a crop of tinselly liturgies. The Catholic Church having abandoned its tradition of festal symbols, parishes, in order to present the Christmas Eucharist as the sense of occasion demands, have adopted the symbol systems of the marketplace.

Ash Wednesday to Ascension was the 'high' period in the whole year). It is against this sense of festal time, and the need to get it right, that we must look at all the arguments about the correct date of Easter and the need to understand the cycles of the Moon and Sun that generated its 'true' date.[8] Equally, the time of a death stood out: the funeral for Columba required three days of special liturgy – so momentous an event just could not be fitted into the regularity of ordinary time.

Cyclical and Linear Movement

One of the distinct features of Judaism and Christianity is that they stress that time is linear: there was a beginning, there will be an end, and we are somewhere in between. This contrasts with Greek speculation about a great wheel of time, and with many eastern religions today. However, in our perceptions of time (leaving aside the bigger philosophical question) we imagine time *both* cyclically *and* linearly. On the one hand we know that we go through the year's 'round of activities', and no sooner are we finished but we seem to be back where we started: 'has that time of year come round again?' So while our ancestors, who were closer to agriculture than we are, had a more developed sense of the seasons and the cycle of planting and harvest, we have this cyclical sense when 'starting back' after holidays, beginning yet another week, realizing that the tax year is starting over, and noting that the time for sending Christmas cards is suddenly coming up on us. On the other hand, we sense time as a line; the past is past, and it never returns. We sense that we are getting older, that ageing is a one-way process; we finish jobs, stages of our lives and even relationships, and know that they are now behind us. The model of car we drive, the computer programs we run, the latest news – all show us movement in time in one direction: new things, never seen before, render other things obsolete and part of the past. Birthdays are curious in this respect. We celebrate them annually (indeed, as we get older they seem 'to come round' with greater rapidity) and we wish one another 'many happy *returns* of the day' – all these perceptions belong to cyclical time; yet, we also know that the numbers on the cards only go in one direction, and a point will come when they stop – perceptions belonging to linear time.

We react in different ways to these perceptions. Festal days that come around annually bring out a conservative streak in our nature: 'we always visit gran on Christmas Day!'[9] while our linear perception

---

8. See ch. 4 above.
9. Liturgists sometimes refer to this as Baumstark's Law: the liturgy is at its most conservative on the great feasts, for then our expectations of continuity are greatest.

brings out either our desire for, or rejection of, the new: for some the past is dull and primitive, today is shining and sophisticated, but for others the new is 'the beginning of the end' as they recall 'the good old days'.

These twin perceptions can be found in early Irish monks: the liturgical year, dovetailed with the seasons and farming, was the great round of offices; going round and round in the cycle was, they hoped, the gradual means of perfecting the image of Christ in their hearts as they recalled again and again the saving mysteries. This is the leitmotiv of the *Nauigatio sancti Brendani*. But equally they knew that they lived in the Sixth Age of the world, and they could date themselves as an exact number of years and days after the creation of Adam.[10] They belonged to the hourglass of history running through the ages preparing in succession for the Christ; now the Christ had come and they were moving through the interval until he would come 'to judge the living and the dead'.[11] In this sequence from Alpha to Omega they could mark their position in linear time from the supposed date of the birth of Jesus. To know that one lives in AD 800 is to know that one is eight hundred annual cycles down a line of time, and this gives one an interest in history, for it is within that span of time that God is constantly intervening with his providence and grace.[12]

Good Times, Bad Times and Neutral Time

Time is also perceived as having a moral quality: there is everyday time which is just 'run-of-the-mill', neither good nor bad, just day following day. But there are also times which are nasty, bad and unfriendly to us: then we refer to 'hard hours', 'dreadful weeks preparing for an audit' or 'being swamped' or having 'unsociable hours' or 'irregular hours' or 'racing for a deadline'. In these situations it is as if time were our enemy and we must just go through it as we cannot avoid it – and time seems to have a special weapon to punish us: it goes slowly. Then there are times which are good, friendly and on our side: 'breaks', periods when things are sunny and we are 'on top' of all the jobs we have to do. The words 'holiday' and 'honeymoon' sum up these periods, short or long, when we are having 'a good time' – but time now seems to play a treacherous trick on us: time moves at the double in these periods.

This moral sense of time was also present in the monastery – our word 'holiday' was then still 'holyday' – when there were friendly

---

10. See T. O'Loughlin, 'The Controversy over Methuselah's Death: Proto-Chronology and the Origins of the Western Concept of Inerrancy', *RTAM* 62 (1995), 182–225.
11. From the Nicene Creed.
12. This was the perspective of Augustine: time provides the opportunity for God to act in human affairs, and history must be studied as the record of his actions.

special times and hard special times. There were moments of penance every day and week, there were the hard days of Lent and times of penance with unsociable hours. There were times of urgency such as Ember and Rogation Days when intercession was made,[13] there were times when one prayed for the dead and which had the character of mourning. There were the specially imposed days of penitence, of fasting in various degrees, which were the response to the illness of sin and which were prescribed by the penitentials and endured like our times of illness or hospitalization.[14] There were also the friendly times of the joyful holydays when fasting and sackcloth were put aside and the singing was full of 'alleluia' and the praise of the goodness of God. It was the mixture of the rejoicing days, the hard days, and the contrast of the days/periods of penitence that made up the complex pattern of the liturgy's cycle, and made the passing of religious time an affair that was comprehended by all the senses. Lent, for instance, affected eyes in its lack of decoration, ears in its sombre chants, the nose in its lack of incense, and the body which felt the time of year in its hungry stomach; what a transformation was felt in the change in the quality of time over just a few hours from the starkness of Holy Saturday evening to the sonorous rejoicing and plenty of Easter morning.

These distinctions may seem obvious, but without paying attention to them we may pass over many of the time cues which we get in insular writings without recognizing that they betoken a fundamentally different perspective on this basic presupposition of all human experience: time. I have laid out four distinctions above in the way humans appreciate time which I believe are common to modern people and those who wrote religious texts more than a millennium ago in the Celtic lands. As features of the perception of time these distinctions overlap (Easter, for example, is an annual, special day within a cycle of time which has a joyful character) and complement one another in what is a unified experience; but by dissecting them as here, we are enabled to see more clearly some of the dynamics of our lives and how they are different from those of someone ringing a bell from a high round tower, or fixing the time of prayer by the fall of a shadow on a sundial or deciding on the contents of a meal by reference to the penitential character of the day.

Discontinuities

We should also note two differences in perception where there is no common experiential ground between us and those insular monks. First, we think of time in terms of a quantity to be filled: it is a

---

13. See chapter 8 above.
14. See chapter 3 above.

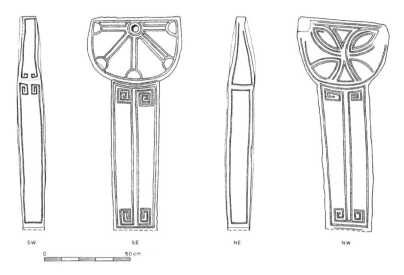

SW   SE   NE   NW

0   50 cm

Sundial at Kilmalkedar, Co. Kerry. Sundials indicated the times of the daytime offices, but also showed that the order in the heavens was reflected in the order of the liturgy in the monastery.

window in which I may chose to act, it is having scope for operations. Our question is: have you got (a sufficient quantity of) time? Earlier Christians perceived history as purposeful from beginning to end as the place where God had given himself scope for operations, for time itself was dependent on his creative action and sustaining will.[15] As such it was the scene of the drama of redemption: the characteristic question was about how much time was left until the 'hour of his coming' when history's purpose would be fulfilled, and this in turn was a prayer that they would be ready 'now and at the hour of [their] death'. This is the very first cue regarding time in Adomnán's *Vita Columbae*.

Second, we experience times as having different sources. Primarily there is 'clock time' and we have a vague notion that it is linked to the seasons (e.g. we move onto 'daylight saving time') and the movement of Sun (for instance our awareness of time zones), but we are so accustomed to all-weather services that if our travel is disrupted, it is newsworthy. Time is one thing, weather and seasons another; and astronomical movements are just a curiosity. Until surprisingly recently (a century or two at most) these were integrated realities: hours of daylight, the seasons, the ability to travel, the availability of foods and the movements of the heavens were experienced as interwoven. One could ignore no one element of time/change, for

---

15. See T. O'Loughlin, 'Tradition and Exegesis in the Eighth Century: The Use of Patristic Sources in Early Medieval Scriptural Commentaries', in T. O'Loughlin (ed.), *The Scriptures and Early Medieval Ireland* (Turnhout 1999), pp. 217–39.

no area of life could escape the consequences of times and seasons.[16] As such the external quality of time, namely that it is not just a system we create, impressed itself on people then in a way that it never affects us.

Now with these distinctions in mind we can look at some texts.

HAGIOGRAPHY

One of the features of portrayals of monks is that they are presented as sensitive to the time-rules of the monastery, and prompt and exacting in their observance. The bell was a holy sound.

The *Vita Columbae*

When we read a saint's life, Adomnán's *Vita Columbae* being a fine example, we have to be aware of just how conscious the author is about time and that he sees the day divided up into sleep, eating, working and prayer where the boundaries between these activities are marked by the hours of the Offices: matins (midnight), lauds, prime, terce, sext, nones and vespers.[17] We know that at each of these points a bell was rung (see *Vita* III, 23) which called the monks from work or their houses to the church (cf. II, 5). But it could also be rung at other times to call them to together to pray for some special need (cf. I, 8; I, 22; III, 13). Adomnán assumes that other monasteries have a similarly regulated day (cf. II, 5), and that even when monks are away from the monastery they should keep the cycle of prayer going wherever they happened to be (cf. I, 37). Having gathered in the night and morning for the Office, they gathered on Sundays (cf. I, 44) and feast days (cf. III, 11 and 12) for the Eucharist at the sixth hour (midday). All these gatherings took place 'according to custom' (*ex more*),[18] so if they were called for the celebration of the Eucharist at an earlier hour, this departure from routine needed a very special reason (cf. III, 12). Later, after nones, they ate their meal (cf. II, 13).

Adomnán also shows other signs of his time-consciousness. He remarks in the Second Preface to the *Vita* that Columba was so conscious of time's passing, and of living in the final days of the world (i.e. the Age of Christ between the Ascension and his Second

---

16. For a sense of how all these were related to one another, one can do no better than to read Bede's *De temporum ratione* (*CCSL* 223B, pp. 263–460).
17. See note 238, p. 323, in Richard Sharpe's translation of the *Vita* which develops this point. We find references at these points in the *Vita*: midnight: II, 5; III, 23; prime: II, 5; third hour: II, 15; sixth hour: II, 45; ninth hour: I, 48; II, 13. For an introduction to the same theme in the life and rules of Columbanus, see J. B. Stevenson, 'The Monastic Rules of Columbanus', in M. Lapidge (ed.), *Columbanus: Studies on the Latin Writings* (Woodbridge 1997), especially pp. 208–9.
18. See I, 37 for an example of how this phrase was used by Adomnán.

Coming), that there was 'never an hour' in which he was not working in some way, and that he was busy 'day and night'. Not surprisingly he refers to Christmas and Easter as the major points in the year, but significant for his sense of the year as a cycle of prayer is his expression to indicate that a lengthy time had passed between two events: 'after the cycles of many years had run' (II, 8). Again, as was standard, the liturgical books were arranged in cycles: thus the hymns for the Office were arranged around a weekly cycle, and in at least one copy this was the exact amount contained in a book (II, 8). However, the routine of ordered time is always liable to interruption through surprises such as guests coming, or crises as when the bell has to be rung for a special gathering for prayer and, of course, for the greatest intruder into time: death. Adomnán remarks that the funeral period for Columba took three days (III, 23). It seems that just as more time than a single day was necessary to mark off the great feasts (hence octaves), so a death – seen by Adomnán as a joyful day – needed a length of time to enable the monks to celebrate the event in a proper manner. It is as if they had to work their way through the death through a course of ritual and prayer.

The *Nauigatio Sancti Brendani*

For an even more spectacular example of how liturgical time can stand in the forefront of understanding, we can examine the *Nauigatio sancti Brendani* which as an allegory of the monastic life sees the sanctification of time as the ongoing task of all the monks it describes.[19] In this tale the characteristic of good monks is that they keep up the daily cycle of praise wherever they are (cf. chapters 6 and 11), and when they meet other monks they join with them for the appropriate Office for that time of day (cf. ch. 1); and on no day is any Office omitted (cf. chapters 11 and 17); the text provides a listing of the correct Psalms to be used at each canonical hour.[20] The island monasteries of those saints which are exemplary are places where the Office is well ordered (cf. chapters 1 and 12), as is the rest of monastic life through the routine use of a bell (cf. ch. 12).

Larger than the day is the cycle of the week, and this is seen in the respite given on Sundays and feasts that had been given to the souls that had been given the bodies of birds (cf. ch. 11), and in good monasteries there are special meals on these days (cf. ch. 12). The essential task that faces Brendan is that he should go through the

19. See T. O'Loughlin, 'Distant Islands: The Topography of Holiness in the *Nauigatio Sancti Brendani*', in Marion Glasscoe (ed.), *The Medieval Mystical Tradition: England, Ireland, Wales* (Woodbridge 1999).
20. See Stevenson, op. cit., p. 214.

cycle of the (liturgical) year with its feasts and fasts in a routine that will last seven years (cf. ch. 15), and then he and his companions will be fit for entry to the New Jerusalem.[21] They fast regularly in standard forty-day periods (ch. 3), in imitation of Christ (cf. Lk 4:2), and they fast for Lent (ch. 8). Then there is the pattern of one island for Holy Thursday and Good Friday, the giant fish Jasconius for the celebration of Easter Sunday (chapters 9 and 15), the Paradise of the Birds for the Easter Octave (ch. 11) and Ailbe's Island for Christmas and its Octave (ch. 12). Round and round they sail from one place to another and back again, round and round they also move in time from Lent to Easter to Pentecost to Christmas. It is the circular journey of a life of penitence and prayer that prepares them for the complete departure from the cycle of time and earthly movement into the Promised Land of the Saints.[22]

So far-reaching is this liturgical ordering of time, for the ordering is God's ordering and his servants' task is to fit in with it, that even those who are being punished (Judas Iscariot in ch. 25) have their punishment lessened and increased with the ups-and-downs of the liturgical cycle. This belief was also shared by Adomnán, for in his *De locis sanctis* 'the gates of hell' thunder more 'on the sixth day [on which Christ was crucified] and on the Sabbath [the day when he first burst in to release the righteous held captive there]' than during the rest of the week.[23] For while the just leave time's limitations behind for the eternity of paradise, those being punished remain within its strictures.

MONASTIC RULES

To become a monk is to become a disciple under a father: which means one accepts a rule. So discipline and regulation of life are the *sine qua non* of monastic holiness, and *a fortiori* if we look at any rule that has survived from the early Irish church we should expect to find many prescriptions with regard to time-ordering and the cycle of prayer within the community. However, instead of looking here at a formal rule, I want to draw attention to the liturgical cycle and time aspects of a text known as *The Teaching of Máel Rúain* which comes from the ninth century.[24] It is interesting as it was some monk's attempt to put together the customs that had been handed down within monasteries of the Céli Dé reform under the name of Máel

---

21. See ch. 10 where this theme of the eschaton in the *Nauigatio* will be explored in greater detail.
22. See Heb 9:15 – the notion of the heavenly reward as the 'promised inheritance' will be discussed in ch. 10.
23. *De locis sanctis* III, vi, 1.
24. The text is found in E. Gwynn (ed.), *The Rule of Tallaght* (Dublin and London 1927); see Kenney, no. 264.

Rúain, and the fact that so much of what he recorded concerns the ordering of time shows how large this aspect loomed in the eyes of anyone seeking to know more about the monastic life.

The work opens by assuming that there is an intrinsic link between what prayers are said, the quantities and nature of the food and drink taken – or not taken – and the annual cycle of feasts focusing on Christmas and Easter (sections 1–3). But having begun with this theme, he keeps returning to it throughout the work (see sections 8–9, 23, 55, 61 and 77). He makes the point that while among other monks there was the practice of special portions on feastdays, no such ease-taking was allowed by Máel Rúain (section 1). It was a serious indulgence that he occasionally – note it is not the regular custom – allowed porridge on Saturdays (section 1). Máel Rúain himself appears here as a rather miserable character – zealously intent on celebrating every detail of the year and its feastdays, without missing even a small prayer (see section 19), but devoid of any spirit of joyful festivity. This penitential obsessiveness can be seen in his reply to a piper who wanted to play music for him: Máel Rúain did not want to have 'his ears delighted with earthly music, for he wanted to await the delights of the music of heaven' (section 50). One suspects that they did not really capture the spirit of the Easter Sunday liturgy that well in Tallaght, which makes a striking contrast with the way Easter morning is approached in the *Nauigatio sancti Brendani*.

Not only was food related to the year, the whole of the religious life seems to be organized in time sequences. Thus there are detailed regulations on when, and under what forms, the Eucharist was to be received (sections 4–5 and 19), which pattern of psalmody was to be used for different vigils (sections 36–8), the hymns for particular times (sections 90–7) and how a Sunday or other feast day is to be treated if it falls within an octave (sections 11 and 72). This last point might strike one as simply the legalism about precedence known to those who still devise church calendars, but it also points to their sense that time varies in quality and dignity – that each day is not the same as every other day – and that this dignity and significance goes up and down with the cycles of the calendar. The sense of a year of saints which can touch them to a greater or lesser extent can be seen in the note that there was a special invocation of Patrick and Brigid in the psalmody on their feastdays (section 42).

Our observer was also interested in the customs that ran in shorter cycles than the year. So once a month, on the last Thursday of the month, they renewed their tonsure (i.e. shaved the crown of their heads in the monastic fashion) (section 83). Each week had its fixed pattern of penances and readings, so each night for a week they read passages from John's gospel, and then in the following week they read passages from Acts, and then reverted to John (section 17). Each day there were fixed times for meals (section 25), there was a formal grace before each meal (section 92), and there were prayers in the refectory after supper on feastdays (section 78).

In recent years the monks of the Céli Dé reform have become popular figures represented as a 'reform' movement within the church that 'brought it back' to some original simplicity far away from a rigid structure of law and regulations. Such romantic creations are so attractive that it is frequently difficult to see just how far they are from historical reality, but observing the Céli Dé on a matter such as time-management illustrates the reality well. They were a group so anxious to use every moment for prayer, penitence and the advancement of holiness that they lost sight of the comedy and fun that are equally part of the Christian year, for comedy must end on a joyful note, and so must all Christian activity, the unworried joyfulness that knows that Christ has conquered.

SUNDAY

The most basic Christian liturgical cycle is the weekly one around the Eucharist on 'the Day of the Lord' – *dies dominica* in Latin, from which we get such names for that day as *dimanche* in French and *domingo* in Spanish. As the Christian day, 'the first day of the week'[25] and 'the Lord's Day',[26] it was already a special day within a decade or two of the beginning of the Christian movement; indeed before any of the four canonical gospels were written it had already a defined liturgical shape in some churches as we see from the *Didache*.[27] As Christianity became the religion of the Empire, from the time of the Council of Nicaea (325) onwards, Sunday also found itself gaining a special status as the public day of rest, and from that time onwards there was a tension in its celebration for Christians. On the one hand it was the 'first day of the week', the day *after* the Sabbath – and the day that had superseded the Sabbath as the Christian church was seen as superseding the Synagogue – and so the day that was primarily one of rejoicing over the resurrection. On the other hand, as more and more Old Testament materials were reused to furnish precedents and guides for Christian law, so the rest aspect of rejoicing became the Sabbath rest and a fear of violating it with work.

By the time Christianity came to Ireland this tension was already present and one of the phenomena we see in the insular material is the rise of the Sabbatarian tendency: Sunday becomes a virtual 'day

---

25. Cf. Mt 28:1; Mk 16:2; 16:9; Lk 24:1; Jn 20:1; 20:19; Acts 20:7; 1 Cor 16:2.
26. Cf. Apoc 1:10.
27. The best overall history of Sunday is still W. Rordorf, *Sunday: The History of the Day of Rest and Worship in the Earliest Centuries of the Christian Church* (ET: A. A. K. Graham, London 1968); however, H. B. Porter, *The Day of Light* (2nd edn, Washington 1987) deserves attention as a basic introduction, as does the collection of essays edited by M. Searle: *Sunday Morning: A Time for Worship* (Collegeville 1982), as they relate the history of the day to the nature of Christian liturgy, past and present.

of fear', for it is so easy to transgress the law on that day.[28] Rest instead of being relaxation becomes, under the watching eye of an exacting God, enforced idleness and extra piety.

The negative 'Sabbatarian' tendency can be seen in an eighth-century Irish text known as the *Cáin Domnaig* ('the law of Sunday') which warns of the penalties that will punish those who transgress the limits of sacred time and carry out ordinary work on Sunday.[29] It is a curious text in three parts. The first claims to be a letter from Jesus laying down the importance of Sunday; then in the next part are found three examples of the frightful punishments that await the one who works on Sunday; and with this, its third part is a law tract which makes precise, and exacting, demands.[30] This has to be seen as part of a wider movement in the western church at the time which saw time-regulation as primarily restrictive.[31] Such texts stand as a warning of how regulations intended to help sanctify our temporal existence can so easily degenerate into viewing time as a medium to test us to see whether or not we can take the rigours of discipleship. When that happens the gatherings that are intended to belong to rejoicing time – friendly time – are transformed into threatening time whereby failure to meet time's demands is a mark against us. This may seem far from modern Christianity, but it is still a problem for many older Catholics with regard to 'holydays of obligation [to hear Mass]'. These were days which were believed to be important – and joyful – feasts. To emphasize this, hierarchies added an 'obligation', and with this the threat that if one failed to meet the 'obligation' one had sinned. Now the emphasis moved from rejoicing on such days to avoiding the committing of a sin by failing to meet the law's demands, and the very idea of the Eucharist became a burden. In turn, the clergy tried to ease the burden by celebrating 'quick Masses' and, in the process, what should have been faith-enhancing became faith-destroying. This modern example is instructive in explaining the process of what happened to the understanding of Sunday in the early Middle Ages, and also with regard to the corruption of time-regulations in many monasteries. What often started as a positive response of joy became inextricably bound up with duties and inviting people to see the Christian life as dodging sins.

For a more positive view of Sunday we can turn to a series of three ninth-century texts intended for use in preaching and teaching, and

---

28. For a summary guide to the history of Sunday in Irish tradition, see M. Maher, 'Sunday in the Irish Church', *ITQ* 61 (1994), 161–84.
29. Cf. J. G. O'Keeffe, 'Cáin Domnaig', *Ériu* 2 (1905), 189–204; V. Hull, 'Cáin Domnaig', *Ériu* 20 (1966), 151–77; Kenney, no. 270 (pp. 476–7); and see M. Herbert and M. McNamara, *Irish Biblical Apocrypha* (Edinburgh 1989), pp. 50–4.
30. For further details, see F. Kelly, *A Guide to Early Irish Law* (Dublin 1988).
31. See C. A. Lees, 'The "Sunday Letter" and the "Sunday Lists" ', *ASE* 14 (1985), 129–51.

known simply as *'Dies dominica'* (the Lord's day).[32] In essence these are lists of the wonders God did on Sunday: God rested after creating the universe, Christ rose from the dead, he sent the Spirit, he gave his first sign at Cana in Galilee, and on a Sunday he shall come again. The lists are long and cover events both before and after Christ's first coming (i.e. the recalled events are recorded in Old and New Testaments), and all are connected in that they are understood as having occurred on this particular day. In effect, Sunday becomes a doorway through time so that to live on this special day now, is to be present in some mystical manner on all the previous occurrences of the day. Sunday encompasses the past in itself. In rejoicing upon it, one celebrates all the mighty works of God. To step out of ordinary time into the special time of Sunday is to step out of the ninth century and be present in many moments in the history of the creation/salvation: it is to be present in the divine rest, the divine deliverance at the Red Sea, the divine care with the manna in the desert and with Christ in all his mysteries.

Sunday is the sacrament of time; to enter its actual finitude now (i.e. the hours between Saturday and Monday) is also to step outside the limitations of time and to stand in the 'today' of the wonders of God. Just as the Eucharist collapses time and space so that the gathering now is also the gathering of the Last Supper, so Sunday collapses temporal separation and one is actually present at the moments of divine deliverance. Travelling forward through time each week towards the consummation of the universe, one is invited by Sunday to step out into a special time when one sees the beginning of history and the opening of the age whose close is expected in hope.

THE YEAR AND ITS COMMUNITY

Many Christians still sing:

> Time, like an ever rolling stream,
> bears all its sons away,
> they fly forgotten, as a dream
> dies at the opening day.[33]

This is a sentiment, despite being based closely on Ps 90:4–5, with which those whose texts we have studied in this book would not have identified. 'The souls of the just are in the hands of God' (Wis 3:1) and far from disappearing from memory they were recalled each day by those Christians who were still living in time. The saints included those who had died long ago and those who had died only recently,

---

32. There is an introductory study of these texts, along with an analysis of the use of Scripture, in T. O'Loughlin, 'The Significance of Sunday: Three Ninth-Century Catecheses', *Worship* 64 (1990), 533–44; for bibliography on these texts, see L&S, 903, 904 and 906.

33. Written by Isaac Watts (1674–1748) (first line: 'O God our help in ages past').

those who had died in distant places whose names were only foreign sounds and those who had died who were members of one's own community or region – and each, great or small, had a day within the year and was recalled on it. The record of all these saints was the martyrology – a list of saints for every day of the year. To pass through the year was a long act of recollection, and this was a holy task in its own right.

From around 830 we possess two martyrologies from the monastery of Tallaght. The first is *The Martyrology of Tallaght* which is a standard western martyrology with the addition of many local saints which allows us to date it, and to see the prehistory of this particular text.[34] From the names included we can see that it was copied for Tallaght from a martyrology that was used in Iona, for it includes abbots of that monastery; and that in turn had been copied from one in use in an Anglo-Saxon monastery, for some saints from Anglo-Saxon England are listed. In the course of living each day, one had to recall the past, and all 'born to eternal life' on that day. This was a matter of recalling the special times not only of saints known to all Christians, such as St Martin, but also those known only to the particular community. A martyrology is at once a very public affair noting the saints who have a special feastday and a more intimate document – a modern equivalent would be a birthday-card list – by which, over the course of a year, a community could ensure that it did not forget anyone significant to it who had entered the communion of saints.[35]

The second Tallaght martyrology, the *Félire Oengusso*, is that created by Oengus in Irish and in verse – one stanza for every day of the year. It picks out the most significant commemorations of each day and, as we should expect, it includes all the apostles, the martyrs of the early church, the pope-saints and the great writers such as Augustine. But it also includes many that have now passed from memory such as the 'holy Maccabees' (1 August),[36] and other medieval curiosities such as 'the seven sleepers of Ephesus' (7 August).[37] However, what is more interesting is its sense that time recalls the saints of one's own place: on 6 August it recalls St Cua from Clondalkin (the monastery whose lands adjoined those of

---

34. See L&S, 540; and for background see: J. Hennig, 'The Function of the Martyrology of Tallaght', *MedS* 26 (1964), 315–28; P. Ó Riain, 'The Tallaght Martyrologies, Redated', *CMCS* 20 (1990), 21–38; and idem, *Anglo-Saxon Ireland: the evidence of the Martyrology of Tallaght* (Cambridge 1993).
35. On the significance of the communion, see the previous chapter.
36. This feast was based on the story of the seven Jewish martyrs in 2 Macc 7, and was alluded to with what became its standard Christian interpretation in Heb 11:35; cf. A. Bévenot, 'The Holy Maccabees', *The Month* 150 (1927), 107–14. It was still an optional celebration in the Roman Rite until 1969; in Stokes's edition, p. 174.
37. See E. Honigmann, 'Stephen of Ephesus (April 15, 448–Oct. 29, 451) and the Legend of the Seven Sleepers', in his *Patristic Studies* (Rome 1953), pp. 125–68.

Tallaght), on 8 August it recalls St Colmán of Inisbofin, and on the following day another saint from Connacht.[38] What we have is a celebration of time and spiritual friendship, a statement of who constituted the world of Oengus mapped out in a cycle of prayer.

TIMES AND SEASONS

To be human is to exist in time, and to be a Christian is to see time as an inherently sacred dimension, for the Word has become flesh in history. This belief was impressed on the Christians of the first millennium every time they deliberately chose to use AD dating, and it was supported by a recognition of the order of the seasons, the recurring cycles of life and the march of time towards death. Time was the characteristic of earthly life, and the destiny of that life lay in an existence greater than time: eternity. But while here they experienced all of time's moods and changes, its ups and downs, since 'for everything there is a season, and a time for every matter under heaven' (Qo 3:1).

FURTHER READING

Texts

Anon, *Cáin Domnaig*.
Anon, *Dies dominica*.
Anon, *The Martyrology of Tallaght*.
Anon, *The Teaching of Máel Rúain*.
Bede, *De temporum ratione*.
Oengus mac Oengobann, *Félire Oengusso*.

Studies

V. Hull, 'Cáin Domnaig', *Ériu* 20 (1966), 151–77.
C. A. Lees, 'The "Sunday Letter" and the "Sunday Lists" ', *ASE* 14 (1985), 129–51.
M. Maher, 'Sunday in the Irish Church', *ITQ* 61 (1994), 161–84.
J. G. O'Keeffe, 'Cáin Domnaig', *Ériu* 2 (1905), 189–204.
T. O'Loughlin, 'The Significance of Sunday: Three Ninth-Century Catecheses', *Worship* 64 (1990), 533–44.
W. Rordorf, *Sunday: The History of the Day of Rest and Worship in the Earliest Centuries of the Christian Church* (London 1968).
J. B. Stevenson, 'The Monastic Rules of Columbanus', in M. Lapidge (ed.), *Columbanus: Studies on the Latin Writings* (Woodbridge 1997), pp. 203–16.

---

38. See Stokes's edition, p. 175.

10 Jerusalem: Our Mother and Home Above

O Jerusalem, O blessed city
Called 'the vision of peace'[1]

So far in this book we have examined individual writers or closely related groups of texts. That done, we can obtain a more rounded picture of how early Irish writers did theology in Latin by following a defined theme through different writers in different kinds of texts over a relatively short time-span. This will enable us to see how the culture at a given period appreciated, took to itself and developed some aspects of the Christian message. Moreover, in any book on Christian theology one element which must feature is eschatology – and appropriately it should come last in the book. To provide a window on eschatology, I have chosen to follow their use of the theme of 'Jerusalem' as a symbol for the final Christian destination, heaven. The time-span of this survey will be roughly from 680 to 810.

To treat heaven separately from the other three 'Last Things' (namely: death, judgement, hell) may seem strange, but this chapter is only intended as a taster, and a proper treatment of early Irish eschatology remains to be written.[2] However, in many of our sources there is a similar segregation of ideas. While we do find speculation about judgement and the torments of the wicked, this is not invariably linked to reflections on heaven; nor do we find that writings on heaven automatically involve images of judgement and

---

1. The opening lines of a sixth- or seventh-century hymn (*Urbs beata Ierusalem*) used throughout the western Church. The description of Jerusalem as the 'vision of peace' is based upon reading Ezek 13:16 out of context: the Hebrew has 'visions'; the Vulgate 'vision'.
2. To date, there is no survey of this theme. However, these items set out the state of the question: St J. D. Seymour, 'The Bringing Forth of the Soul in Irish Literature', *JTS* 22 (1921), 16–20; idem, 'The Signs of Doomsday in the *Saltair na Rann*', *PRIA* 36c (1923), 154–63; idem, 'The Eschatology of the Early Irish Church', *ZCP* 14 (1923), 179–211; W. W. Heist, *The Fifteen Signs Before Doomsday* (East Lansing 1952); idem, 'The Fifteen Signs before the Judgement: Further Remarks', *MedS* 22 (1960), 192–203; and B. Grogan, 'Eschatological Teaching of the Early Irish Church', in M. McNamara (ed.), *Biblical Studies: The Medieval Irish Contribution* (Dublin 1975), pp. 46–58.

punishment as their counterpoint. This absence of the 'carrot-and-stick' approach – entice with heaven while threatening with hell – has left us with two distinct pictures. On the one hand, there are pleasant vistas of the New Jerusalem without apocalyptic terrors – an aspect of these texts that makes them appealing today; while on the other we have the descriptions of the gates of hell and lists of 'the signs before the doom'. Indeed, they seem to have appreciated – probably through reading Gregory the Great – that heaven and hell are not symmetrical either as human destinies or as objects of human knowledge.[3] As such they had to speculate about them separately and preach/teach about them in different ways.

THE BACKGROUND

One continuous strand of Christian imagery, derived from Judaism, concerns Jerusalem. The city in Palestine became the type for the Christian community in the last days of the world. 'Jerusalem' would be the designation of the complete and perfect church, the fatherland of all who have been ransomed by Christ.[4] The 'new Jerusalem' would be 'a holy city' and would be so built that it would relate to God 'as a bride adorned for her husband'.[5] Today this theme of the 'new Jerusalem' is firmly on the fringes of Christianity – invoked usually by those of a millenarian/apocalyptic frame of mind; but throughout the Middle Ages, Jerusalem was a powerful religious symbol within the different time-frames through which Christians sought to understand their beliefs and world. Some idea of the importance of this symbol can be grasped from that fact that 'Jerusalem' was used by Jerome and Cassian as the ideal example of the levels of meaning that were in Scripture. Jerome in his *Commentary on Ezekiel* pointed out that 'Jerusalem'

> could be understood in four ways: either [first] this is the city which was burned by the forces of Babylon and Rome; or [second] the heavenly 'first-born' [of the church];[6] or [third] the church which is referred to as 'the vision of peace' [Ezek 13:16]; or [fourth] the souls of individuals who by faith seek God[7]

and he noted that one had to judge which meaning was appropriate.

---

3. See T. O'Loughlin, ' "The Gates of Hell": From Metaphor to Fact', *MS* 38 (1996), 98–114.
4. Cf. Heb 12:22.
5. Apoc 21:2.
6. Jerome uses the phrase *coelestis primitiuorum* which is an echo of Heb 12:23 (*ecclesia primitiuorum*/church of the first-born), but the contrast with the third meaning demands that this be the church, the first-born, here 'who are enrolled in heaven' (Heb 12:23).
7. *Commentariorum in Ezechielem* 4, 16 (*PL* 25, 125); and cf. R. E. McNally, *The Bible in the Middle Ages* (Westminster, MD 1959), p. 54.

When John Cassian wanted to show that there were levels of meaning beyond the literal he pointed out that literally 'Jerusalem' was the Jewish city, but it also could refer to the Church, the heavenly city and the human soul as a moral subject.[8] Such references only enhanced the significance of Jerusalem within the symbolic universe of Christians. Thus by the time of the first author we wish to look at here, the centuries of reading Scripture, and the commentaries and homilies on Scripture, had left their mark and the very name had a magic attached to it: pointing backwards to the times of the prophets and of Christ, pointing forwards to the Eschaton, and bringing up a wealth of liturgical imagery, for whenever people gathered in a church-building they were somehow not just there, but also in Jerusalem.

Jerusalem is mentioned 966 times in the Scriptures.[9] In the case of most of these references the interest lies in the historical city, albeit one where the power of what happened there was still alive and could be accessed in the present by the pilgrim. In these situations 'Jerusalem' was, in essence, historical and past. The biblical references to Jerusalem that are directly of interest here are a well-defined sub-group where the referent is a city of the future, which is to be awaited and which, while somehow 'linked' to the city in Palestine, also belongs to another realm to that in which we live now. This future city is to be viewed by the Christian exegete 'mystically' rather than 'historically'.[10] This sub-group is composed primarily of just three texts – although, as we shall see, they associate other passages to them – but such is their visual and exegetical force that they justified the eschatological understanding of 'Jerusalem' as prescribed by Jerome and Cassian, and can be seen as basic to the Irish texts being considered here.

The first two texts (Gal 4:24–6 and Heb 12:22) both use Jerusalem as a metaphor for the Church both now and in the future. In Gal 4:24 Paul wants to contrast the Jews and the Christians and does so by an 'allegory' on the story of Sarah and Hagar from Genesis: 'Now Hagar [= the Jews] is Mount Sinai in Arabia and corresponds to the present Jerusalem, for she is in slavery with her children. But the other woman [Sarah = the Church] corresponds to the Jerusalem above; she is free, and she is our mother' (Gal 4:25–6). There is another, supernal and future Jerusalem and this is the city of the Christians, their source of life (mother) and their destination when delivered from slavery (i.e. saved). The author of Hebrews also invokes Jerusalem as a metaphor for the destination of Christians – it is a city, not on earth but in heaven, and the place of the angels: 'But you have come to Mount Zion and to the city of the living God, the

---

8. *Conlatio* 14, 8 (*CSEL* 13, 2, pp. 404–6).

9. That is, using the large canon as found in Augustine.

10. See T. O'Loughlin, *Teachers and Code-Breakers: The Latin Genesis Tradition, 430–800* (Turnhout 1999), ch. 5.

heavenly Jerusalem, and to innumerable angels in festal gathering'
(12:22). In both texts there is a tension between now and the future:
the heavenly Jerusalem is the Church now in contrast with the Jews,
the mother now, but also above and in the future; it is the place they
have come to with its festal gathering of the angels – a point that
stands behind the image of the liturgy as entering the heavenly
Jerusalem now – but it is also the place of those who have been
ransomed by Christ's blood, the first-born (12:23), and the city of God
whose number is not yet complete. This tension recurs within the
tradition.

The third text is what is said about Jerusalem in the Apocalypse of
John. There is an early reference to Jerusalem at 3:12 ('the city of my
God, the new Jerusalem that comes down from my God out of
heaven'), but the most important material is in the seer's final vision:
'And I saw the holy city, the new Jerusalem, coming down out of
heaven from God' (21:2). The vision describes its walls, gates,
foundations and the other wonders in this heavenly place (21:2–
22:5). This vision is wholly other-worldly and held out as a vision of
the future abode for the seer. Its details – especially its numerical
details – were a source of fascination to many writers,[11] but the
overall description also provoked a sustained effort to envisage the
city as seen by John. And, as the vision in the Apocalypse itself drew
on earlier visions, especially Ezek 48, so medieval authors strove to
draw all these references together to form an even more exact
composite. This process, moreover, was not one of stringing
similarities into a chain but the careful composition of details, for
they took for granted that each seer (Ezekiel and John) saw the same
reality. Hence the Christian reader does not have two visions, nor
simply two specific instances of a genus, but two reports of the same
reality differing in depth and intensity, where each reporter adds to
the other. All three of the 'pictures' considered in this chapter are
such composites, and from the standpoint of their authors are so
much the better for this: as exegetes they had carefully gathered the
evidence from each witness, and the reader has the benefit of their
careful collation of the details.

Now we can proceed to examine how this symbol of Jerusalem was
used, developed and imagined in three Irish texts: the *De locis*

---

11. An early example of this is the fascination with Apocalyptic numbers in Tyconius
(see P. Bright, *The Book of Rules of Tyconius: Its Purpose and Inner Logic* (Notre
Dame, IN 1988)) and the presence of 'decoding' in early medieval manuals of
exegesis such as that by Eucherius of Lyons (see V. F. Hopper, *Medieval Number
Symbolism* (New York 1938); and J. MacQueen, *Numerology* (Edinburgh 1985)).
To see the extent of this kind of interest in Hiberno-Latin writings one could look
at the Irish *Liber de numeris* (L&S, no. 778) or the, now more accessible,
Collectanea attributed to Bede (L&S, no. 1257) and the section *De duodecim
lapidibus* ('On the twelve stones [found in the New Jerusalem's foundations]'),
nos 305–16.

sanctis of Adomnán from the late seventh century,[12] the *Nauigatio sancti Brendani*[13] which probably dates from the late eighth century,[14] and the illustration of the New Jerusalem from the Book of Armagh from the early years of the ninth century.[15] All three can be seen as explorations of the single motif of the shining, final city in the immediate divine presence; and as such it characterizes a developed, and virtually unexplored, theme within Irish religious thought at the time.

JERUSALEM IN ADOMNÁN'S *DE LOCIS SANCTIS* I

That Jerusalem was the holy city of the Jews, the place of the Temple and the place of the dramatic final days of Jesus's life would have been enough to ensure that Christians would have an interest in this city as a place of special holiness. Of all the *martyria* – places that bore witness to sacred events that happened there – none was more sacred than Jerusalem: the whole city was a relic where the pilgrim could walk where Jesus had walked, sit where he sat and kneel where he suffered. But this historical, relic-style interest apart, Jerusalem was also of interest as a place met day-by-day and year-by-year in the liturgy. Not only in scriptural readings, for it was also a theme in prayer through texts such as: 'I was glad when they said to me, "Let us go to the house of the Lord!" Our feet have been standing within your gates, O Jerusalem!' (Ps 122:1–2) where the whole Psalm praises the city, and the liturgical space itself was seen as a sacramental Jerusalem. A place recalling the past, and by being in that liturgical space they were anticipating, and preparing for, the End. So curiosity about Jerusalem by the monks of Iona answered questions on many levels. We know that they had books on the subject in their library, and now their abbot added to their resources on that distant city.[16] Indeed, the whole first book, more than a third of the whole, of Adomnán's *De locis sanctis* is devoted to the city.

The *De locis sanctis* was written as a exegetical handbook and enjoyed popularity for several centuries in that role.[17] More recently,

---

12. The text was written sometime between 680 and 704; cf. D. Meehan's introduction to his edition, pp. 9–11.
13. L&S, no. 362.
14. The date of its composition has been a matter of controversy; however, this is the most widely accepted date. Cf. J. Carney's review of Selmer's edition of the *Nauigatio* in *MA* 32 (1963), 37–44 at 40 which dated it about AD 800, and the precision of dating to the final decades of the eighth century is due to the work of D. N. Dumville, 'Two approaches to the dating of "Nauigatio Sancti Brendani" ', *SM* 29 (1988), 87–102.
15. See R. Sharpe, 'Palaeographical Considerations in the Study of the Patrician Documents in the Book of Armagh', *Scriptorium* 36 (1983), 3–28.
16. Cf. T. O'Loughlin, 'The Library of Iona in the Late Seventh Century: The Evidence from Adomnán's *De Locis Sanctis*', *Ériu* 45 (1994), 33–52.
17. See ch. 4 above.

it has become a medieval travelogue for details about Palestine in the seventh century. One curious by-product of this reduction of Adomnán's labour to being the amanuensis for a pilgrim's account is that it is treated as a factual guide demanding little critical awareness. However, as an exegetical work its task in relation to Jerusalem is as complex as the notion of Jerusalem is in the writings of Jerome and Cassian. Thus while Adomnán must look backwards in time to 'the city of the Jews' in order to resolve exegetical difficulties relating to events there mentioned in scripture; he must also look at that city in terms of the scriptural references to the other Jerusalem which is to come. In the first exegetical situation, Jerusalem is a witness-place after the event, a relic allowing the historian to understand obscure texts. In the latter, the city now is an antetype to the future city. The rationale for this belief that the present city somehow anticipates the heavenly one is fully in line with Adomnán's sacramental understanding of reality. That there is to be some link between the present and future cities is, for Adomnán, obvious or they would not share the same name: the latter must somehow be a fulfilment of the former, so a study of the former should somehow point toward the latter.[18] The case of Jerusalem is not an isolated one: the perfect example of such a relationship is, for him, laid out in Paul between Adam ('a living being') and the 'new'/'last Adam' – Jesus Christ ('a life-giving spirit').[19] Christ would not have been given this title of 'Last Adam', if (the first) Adam did not somehow point forward to him. In cases of something earthly pointing to something in the future that will be more-than-earthly (e.g. Adam–Christ, or the earthly Jerusalem–the heavenly city), the first elements in the couplets are to be seen as signs (*signa*), the latter as realities (*res*). Since the task of the Christian teacher is to study the *signa* as pointing from themselves to that which they betoken and anticipate, so the scholar looking at the holy places in the Scriptures must look at the present city of Jerusalem for help in understanding what the Scriptures say about the one that 'will come down from heaven'.[20]

Adomnán's interest in this future aspect is not a major concern in *De locis sanctis*, but it is present. He recounts two miraculous aspects of the city which point to the future with keen sympathy. The first 'wonder'[21] which separates Jerusalem now from other cities is its miraculous annual cleansing so that no filth can remain in the city

---

18. This is based on Eucherius of Lyons who devoted a section of his work on interpreting the Scriptures to the theme of Jerusalem. On its sacramental logic, see T. O'Loughlin, 'The Symbol gives Life: Eucherius of Lyons' Formula for Exegesis', in T. Finan and V. Twomey (eds), *Scriptural Interpretation in the Fathers: Letter and Spirit* (Dublin 1995), pp. 221–52.

19. 1 Cor 15:45.

20. Cf. Apoc 21:2 and 10. 'Coming down from heaven' is an apocalyptic image, see Apoc 10:1; 18:1; 20:1 or Dan 4:23.

21. Note his use *mirum dictu!* at I, i, 10 – this supine can best be translated as 'Wow!'

after the annual fair on 12 September.[22] At first sight it appears to be a medieval wonder of the sort that causes us to label medieval Christians as 'gullible'. But if we suspend judgement on the fact of the annual miraculous cleansing, and look at the details of what Adomnán believed to happen, then we can see the number of details that are present anticipations of the New Jerusalem. The first point is that the ordure and stench are not caused by the local inhabitants nor those who simply come there from round about, but by people 'from diverse nations' – already, today, the city is a focus gathering the nations. That the nations shall all be gathered to Jerusalem is a theme found in many places in the prophets in the Old Testament on the subject of what the Lord will do at the future time of deliverance when Jerusalem will be the focus of the nations.[23] From Adomnán's perspective in time, those future predictions now relate to the Eschaton when Christ will come again in glory.[24] This theme – that all the people will be gathered – is further expressed in terms of the gathering of the 144,000 in Apoc 14 – the Lamb who presides in the city (Apoc 21:22) is the one 'worthy . . . to take the scroll and to open its seals, for you were slain and by your blood you ransomed men for God from every tribe and tongue and people and nation' (Apoc 5:9).[25] However, the exact verse that Adomnán has in mind is immediately after the description of the New Jerusalem in Apoc 21: 'The nations will live and move in its radiance; the kings of the earth will bring it their tribute and honour. All day the gates will be open, and there is no night there [for Adomnán the gates are open at night for the waters to flood through the gates (I, i, 11)], as the nations flock into it with their honour and praise. Nothing that is unclean, no source of corruption or deceit can ever hope to find its way in there, there is entrance only for those whose names are in the Lamb's book of life' (Apoc 21:24–7). That no filth remains now in Jerusalem from the gathering of the traders who come with goods, not yet tribute, is an anticipation of the clean city of the end of time.

However, just as the biblical text has in Adomnán's eyes many details that need to be teased out for the whole of its message, so this sacramental miracle has other details that relate to the Eschaton. The 'immense downpour of rain from the clouds' (I, i, 10) becomes on the ground 'just like rivers' flowing through the city (I, i, 11), and so can be called 'celestial waters' (I, i, 12), which flow from the east, for they go through the eastern gates (I, i, 12) and carry everything off to the valley of Josaphat (I, i, 12), for that is the way that the watershed

---

22. The story is found in the first chapter of the first book of *De locis sanctis*.

23. See, for example, Isa 25:6; 56:7; Ezek 11:17; 20:34–5; Zech 8:23; or Zeph 3:20.

24. On his time perspective for reading the Old Testament as still predictive of the future, see T. O'Loughlin, 'Christ and the Scriptures: the Chasm between Modern and Pre-modern Exegesis', *The Month* 259 (1998), 475–85.

25. The phrase 'from every tribe and tongue and people and nation' is also used at Apoc 13:7 and 14:6.

of the city has been disposed by God (I, i, 11) – i.e. it is a work of divine Providence. Why all these details? The key lies in the linking made in Christian traditions (in both exegesis and liturgy) between the visions of Jerusalem in Ezek 47–8 and Apoc 21–2. The city of Apoc 21 was that of Ezek 48, while the river of Apoc 22 was the same as the waters of Ezek 47:1–2 when the seer looked to the east and saw abundant waters flowing towards the temple to the south.[26] This may seem an obscure detail, but it formed the basis for one of the major Eastertide antiphons (*Vidi aquam*) which linked the hope of the Christian people with the new Jerusalem and the flowing miraculous waters of baptism. Each year during Easter Adomnán and his community would have prayed: 'I saw water flowing from the right side of the temple. It brought God's life and salvation, and the people sang in joyful praise: Alleluia.'[27] So the reader of *De locis sanctis* would now know that this deliverance which he would fully share in at the End is taking place now by way of a foretaste. Likewise, the waters flow towards the Valley of 'Josaphat' (= 'Jehoshaphat' in modern translations). This might seem just a curious geographical detail, except that this name was invariably linked in Jewish and Christian (and later Muslim) thought with the last judgement.[28] The basic text is two verses from Joel read in combination: 'I will gather all the nations and bring them down to the valley of Jehoshaphat, and I will enter into judgement with them there, on account of my people and my heritage Israel, because they have scattered them among the nations' (3:2) and 'Let the nations rouse themselves, and come up to the valley of Jehoshaphat; for there I will sit to judge all the neighbouring nations' (3:12).[29] So just as the nations are gathered now near this valley for trade, so at the End they will be gathered for judgement.

The opening chapter of *De locis sanctis* introduces us to three cities: the one which is there now and its annual activities; this is a witness to the time in the past when the key events of the history of salvation took place there, and so ever more it is a chosen place of God's presence. But because of this divine involvement it is also the place of the future seen now dimly through signs, wonders, pointers and foretastes which beckon the reader to wait in hope. This is the place honoured by the Father on account of his Son's cross and resurrection, and so it is important for Adomnán to note its honours with care (I, i, 13). Hence the detail of the miraculous cleansing

---

26. The Vulgate conveys this impression, but modern translations make it clear that the water is not coming from the east.
27. In the present Roman Missal this text is sourced thus: 'Cf. Ezek. 47:1–2, 9.'
28. See W. H. Mare, 'Jehoshaphat, Valley of', *ABD* 3, pp. 668–9 who traces its role as a motif pointing to the final judgement.
29. There are two numerations used in Joel: I have followed the Vulgate which is followed by most English translations, but in some texts these verses may appear as 4:2 and 4:12.

which he can describe as 'the baptizing of Jerusalem' (*Hierusolimi-tanam baptizationem*) (I, i, 12). This is no pious metaphor such as when we refer to 'a baptism of fire' – medieval theologians always refer to baptism with the utmost respect; rather, it is a statement that this washing each September is a purification of the city so that it can stand as the holy city in the presence of the Lord. So purified, it is now 'the gate of heaven' (Gen 28:17), the vessel worthy of the Lord's dwelling within it. Moreover, just as the individual when baptized is set on a path that leads to standing among the saints at the End, so too the city is given, symbolically, baptism each year to remind those who see or learn of the event that it will be the final destination of the saints. The striking image of the miracle of the annual baptismal rains is intended to produce spiritual effects in Adomnán's readers/listeners: you must not think of Jerusalem without remembering its mystagogic meaning, for the New Jerusalem is the destination towards which all your discipleship is directed.

BARRIND'S ISLAND IN THE *NAUIGATIO SANCTI BRENDANI*

Recently I have argued[30] – building on the work of Kenney,[31] Carney[32] and others[33] – that the *Nauigatio* was not just an allegory of the monastic life, but a tale about Christian holiness presented through a series of pictures, and that the author, somewhat in the manner of John Bunyan or C. S. Lewis, deliberately chose a fictional form as this was ideally appropriate to the nature of the subject matter. In describing the place of Christian destiny prepared for them by God, the imagery of the New Jerusalem is invoked on many occasions in the work. However, just as in the *De locis sanctis* we looked at just one image, so we shall look at only one instance from this text: the self-contained tale within the tale of Barrind's voyage.[34] Barrind travels to an island monastery in Donegal named the Island of Delights where his disciple Mernóc is abbot. There follows a description of an ideal monastery – the model each monastery in

30. 'Distant Islands: The Topography of Holiness in the *Nauigatio Sancti Brendani*', in Marion Glasscoe (ed.), *The Medieval Mystical Tradition: England, Ireland, Wales* (Woodbridge 1999), pp. 1–20.
31. J. F. Kenney, 'The Legend of St Brendan', *TRSC* 14 (1920), 51–67; and taken up by him in Kenney, pp. 414–17.
32. See J. Carney, *Studies in Irish Literature and History* (Dublin 1955), pp. 276–323.
33. For example: C. Bourgeault, 'The Monastic Archetype in the *Navigatio* of St. Brendan', *MonS* 14 (1983), 109–22; D. A. Bray, 'A Note on the Life of St Brendan', *CS* 20 (1985), 14–20, and 'Allegory in the *Navigatio Sancti Brendani*', *Viator* 26 (1995), 1–10; and B. Hillers, 'Voyages Between Heaven and Hell: Navigating the Early Irish *Immran* Tales', *PHCC* 13 (1995), 66–81.
34. *Nauigatio* 1.

Ireland at the time should imitate. But Barrind has to set off again westwards, and in the course of his travels he moved from the historical to the spiritual realm, a trip analogous to moving from the earthly to the heavenly Jerusalem. Barrind moved from historical space (i.e. such as we know with the senses) on the western edge of Mernóc's island into a veil of fog where both time and space are beyond direct measure. Beyond the veil of fog he approaches a land unlike any in the experience of the audience: this is the Promised Land of the Scriptures, not the earthly land of the Old Testament but the eschatological destiny of which, for Christians, it was an antetype.[35] The scriptural echoes show it to be a place similar in structure to the visions of Jerusalem.

Before arriving on the island Barrind notices its light: it has a brightness unlike any other in that it shines right around the island. In the ordinary material world the *luminaria* of that creation (Gen 1:14–16) cannot shine all around; they always leave places in shadow due to the density of matter and their own limited material natures: the sun and moon can only shine outward and their light can be easily blocked out. This island's light is exactly like that of the New Jerusalem which needs neither sun nor moon, for God himself – and not a material creature – shines on its inhabitants (Apoc 22:4–5).[36] Then, when Barrind has landed, we are given more details. First, the island's flora are always in both flower and fruit, this is 'the tree that gives life' which is not affected by the seasons and gives twelvefold fruit, one yield each month of the year (Apoc 22:2). The island is, like the final Christian destination, a place without shadow and free from decay or want. Second, the stones of the island are precious, just as the new Jerusalem shines like a precious stone (Apoc 21:11) and its foundations are precious stones (Apoc 21:19–21). Third, the island has a river running through its middle from east to west – we have already seen this theme in Adomnán, but we should remember that east stands for the beginning and west for the end and so both directions together are like Christ, the Alpha and Omega (Apoc 21:6 and 22:13) – and so too has the heavenly city a river flowing through its middle (Apoc 22:1). Fourth, on the island there is no physical need, neither hunger nor thirst, nor need of clothing: all such needs are indicative of the imperfection and corruption of sin.[37] In the heavenly city there are no such signs of imperfection, for sin has no place there whatsoever (Apoc 21:27). Fifth, on the island Barrind is

---

35. The phrase *terra repromissionis* occurs only once in the Vulgate, at Heb 11:5. The familiar Old Testament phrase 'the promised land' is only found in English versions; on those occasions the Vulgate uses phrases such as this: *et eduxit nos inde ut introductis daret terram super qua iurauit patribus nostris* ('the land he promised to our fathers') (Deut 6:23).
36. Bray, 'Allegory', pp. 7–8, drew attention to this point.
37. These material needs were perceived as being part of the punishment of Adam's sin: clothing is mentioned in Gen 3:7 and 21; the need to labour in order to have food in Gen 3:18–19.

approached by an angelic figure – a man of great splendour – who recognizes him, greets him and gives him information about the place. Similarly in the Apocalypse (e.g. at 21:9) an angel appears to John, knows his name and gives him further information about the vision he sees. A sixth detailed point of comparison between the island and the heavenly city concerns day and night. The island being not illumined by a material light knows no night (*Dies namque est semper*); this is exactly as in the Apocalypse: 'And there will be no more night; they need no light of lamp or sun, for the Lord God will be their light, and they will reign for ever and ever' (22:5). Likewise, on the island 'our Lord Jesus Christ is' himself 'the light'. This identification with Christ is directly based on Apoc 21:23 where the lamp of the city is the Lamb.

A less obvious link between the Promised Land and the Apocalypse concerns the number 'fifteen' which is mentioned twice in the account. That these numbers may have a symbolic meaning within the narrative has been pointed out by several who have written on the *Nauigatio*,[38] but trying to establish what such numbers actually are intended to convey in medieval texts is always problematic.[39] However, it is possible that this use of 'fifteen' is taken from Eucherius of Lyons' *Formulae spiritalis intellegentiae*, one of the most widely used – certainly used frequently in Ireland – handbooks of exegesis in the period. In the chapter on numbers he says this about 'fifteen': 'this refers to the fifteen steps of Solomon's temple, for there are fifteen Psalms which are called "step [gradual] psalms": [he supplies the opening line of the first (Ps 119) and last (Ps 133) of these psalms]'.[40] That this may be in the author's mind is also suggested by his own reference to these psalms in *Nauigatio*, ch. 17. If this interpretation of 'fifteen' is accepted then the island itself, which it takes fifteen days to walk around without meeting its end, is to be seen as being itself equivalent to a temple. However, it does not need a temple, and Barrind makes no mention of a temple, as the Christ himself is present and is its temple. Similarly, John does not see a temple in the heavenly city: it does not need one, 'for its temple is the Lord God the Almighty and the Lamb' (Apoc 21:22).

Clearly, in the author's imagination, the island visited by Barrind is what is promised to the saints judged deserving of it; and for this his fundamental source is the image of the New Jerusalem. In effect, he has taken the image of Jerusalem as a reality rather than as a metaphor, and then has had to create a new allegory to bring it

---

38. Cf. O'Meara's translation of the text, p. xvii; and Bray, 'Allegory', pp. 3–4.
39. Cf. Hopper, op. cit. and MacQueen, op. cit.
40. The critical edition of this work is in *CSEL* 31 (and part of the passage quoted is on p. 60); however, there are times, as here, when the older edition printed in *PL* is to be preferred, where this quotation can be found in *PL* 50, 771 (for the reasons for using this older edition, cf. my 'The Symbol gives Life: Eucherius of Lyons' Formula for Exegesis', pp. 250–1).

within his allegory of the Christian life.[41] In addition, we see another aspect of the interest in the New Jerusalem: not only is it conceived of as the eschatological reward, but it is conceived as the form of the mystical state – although the author carefully emphasizes that that is a state which is entered sacramentally – which is the goal of monastic life: there one encounters the uncreated light of Christ.[42] So not only is the New Jerusalem the final destination, it is also the place the Christian soul must long for throughout life, but also a state/place which may be reached even now through a holy life. A place where one can savour a foretaste and catch a glimpse of 'the inheritance of the saints in light' (Col 1:12).

THE PLAN OF NEW JERUSALEM IN THE BOOK OF ARMAGH

The Book of Armagh, as one the monuments of the early Irish church, has attracted much attention over the years,[43] and in particular its biblical text has been studied intensely by those interested in early Irish scriptural studies. However, one aspect of its biblical apparatus has received almost no attention to date: the plan of the New Jerusalem that follows the text of the Apocalypse on fol. 141r. It was described by John Gwynn thus:

> The last four lines of the text [of the Apocalypse] are in 171$r°$, extending across the width of the page. . . . The rest of the page is taken up by a strange design, – a rectangular diagram representing the city that 'lieth foursquare', the 'Jerusalem' of Rev. xxi. 10–16, with its twelve gates, each bearing the name of its precious stone, its tribe, and its Apostle.[44]

Since the diagram contains the decorative feature of interwoven straps in its representation of the walls of the city – in contrast to the explicitly explicative diagrams found in the manuscripts of other works, e.g. Adomnán's *De locis sanctis* – it would seem that here we have little more than a decorative filler for a page that would otherwise remain blank. However, an analysis of its contents reveals that it is an exegetical tool in its own right, that it is a copy of an already established diagram and that it served a practical purpose in

---

41. This is a process within symbol systems that has often been noted with regard to the liturgy.
42. This is the theme of God dwelling in 'inaccessible light' (the phrase is derived from 1 Tim 6:16) which would play such a prominent role in the thought of John Scottus Eriugena.
43. There is a facsimile by J. Gwynn, *Liber Ardmachanus: The Book of Armagh edited with Introduction and Appendices* (Dublin 1913); for bibliography on the manuscripts, see L&S, nos 354–60, 526, 538–9 and 616; and Sharpe, loc. cit.
44. Gwynn, op. cit., p. cxxix.

this manuscript and in any other copy of the Apocalypse with which it was included.[45]

At the beginning of the text of the Apoc, fol. 160v, there is a survey of the book, which incidentally divides it into a system of *capitula* (chapters), drawn from 'John's words' setting out what was seen by the person responsible for the production of this manuscript as the internal structure of the text. The last part of the Book of the Apocalypse is seen as the culmination of a series of revelations. And in this scheme our last two chapters are seen to be one-seventh (sections xiii and xiiii) of the book's content: 'And I saw a new heaven and a new earth [Apoc 21:1] / [and] he showed me the river of the water of life, sparkling [as crystal] [Apoc 22:1].' So the book's purpose is to make plain to the readers what the seer saw in the vision of the new heaven and earth (21:1), and this is named by the text, the new Jerusalem (21:2). However, once one starts to read that text with its many instances of 'twelve this' linked with 'twelve that' along with 'twelve something else', a sense of confusion arises as to how all these elements fit together, and may accord with other such visions – especially Ezek 48 upon which Apoc 21–22:5 is based. The diagram, carefully including each element, then 'makes sense' of the information in a particular way. The text's language with its many physical details, its precise numbers and its geometrical references seems to call out for the reader to pick up a pen and try to sketch out what is being described, but no sooner does one begin this process than it appears hopelessly complex. What the designer of this diagram did was to produce a solution that integrated as many of the complexities as possible and then offer it as a ready-made solution to the reader's desire to try 'to sketch it out'. The solution is not perfect, *and none could be*, in that the 'twelve foundations' are assumed to correspond to the five other sets of twelve: angels, gates, tribes and apostles / precious stones, but the text now seems far more intelligible. It is only by using it as an aid to reading that we can appreciate it (and, incidentally, realize that it cannot be reduced to the status of a decorative figure). It is both a tool of exegesis and, within the book's layout, a celebration of its content, for the text tells us that we shall be shown the new heaven and, through text with diagram, we are helped to glimpse this. So keeping an eye on the drawing (see overleaf), we read the scriptural text.

John 'saw the holy city, new Jerusalem' (21:2), the 'dwelling of God' (21:3), 'coming down out of heaven from God. It has the glory of God and a radiance like a very rare jewel, like jasper, clear as crystal' (21:10–11). It is at this point that the diagram begins to make things easier to follow and to help us keep track of what we have read.

The city 'has a great, high wall with twelve gates, and at the gates

---

45. I have examined it in detail in 'The Plan of the New Jerusalem in the Book of Armagh', *CMCS*, forthcoming.

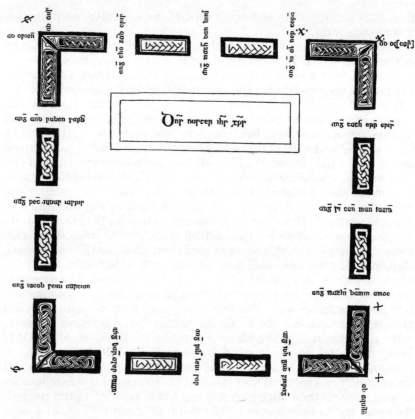

Plan of the New Jerusalem from the Book of Armagh

twelve angels, and on the gates are inscribed the names of the twelve tribes of Israel' (21:12). The diagram has the wall, twelve gates and the word *ang*[*elus*] written at each gate to remind us of these angels. In the same locations we have the first additional help made by the diagram in that it fills in at each gate the name of one of the twelve tribes. But here, also, we have the first exegetical addition. The notion that the number of tribes was twelve was a particular development within Judaism, and even in those places where the number is fixed at twelve, there were differences as to what names made up the twelve.[46] As well, the order in which they were recounted varied from list to list. The list used in the diagram does not correspond to any of the existing lists in the canonical scriptures, even the list given in Apoc 7:5–8, but is a combination of elements from two specific lists (Apoc and Ezek 48:1–28) which are distinct in their contents. Furthermore, the resulting list is not just one that is

---

46. Cf. C. U. Wolf, 'Tribe', *IDB*, 4, pp. 698–701.

common from memory, but one specifically linked to the visionary material relating to the New Jerusalem. At this point it might be wondered how we know in which order the designer of the diagram placed the names of the tribes within his list, since the names are not numbered and my list is not based on some arbitrary convention such as going 'clockwise', but this will become clear shortly.

The city has 'on the east three gates, on the north three gates, on the south three gates, and on the west three gates' (21:13). These are shown directly on the diagram as gaps in the walls, and the orientations of each wall are given in writing.

'And the wall of the city has twelve foundations, and on them are the twelve names of the twelve apostles of the Lamb' (21:14). The twelve apostles' names are then shown on the diagram, not by some attempt to draw layers beneath the walls, but between the word *angelus* and the tribe name at each gate. This, along with the addition of the names of precious stones which decorate the foundations as if they decorated the gates, might appear to be simply carelessness such that if several sets of twelve have been linked to the gates, so too should this set of twelve. However, it actually solves a conundrum. The twelve apostles were normally seen as the New Testament equivalent of the twelve tribes, a point explicitly made with reference to the final times in Mt 19:28: 'Jesus said to them, "Truly I tell you, at the renewal of all things, when the Son of Man is seated on the throne of his glory, you who have followed me will also sit on twelve thrones, judging the twelve tribes of Israel." ' Here, this verse accounts for placing these names not beneath the city, but around the throne, each one linked to a new cohort of twelve thousand people from each of 'the twelve tribes of the dispersion' (Apoc 7:4–8).

As with the tribes, but to a lesser extent, there is some disparity in the New Testament as to the names of the apostles. The diagram, however, draws solely upon Mt 10:2–4 in its content and its ordering of the names, except that in the heavenly city Judas Iscariot has no place, and the twelfth apostle is his replacement: Matthias (cf. Acts 1:26).

'The city lies foursquare, its length the same as its width' (21:16). Just as with the city in Ezek 48:30–35, the seer's city is a square, as is the diagram. The biblical text continues by giving dimensions: a perfect cube with sides of 12,000 × 12,000 × 12,000 *stadia*; and then, confusingly, it says that its wall (up to now the wall's and the city's dimensions seemed coterminous) is 144 cubits (presumably high), and 'built of jasper, while the city is pure gold, clear as glass' (21:16–18). There was no attempt in the diagram to show these measurements, the difference between the city and the wall, or 'gold, clear as glass'. However, we may wonder how many readers were lulled into thinking that the text was consistent simply by the presence of the diagram nearby, and by the assumption that 'it' had explained these difficulties!

'The foundations of the wall of the city are adorned with every jewel; the first was jasper, the second sapphire, the third agate, the fourth emerald, the fifth onyx, the sixth carnelian, the seventh chrysolite, the eighth beryl, the ninth topaz, the tenth chrysoprase, the eleventh jacinth, the twelfth amethyst' (21:19–20). This text not only gives the names of the stones that are placed beside each gate (the logic being that each stone is linked to a foundation, each foundation to an apostle; and that the apostles had already been linked to the tribes who are linked to the gates), but by giving the names in a numbered order we can see the order in which he arranged the apostles and tribes, and thereby we have an indicator to which particular list of tribes the diagram's author had in mind. In addition, because of discrepancies between the list of stones in the text of the Apocalypse in the Book of Armagh and that in the Vulgate text[47] we can assert – since in one case it is clear that the diagram's author was using the Vulgate – that the diagram was taken from elsewhere and not simply made for this manuscript.

The numbered stones were distributed around the gates in the order in which the sides were listed in Apoc 21:13, so stones 1–3 were on the east, 4–6 on the north, 7–9 on the south, and 10–12 on the west, the only exception being that the first stone, and so the apostle Peter, was placed at the centre of the eastern wall in the position of respect. The stones – and, following their order, the apostles – are in this sequence:

	7		8	9
2		**S**		10
1	**E**		**W**	11
3		**N**		12
	6	5	4	

The remainder of the description of the city (21:21–22:5) is not reflected in the diagram, so there is no attempt to show that 'the twelve gates are twelve pearls, each of the gates is a single pearl' (21:21). But there is an exception. The city is focused around 'the throne of God and of the Lamb' (22:3). This is represented in the diagram by placing *Dominus noster Iesus Christus* ('Our Lord Jesus Christ') in its centre. The city has 'no temple in the city, for its temple is the Lord God the Almighty and the Lamb' (21:22) so this Christ is placed there as the temple – possibly this is the significance of the two rectangles around the name. And Christ is its lamp replacing sun and moon (cf. 21:23). Moreover, it is this name that 'will be on' the 'foreheads' of the just who will be allowed to enter that city (22:4).

---

47. This variation of Armagh from other Vulgate manuscripts was noted by Gwynn, op. cit., p. cclvi.

One significant omission from the diagram is that it does not mention the river flowing through it nor the multi-fruited tree of life, while the introduction to the Apoc in Armagh mentions this river as a major element in the final vision. This omission probably reflects the different interests of the writer of the introduction who was interested in both parts of the description of the New Jerusalem (21:10–22:5), while the diagram's author was concerned solely with the complex description of the walls and gates (21:10–21).

Reading this strange text while keeping an eye on the diagram is a most curious experience: it is as if the diagram brings the text to life and brings it close to one. As such this little bit of exegetical scholarship produced probably in the eighth century (for it already existed in 806), perhaps at the same time as the *De locis sanctis* or the *Nauigatio*, is more than a decoding device; it actually functions sacramentally by helping the human mind to a more real appreciation of 'the things of God'.

FROM 'THE GATE OF HEAVEN' TO 'THE GATES OF HELL'

There is no shortage of other texts in both Latin (such as homilies[48]) and Irish (for instance, the famous *Fis Adomnáin*[49]), nor of themes (for example, early Irish attitudes to burials[50]), which could help us draw out in greater detail their beliefs about the final Christian destiny.[51] This chapter is no more than a curtain-raiser to show some of the diversity and richness of the material.

As a conclusion we can do no better than to look again at *De locis sanctis*. Adomnán framed his book with two eschatological images: it opens with a description of the gates of heaven (cf. Gen 28:17), and a miraculous foretaste of the heavenly city, and closes with a description of 'the gates of hell' (Mt 16:18) and an equally 'beyond-the-senses' account of the place of final torment (III, vi). Arculf is presented as walking and sailing in real space between Jerusalem and Sicily on a trip the reader is not expected to take; but he is also travelling between the portals of two destinations of a more real journey upon which all the book's readers are making their way. The work's initial audience would have been more than aware that they would end their journeys either in the city above or the fire beneath;

---

48. See T. O'Loughlin, 'The Celtic homily: Creeds and Eschatology', *MS* 41 (1998), 99–115.

49. See C. S. Boswell, *An Irish Precursor of Dante* (London 1908); and Kenney, no. 226.

50. See T. O'Loughlin, 'The Tombs of the Saints: their significance for Adomnán', in M. Herbert (ed.), *Proceedings of the 1997 International Hagiography Conference* (Dublin 2000).

51. For a survey of the genre of visions, see E. Gardiner, *Medieval Visions of Heaven and Hell: A Sourcebook* (New York/London 1992).

here they found depictions of each, and it was to assist them in their travelling that Adomnán wrote his book. As many Christians today seek to look back to this period for refreshment, inspiration or understanding of where, in part, they have come from, they might reflect that they too are on the same journey, but would they imagine their destinations (or destination?) using any of these powerful images?

FURTHER READING

Texts

Adomnán, *De locis sanctis*.
Anon, *Nauigatio sancti Brendani*.

Bibliography

E. Gardiner, *Medieval Visions of Heaven and Hell: A Sourcebook* (New York/London 1992).

Studies

B. Grogan, 'Eschatological Teaching of the Early Irish Church', in M. McNamara (ed.), *Biblical Studies: The Medieval Irish Contribution* (Dublin 1975), pp. 46–58.
W. W. Heist, *The Fifteen Signs Before Doomsday* (East Lansing 1952).
T. O'Loughlin, ' "The Gates of Hell": From Metaphor to Fact', *MS* 38 (1996), 98–114.
—— 'Distant Islands: The Topography of Holiness in the *Nauigatio Sancti Brendani*', in Marion Glasscoe (ed.), *The Medieval Mystical Tradition: England, Ireland, Wales (Exeter Symposium VI)* (Woodbridge 1999), pp. 1–20.
—— 'The Plan of the New Jerusalem in the Book of Armagh', *CMCS*, forthcoming.

11 Conclusion

> *O Lord Jesus Christ,*
> *Guard us in all our good works.*
> *O God, fountain and source of all good things,*
> *take from us all our vices and fill us with good powers,*
> *through you, O Jesus Christ.* [1]

Recent years have seen unparalleled interest in the medieval religion of Celtic lands. On the one hand there is a romantic religiosity that reduces the men and women of the Celtic lands in the first millennium to pretty, sentimental figures. This is a tradition of interpretation that can be traced back to the nineteenth-century writers. [2] On the other hand, there are the proponents of differing religious interest groups who use this period as a means of defining difference, and in the process foist on medieval writers concerns and beliefs that never entered their minds. This is a concern to claim 'Celtic Christianity' for a place or a people the lineage of which goes back to the debates of the age of James Ussher. And there is the bizarre interest of those who would strip early medieval people of their ethnic identity and Christianity by presenting them as models for modern neo-pagan rituals. [3] In the 'pick 'n' mix' cultural milieu of modern belief there seems room for a bit of everything: a bit of 'Celtic', a bit of 'Celtic nature poetry', some Celtic myths and legends, a few ghosts, and even a scattering of assorted superstitions repackaged as 'alternative wisdom'.

However, amid this plethora I hope there is room for a book which looks at some of the material within the more sedate parameters of historical theology. Scholarship is only beginning to address this material in terms of its theological content. [4] My aim here has been to

---

1. From the visitation of the sick in the Book of Deer (H&S, vol. 2, p. 275).
2. See P. Sims-Williams, 'The Medieval World of Robin Flower', in M. de Mórdha (ed.), *Bláithín: Flower* (Dingle 1998), p. 81.
3. See for example: A. Kondratiev, *The Apple Branch: A Path to Celtic Ritual* (Cork 1998); and my review of this book in *ISR* 7 (1999), 399–400.
4. See the list of *desiderata* in T. O'Loughlin, 'The Latin Sources of Medieval Irish Culture', in K. McCone and K. Simms (eds), *Progress in Medieval Irish Studies* (Maynooth 1996), pp. 91–105.

provide a series of explorations of particular texts to show (1) that there is a theological dimension to all these topics which deserves formal attention; (2) that early Irish theology survives in a rich diversity of forms and that its examination requires a measure of creative sympathy on the part of the enquirers to see the texts as tokens of a larger theology whose products have not survived; (3) that any work with these materials requires an interdisciplinary approach by theologians, text scholars, biblical exegetes, historians, linguists, archaeologists and those who work in the phenomenology of religion; (4) that in the historical reconstruction of these long-dead people's theology, the methodological restrictions of no single discipline can be allowed to determine, a priori, the value of the evidence; and (5) that the field of examination is a very broad one that deserves the attention of many labourers.

Earlier generations of scholars were dismissive of the notion that there was such a topic for investigation as an 'Irish theology' or even that there was much theology in early Christian Ireland. For one group, the Celts were a people of imagination and feeling, not reason and careful scholarship. Emotion and feeling, an intuitive sense of mystery, belonged to the early monks in this vision, with their harsh discipline and awe-inspiring surroundings, while dialectic, analysis and systematic preaching were alien notions better suited to more earthbound types. The assumption even led to sympathy: 'One may imagine that the dull task of transcribing theological and grammatical texts fretted these exuberant minds, and their impatient and erratic fancy overflowed into the margins.'[5] This tells us far more about twentieth-century attitudes to theology than about the early Middle Ages. Even if we had not moved beyond the implicit racism of such comments, the sheer weight of evidence that those writers sought out and eagerly copied every theological and grammatical text they could lay their hands on has changed our picture of early Ireland.

For another group, theology was something that was done in only one manner: the systematic textbook and the scriptural commentary, and the mark of theological significance was that its author was still cited as an *auctoritas* 'in the schools'. To generations of clerical scholars raised in this debased scholasticism (and note that this was equally prevalent on both sides of the Reformation divide) there was no theology from Ireland – and even Eriugena did not count as he did not leave a position with his name attached to it to be either cited or attacked. To this group, the Irish produced only materials of an inferior intellectual sort: saints' lives, devotional works and pastoral materials. Sadly, this group still have supporters. In only the last decade I have heard a historian of systematic theology declare to a class in Ireland that there was 'no evidence whatsoever for

---

5. Robin Flower quoted in Sims-Williams, loc. cit., p. 83.

systematics in Ireland – Eriugena was trained by the Carolingians' and when challenged with the fact that the *Collectio canonum hibernensis* is one of the earliest systematic collections of canon law and so we must presume a context of systematic teaching, he replied that 'it was a collection of local customs'.[6] If having read this book you now consider both these groups to be wide of the mark, I have achieved my goal.

The material examined in this book is just the tip of an iceberg. These expressions of theology – not one of them taking the form of a treatise in systematics – could only have appeared in a well-established and wide-ranging theological culture. I have deliberately chosen the more run-of-the-mill texts so that the depth and extent of that culture can become clear. It is not the peaks that stand proud of the plain that give the measure of the theological culture of a period, but the everyday texts that were produced for pastoral work, the ordinary liturgy of groups and monasteries, and the texts that were used to train clergy. I have only touched upon a few of these sources; there are many others awaiting investigation ranging from explicitly theological materials like homilies to materials which look anything but theological, the annals, but which incorporate a particular religious view of history.

The theological writers who lived in the Celtic lands in the early Middle Ages were conscious, every time they wrote a sentence in Latin, that they were part of a great Christian family. They drew life from that family and contributed to its development in personnel and ideas. They were also conscious, every time they spoke to someone nearby, that they had a native culture and that they belonged to a people who had converted to Christianity, and – at a time before this was widely felt on the continent – that Christianity's Latin culture was a deliberately assumed culture. Like Christians everywhere they relied on those close by for teaching, explanation and access to books, and so naturally they developed common habits of reflection and expression, shared a common pool of ideas, and felt bound to one another as only those who see themselves as disciples within a tradition can. The result was a local theology: a specific, local slant to its picture of Christianity that reflects its particular concerns, background and tradition of teaching. As such it is part of the intellectual history of those Celtic lands, and a part of the mosaic of local theologies that make up the theology of the western church, and a chapter in the general history of Christian thought.

---

6. See ch. 6 above; and note the comment of A. M. Stickler in ch. 3, p. 48.

Bibliography

PRIMARY SOURCES

Adomnán, *Cáin / Lex innocentium* (K. Meyer (ed. and trans.), *Cáin Adomnáin: An Old-Irish Treatise on the Law of Adamnan* (Oxford 1905).
——*De locis sanctis* (D. Meehan with L. Bieler (eds), Dublin 1958) [Latin text with facing ET; *SLH* 3].
——*Vita Columbae* (A. O. Anderson and M. O. Anderson (eds and trans), *Adomnan's Life of Columba*, Edinburgh 1961, 2nd edn Oxford 1991; and R. Sharpe (trans.), *Adomnán of Iona: Life of St Columba*, Harmondsworth 1995).
——*Canones* (L. Bieler (ed.), *The Irish Penitentials* (Dublin 1975), pp. 176–81) [Latin text with facing ET: *SLH* 5].
Ambrose, *Epistulae* [Latin text: *CSEL* 82; ET: *FC* 26].
Anon, *Cáin Domnaig* (J. G. O'Keeffe, 'Cáin Domnaig', *Ériu* 2 (1905), 189–204 [Irish text with ET]; V. Hull, 'Cáin Domnaig', *Ériu* 20 (1966), 151–77) [Irish text with ET]; and for the work in ET only: M. Herbert and M. MacNamara, *Irish Biblical Apocrypha: Selected Texts in Translation* (Edinburgh 1989), pp. 50–4).
——*Dies dominica* (R. E. McNally (ed.), *CCSL* 108B, pp. 175–86; ET: T. O'Loughlin, 'The Significance of Sunday: Three Ninth-Century Catecheses', *Worship* 64 (1990), 533–44).
——Litanies *see* C. Plummer (ed.), *Irish Litanies: Text and Translation* (London 1925) [*HBS* 62].
——The *Collectio Canonum Hibernensis* (H. Wasserschleben (ed.), *Die irische Kanonensammlung*, 2nd edn, Leipzig 1885).
——*The Irish Liber Hymnorum* (J. H. Bernard and R. Atkinson (eds), London 1898) [Latin text: *HBS* 13 and 14; no collected ET].
——*The Martyrology of Tallaght* (H. J. Lawlor and R. I. Best (eds), London 1931) [*HBS* 68].
——The *Nauigatio Sancti Brendani* (C. Selmer (ed.), *Navigatio Sancti Brendani Abbatis*, Notre Dame, IN 1959) [Latin text; ET: J. J. O'Meara, *The Voyage of St Brendan: Journey to the Promised Land*, Dublin 1976].
——The *Stowe Missal* (G. F. Warner (ed.), London 1906 and 1915) [*HBS* 31 and 32 (rept in one vol., 1989)].

——*The Teaching of Máel Rúain* (E. Gwynn (ed.), *The Rule of Tallaght* (Dublin and London 1927)) [Irish text with facing ET].

Augustine, *De bono coniugali* [Latin text: *CSEL* 41, pp. 185–231; ET: C. T. Wilcox, in R. J. Deferrari (ed.) *St Augustine: Treatises on Marriage and Other Subjects* [*FC* 27] (Washington 1995), pp. 3–51.]

—— *De ciuitate Dei* [Latin text: *CCSL* 47 and 48; ET: R. W. Dyson, *Augustine: The City of God against the Pagans* (Cambridge 1998)].

—— *De sermone Domini in monte* [Latin text: *CCSL* 35; ET: D. J. Kavanagh, Saint Augustine: Commenary on the Lord's Sermon on the Mount [*FC* 11] (Washington 1951).]

——*Tractatus in Ioannis euangelium* XXXIII, 7.

Bede, *Historia ecclesiastica gentis anglorum* (B. Colgrave and R. A. B. Mynors (eds), Oxford 1969) [Latin text with facing ET; and see the notes in C. Plummer's edition (Oxford 1896)].

——*De temporum ratione* (*CCSL* 223B, pp. 263–460; ET: F. Wallis, *Bede: The Reckoning of Time* (Liverpool 1999)).

Ps-Bede, *Collectanea* (M. Bayless, M. Lapidge, *et al.* (eds), Dublin 1998) [Latin text with facing ET: *SLH* 14].

Blathmac, *The Poems of Blathmac Son of Cú Brettan together with the Irish Gospel of Thomas and a poem on the Virgin Mary* (J. Carney (ed.), Dublin 1964) [Irish text with facing ET; *ITS* 47].

Cassian, J. *Conlationes* [Latin text: *CSEL* 13; ET: B. Ramsey, *John Cassian: The Conferences* (ACW 57) (NY 1997).]

Columbanus, *Paenitentiale* (L. Bieler (ed.), *The Irish Penitentials* (Dublin 1975), pp. 96–107) [Latin text with facing ET; *SLH* 5].

——*Regula coenobialis* (G. S. M. Walker (ed.), *Sancti Columbani opera* (Dublin 1957), pp. 142–68) [Latin text with facing ET; *SLH* 2].

Cummean, *Penitential* (L. Bieler (ed.), *The Irish Penitentials* (Dublin 1975), pp. 108–35) [Latin text with facing ET; *SLH* 5].

——*De controversia paschali* (D. Ó Cróinín and M. Walsh (eds), *Cummian's Letter De controversia paschali and the De ratione computandi*, Toronto 1988).

Eucherius of Lyons, *Formulae spiritalis intellegentiae* (*CSEL* 31, pp. 3–62).

Finnian [Vinnianus], *Penitential* (L. Bieler (ed.), *The Irish Penitentials* (Dublin 1975), pp. 74–95) [Latin text with facing ET: *SLH* 5].

Isidore of Seville, *Etymologiae* (W. M. Lindsay (ed.), Oxford 1911).

—— *In Genesim, PL* 83, 207–88.

Jerome, *Aduersus Heluidium* [Latin text : *PL* 23, 183–206; ET: J. N. Hritzu, *Saint Jerome: Dogmatic and Polenical Works* [*FC* 53] (Washington 1965), pp. 3–43.

—— *Aduersus Iouinianum* [Latin text: *PL* 23, 211–338; ET: *NPNF*, vol. 6, pp. 346–416].

——*Epistola XXII* [Latin text: *CSEL* 54; *NPNF*, vol. 6, pp. 22–41].

Muirchú moccu Machthéni, *Vita Patricii* (L. Bieler (ed.), *The Patrician Documents in the Book of Armagh* (Dublin 1979), pp. 62–125) [Latin text with facing ET: *SLH* 10; and see the translation by T. O'Loughlin in O. Davies with T. O'Loughlin (eds), *Celtic Spirituality* (Mahwah NJ 1999) which provides a scriptural apparatus].

Oengus mac Oengobann, *Félire Oengusso* (*The Martyrology of Oengus the Culdee*, W. Stokes (ed.), London 1905) [Irish text with facing ET: *HBS* 29 (rept Dublin 1984)].

Patrick, *Confessio* (N. J. D. White (ed.), 'Libri Sancti Patricii: The Latin Writings of St Patrick', *PRIA* 25c (1905), 201–326; or L. Bieler, *Libri Epistolarum Sancti Patricii Episcopi* (Dublin 1952); and see T. O'Loughlin, *Saint Patrick: The Man and His Works* (London 1999) for an annotated ET).

—— *Epistola ad milites Corotici* (as for the *Confessio*).

Prosper of Aquitaine, *De gratia Dei et libero arbitrio contra Collatorem* (*PL* 51, 213–76).

—— *Epitoma Chronicorum* (T. Mommsen (ed.), *Chronica minora* (Berlin 1892), vol. 1, pp. 385–485).

Vincent of Lérins, *Commonitorium* (R. Demeulenaere (ed.), Turnhout 1985) [Latin text: *CCSL* 64; ET: *NPNF* 2, 11].

Vinnianus, *see* Finnian.

Willibrord, *Calendar* (H. A. Wilson (ed.), *The Calendar of St. Willibrord from MS. Paris. Lat. 10837* (London 1918; rept Woodbridge, Suffolk 1998) [*HBS* 55].

SECONDARY LITERATURE

Allard, G. H., *Johannis Scoti Eriugenae Periphyseon Indices Generales* (Montréal and Paris 1983).

Anderson, A. O., *Early Sources of Scottish History: AD 500–1286* (Edinburgh 1922/Stamford 1990).

Avery, M., 'The Beneventan Lections for the Vigil of Easter and the Ambrosian Chant Banned by Pope Stephen IX at Montecassino', *SG* 1 (1947), 433–58.

Bagley, C. H., 'Litany of Loreto', *NCE* 8, 790–1.

Baumstark, A., *Comparative Liturgy* (rev. edn, B. Botte, ET: F. L. Cross, London 1958).

Bavel, T. van, 'The "Christus Totus" Idea: A Forgotten Aspect of Augustine's Spirituality', in T. Finan and V. Twomey (eds), *Studies in Patristic Christology* (Dublin 1998), pp. 84–94.

Beck, H. G. J., *The Pastoral Care of Souls in South-East France During the Sixth Century* (Rome 1950).

Bévenot, A., 'The Holy Maccabees', *The Month* 150 (1927), 107–14.

Bhreathnach, E., 'Temoria: Caput Scotorum?' *Ériu* 47 (1996), 67–88.

Bieler, L., 'The "Creeds" of St Victorinus and St Patrick', *TS* 9 (1948), 121–4.

——'The Celtic Hagiographer', *SP* 5 (1962), 241–65.

—— 'Hibernensis Collectio', *NCE* 6 (New York 1967), 1095.

——'Muirchú's Life of Patrick as a work of literature', *MA* 43 (1974), 219–33.

——'Hagiography and Romance in Medieval Ireland', *M&H* 6 (1975), 13–24.

——'Ancient Hagiography and the Lives of St Patrick', in F. Paolo and M. Barrera (eds), *Forma Futuri: Studi in onore del Cardinale Michele Pellegrino* (Turin 1975), pp. 650–5.

Billy, D., 'The Penitentials and "The Making of Moral Theology" ', *LS* 14 (1989), 143–51.

Binchy, D. A., 'Patrick and His Biographers, Ancient and Modern', *SH* 2 (1962), 7–173.

Bishop, E., 'The Litany of the Saints in the Stowe Missal', *Liturgica Historica: Papers on the Liturgy and Religious Life of the Western Church* (Oxford 1918), pp. 137–64 [= *JTS* 7 (1906), 122–36].

Bloch, M., *The Historian's Craft* (ET: P. Putnam, Manchester, rept 1992).

Boswell, C. S., *An Irish Precursor of Dante* (London 1908).

Bourgeault, C., 'The Monastic Archetype in the *Navigatio* of St. Brendan', *MonS* 14 (1983), 109–22.

Bourke, C., 'The Work of Angels?', *IR* 50 (1999), 76–9.

Bradley, I., *Celtic Christianity: Making Myths and Chasing Dreams* (Edinburgh 1999).

Bray, D. A., 'A Note on the Life of St Brendan', *CS* 20 (1985), 14–20.

——'Allegory in the *Navigatio Sancti Brendani*', *Viator* 26 (1995), 1–10.

Breatnach, L., 'Canon Law and Secular Law in Early Ireland: The Significance of *Bretha Nemed*', *Peritia* 3 (1984), 439–59.

——'Law', in K. McCone and K. Simms (eds), *Progress in Medieval Irish Studies* (Maynooth 1996), pp. 107–21.

Brennan, M., *A Guide to Eriugenian Studies: A Survey of Publications 1930–1987* (Fribourg and Paris 1989).

Bright, P., *The Book of Rules of Tyconius: Its Purpose and Inner Logic* (Notre Dame, IN 1988).

Brock, S., 'The Queen of Sheba's Questions to Solomon: A Syriac Version', *Le Muséon* 92 (1979), 331–45.

Brooke, C., *The Medieval Idea of Marriage* (Oxford 1989).

Brundage, J. A., *Medieval Canon Law* (London 1995).

Bullough, D. A., 'Columba, Adomnán, and the Achievement of Iona', *SHR* 43 (1964), 111–30 and 44 (1965), 17–33.

Bury, J. B., *The Life of St Patrick and his Place in History* (London 1905).

Cahill, T. *How the Irish Saved Civilization: The Untold Story of Ireland's Heroic Role from the Fall of Rome to the Rise of Medieval Europe* (London 1995).

Carney, J., *Studies in Irish Literature and History* (Dublin 1955).

——*The Problem of St. Patrick* (Dublin 1961).

——Review of Selmer's edition of the *Nauigatio, MA* 32 (1963), 37–44.

Carr, E. H., *What is History?* (Harmondsworth 1964).

Charles-Edwards, T., 'Palladius, Prosper, and Leo the Great: Mission and Primatial Authority', in D. N. Dumville, *et al.* (eds), *Saint Patrick, AD 493–1993* (Woodbridge 1993), pp. 1–12.

——'The Construction of the *Hibernensis*', *Peritia* 12 (1998), 209–37.

Clancy, F. G., 'The Irish Penitentials', *MS* 21 (1988), 87–109.

Clancy, T. O., and Márkus, G., *Iona: The Earliest Poetry of a Celtic Monastery* (Edinburgh 1995).

Conneely, D., *The Letters of Saint Patrick* (Maynooth 1993).

Connolly, H., *The Irish Penitentials and their Significance for the Sacrament of Penance Today* (Dublin 1995).

Cross, F. M., *The Ancient Library of Qumran* (3rd edn, Sheffield 1995).

Cusack, P., *An Interpretation of the Second Dialogue of Gregory the Great: Hagiography and St. Benedict* (Lampeter 1993).

Daniel-Rops, H., *The Miracle of Ireland* (ET: The Earl of Wicklow, Dublin 1959).

Davies, W., 'The Myth of the Celtic Church', in N. Edwards and A. Lane (eds), *The Early Church in Wales and the West: Recent Work in Early Christian Archaeology, History and Place-Names* (Oxbow Monograph 16) (London 1992).

Delehaye, H., *The Legends of the Saints* (Brussels 1905; ET: London 1962; rept Dublin 1998).

de Paor, L., *Saint Patrick's World* (Dublin 1993).

Department of the Environment for Northern Ireland, *Historic Monuments of Northern Ireland* (Belfast 1983).

Dix, G., *The Shape of the Liturgy* (London 1945).

Duchesne, L., *Christian Worship: Its Origins and Evolution* (ET: M. L. McClure, 5th edn London 1923).

Dumville, D. N., 'Latin and Irish in the Annals of Ulster, AD 431–1050', in D. Whitelock, R. McKitterick, D. Dumville (eds), *Ireland in Early Medieval Europe* (Cambridge 1982), pp. 320–41.

——'Gildas and Uinniau', in M. Lapidge and D. Dumville (eds), *Gildas: New Approaches* (Woodbridge 1984), pp. 207–214.

——'Two approaches to the dating of "Nauigatio Sancti Brendani" ', *SM* 29 (1988), 87–102.

Duncan, A. A. M., 'Bede, Iona, and the Picts', in R. H. C. Davis and J. M. Wallace-Hadrill (eds), *The Writing of History in the Middle Ages: Essays Presented to Richard William Southern* (Oxford 1981), pp. 1–42.

Evans, G. R., *The Logic and Language of the Bible: The Earlier Middle Ages* (Cambridge 1984).

Finegan, J., *Handbook of Biblical Chronology* (rev. edn, Peabody MA 1998).

Fitzgerald, W., 'Father Moore's Well at Rathbride, County Kildare', *JCKAS* 7 (1912–1914), 329–32.

Fournier, P., and Le Bras, G., *Histoire des collections canoniques en Occident depuis les fausses décrétales jusqu'au Décret de Gratien* (2 vols, Paris 1931–32).

Frantzen, A. J., 'The Significance of the Frankish Penitentials', *JEH* 30 (1979), 409–21.

Gardiner, E., *Medieval Visions of Heaven and Hell: A Sourcebook* (New York/London 1992).

Gingras, G. E., *Egeria: Diary of a Pilgrimage* (New York 1993).

Gogan, L. S., *The Ardagh Chalice* (Dublin 1932).

Gorman, M. M., 'A Critique of Bischoff's Theory of Irish Exegesis', *JML* 7 (1997), 178–233.

Grant, R. M., 'Paul, Galen, and Origen', *JTS* ns 34 (1983), 533–6.

Gratsch, E. J., 'Litany, Liturgical use of', *NCE* 8, 789–90.

Grogan, B. 'Eschatological Teaching of the Early Irish Church', in M. McNamara (ed.), *Biblical Studies: The Medieval Irish Contribution* (Dublin 1975) [= *PIBA* 1], pp. 46–58

Gwynn, A., 'The Problem of the *Dicta Patricii*', *SA* 8 (1975–7), 69–80.

Gwynn, J., *Liber Ardmachanus: The Book of Armagh edited with Introduction and Appendices* (Dublin 1913).

Hanson, R. P. C., 'Witness from St. Patrick to the Creed of 381', *AnB* 101 (1983), 297–9.

——*The Life and Writings of the Historical Saint Patrick* (New York 1983).

——'The Mission of St Patrick', in J. Mackey (ed.), *An Introduction to Celtic Christianity* (Edinburgh 1989), pp. 22–44.

Harbison, P., *Guide to the National Monuments in the Republic of Ireland* (Dublin 1970).

Hay, D., *Annalists and Historians: Western Historiography from the Eighth to the Eighteenth Century* (London 1977).

Heist, W. W., *The Fifteen Signs Before Doomsday* (East Lansing 1952).

——'The Fifteen Signs before the Judgement: Further Remarks', *MedS* 22 (1960), 192–203.

Hennig, J., 'The Function of the Martyrology of Tallaght', *MedS* 26 (1964), 315–28.

Herbert, M., *Iona, Kells and Derry: the History and Hagiography of the Monastic* familia *of Columba* (Oxford 1988).

——and M. McNamara, *Irish Biblical Apocrypha: Selected Texts in Translation* (Edinburgh 1989).

Hillers, B., 'Voyages Between Heaven and Hell: Navigating the Early Irish *Immran* Tales', *PHCC* 13 (1995), 66–81.

Honigmann, E., 'Stephen of Ephesus (April 15, 448–Oct. 29, 451) and the Legend of the Seven Sleepers', in *Patristic Studies (Studi e Testi 173)* (Rome 1953), pp. 125–68.

Hopper, V. F., *Medieval Number Symbolism: Its Sources, Meaning, and Influence on Thought and Expression* (New York 1938).

Howlett, D., *The Book of Letters of Saint Patrick the Bishop* (Dublin 1994).

Hughes, K., 'On an Irish Litany of Pilgrim Saints compiled *c.* 800', *AnB* 77 (1959), 305–31.

——*The Church in Early Irish Society* (London 1966).

——*Early Christian Ireland: Introduction to the Sources* (Cambridge 1972).

——'The Celtic Church: Is This a Valid Concept?', *CMCS* 1 (1981), 1–20.

——and A. Hamlyn, *The Early Traveller to the Early Irish Church* (London 1977).

Ireland, C., 'Aldfrith of Northumbria and the Learning of a *Sapiens*', in K. A. Klar, E. E. Sweetser and C. Thomas (eds), *A Celtic Florilegium: Studies in Memory of Brendan O Herir* (Lawrence MA 1996), pp. 63–77.

Jackson, P., 'The Holy Wells of Co. Kildare', *JCKAS* 16 (1979–1980), 133–61.

Jardine Grisbrooke, W., 'Litany', in J. G. Davies (ed.), *A Dictionary of Liturgy and Worship* (London 1972), pp. 215–16.

——'Litany', in J. G. Davies (ed.), *A New Dictionary of Liturgy and Worship* (London 1986), pp. 305–7.

Johnston, L. T., 'Imagining the World Scripture Imagines', *Modern Theology* 14 (1998), 165–80.

Jones, C. W., 'Some Introductory Remarks on Bede's Commentary on Genesis', *SE* 19 (1969), 115–98.

Kelly, F., *A Guide to Early Irish Law* (Dublin 1988).

——*Early Irish Farming* (Dublin 1997).

Kelly, J. F., 'Hiberno-Latin Exegesis and Exegetes', *AM* 22 (1981), 46–60.

——'The Escape of Saint Patrick from Ireland', *SP* 18 (1985), 41–5.

——'A Catalogue of Early Medieval Hiberno-Latin Biblical Commentaries (II)', *Traditio* 45 (1989–90), 393–434.

Kelly, J. N. D., *Early Christian Creeds* (London 1950).

Kenney, J. F., 'The Legend of St Brendan', *TRSC* 14 (1920), 51–67.

——*The Sources for the Early History of Ireland* (New York 1929).

Kilmartin, E. J., *The Eucharist in the West: History and Theology* (Collegeville, MN 1998).

Klingshirn, W., 'Charity and Power: Caesarius of Arles and the Ransoming of Captives in Sub-Roman Gaul', *JRS* 75 (1985), 183–203.

Knowles, M. D., 'Jean Mabillon', *JEH* 10 (1959), 153–73.

——*Great Historical Enterprises* (London 1963).

Kondratiev, A., *The Apple Branch: A Path to Celtic Ritual* (Cork 1998).

Kuttner, S. G., *Harmony from Dissonance: An Interpretation of Medieval Canon Law* (Latrobe 1960).

Ladner, G. B., *The Idea of Reform: Its Impact on Christian Thought and Action in the Age of the Fathers* (Cambridge, MA 1959).

Laeuchli, S., *Power and Sexuality: The Emergence of Canon at the Synod of Elvira* (Philadelphia 1972).

Lapidge, M. and Sharpe, R., *A Bibliography of Celtic-Latin Literature 400–1200* (Dublin 1985).

Lees, C. A., 'The "Sunday Letter" and the "Sunday Lists" ', *ASE* 14 (1985), 129–51.

McCready, W. D., *Miracles and the Venerable Bede* (Toronto 1994).

McGregor, A. J., *Fire and Light in the Western Triduum: Their Use at Tenebrae and at the Paschal Vigil* (Collegeville MN 1992).

McHugh, J., *The Mother of Jesus in the New Testament* (London 1975).

Mackin, T., *The Marital Sacrament* (New York 1989).

McNally, R. E., *The Bible in the Middle Ages* (Westminster, MD 1959).

McNeill, J. T., 'Medicine for Sin as Prescribed in the Penitentials', *CH* 1 (1932), 14–26.

——and Gamer, H. M., *Medieval Handbooks of Penance* (New York 1938).

Macquarrie, A., *The Saints of Scotland: Essays in Scottish Church History AD 450–1093* (Edinburgh 1997).

MacQueen, J., *Numerology: Theory and Outline History of a Literary Mode* (Edinburgh 1985).

Maher, M., 'Sunday in the Irish Church', *ITQ* 61 (1994), 161–84.

Mare, W. H., 'Jehoshaphat, Valley of', *ABD* 3, pp. 668–9.

Martínez Díez, G., 'Hispana Collectio (Isidoriana)', *NCE* 7, 1.

Mathisen, R. W., 'Prosper of Aquitaine', *DMA* 10, 153–4.

Maude, J. H., 'Litany', *ERE* 8, pp. 78–81.

Meek, D. E., 'Modern Celtic Christianity: The Contemporary Revival and its Roots', *SBET* 10 (1992), 6–31.

——'Modern Celtic Christianity', in T. Brown (ed.), *Celticism. Studia Imagologica: Amsterdam Studies on Cultural Identity* 8 (1996), 143–57 (Amsterdam 1996).

——'Surveying the Saints: Reflections on Recent Writings on "Celtic Christianity" ', *SBET* 15 (1997), 50–60.

Moore, C. A., *Daniel, Esther and Jeremiah: The Additions* (New York 1977).

Moran, D., *The Philosophy of John Scottus Eriugena: A Study of Idealism in the Middle Ages* (Cambridge 1989).

Muldoon, J., 'Medieval Canon Law and the Formation of International Law', *ZSSR* 112 (1995), 64–82.

Murray, R., 'Hebrew Bible, Jewish Scriptures, Christian Old Testament', *The Month* 259 (1998), 468–74.

Nagy, J. F., *Conversing with Angels and Ancients* (Dublin 1997).

Ní Chatháin, P., 'The Liturgical Background of the Derrynaflan Altar Service', *JRSAI* 110 (1980), 127–48.

Ní Dhonnchadha, M., 'The Guarantor List of *Cáin Adomnáin*, 697', *Peritia* 1 (1982), 178–215.

——'The *Lex Innocentium*: Adomnán's Law for Women, Clerics and Youths, 697 AD', in M. O'Dowd and S. Wichert (eds), *Chattel, Servant or Citizen: Women's Status in Church, State and Society* (Belfast 1995), pp. 58–69.

Nodet, É., and Taylor, J., *The Origins of Christianity: An Exploration* (Collegeville, MN 1998).

Oakley, T. P., 'Cultural Affiliations of early Ireland in the penitentials', *Speculum* 8 (1933), 489–500.

—— 'The Penitentials as Sources for Medieval History', *Speculum* 15 (1940), 210–23.

Ó Corráin, D., 'Irish Law and Canon Law', in P. Ní Chatháin and M. Richter (eds), *Irland und Europa: Die Kirche im Frühmittelalter* (Stuttgart 1984), pp. 157–66.

——, Breatnach, L., and Breen, A., 'The Laws of the Irish', *Peritia* 3 (1984), 382–438.

Ó Cróinín, D., and Walsh, M. (eds), *Cummian's Letter De controversia paschali and the De ratione computandi* (Toronto 1988).

O'Donoghue, N. D., *Aristocracy of Soul: Patrick of Ireland* (London 1987).

O'Loughlin, T., 'Knowing God and Knowing the Cosmos: Augustine's Legacy of Tension', *IPJ* 6 (1989), 27–58.

——'The Significance of Sunday: Three Ninth-Century Catecheses', *Worship* 64 (1990), 533–44.

——'Newman, Vincent of Lérins and Development', *ITQ* 58 (1991), 147–66.

——'The Exegetical Purpose of Adomnán's *De Locis Sanctis*', *CMCS* 24 (1992), 37–53.

——'Adam's Burial at Hebron: Some Aspects of its Significance in the Latin Tradition', *PIBA* 15 (1992), 66–88.

——'Adam's Rib and the Equality of the Sexes: Some Medieval Exegesis of Gn 2:21–22', *ITQ* 59 (1993), 44–54.

——'Julian of Toledo's *Antikeimenon* and the Development of Latin Exegesis', *PIBA* 16 (1993), 80–98.

——'The Library of Iona in the Late Seventh Century: The Evidence from Adomnán's *De Locis Sanctis*', *Ériu* 45 (1994), 33–52.

——'St Patrick and an Irish Theology', *D&L* 44 (1994), 153–9.

——'The Latin Version of the Scriptures in use on Iona', *Peritia* 8 (1994), 18–26.

——'The Symbol gives Life: Eucherius of Lyons' Formula for Exegesis', in T. Finan and V. Twomey (eds), *Scriptural Interpretation in the Fathers: Letter and Spirit* (Dublin 1995), pp. 221–52.

——'Adomnán the Illustrious', *IR* 46 (1995), 1–14.

——' "The Waters above the Heavens": Isidore and the Latin Tradition', *MS* 36 (1995), 104–17.

——'The Controversy over Methuselah's Death: Proto-Chronology and the Origins of the Western Concept of Inerrancy', *RTAM* 62 (1995), 182–225.

——'Newman and *Doing* Theology', *NB* 76 (1995), 92–8.

——'The Latin Sources of Medieval Irish Culture', in K. McCone and K. Simms (eds), *Progress in Medieval Irish Studies* (Maynooth 1996), pp. 91–105.

——'The View from Iona: Adomnán's Mental Maps', *Peritia* 10 (1996), 98–122.

——'Adomnán and *mira rotunditas*', *Ériu* 47 (1996), 95–9.

——' "The Gates of Hell": From Metaphor to Fact', *MS* 38 (1996), 98–114.

——'Biblical Contradictions in the *Periphyseon* and the Development of Eriugena's Method', in G. Van Riel, C. Steele and J. McEvoy (eds), *Iohannes Scottus Eriugena: The Bible and Hermeneutics* (Leuven 1996), pp. 103–26.

——'Adomnán and Arculf: The Case of an Expert Witness', *JML* 7 (1997), 127–46.

——'*Res, tempus, locus, persona*: Adomnán's exegetical method', *IR* 48 (1997), 95–111.

——'Marriage and Sexuality in the *Hibernensis*', *Peritia* 11 (1997), 188–206.

——'Adomnán's *De Locis Sanctis*: A Textual Emendation and an Additional Source Identification', *Ériu* 48 (1997), 37–40.

——'Living in the Ocean', in C. Bourke (ed.), *Studies in the Cult of Saint Columba* (Dublin 1997), pp. 11–23.

——'The Mysticism of Number in the Medieval Period before Eriugena', in J. J. Cleary (ed.), *The Perennial Tradition of Neoplatonism* (Leuven 1997), pp. 397–416.

——'Individual Anonymity and Collective Identity: the Enigma of Early Medieval Latin Theologians', *RTPM* 64 (1997), 291–314.

——'Medieval Church History: Beyond apologetics, after development, the awkward memories', *The Way* 38 (1998), 65–76.

——'The Celtic homily: Creeds and Eschatology', *MS* 41 (1998), 99–115.

——'Christ as the focus of Genesis Exegesis in Isidore of Seville', in T. Finan and V. Twomey (eds), *Studies in Patristic Christology* (Dublin 1998), pp. 144–62.

——'Rhygyfarch's *Vita Dauidis*: An Apparatus biblicus', *StC* 32 (1998), 179–88.

——'Christ and the Scriptures: the Chasm between Modern and Premodern Exegesis', *The Month* 259 (1998), 475–85.

——'Tradition and Exegesis in the Eighth Century: The Use of Patristic Sources in Early Medieval Scriptural Commentaries', in T. O'Loughlin (ed.), *The Scriptures and Early Medieval Ireland* (Turnhout 1999), pp. 217–39.

——*Saint Patrick: The Man and His Works* (London 1999).

——*Teachers and Code-Breakers: The Latin Genesis Tradition, 430–800* (Turnhout 1999).

——'The List of Illustrious Writers in the Pseudo-Bedan Collectanea', in H. Conrad O'Briain, A. M. D'Arcy and J. Scattergood (eds), *Text and Gloss: Studies in Insular Learning and Literature Presented to Joseph Donovan Pheiffer* (Dublin 1999), pp. 34–48.

——'Distant Islands: The Topography of Holiness in the *Nauigatio Sancti Brendani*', in Marion Glasscoe (ed.), *The Medieval Mystical Tradition: England, Ireland, Wales (Exeter Symposium VI)* (Woodbridge 1999), pp. 1–20.

——'Penitentials and Pastoral Care', in G. R. Evans (ed.), *A History of Pastoral Care* (London 2000), pp. 93–111.

——'The Tombs of the Saints: their significance for Adomnán', in M. Herbert (ed.), *Proceedings of the 1997 International Hagiography Conference* (Dublin 2000).

——'The Diffusion of Adomnán's *De locis sanctis* in the Medieval Period', in C. Swift, *et al.* (eds), *Proceedings of the 1997 Derry Conference on Columba*, forthcoming.

——'Palestine in the aftermath of the Arab conquest: the earliest Latin account', in R. N. Swanson (ed.), *Studies in Church History*, forthcoming.

——'A Woman's Plight and the Western Fathers', in L. J. Kreitzer (ed.), *Scribblings in the Sand: Interpretations of the Adulterous Woman (John 7:53–8:11)*, forthcoming.

——'The Plan of the New Jerusalem in the Book of Armagh', *CMCS*, forthcoming.

——'Master and Pupil: Christian Perspectives', in *The Encyclopedia of Monasticism*, forthcoming.

——and H. Conrad-O'Briain, 'The "baptism of tears" in early Anglo-Saxon sources', *ASE* 22 (1993), 65–83.

O'Meara, J. J., *Eriugena* (Oxford 1988).

O'Rahilly, T. F., 'The History of the Stowe Missal', *Ériu* 10 (1926), 95–109.

O'Reilly, J., 'Exegesis and the Book of Kells: the Lucan genealogy', in T. Finan and V. Twomey (eds), *Scriptural Interpretation in the Fathers: Letter and Spirit* (Dublin 1995), pp. 315–55.

——'Gospel Harmony and the Names of Christ: Insular Images of a Patristic Theme', in J. Sharpe and K. Van Kampen (eds), *The Bible as Book: The Manuscript Tradition* (London 1998), pp. 73–88.

Ó Riain, P., 'The Tallaght Martyrologies, Redated', *CMCS* 20 (1990), 21–38.

——*Anglo-Saxon Ireland: the evidence of the Martyrology of Tallaght* (Cambridge 1993).

Osborne, K. B., *Reconciliation and Justification: The Sacrament and its Theology* (New York 1990).

Pagels, E. H., *Adam, Eve, and the Serpent* (London 1988).

——' "Freedom from Necessity": Philosophic and Personal Dimensions of Christian Conversion', in G. A. Robbins (ed.), *Genesis 1–3 in the History of Exegesis: Intrigue in the Garden* (Lewiston NY 1988), pp. 69–97.

Payer, P. J., 'The Humanism of the Penitentials and the Continuity of the Penitential Tradition', *MedS* 46 (1984), 340–54.

——*Sex and the Penitentials: The Development of a Sexual Code 550–1150* (Toronto 1984).

Plummer, C. (ed.), *Irish Litanies: Text and Translation* (London 1925).

Porter, H. B., *The Day of Light* (2nd edn, Washington 1987).

Poschmann, B., *Penance and the Anointing of the Sick* (ET: F. Courtney, London 1963).

Rambaud-Buhot, J., 'Hadriana Collectio', *NCE* 4, 876.

Ramsey, M., *The Narratives of the Passion* (London 1962).

Ranke-Heinemann, U., *Eunuchs for the Kingdom of Heaven* (ET: P. Heinegg, Harmondsworth 1990).

Ray, R. D., 'What do we know about Bede's Commentaries?' *RTAM* 49 (1982), 5–20.

Reynolds, P. L., *Marriage in the Western Church: The Christianization of Marriage During the Patristic and Early Medieval Periods* (Leiden 1994).

Reynolds, R. E., 'Unity and Diversity in Carolingian Canon Law Collections: The Case of the *Collectio Hibernensis* and Its

Derivatives', in U.-R. Blumenthal (ed.), *Carolingian Essays: Andrew W. Mellon Lectures in Early Christian Studies* (Washington 1983), pp. 99–135.

Ricci, C., *Mary Magdalene and Many Others* (ET: P. Burns, London 1994).

Richard, M., 'Enfer', *DTC* 5, cols 47–49.

Richardson, H., and J. Scarry, *An Introduction to Irish High Crosses* (Cork 1990).

Richter, M., *Ireland and her Neighbours in the Seventh Century* (Dublin 1999).

Rordorf, W., *Sunday: The History of the Day of Rest and Worship in the Earliest Centuries of the Christian Church* (ET: A. A. K. Graham, London 1968).

Ryan, D., 'Perpetual Virginity', in K. McNamara (ed.), *Mother of the Redeemer* (Dublin 1959), pp. 104–34.

Ryan, J., 'The *Cáin Adomnáin*', in D. A. Binchy (ed.), *Studies in Early Irish Law* (Dublin 1936), pp. 269–76.

——'The Mass in the Early Irish Church', *Studies* 50 (1961), 371–84.

Ryan, J. J., 'Observations on pre-Gratian canonical collections: Some recent work and present problems', *Congrès de Droit Canonique Médiéval, Louvain et Bruxelles: 22–26 Juillet* (Louvain 1959), pp. 88–103.

Ryan, M., 'The Derrynaflan and other early Irish eucharistic chalices: some speculations', in P. Ní Chatháin and M. Richter (eds), *Irland und Europa: Die Kirche im Frühmittelalter* (Stuttgart 1984), pp. 135–48.

——'The Derrynaflan Hoard and Early Irish Art', *Speculum* 72 (1997), 995–1017.

—— (ed.), *The Derrynaflan Hoard I: A Preliminary Account* (Dublin 1983).

Sabourin, L., *The Psalms: Their Origin and Meaning* (New York 1974).

Sandelin, S., 'The Date and Provenance of the "Litany of Irish Saints – II" (The Irish Litany of Pilgrim Saints)', *PRIA* 75c (1975), 251–62.

Schwartz, W., 'The Meaning of *Fidus interpres* in Medieval Translation', *JTS* 45 (1944), 73–8.

Searle, M. (ed.), *Sunday Morning: A Time for Worship* (Collegeville 1982).

Seymour, St J. D., 'The Bringing Forth of the Soul in Irish Literature', *JTS* 22 (1921), 16–20.

——'The Signs of Doomsday in the *Saltair na Rann*', *PRIA* 36c (1923), 154–63.

——'The Eschatology of the Early Irish Church', *ZCP* 14 (1923), 179–211.

Sharpe, R., 'Palaeographical Considerations in the Study of the Patrician Documents in the Book of Armagh', *Scriptorium* 36 (1983), 3–28.

Sims-Williams, P., 'Celtomania and Celtoscepticism', *CMCS* 36 (1998), 1–35.

——'The Medieval World of Robin Flower', in M. de Mórdha (ed.), *Bláithín: Flower* (Dingle 1998), pp. 73–96.

Smith, J. Z., *Divine Drudgery: On the Comparison of Early Christianities and the Religions of Antiquity* (London 1990).

Somerville, R., and Brasington, B. C., *Prefaces to Canon Law Books in Latin Christianity: Selected Translations 500–700* (New Haven, Conn. 1998).

Stevenson, J. B., 'The Monastic Rules of Columbanus', in M. Lapidge (ed.), *Columbanus: Studies on the Latin Writings* (Woodbridge 1997), pp. 203–16.

Stewart, C., *Cassian the Monk* (Oxford 1998).

Stickler, A. M., *The Case for Clerical Celibacy* (San Francisco 1995).

Stokes, W., and Strachan, J., *Thesaurus Palaeohibernicus: A Collection of Old-Irish glosses, scholia, prose and verse* (2 vols, Cambridge 1901–3) with a *Supplement* (Halle 1910) (the whole work was reprinted in 2 vols, Dublin 1975).

Straw, C., *Gregory the Great: Perfection in Imperfection* (Berkeley 1988).

Thompson, E. A., *The Visigoths in the Time of Ulfila* (Oxford 1966).

——'St. Patrick and Coroticus', *JTS* n.s. 31 (1980), 12–27.

van der Meer, F., *Augustine the Bishop* (London 1961).

Van Riel, G., Steele, C. and McEvoy, J. (eds), *Iohannes Scottus Eriugena: The Bible and Hermeneutics* (Leuven 1996).

Verbraken, P., 'Une "Laus cerei" africaine', *RB* 70 (1960), 301–12.

Voll, U., 'Sins, Capital', *NCE*, vol. 13, pp. 253–4.

Warren, F. E., *The Liturgy and Ritual of the Celtic Church* (London 1881; 2nd edn, with introduction and bibliography by J. Stevenson, Woodbridge 1987).

Wasserschleben, F. W. H., *Die Bussordnungen der abendländischen Kirche nebst einer rechtgeschichtlichen Einleitung* (Halle 1851).

Wolf, C. U., 'Tribe', *IDB* (1962), 4, pp. 698–701.

Index of Biblical References

General Index

Daniela Folco

Mistero a Roma

di Ivan Canu

Redazione: Daniela Difrancesco
Progetto grafico e direzione artistica: Nadia Maestri
Grafica al computer: Carlo Cibrario-Sent, Simona Corniola
Ricerca iconografica: Alice Graziotin

© 2014 Cideb

Prima edizione: gennaio 2014

Crediti: Istockphoto; Dreams Time; Shutterstock Images; DeAgostini
Picture Library: 13, 14; Tips Images: 16, 66.

Saremo lieti di ricevere i vostri commenti o eventuali suggerimenti,
e di fornirvi ulteriori informazioni sulle nostre pubblicazioni:
info@blackcat-cideb.com

Le soluzioni degli esercizi sono disponibili sul sito:
blackcat-cideb.com

Member of CISQ Federation

RINA
ISO 9001:2008
Certified Quality System

IQNet

The design, production and distribution of educational materials
for the CIDEB brand are managed in compliance with the rules of
Quality Management System which fulfils the requirements of the
standard ISO 9001 (Rina Cert. No. 24298/02/S - IQNet Reg. No. IT-80096)

ISBN 978-88-530-1434-4   libro + CD

Stampato in Italia da Litoprint, Genova

Indice

Questi simboli indicano l'inizio e la fine dei brani collegati ad attività di ascolto.

Esercizi in stile CELI 2 (Certificato di conoscenza della lingua italiana), livello B1.

Personaggi

Da sinistra a destra: l'investigatore Lucio Silvi e la sua segretaria, Giusi Rosso; Mark Staub
e la sua segretaria, Elisa Bondi; il commissario Felisi; il professor Francesco Peltri;
il mercante d'arte Dino Aussone; Fausto Giovannelli, ladro di opere d'arte.

Prima di leggere

1 Troverai queste parole nel capitolo 1. Associa ogni parola all'immagine corrispondente.

a luna   d furgone   g coperchio

b pila   e poltrona   h statua

c cassa   f scrivania   i pugno

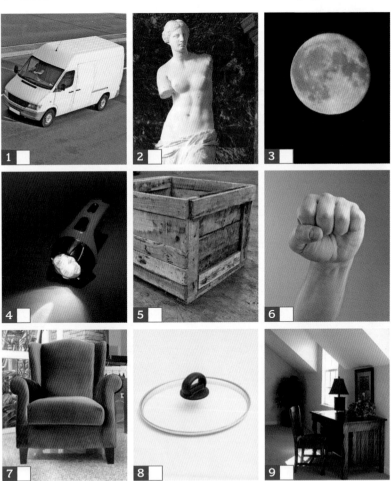

Un furto nella notte

notte. La luna brilla in cielo. Figure scure camminano
lungo la via Appia. La prima è di un uomo alto e magro.

Gli uomini scavalcano [1] un recinto. Scendono alcuni
scalini ed entrano in una tomba romana, scoperta di
recente.

"Attenzione!" sussurra il primo con una pila in mano.

La luce si muove sulle pareti e sul pavimento. Gli uomini
camminano adagio.

"Là!" indica uno.

Gli uomini si chinano. Tolgono terra e sabbia, sollevano il
coperchio di una cassa.

---

1. **scavalca** : oltrepassa, attraversa, supera.

CAPITOLO 1

"Muovetevi!"

Qualcosa brilla: un braccio e una mano d'oro.

"Svelti! Svelti! È la statua di Apollo che abbiamo trovato ieri" spiega la voce. "E domani sarà già all'estero..."

Sotto la luna brilla la statua d'oro. Gli uomini corrono via. Un furgone sparisce nella notte...

Il giorno seguente il sole splende su Roma. La luce entra dalla finestra e illumina un ufficio come tanti: ci sono una vecchia poltrona, una vecchia sedia e un giovane uomo, seduto ad una scrivania. Il detective privato Lucio Silvi, un bel ragazzo sui trentacinque anni, beve un caffè. Ha splendidi occhi azzurri, un sorriso simpatico e un cuore gentile.

La sua segretaria, Giusi Rosso, gli porta la posta. E in quel momento pensa: 'Da settimane non ci sono clienti...'

Silvi sospira, preoccupato: "Solo conti da pagare!"

Apre il giornale per leggere le ultime notizie.

Giusi aspetta paziente gli ordini dal capo. Ha una maglietta rosa e un paio di jeans nuovi, ma pensa che Silvi non se ne accorgerà, perché la considera solo come una brava aiutante. Giusi però non sa che, in realtà, lui non vuole confessare di apprezzarla, anzi, di volerle bene...

Silvi di colpo esclama: "Un altro furto!"

"Cos'hanno rubato?" chiede Giusi.

"Una statua del dio Apollo" risponde il detective, e spiega: "Gli archeologi l'avevano appena trovata. È sparita!"

"Chi l'ha rubata?" chiede la ragazza.

"Oh, i soliti furfanti. C'è un florido[2] mercato di oggetti antichi, sai?"

---

2. **florido** : ricco, grande, notevole.

CAPITOLO 1

"Cioè?"

"Statue e anfore romane sono molto richieste dai commercianti di antichità."

Proprio in quel momento Mark Staub, direttore di un famoso museo di Berlino, si trova in un elegante ristorante di via Condotti. È molto arrabbiato.

"Non voglio più nulla e soprattutto non voglio questa statua!" grida all'uomo alto e magro che gli sta davanti.

I clienti del ristorante li osservano stupiti.

Fausto Giovannelli guarda Max Staub con un'espressione minacciosa.

"Hai ordinato tu il furto della statua, perché non la vuoi più?" chiede a voce bassa, agitando i pugni.

"Stai calmo, non vedi che tutti ci guardano?" dice Staub, che non desidera attirare l'attenzione. "C'è troppa polizia in giro: è pericoloso!"

"Non parlerai, vero?" gli chiede Giovannelli, stringendogli il braccio.

"Certo che parlerò, se necessario. Mi difenderò... dirò tutto e farò i nomi di chi mi ha offerto oggetti di incerta provenienza."

"Non ne uscirai vivo!" lo minaccia l'altro. Poi esce dal ristorante sbattendo la porta. Vendere la statua è per lui una questione di vita o di morte...

Mark Staub guarda preoccupato il cielo e le nuvole.

'Devo stare molto attento!' pensa mentre cammina lungo via Condotti, una delle strade più note di Roma.

Comprensione scritta e orale

1 Rileggi il capitolo e indica se le seguenti affermazioni sono vere (V) o false (F).

		V	F
1	A mezzogiorno alcuni uomini entrano in una tomba.	☐	☐
2	Un uomo grida: "Ecco i panini!"	☐	☐
3	Un autobus sparisce nella notte.	☐	☐
4	L'ufficio di Silvi è molto elegante.	☐	☐
5	Lucio Silvi ha splendidi occhi azzurri.	☐	☐
6	Giusi Rosso fa l'infermiera.	☐	☐
7	Mark Staub è il direttore di un museo.	☐	☐
8	La segretaria di Lucio Silvi si chiama Maria.	☐	☐

2 Completa ogni frase con il nome di un personaggio.

1 .... è una ragazza carina.

2 .... è molto arrabbiato.

3 .... è il direttore di un museo.

4 .... è un detective.

5 .... commenta sui recenti furti.

6 .... porta la posta.

Competenze linguistiche

1 Indica l'intruso.

	a			b			c			d		
1	a	☐ camminare	b	☐ nuotare	c	☐ correre	d	☐ leggere
2	a	☐ via	b	☐ strada	c	☐ vicolo	d	☐ stazione
3	a	☐ simpatico	b	☐ magro	c	☐ grasso	d	☐ alto
4	a	☐ cucchiaio	b	☐ forchetta	c	☐ pila	d	☐ coltello
5	a	☐ braccio	b	☐ mano	c	☐ testa	d	☐ finestra
6	a	☐ domani	b	☐ ieri	c	☐ oggi	d	☐ giorno

Grammatica

Gli aggettivi interrogativi

Gli aggettivi interrogativi sono: **che, quale/quali, quanto, quanti, quante.**

L'aggettivo interrogativo **che** è invariabile. Il plurale dell'aggettivo interrogativo **quale** è **quali.** Il plurale dell'aggettivo interrogativo **quanto** è **quanti** per il maschile e **quante** per il femminile.

Che tempo fa?   *Che ore sono?*   *Che cosa vuoi fare?*

Quale libro mi consigli?   *Quali vestiti hai scelto?*   *Quali ragazze verranno?*

Quanto denaro hai speso?   *Quanti anni compi?*   *Quante sorelle hai?*

1 Completa le frasi con gli aggettivi interrogativi. In alcuni casi, è possibile più di una risposta corretta.

1 .... gatti ci sono su quell'albero?

2 Di .... matite hai bisogno per fare il disegno?

3 Oggi .... amica viene a trovarti?

4 .... cosa hai messo nel caffè? Mi sembra amaro!

5 .... spazio posso usare per il computer?

6 .... vasi devo spostare?

7 .... monumenti hai visitato a Roma?

8 Non so dirti .... tempo avremo per pranzare.

9 Mi piacerebbe sapere .... scuse ha trovato Paolo questa volta.

10 .... significato ha questo biglietto?

Produzione scritta e orale

CELI 2

1 Racconta un episodio della tua vita in cui ti sei sentito preoccupato. (Max 100 parole).

Piazza di Spagna e Trinità dei Monti in un dipinto del XVII secolo.

Paesaggi romani

Una gita a Roma è il sogno di milioni di turisti. Da tutto il mondo
americani, giapponesi, cinesi, russi, francesi, inglesi, tedeschi,
scandinavi… volano a Roma.

E Roma offre un caloroso benvenuto a tutti. Chi la sceglie come meta
per il viaggio di nozze non sarà deluso: soprattutto in primavera e
all'inizio dell'estate, la città eterna regala scorci indimenticabili. Ecco
qualche esempio.

La Santissima Chiesa di Trinità dei Monti

Questa chiesa è famosa per la sua posizione. Infatti, si trova davanti
alla scalinata che porta a Piazza di Spagna. Dal suo sagrato[1] si gode
uno splendido panorama su Roma.

---

1. **sagrato** : piazzale davanti alla chiesa.

Nel 1494 San Francesco da Paola, un frate che veniva dalla Calabria, ebbe da Papa Alessandro VI il permesso di costruire un monastero.

Poi, nel 1502, il re francese Luigi XII iniziò la costruzione della Chiesa della Trinità, accanto a questo monastero. In seguito, un'altra chiesa fu costruita al suo posto e venne inaugurata da Papa Sisto V, nel 1585.

La scalinata di Trinità dei Monti

Questa scalinata, di 135 gradini, è uno degli scenari più affascinanti della città. Fu costruita da Francesco De Sanctis nel 1723-26, su ordine di Papa Innocenzo XIII.

In primavera e in estate è piena di fiori e offre a chi passa un'immagine indimenticabile. Nessuno lascia Roma senza una foto di Trinità dei Monti, con i suoi scalini bianchi, i fiori di tutti i colori, la chiesa e lo sfondo del cielo di uno straordinario azzurro.

La fontana della Barcaccia di Pietro e Gian Lorenzo Bernini, in Piazza di Spagna.

Piazza di Spagna e la fontana della Barcaccia

Partendo dall'alto, cioè dal sagrato della chiesa, la scalinata di Trinità dei Monti arriva in Piazza di Spagna, una delle piazze più famose di Roma.

Chi non ricorda Audrey Hepburn e Gregory Peck nel film *Vacanze romane*? Una scena ritrae proprio questa piazza, simile alle ali di una farfalla: è infatti formata da due triangoli con il vertice in comune.

La piazza deve il suo nome al Palazzo di Spagna, residenza dell'ambasciatore spagnolo.

Al centro della piazza si trova la fontana della Barcaccia, costruita nel 1629 da Pietro Bernini e dal figlio Gian Lorenzo. Il nome di questa fontana deriva dalla sua caratteristica forma a barca, che la rende davvero unica e particolare. Sempre in Piazza di Spagna, si trovano la casa museo del poeta inglese John Keats e la Colonna dell'Immacolata Concezione, innalzata nel 1856.

La fontana del Nettuno di Giacomo Della Porta, in Piazza Navona.

Piazza Navona

Se si è a Roma, non si può non visitare Piazza Navona. Fu costruita sopra l'antico stadio dell'imperatore Domiziano, del quale mantiene la forma. Lo stadio era lungo più di 270 m e largo circa 55 m. Costruito verso l'86 d.C., poteva contenere fino a 33.000 persone e vi si svolgevano gare di atletica.

Una traccia degli eventi che si svolgevano qui si trova nell'antico nome della piazza, che era *in agone*. Questa espressione in latino vuol dire appunto 'in gara' e si ritrova ancora oggi nel nome della chiesa di Santa Agnese in Agone, situata davanti alla fontana del Bernini.

L'odierna piazza, voluta da Papa Innocenzo X, ha tre fontane: la Fontana del Nettuno, la Fontana del Moro e la Fontana dei Quattro Fiumi. Quest'ultima, la più importante, venne realizzata da Gian Lorenzo Bernini fra il 1648 e il 1651. I fiumi in essa rappresentati sono il Danubio, il Gange, il Nilo e il Rio della Plata.

Piazza Navona è sempre piena di gente. I turisti si fermano davanti agli artisti che fanno dei ritratti o girano fra le tante bancarelle colorate che vendono ogni genere di oggetti. La gente, le bancarelle, i monumenti fanno di questa piazza un luogo animato, vivace e dall'atmosfera gioiosa.

Prima di leggere

1 Troverai queste parole nel capitolo 2. Associa ogni parola all'immagine corrispondente.

a	indice	d	fronte	g	folla
b	camicia	e	cellulare	h	articolo
c	biglietto	f	scalinata	i	albergo

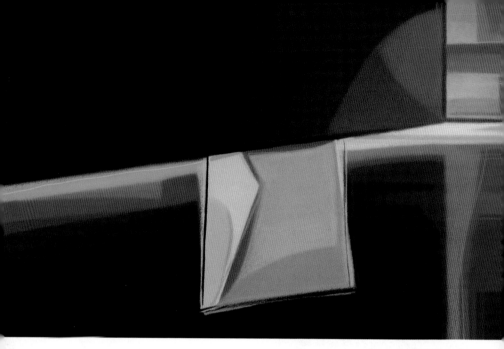

Insidie a Roma

L a scalinata di Trinità dei Monti è straordinaria sotto il cielo azzurro di Roma. Mark Staub aspetta la sua segretaria Elisa, che è in ritardo. Lei arriva di corsa.

"Ci sono i giornalisti!" grida.

Mark Staub ed Elisa corrono via. Il direttore del museo è un uomo famoso e i giornalisti non lo lasciano mai tranquillo. Lui ed Elisa fuggono salendo gli scalini di Trinità dei Monti. Un giornalista urla: "Che ne pensa dei recenti furti, direttore?"

Ma i due sono già in cima alla scalinata e si perdono tra la folla. FINE

Lontano dai giornalisti, ricominciano a camminare tranquillamente.

'Ora o mai più' pensa Elisa e dice: "Vorrei un aumento."

Mark Staub la guarda stupito.

"Elisa guadagni molto, sai? Non puoi chiedermi un aumento!"

"Non guadagno molto e ci sono troppe spese..." risponde lei.

"Anch'io ho tante spese. No, cara, non posso proprio!"

E aggiunge: "Avrai molti soldi. Non ricordi l'assicurazione in tuo favore? Alla mia morte sarai ricca!"

"Sì, certo. È stato generoso perché sperava di sposarmi. Ma io non la amo!" ribatte Elisa.

Le brillano gli occhi dalla rabbia, stringe i pugni: "Se non avrò l'aumento, mi licenzierò, e la lascerò nei guai, un mare di guai!"

All'improvviso si sente gridare: "Sì, sei in un mare di guai, Staub! Maledetto, ancora in Italia, a portarci via opere d'arte!"

Mark si trova davanti il famoso professore di storia dell'arte Francesco Peltri. Elisa intanto si allontana. Peltri, che è anche un archeologo, accusa Staub di aver rubato importanti opere d'arte.

"Sono certo che l'ultimo furto sia opera tua!" conclude.

Il direttore del museo è fuori di sé.

"Senti, calmati!" grida, e lo minaccia con l'indice. "O tieni a freno la lingua,[1] o dirò a tutti da dove hai copiato i tuoi articoli."

"Maledetto!" urla Francesco Peltri, che si allontana rapido. La minaccia di Staub è andata a segno[2].

Più tardi Mark Staub è in un lussuoso albergo della capitale. Sdraiato sul letto, sbottona il colletto della camicia. Chiude gli occhi e ripensa alla giornataccia che ha avuto. Si addormenta per un po'. Quando riapre gli occhi, le sorprese non sono finite. Vede una busta che qualcuno ha infilato sotto la porta mentre lui riposava.

"Attento a quello che fai! Uno sbaglio e sei morto!" legge sul

---

1. **tieni a freno la lingua** : stai attento a quello che dici.
2. **è andata a segno** : ha avuto effetto, è stata efficace.

biglietto che ha tirato fuori dalla busta, e gli tremano le mani. Poco dopo compone un numero sul cellulare. Il detective Lucio Silvi risponde subito.

"Lucio, carissimo" dice Staub "sono nei guai, ho bisogno del tuo aiuto. Quando possiamo incontrarci?"

"Fra un quarto d'ora in Piazza Navona, ti va bene?" chiede l'investigatore.

"Ci sarò" risponde Staub.

In un bar di Piazza Navona Mark, Lucio e Giusi discutono animatamente. Lucio è convinto che il biglietto sia una minaccia seria, ma Mark non gli crede.

"Sono il direttore di un museo, non un delinquente, chi mai..."

"Dottor Staub" interrompe Giusi "è meglio non correre rischi."

"Giusi ha ragione" dichiara il detective. "Devi dirmi chi sono i tuoi nemici, prima che..."

Mark Staub insiste: "Non ho nemici."

"C'è qualcuno con cui hai litigato di recente?"

"Non si tratta di litigi veri e propri... Stamattina, per esempio, ho negato un aumento di stipendio alla mia segretaria."

Mark Staub sospira e si passa una mano sulla fronte.

"Poi ho minacciato un archeologo di rivelare da dove ha copiato i suoi articoli. Lui mi accusava di aver commissionato il furto della statua del dio Apollo..."

Lucio Silvi scambia uno sguardo con Giusi. "Si può morire per molto meno. E questi furti sono davvero un enigma da risolvere, come quello del mittente [3] del biglietto."

Nessuno ancora lo sa, ma quello è il messaggio di un assassino.

---

3. **mittente** : colui che invia una lettera, un biglietto o altro.

Comprensione scritta e orale

1 Ascolta il capitolo e metti in ordine gli eventi.

a ☐ Lucio Silvi siede in un bar di Piazza Navona con l'amico Mark Staub.

b ☐ Qualcuno lascia un biglietto sotto la porta di Mark Staub.

c ☐ Il professor Peltri litiga con Mark Staub.

d ☐ Mark Staub è in un lussuoso albergo.

e ☐ Francesco Peltri accusa il direttore del museo.

f ☐ "Vorrei un aumento" dice Elisa.

g ☐ Mark Staub telefona a Lucio Silvi.

h ☐ Il detective dice: "Si può morire per molto meno."

2 Ascolta di nuovo l'inizio del capitolo e sottolinea le parole sbagliate. Scrivi quelle giuste sotto il brano.

La scalinata di Trinità dei Monti è straordinaria sotto il cielo di Genova. Mark Staub aspetta sua moglie Elisa, che è in anticipo. Lei arriva adagio. "Ci sono i pompieri!", grida.
Mark Staub ed Elisa si siedono su una panchina. Il direttore del museo è un uomo famoso e i pompieri non gli badano. Lui ed Elisa guardano il cielo salendo gli scalini di Trinità dei Monti.
Un giornalista urla: "Che ne pensa dei recenti incendi, direttore?"
Ma i due sono già in cima alla scalinata e si comprano un gelato.

(1) ....

(2) ....

(3) ....

(4) ....

(5) ....

(6) ....

(7) ....

(8) ....

(9) ....

(10) ....

Competenze linguistiche

1 Indica il significato delle seguenti parole e espressioni.

1 *Essere in ritardo*
   - a ☐ Aspettare
   - b ☐ Superare l'orario previsto
   - c ☐ Camminare in fretta

2 *Prendere sul serio*
   - a ☐ Non ridere
   - b ☐ Dare importanza e attenzione
   - c ☐ Avere un'espressione seria

3 *Essere in un mare di guai*
   - a ☐ Nuotare in un posto pericoloso
   - b ☐ Essere in pericolo
   - c ☐ Avere tanti problemi e difficoltà

4 *Stringere i pugni*
   - a ☐ Avere le mani bianche
   - b ☐ Mostrare grande ira con un gesto delle mani
   - c ☐ Bendarsi le mani

5 *Scambiare un'occhiata*
   - a ☐ Prestare a qualcuno qualcosa
   - b ☐ Scambiarsi delle idee
   - c ☐ Guardarsi negli occhi

6 *Enigma*
   - a ☐ Domanda difficile
   - b ☐ Fatto inspiegabile, poco chiaro
   - c ☐ Risposta incompleta

7 *Mittente*
   - a ☐ Chi riceve una lettera
   - b ☐ Chi legge una lettera
   - c ☐ Chi manda una lettera

Prima di leggere

1 Troverai queste parole nel capitolo 3. Associa ogni parola all'immagine corrispondente.

a   sciarpa

b   pino

c   neonato

d   colonna

e   edificio

f   reperto

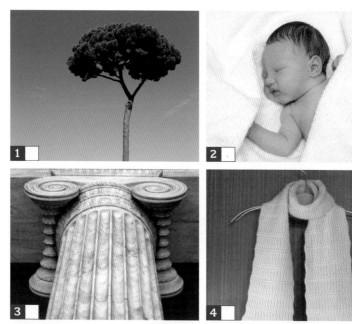

I Fori Imperiali

Roma riserva sempre grandi sorprese per il turista. Una visita alla zona dei Fori Imperiali vi sorprenderà per la lunghezza del percorso e la quantità di opere da ammirare.

I Fori Imperiali sono un insieme di varie piazze costruite tra il 46 a.C. e il 113 d.C. nel cuore di Roma, come dice il nome, dai più importanti imperatori della storia romana. I resti delle imponenti costruzioni che sono arrivati fino a noi danno ancora oggi l'idea della lontana grandezza degli originali.

Il Foro di Cesare

Giulio Cesare, per celebrare la vittoria ottenuta a Farsalo contro Pompeo nel 48 a.C., fece costruire una grande piazza vicino al vecchio Foro Romano. Il foro venne inaugurato nel 46 a.C., ma i lavori furono terminati sotto Augusto.

Il Foro di Cesare era costituito da una piazza rettangolare che sul lato nord-occidentale era dominata dal tempio di Venere Genitrice. Questo magnifico tempio aveva otto colonne sul davanti e nove sui lati.

Fu distrutto da un incendio nell'80 d.C. e venne ricostruito dall'imperatore Traiano nel 113 d.C.

Il Foro di Augusto

Come Giulio Cesare, anche l'imperatore Augusto acquistò con i propri soldi l'area per realizzare il foro in suo onore, che venne inaugurato nel 2 a.C.

Il Tempio delle Vestali, presso il Foro Romano.

Inoltre, dopo la battaglia di Filippi (42 a.C.) contro Bruto e Cassio, Augusto decise di innalzare un tempio a Marte Ultore. Il tempio venne circondato, come il foro, da un muro di 33 m per proteggerlo dagli incendi. Era un grande edificio di marmo bianco, con otto colonne sul davanti e sette sui lati. Nei portici di fianco al tempio si trovavano le statue della famiglia Giulia. Al centro della piazza c'era la statua di Augusto, che purtroppo è andata perduta nel corso dei secoli.

Il Foro della Pace

Nel 71 d.C. l'imperatore Vespasiano iniziò i lavori per la costruzione del Foro della Pace, per celebrare la sua vittoria sugli Ebrei. Il foro prese il posto del Macellum, il mercato che era stato distrutto da un incendio scoppiato sotto Nerone nel 64 d.C. Dopo la morte di Vespasiano i lavori furono portati avanti da Domiziano e l'inaugurazione avvenne nel 75 d.C.

Il Foro della Pace venne definito dallo storico romano Plinio, "una meraviglia del mondo". E doveva essere davvero particolare per la grande piazza piena di fiori, fontane e statue e per lo splendido Tempio della Pace, che custodiva opere d'arte provenienti dalla Grecia, dall'Asia Minore e dal bottino della guerra contro gli Ebrei.

Nel V secolo d.C. un incendio distrusse il tempio. Tra quanto ci rimane è molto interessante la Forma Urbis Romae, una piantina di Roma incisa sul marmo: è il documento più importante per comprendere come era fatta anticamente la città.

Il Foro di Nerva o Transitorio

L'imperatore Domiziano decise di unire i fori precedenti e fece costruire un'altra piazza. Dopo la sua morte, questo foro fu terminato nel 98 d.C. da Nerva.

Si tratta di una piazza rettangolare che presenta il Tempio di Minerva, protettrice di Domiziano, su uno dei lati. La piazza serviva come passaggio tra il Foro Romano, il più antico di Roma, e il quartiere della Suburra. Da questa funzione deriva il nome di Foro Transitorio.

Il Foro di Traiano

È l'ultimo dei Fori Imperiali e il più grande. Venne inaugurato nel 112-113 d.C. Nella piazza, circondata da portici, c'era una statua dell'imperatore a cavallo. Sul fondo si trovava la Basilica Ulpia e dietro ad essa la Colonna Traiana. Questa colonna, alta 39.81 m, celebra la conquista della Dacia (attuale Romania) da parte dell'imperatore, avvenuta tra il 101 e il 106 d.C.

È decorata con più di 2.500 figure che celebrano le imprese dei soldati romani. Nel suo basamento si trova la tomba di Traiano.

La Colonna Traiana.

28

Pericolo ai Fori Imperiali

I giorno dopo Lucio e Giusi passeggiano con il direttore del museo lungo i Fori Imperiali. Staub ammira il paesaggio e quel che resta degli antichi edifici costruiti dai Romani. Mentre osserva alcune colonne, lo raggiunge la sua segretaria Elisa.

"Oh, Elisa! Spero di non averti delusa negandoti l'aumento" le dice sorridendole. "Forse sono stato un po' brusco [1], ma non volevo offenderti, sai?"

Elisa decide di essere gentile e i due si riconciliano quasi subito.

Poco lontano, Francesco Peltri è insieme ad alcuni studenti.

"Oggi visiteremo una serie di piazze realizzate dagli imperatori romani tra il 46 a. C. e il 113 d. C. nel cuore della città."

---

1. **brusco** : aspro, duro.

Una ragazza lo guarda con aria preoccupata. "Sto morendo di sete. Che noia!" mormora all'amica.

Il professore si volta con l'intenzione di sgridarla, ma qualcosa lo interessa molto di più. Ha infatti notato la presenza di Mark Staub e non stacca gli occhi dal direttore del museo e dai suoi amici.

Uno studente chiede se ci sono pericoli per i monumenti antichi.

"Certo che ce ne sono!" esclama il professore e alza la voce per farsi sentire dal direttore del museo.

"Ecco, guardate, quel signore laggiù, con il cappello bianco e la sciarpa celeste. Quello è un vero furfante! Pare che ci sia lui dietro ai tanti furti di opere d'arte di cui parlano i giornali."

I ragazzi sono stupiti. Qualcuno chiede: "Come mai non è in prigione?"

"Be', è il direttore di un museo, ha tante amicizie importanti ed è molto furbo. Nessuno è mai riuscito trovare prove contro di lui."

"Allora la statua del dio Apollo è nelle sue mani?" chiede una ragazza.

"Ci scommetterei la testa [2]!" risponde il professore, e si dirige a grandi passi verso Staub, che viene presto circondato dagli studenti, incuriositi dalle accuse.

Il professore gli afferra un braccio e urla: "Ladro! Sei qui per scegliere altri reperti da portare via?"

Staub cerca di liberarsi. Grida a sua volta: "Mi lasci! Mi lasci!"

Peltri lo colpisce con un pugno che lo fa cadere a terra.

Lucio giunge in aiuto dell'amico e trascina via il professore minacciandolo di chiamare la polizia.

"Si calmi, per favore!" dice Lucio a Peltri, e Giusi commenta: "Che figura! Comportarsi così davanti agli studenti, poi!"

---

2. **Ci scommetterei la testa** : ne sono assolutamente sicuro.

Elisa, intanto, aiuta il suo capo a rialzarsi e a raccogliere il cappello.

Mark Staub si allontana, amareggiato e spaventato, mentre Elisa e Giusi lo seguono, preoccupate e perplesse. Nel frattempo Lucio discute con il professor Peltri.

"Se non ci sono le prove del furto, non si può fare nulla, mi creda" osserva.

L'altro fa un cenno con la testa. L'investigatore forse lo ha convinto.

"Vede, lei si mette dalla parte del torto[3] comportandosi così."

Gli studenti non partecipano alla discussione. Si sono seduti sotto un pino e approfittano della pausa per mangiare dei panini.

Il professore guarda la strada e le rovine, poi osserva il cielo. "Forse ha ragione. Tutta colpa dell'ira, che a volte mi prende quando si tratta di difendere la nostra storia e le nostre antichità." Ringrazia, saluta e si allontana velocemente, quasi di corsa.

L'investigatore è sorpreso. 'Quanta fretta!' pensa. Sorride a un neonato, che lo guarda in braccio alla mamma. Ma quel sorriso gli si spegne sulle labbra.

Da lontano giungono delle grida. La folla accorre sul posto e anche Lucio Silvi si mette a correre, con il fiato in gola. Si vedono una nuvola di polvere e tante pietre, pezzi di muro ovunque. Il cuore gli batte all'impazzata[4].

Un muro è crollato. Giusi è sotto le macerie e qualcuno sta cercando di soccorrerla. Il direttore del museo è steso a terra, mentre Elisa non smette di urlare con le mani sul viso.

---

3. **dalla parte del torto** : dalla parte di chi sbaglia, di chi non ha ragione.
4. **batte all'impazzata** : batte fortissimo.

Comprensione scritta e orale

1 Ascolta e leggi il capitolo 3 e rispondi alle seguenti domande.

1 Con chi è Mark Staub durante la visita ai Fori Imperiali?

2 Con chi è il professor Peltri?

3 Una studentessa si lamenta. Cosa dice?

4 Cosa fa Peltri quando vede Mark Staub?

5 Come si sente Mark Staub dopo l'incontro con Peltri?

6 Come si sentono Elisa e Giusi dopo la lite tra Staub e Peltri?

7 Cosa fanno gli studenti mentre Lucio cerca di calmare Peltri?

8 Cosa succede alla fine del capitolo 3?

2 Rileggi il testo e scrivi il nome del personaggio corrispondente alla descrizione.

1 Ha ricevuto un pugno ed è preoccupato e amareggiato. ....

2 Ha deciso di essere gentile con Mark Staub. ....

3 Dice che Mark Staub è un ladro. ....

4 Va in aiuto di Mark Staub, allontanando Peltri. ....

5 Urla con le mani sul viso. ....

Competenze linguistiche

1 Collega ogni aggettivo al suo contrario.

1	☐	steso	a	moderno
2	☐	lontano	b	brutto
3	☐	preoccupato	c	sciocco
4	☐	veloce	d	vicino
5	☐	furbo	e	lento
6	☐	grazioso	f	tranquillo
7	☐	antico	g	alzato

Produzione scritta e orale

CELI 2

1 Immagina di essere il detective Silvi. Scrivi un rapporto sulla visita ai Fori Imperiali. Inserisci nel tuo testo i seguenti elementi, basandoti anche sulla tua fantasia:

- condizioni atmosferiche
- partecipanti
- incontri
- descrizione dell'incidente
- conclusioni

Prima di leggere

1 Troverai queste parole nel capitolo 4. Associa ogni parola all'immagine corrispondente.

a	martello	**c**	palma
b	mazzo di rose	**d**	infermiera

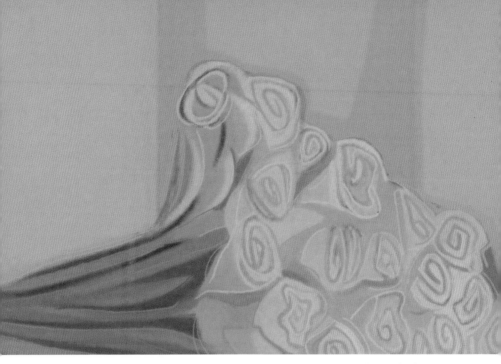

È tutto chiaro

ono le quattro di un pomeriggio afoso [1]. Fa caldo
anche nella stazione di polizia. Lucio guarda con aria
interrogativa il commissario Felisi, silenzioso e serio
dietro la sua scrivania. Il commissario sposta dei fogli
e prende tempo, incerto se raccontare all'investigatore
privato le ultime notizie sull'incidente ai Fori Imperiali.
Poi pensa che forse Silvi può aiutarlo.

"Vede, è tutto chiaro" comincia il commissario.

Lucio aspetta paziente e l'altro prosegue: "Non si tratta di un
incidente. È tentato omicidio [2]."

---

1. **afoso** : molto caldo.
2. **tentato omicidio** : un'uccisione tentata ma non riuscita.

Il detective si china in avanti, sorpreso. Non si aspettava una cosa del genere. Ora è ansioso di sapere. Non stacca gli occhi dal viso del commissario. Felisi si volta verso la finestra, sospira. 'Poteva anche capirlo da solo che si trattava di un agguato[3]' pensa. Sorride e continua a riflettere: 'Sono cambiati i tempi, i giovani d'oggi hanno poco intuito.'

L'investigatore si sta innervosendo. 'Parli o non parli?' pensa impaziente.

Il commissario torna alla realtà e decide di parlare: "Il muro che è crollato sulla signorina Giusi è stato spinto, buttato giù da qualcuno, volontariamente..."

"Si spieghi meglio" chiede l'investigatore, poco interessato a muri antichi.

"Ma come? Non capisce?"

"No, mi spieghi, per favore."

"Dunque, qualcuno vuole uccidere qualcun altro e sceglie proprio i Fori Imperiali... Ma non vuole essere scoperto. Secondo lei cosa fa?"

"Ho capito... Provoca un crollo per farlo sembrare un semplice incidente."

"Proprio così, collega."

"Sì, in effetti, è possibile. Bastava un attrezzo, una mazzetta, un martello..." conclude Silvi.

"Vede, in realtà è un gioco da ragazzi. Il muro crolla, e investe la signorina Giusi" aggiunge Felisi.

"Comunque, commissario, qualcosa non torna[4]."

"Cosa?"

---

3. **agguato** : attacco, aggressione.
4. **qualcosa non torna** : c'è un errore o una contraddizione.

"La mia segretaria non ha nemici. Non ha mai fatto del male a nessuno... Chi può volerla morta? Nessuno, commissario."

"Ha ragione, Silvi. Allora, sa cosa penso? Penso che l'assassino abbia sbagliato."

All'investigatore sfugge un 'Ah!' di sorpresa.

"Sì, non era la sua segretaria che doveva morire, ma qualcun altro..."

"Vicino a Giusi c'erano solo Elisa e Mark Staub" osserva il detective, pensieroso.

"Secondo me l'obiettivo era Staub" aggiunge il commissario. "Ora non ci resta che scoprire chi voleva ucciderlo."

Il giorno seguente Lucio Silvi stringe tra le mani un mazzo di piccole rose gialle. Cammina lungo il corridoio dell'ospedale e quel luogo lo fa sentire a disagio: visi tristi, odore di disinfettante, porte tutte uguali. Bussa a una, in fondo al corridoio.

Una voce debole gli risponde: "Entra, entra."

Giusi è in un letto, con le gambe e un braccio ingessati. Quando vede entrare il capo, però, sorride e il viso le si illumina. Non si aspettava questa visita...

"Ciao, come stai?" le chiede Lucio. Mette le rose in un vaso, e poi le sfiora la mano.

"Come vuoi che stia? Voglio andare a casa."

"Non essere testarda[5], andrai a casa non appena starai meglio" le dice Lucio, incoraggiandola. Giusi fa una smorfia[6].

"Hai le gambe e un braccio rotti. Come puoi pretendere di andare via?"

---

5. **testarda**: cocciuta, irremovibile, decisa a non cambiare parere.
6. **fa una smorfia**: contrae il viso.

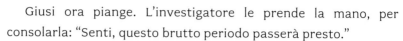

Giusi ora piange. L'investigatore le prende la mano, per consolarla: "Senti, questo brutto periodo passerà presto."

"E tu come farai in ufficio?"

"Non ti preoccupare, me la caverò. Forse imparerò a essere meno disordinato..."

Il detective riprende a parlare e vorrebbe restare a lungo, ma un'infermiera si affaccia dalla porta e annuncia che l'orario per le visite sta per finire.

Lucio Silvi cammina nel parco dell'ospedale. Si dirige all'auto, posteggiata vicino a delle palme. Alcuni colombi volano via. 'No, non me la caverò senza Giusi. Lei mi mancherà da morire' pensa addolorato.

Quella sera l'investigatore va a una festa in casa del mercante d'arte Dino Aussone. Silvi è contento: ha un'ottima occasione per indagare e forse scoprire chi ha tentato di uccidere Giusi e Mark Staub.

Il mercante d'arte ha invitato i più noti archeologi, giornalisti e professori universitari per inaugurare la sua nuova galleria. Nella sala, piena di gente, tutti parlano dei recenti furti. I camerieri posano sui tavoli piatti con tramezzini, pizzette, salatini, dolci e frutta. In un angolo, vicino alla porta-finestra, si trovano i bicchieri e le bevande.

Oltre la porta-finestra, sul terrazzo davanti al parco della villa, il padrone di casa parla a bassa voce con Mark Staub.

"Ho una cosa fantastica per te" gli dice.

Staub ha già capito di cosa si tratta.

'Giovannelli deve essere riuscito a vendere la statua del dio Apollo' pensa.

Risponde, deciso: "Non compro niente senza sapere da dove viene: voglio il nome di chi la vende."

"Sai bene che non è il caso di fare gli schizzinosi [6]" ribatte Aussone. "Questa statua è bellissima... un giovane dio..."

"Non mi interessa. Non compro più nulla che abbia provenienza incerta."

"Ma questi non sono i patti tra noi! Hai sempre detto che avresti acquistato tutto..."

Aussone sta sudando, è rosso in volto e capisce di aver attirato l'attenzione di molti presenti.

"Una volta, ma ora i tempi sono cambiati: c'è troppa polizia in giro. Non voglio guai" conclude Staub.

"Te ne pentirai, ti assicuro che te ne pentirai!" gli dice il mercante, mentre si allontana.

Elisa e un altro invitato, dietro la porta-finestra, hanno sentito la minaccia. L'uomo è molto colpito e non capisce la reazione violenta di Aussone nei confronti di Staub.

"Non deve stupirsi, il mio capo ha molti nemici" dice Elisa. "Anch'io ho iniziato a detestarlo, ma devo ancora trovare la forza per fargliela pagare."

Nessuno si aspettava che durante una delle celebri e spensierate feste a casa di Dino Aussone la tensione potesse salire fino a questo a punto.

---

6. **schizzinosi** : troppo esigenti, critici.

Comprensione scritta e orale

1 Ascolta il capitolo e rispondi alle seguenti domande.

1 Cosa pensa Lucio Silvi del commissario Felisi?
2 Che atteggiamento ha Felisi nei confronti del detective?
3 Cosa dice Lucio Silvi della sua segretaria?
4 Cosa succede in ospedale?
5 Chi ha organizzato una festa a casa sua?
6 Con chi parla il mercante d'arte Dino Aussone sul terrazzo della sua villa?
7 Cosa dice Elisa di Mark Staub?

Competenze linguistiche

1 Indica il significato delle seguenti parole e espressioni.

1 *Cavarsela*
   a ☐ Tirare fuori qualcosa
   b ☐ Riuscire ad andare avanti, nonostante le difficoltà o la mancanza di mezzi
   c ☐ Avere successo

2 *Con aria interrogativa*
   a ☐ Con la mano alzata per fare una domanda
   b ☐ Con un'espressione del viso che indica dubbio
   c ☐ Con un'espressione del volto che indica cattiveria

3 *Non staccare gli occhi*
   a ☐ Fissare senza interruzione
   b ☐ Cucire gli occhi a un giocattolo di pezza
   c ☐ Osservare di nascosto

4 *Un gioco da ragazzi*
   a ☐ Un gioco adatto ai bambini
   b ☐ Una cosa semplicissima
   c ☐ Un'attività amata dai ragazzi

5 *Qualcosa non torna*
   a ☐ Qualcuno non ha restituito qualcosa
   b ☐ Qualcosa è andato perduto
   c ☐ C'è un errore o un aspetto che non corrisponde alla verità

Grammatica

Comparativi e superlativi

Il **comparativo** si usa per confrontare più elementi fra loro e può essere di **maggioranza**, di **minoranza** e di **uguaglianza**.

Sono più alto di te. (comparativo di maggioranza)

Carla è meno studiosa di Lucia. (comparativo di minoranza)

Roma è bella (tanto) quanto/(così) come Firenze. (comparativo di uguaglianza)

Il **superlativo relativo** esprime la qualità di qualcosa nel suo grado più alto, mettendola in relazione con gli elementi di un insieme.

Tu sei il più alto della squadra. (superlativo relativo di maggioranza)

Io e mio fratello siamo i meno sportivi della famiglia. (superlativo relativo di minoranza)

Il **superlativo assoluto** indica una qualità nel suo grado più alto, ma senza confronti. Si forma aggiungendo *-issimo.*

Elisa è bellissima e intelligentissima.

Gli aggettivi indicati in tabella hanno, oltre alle forme regolari, anche un comparativo di maggioranza e un superlativo assoluto irregolari.

Aggettivo (grado positivo)	Comparativo di maggioranza	Superaltivo assoluto
buono	migliore	ottimo
cattivo	peggiore	pessimo
grande	maggiore	massimo
piccolo	minore	minimo

1 Crea frasi comparative o superlative basandoti sulle tracce e sull'indicazione data tra parentesi.

1 Monumenti di Roma/antichi (+)/monumenti della tua città.

2 Il nostro lavoro/interessante (-)/lavoro di Roberta.

3 La festa di ieri/divertente (-)/tutte le feste di quest'anno.

4 La mia famiglia/numerosa (=)/la vostra famiglia.

5 *I Promessi Sposi*/il romanzo/noioso (+)/abbia mai letto.

2 Inserisci i comparativi irregolari corretti nelle seguenti frasi.

1 "Questo è il caso (brutto) .... che mi sia capitato" dice il commissario Felisi.
2 "Il furto della statua è il danno (piccolo) .... rispetto alla morte del mio amico" dice Lucio Silvi.
3 "Spero in un futuro (buono) ...." dice Elisa.
4 Giusi Rosso sa che dovrà curarsi con (grande) .... attenzione.

3 Inserisci nelle seguenti frasi i superlativi irregolari corretti.

1 Il commissario fa il (grande) .... sforzo per scoprire l'assassino.
2 Giusi Rosso è un' (buona) .... segretaria.
3 Lucio Silvi ha una (cattiva) .... abitudine: è molto disordinato.

Prima di leggere

1 Troverai queste parole nel capitolo 5. Associa ogni parola all'immagine corrispondente.

a pipistrello   b balaustra   c civetta   d gabbia

Troppo tardi!

Nella villa di Dino Aussone sono presenti anche alcuni studenti del professor Peltri. Ai valzer seguono pezzi più moderni e loro ballano con gioia. Ridono felici. Ma l'atmosfera si guasta[1] quando dal terrazzo si sente urlare: "Maledetto!" e poi: "Te ne pentirai, presto, molto presto!"

I ragazzi smettono di ballare, si avvicinano alle finestre e guardano il terrazzo. È buio, però capiscono che l'uomo che ora sta camminando avanti e indietro, con aria cupa[2], ha dei problemi.

Riconoscono il direttore del museo, Mark Staub.

'Il signor Staub è una persona con molti nemici' pensano gli studenti. Poi riprendono a ballare.

---

1. **si guasta** : cambia in peggio.
2. **aria cupa** : espressione pensierosa, tormentata.

Troppo tardi!

Una biondina mormora all'orecchio del suo compagno: "Non vorrei essere nei suoi panni [3], poverino. Tutti lo odiano, persino quella donna parlava male di lui."

Intanto il loro professore, Francesco Peltri, sembra molto angosciato. Con un bicchiere in mano, osserva gli invitati in un angolo della sala.

Un uomo grosso e calvo gli si avvicina.

"Che piacere, professore, incontrarla" gli dice. "Leggo tutti i suoi articoli. Sono davvero interessanti. Chi è stato il suo maestro?"

Peltri non gli risponde, solleva le spalle e sbuffa [4]. L'altro continua a disturbarlo e gli chiede: "Posso chiederle di cosa ha intenzione di occuparsi prossimamente?"

"No, non posso dirlo" risponde Peltri, infastidito. Ha paura che le domande possano diventare più imbarazzanti e vuole essere lasciato in pace.

Una donna bruna, che accompagna lo sconosciuto, guarda con ammirazione il professore.

"Cara, ti presento..." dice l'uomo, ma Peltri si è alzato e già si fa largo fra gli ospiti. Ad un tratto si china, come per raccogliere qualcosa da terra. Poi esce sul terrazzo e scende lungo la scalinata che porta al parco.

"Che maleducato!" commenta la donna.

Nel frattempo Mark Staub non è ancora riuscito a calmarsi. 'Imbroglione! Maledetto imbroglione! Vuole vendere statue rubate...' riflette, ripensando alla conversazione avuta con il padrone di casa.

Cammina avanti e indietro sul terrazzo, come un leone in gabbia.

---

3. **essere nei suoi panni** : essere al posto suo.
4. **sbuffa** : soffia, emette fiato dalla bocca.

CAPITOLO 5

Poi si accorge che dalla sala alcuni ospiti lo osservano incuriositi. Si appoggia alla balaustra e fissa la notte buia. Il parco è pieno di vita: civette, gatti e anche dei pipistrelli. Lui si sente stanchissimo... All'improvviso il silenzio è interrotto dagli squilli del cellulare.

"Pronto?" dice Mark Staub. Resta in ascolto per alcuni secondi.

"Va bene, va bene... per scusarsi e dirmi una cosa importante? Alla fontana? D'accordo, arrivo" dice, e infila il telefonino nella tasca. Scende i gradini adagio...

Un'ombra furtiva si aggira attorno alla fontana con la statua di Venere al centro... Vedendo Mark Staub dirigersi verso il parco, Lucio ha un brutto presentimento[5].

"Mark! Mark, aspettami!" grida, ma teme che sia troppo, tardi...

Succede tutto in un attimo. Corre e mentre si avvicina sente lo sparo.

Due ore dopo la polizia è alle prese[6] con un cadavere. Mark Staub è stato assassinato. Un proiettile gli ha centrato il cuore. E la pistola da cui è partito è nella fontana, circondata dai pesci rossi.

Gli ospiti se ne sono andati. Solo Elisa è ancora lì perché il commissario Felisi l'ha pregata di restare. Dino Aussone è sotto shock. Lucio è senza parole.

'Non ho saputo difenderlo' pensa. 'Però il suo assassino non mi sfuggirà. Glielo devo[7] come amico.'

---

5. **presentimento** : il sentire in anticipo quello che accadrà.
6. **è alle prese con** : ha a che fare con, lavora su qualcosa.
7. **glielo devo** : è mio dovere farlo.

Comprensione scritta e orale

1 **Rispondi alle seguenti domande.**

1 Durante la festa che atteggiamento ha il professor Peltri?

2 Chi cerca di avere una conversazione con lui?

3 Come reagisce Peltri?

4 Dove si trova e cosa fa Mark Staub poco prima di essere ucciso?

2 **Ascolta l'inizio del capitolo e inserisci le parole corrette.**

Nella villa di (**1**) .... anche alcuni studenti del
professor Peltri. Ai valzer seguono pezzi più moderni e loro ballano con
gioia. Ridono felici. Ma l'atmosfera si guasta quando dal
(**2**) .... si sente urlare: "Maledetto!" e poi: "Te ne
pentirai, presto, molto presto!"
I ragazzi (**3**) .... di ballare, si avvicinano alle
finestre e guardano il terrazzo. È buio, però capiscono che l'uomo che
ora sta camminando avanti e indietro, con aria cupa, ha dei problemi.
Riconoscono il (**4**) .... , Mark Staub.
'Il signor Staub è una persona con molti (**5**) ....
pensano gli studenti. Poi riprendono a ballare.
Una (**6**) .... mormora all'orecchio del suo
compagno: "Non vorrei essere nei suoi panni, poverino. Tutti lo odiano,
persino quella donna (**7**) .... di lui."
Intanto il loro professore, Francesco Peltri, sembra molto
(**8**) .... Con un bicchiere in mano, osserva gli
invitati in un (**9**) .... della sala.
Un uomo grosso e (**10**) .... gli si avvicina.
"Che piacere, professore, incontrarla" gli dice. "Leggo tutti i suoi
(**11**) .... Sono davvero interessanti. Chi è stato il
suo maestro?"
Peltri non gli risponde, solleva le spalle e sbuffa. L'altro continua a
disturbarlo e gli chiede: "Posso chiederle di cosa
(**12**) .... occuparsi prossimamente?"

Competenze linguistiche

1 Indica l'intruso.

1 a ☐ magro   c ☐ felice
   b ☐ angosciato   d ☐ triste

2 a ☐ agile   c ☐ calvo
   b ☐ bruno   d ☐ biondo

3 a ☐ avvicinarsi   c ☐ fermarsi
   b ☐ mangiare   d ☐ allontanarsi

4 a ☐ leggere   c ☐ nuotare
   b ☐ scrivere   d ☐ contare

5 a ☐ prima   c ☐ accanto
   b ☐ vicino   d ☐ dietro

6 a ☐ ora   c ☐ attimo
   b ☐ bicicletta   d ☐ secondo

7 a ☐ scalinata   c ☐ gradini
   b ☐ altalena   d ☐ scala

8 a ☐ villano   c ☐ maleducato
   b ☐ gentile   d ☐ scortese

Produzione scritta e orale

CELI 2

1 Scrivi messaggio email a un amico. Raccontagli come hai passato il sabato, dove sei stato/a, chi hai incontrato, chi ti ha telefonato, che musica hai ascoltato e tutto ciò che ritieni interessante.

CELI 2

2 Parla con i tuoi compagni del problema dei furti di opere d'arte. Provate ad elencare i mezzi su cui si può contare per impedire che il fenomeno continui. Trova in internet informazioni su alcuni furti celebri e confrontali con quelli trovati dai tuoi compagni.

Prima di leggere

1 Troverai queste parole nel capitolo 6. Associa ogni parola all'immagine corrispondente.

a cameriere   d orecchino

b fontana   e pollice

c poliziotto   f divano

CAPITOLO **6**

Una segretaria nei guai

ono le tre di notte. Nella sala della festa due camerieri puliscono i tavoli e sistemano le sedie.

"Andate pure a casa" suggerisce Dino Aussone. "Continuerete domani."

"Caro, andiamo a dormire" gli dice la moglie.

"Va' tu. Appena la polizia finisce, ti raggiungo."

"Sei esausto, non tardare."

Elisa entra nella sala dalla porta-finestra. È pallida e si accascia[1] su un divano. Si copre il viso con le mani. Chiude gli occhi per non piangere.

"Come mai è ancora qui?" le chiede il padrone di casa.

---

1. **si accascia** : crolla, si lascia cadere.

51

"Non so... Il commissario Felisi mi ha detto di aspettare" risponde lei con un filo di voce.

"Le farò compagnia" dichiara Aussone.

Il commissario entrando nella sala annuncia che nel parco i poliziotti hanno finito.

"Be', allora può andarsene" dice il padrone di casa a Elisa, sorridendole.

"No, non può andarsene!" dichiara il commissario.

"Perché?" domandano Elisa e Aussone.

Il commissario risponde con una domanda: "È suo questo?"

Fa dondolare ² un orecchino. Tutti guardano Elisa: le manca un orecchino, uguale a quello che il commissario stringe fra il pollice e l'indice.

"Sì, è mio. Devo averlo perso ballando" dichiara la donna, contenta di averlo ritrovato.

"Allora deve seguirmi al commissariato" le annuncia il commissario.

"Ehi, un momento, la signorina è una mia ospite, non può arrestarla solamente perché ha perso un orecchino..."

"Voglio solo interrogarla. Questo orecchino si trovava accanto al corpo di Mark Staub" dichiara Felisi.

"E con ciò?" chiede Lucio.

"Amico mio, per me questo basta per voler parlare con la signorina, a lungo. Sento che nasconde qualcosa."

Elisa scoppia a piangere e mormora tra i singhiozzi: "Lo odiavo, ma non sono stata io a ucciderlo!"

Il mattino dopo Lucio Silvi è al commissariato.

---

2.   **dondolare** : muovere in qua e in là, far oscillare.

CAPITOLO 6

"Guardi, Silvi, che oggi non è la giornata buona per farmi perdere tempo" gli dice brusco il commissario.

"Senta, voglio solo convincerla che la signorina Elisa è innocente."

Il commissario alza lo sguardo dal computer. "Ho in mano una prova evidente..."

Silvi lo interrompe: "È troppo evidente per non destare sospetti. Come può, commissario, non capire che l'orecchino poteva essere lì per caso, oppure che l'assassino l'ha lasciato accanto al cadavere per sviare[3] le indagini?"

"No Silvi, lei non mi convince, sa? E le spiego subito perché. Vede, poche persone, come la signorina Elisa, avevano un buon motivo per desiderare la morte di Mark Staub."

"Non vedo come..."

"Oh, glielo spiego io il come e il perché" annuncia il commissario. "Il come è semplice: un colpo di pistola dritto al cuore e il perché..." Il commissario apre un cassetto della scrivania.

"Il perché è in questa assicurazione: nell'ultima riga c'è scritto: 900.000 euro in caso di morte alla mia segretaria, la signorina Elisa Bondi!"

Lucio rimane senza fiato. Boccheggia[4]. Si abbandona sulla sedia davanti alla scrivania.

Un quarto d'ora più tardi Lucio incontra Elisa nell'ufficio del commissario. La saluta e cerca di tranquillizzarla.

"Farò tutto il possibile per lei" le dice.

Elisa è stanca e disperata. Si mette a piangere, mentre parla

---

3. **sviare** : distogliere l'attenzione, allontanare dalla strada giusta.
4. **boccheggia** : respira affannosamente.

con il commissario: "Lei non mi crede, commissario, ma non sono scesa nel parco, non ho perso l'orecchino lì."

Il commissario non dice nulla. Aspetta il momento adatto per il colpo di scena.

Intanto, da dietro la porta, si sentono delle voci di ragazzi. Elisa si asciuga gli occhi e si rivolge al detective: "Glielo dica lei, Silvi, che sono innocente. Non ho la forza di tenere in mano una pistola, non potevo ucciderlo."

A questo punto il commissario interviene con durezza: "In preda all'ira, anche le persone più deboli fanno cose incredibili e lei, cara signorina Elisa, era molto arrabbiata ieri sera..."

"Non è vero!" grida Elisa.

"Ecco, l'ho messa alla prova, e ho scoperto che lei mente!" dice il commissario aprendo la porta a due ragazzi che aspettavano nel corridoio.

Il commissario, che ha già avuto modo di interrogarli prima dell'arrivo di Silvi, chiede ai due: "E adesso, per cortesia, ripetete cosa ha detto la signorina riguardo al signor Staub ieri, alla festa."

I ragazzi rispondono decisi: "Che voleva fargliela pagare."

Nella stanza scende il silenzio.

Comprensione scritta e orale

1 Chi ha pronunciato le seguenti frasi?

a   Lucio Silvi

b   il commissario Felisi

c   Dino Aussone

d   Elisa

1 ☐ "Non può andarsene!"

2 ☐ "La signorina è una mia ospite, non può arrestarla."

3 ☐ "Devo averlo perso ballando."

4 ☐ "Voglio solo convincerla che la signorina Elisa è innocente."

5 ☐ "Glielo dica lei, Silvi, che sono innocente."

6 ☐ "Continuerete domani."

7 ☐ "Farò tutto il possibile per lei."

Competenze linguistiche

1 Completa il testo con le parole elencate.

> indagini   orecchino   tempo   sospetti
> computer   commissariato   innocente

Il mattino dopo Lucio Silvi è al (**1**) ....

"Guardi, Silvi, che oggi non è la giornata buona per farmi perdere
(**2**) .... " gli dice brusco il commissario.

"Senta, voglio solo convincerla che la signorina Elisa è
(**3**) ...."

Il commissario alza lo sguardo dal (**4**) .... "Ho in
mano una prova evidente..."

Silvi lo interrompe: "È troppo evidente per non destare
(**5**) .... Come può, commissario, non capire
che l'(**6**) .... poteva essere lì per caso, oppure
che l'assassino l'ha lasciato accanto al cadavere per sviare le
(**7**) .... ?"

Produzione scritta e orale

1 Immagina di essere un famoso scrittore di gialli. Inventa lo schema di un poliziesco. In 10-15 righe devi indicare:

- · la vittima
- · l'assassino
- · il movente

- · l'investigatore
- · gli altri personaggi
- · l'ambientazione

Puoi prendere spunto dalla seguente tabella.

Vittima	Assassino	Investigatore	Ambientazione
Mark Staub, direttore di un museo	Francesco Peltri (?) Possibile movente: un segreto che, se svelato, potrebbe rovinargli la vita. Elisa (?) Possibile movente: denaro e rancore personale.	Lucio Silvi	Roma ai giorni nostri

2 Discuti con un compagno. Rispondete alle seguenti domande e parlate dei vostri gusti in fatto di lettura.

1   Ti piace leggere gialli?

2   Quali sono i tuoi giallisti preferiti?

3   Quale libro del tuo autore preferito consiglieresti di leggere per primo? Perché?

4   Qual è l'ultimo giallo che hai letto? Di cosa parla?

5   C'è un libro giallo che hai iniziato ma non sei riuscito a finire, oppure che ti ha deluso?

6   C'è un film tratto da un libro giallo che ti è piaciuto particolarmente? Qual è?

Prima di leggere

1 Troverai queste parole nel capitolo 7. Associa ogni parola all'immagine corrispondente.

a cipresso

b tazzina

c appunti

d esca

e taccuino

f lavastoviglie

CAPITOLO 7

Lungo la via Appia

ualche giorno dopo, Francesco Peltri e i suoi studenti
camminano lungo la via Appia. Il professore spiega
entusiasta che molte erano le vie che collegavano la città
al resto dell'impero romano.

"Vedete, ragazzi, la via Appia collegava Roma a Brindisi,
il più importante porto per la Grecia e l'Oriente..."

Meno contento è l'investigatore Lucio Silvi, che li segue da
vicino. 'Questo Peltri, non mi convince' pensa. 'È famoso e ricco,
molto ricco... troppo per il lavoro che fa. Da dove prende i soldi per
fare viaggi, stare nei migliori alberghi, collezionare oggetti antichi,
organizzare scavi e spedizioni?'

Di colpo l'investigatore si ferma perché ha visto un uomo che
conosce bene: Dino Aussone.

59

"Carissimo, che piacere rivederla" gli dice il mercante d'arte, mentre il professor Peltri li raggiunge. Gli studenti ne approfittano per fare alcune foto.

'Non potrei essere più fortunato: due persone a cui gettare un'esca...' riflette l'investigatore.

"Come vanno le indagini?" gli chiede il professor Peltri.

"In ufficio ho delle prove che darò alla polizia" annuncia Silvi.

Peltri e Aussone sono stupiti. Quest'ultimo osserva: "Ha già trovato il colpevole?"

"Mi manca poco, qualche dettaglio. A proposito, dove eravate alle ventitré dell'altra sera?" chiede l'investigatore.

Peltri dichiara che era alla festa, nella sala da ballo, con gli studenti. Aussone dice di non ricordare e che forse stava ballando con sua moglie o chiacchierando con qualcuno.

Il detective prende nota delle risposte.

"Bravo! Lei è un bravo detective" gli dice Aussone, e si allontana con il professor Peltri. A voce bassa il mercante d'arte commenta: "È una persona pericolosa, devo vendere subito..."

I due raggiungono un gruppo di cipressi, mentre gli studenti osservano la tomba di Cecilia Metella e prendono appunti sui loro quaderni.

"Non parlarmi qui! Non ora. Non vedi che Silvi non si è ancora allontanato?" dice in malo modo Peltri.

"Non ho tempo per aspettare. Ho una splendida statua, devo liberarmene in fretta."

"Non voglio mettermi nei guai, per me non è il momento di comprare" risponde Peltri.

Intanto l'investigatore è arrivato dagli studenti.

"Ragazzi eravate con il professore, alle ventitré, l'altra notte?"

Tutti si guardano stupiti per qualche secondo. Poi una biondina dice: "Sì, certo, eravamo con lui."

Quei secondi di incertezza sono serviti all'investigatore per capire che probabilmente gli studenti mentono per fornire un alibi[1] al loro professore.

Un'ora dopo Dino Aussone incontra Fausto Giovannelli, il ladro di opere d'arte, in un bar poco distante dalla via Appia. Hanno bevuto una tazza di caffè e parlano in un angolo della sala. Non ci sono altri clienti e la barista, dietro il bancone, sta riempiendo la lavastoviglie con piattini, piatti e bicchieri.

"Te l'ho detto" dice il mercante d'arte "questa è merce che scotta[2]!"

L'altro gli lancia un'occhiata di odio.

"Lo so bene e voglio essere pagato presto."

Aussone sospira e ribatte: "Senti, ho fatto il possibile per vendere subito. Mark comprava sempre tutto... e ora abbiamo perso il miglior cliente."

"Cerca qualcun altro" consiglia Giovannelli. "Hai già provato con il professor Peltri?"

"Sì, ma anche lui non vuole comprare. Non si può far altro che aspettare e tenere la bocca chiusa."

"Ti do quindici giorni, non di più. Poi voglio i miei soldi."

Giovannelli si alza, esce dalla porta con passo deciso. L'altro rimane al tavolo con un'aria preoccupata. 'Devo fare qualcosa' si dice. 'Ma cosa?'

---

1. **alibi** : giustificazione.
2. **che scotta** : molto pericolosa, compromettente.

Comprensione scritta e orale

1 **Rileggi il capitolo e indica l'affermazione corretta.**

1   Dove è Lucio Silvi?

a ☐ In ufficio.

b ☐ Lungo la via Appia.

c ☐ Alla stazione.

2   Con chi è il professor Peltri?

a ☐ Con i figli.

b ☐ Con un gruppo di archeologi.

c ☐ Con i suoi studenti e con Aussone.

3   Cosa fanno gli studenti?

a ☐ Scattano foto.

b ☐ Leggono libri.

c ☐ Prendono appunti.

4   Cosa pensa Dino Aussone dell'investigatore Lucio Silvi?

a ☐ Che è un uomo pericoloso.

b ☐ Che non troverà mai l'assassino.

c ☐ Che è un uomo pigro.

5   Cosa chiede Lucio ad Aussone e Peltri?

a ☐ "Cosa avete mangiato in quel ristorante?"

b ☐ "Dove eravate l'altra sera alle ventitré?"

c ☐ "Conoscevate Mark Staub?"

6   Cosa succede al bar tra Aussone e Giovannelli?

a ☐ Scoppia una violenta lite e arriva la polizia.

b ☐ C'è una discussione sulla statua che Aussone non riesce a vendere.

c ☐ I due trovano un accordo e brindano.

2 Ascolta il capitolo e correggi gli errori contenuti nelle seguenti frasi.

1 Francesco Peltri e i suoi studenti camminano lungo la via Torino.

....

2 L'investigatore solleva il braccio e sventola un fazzoletto perché ha visto un uomo che conosce bene: Dino Aussone.

....

3 "Come va il trasloco?" chiede Francesco Peltri al detective Silvi.

....

4 "In macchina ho delle prove che darò alla polizia" annuncia Silvi.

....

5 "A proposito, cosa avete mangiato ieri sera?" chiede l'investigatore ai due uomini.

....

6 Peltri dichiara che era in un'aula dell'università con gli studenti.

....

Produzione scritta e orale

CELI 2

1 Racconta una gita scolastica descrivendo la partenza, il viaggio, i luoghi visitati, i compagni, il ritorno.

CELI 2

2 Immagina di essere una guida turistica. Come presenteresti la via Appia al gruppo di turisti che accompagni? Che cosa diresti dei Fori Imperiali, della scalinata di Trinità dei Monti, di Piazza Navona e della Fontana di Trevi?

Prima di leggere

1 Troverai queste parole nel capitolo 8. Associa ogni parola all'immagine corrispondente.

a lampada

b armadio

c sportello

d giacca

e matita

f pavimento

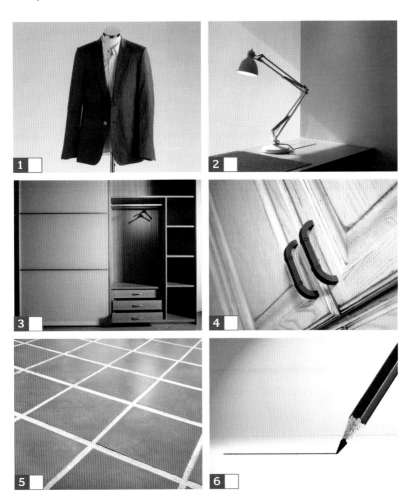

La via *Appia Antica*

Il sito archeologico di Minturno, lungo la via Appia Antica.

Oltre a visitare piazze e monumenti, a Roma può valere la pena di fare una gita lungo la via Appia Antica.

Costruita dai Romani, questa strada collegava Roma a Brindisi, il più importante porto per l'Oriente. La sua costruzione iniziò nel 312 a.C per volere del console Appio Claudio Cieco e continuò fino al 190 a.C. Gli imperatori Augusto, Vespasiano, Adriano e Traiano la allargarono e migliorarono, ma dopo la caduta dell'Impero Romano non fu più usata per secoli. Quel poco che oggi rimane si è conservato grazie all'istituzione, nel 1534, per volere di Papa Paolo III del Commissariato delle Antichità per la salvaguardia dei beni storici. Inoltre, nel 1777, Papa Pio VI ne fece restaurare una parte.

Attualmente è inserita nel Parco Naturale Regionale dell'Appia Antica e tocca le seguenti regioni: Lazio, Campania, Puglia e Basilicata.

Una delle torri del
Circo di Massenzio.

Caratteristiche

La via Appia antica è quasi sempre rettilinea. Larga circa 4 m, permetteva di circolare in entrambi i sensi. Già al tempo dei Romani si poteva percorrere anche a piedi, poiché era dotata di marciapiedi. Inoltre, oggi è possibile affittare una bicicletta e attraversare su due ruote una delle zone archeologiche più importanti d'Italia. Vi si trovano infatti molte tombe romane, terme, chiese e monumenti che raccontano la storia di Roma. I luoghi più frequentati sono: il circo di Massenzio, la tomba di Cecilia Metella, la villa dei Quintili.

La Villa dei Quintili.

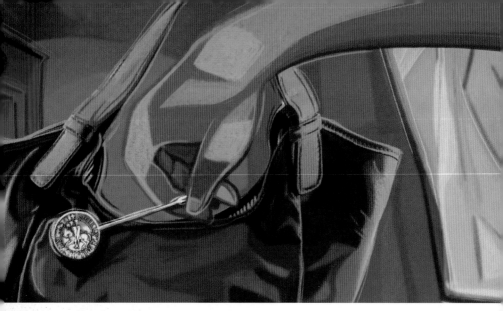

La prova decisiva

ue giorni dopo, Lucio Silvi trova l'ufficio nel caos più completo: schedari[1] a terra, scrivania rovesciata, armadio sfondato, cartellette e fogli dappertutto. L'investigatore sistema la sedia e la scrivania. Raccoglie da terra la lampada, le matite e le penne. Si siede e porta le mani alla fronte.

'Che disastro!' pensa.

Si guarda intorno e si chiede chi può essere entrato e che cosa volesse rubare, tanto più che nel suo ufficio non ci sono oggetti di valore. Un sospetto gli attraversa la mente, ma decide di pensarci più tardi e si alza per controllare se manca qualcosa. Anche il bagno è stato passato al setaccio[2]. Lo sportello dell'armadietto è aperto, il contenuto sparso pavimento. Però, a parte il tremendo disordine, non manca nulla.

1. **schedari** : archivi, mobili da ufficio.
2. **passato al setaccio** : controllato in ogni angolo.

'Senza Giusi ci vorrà un secolo per sistemare tutto. Quanto mi manca!' sospira.

Ad un tratto si dirige alla porta. La chiude. Scende le scale di corsa e, sempre di corsa, si dirige all'auto, perché sente di aver bisogno di lei, un grandissimo bisogno.

Mezz'ora più tardi l'investigatore è in ospedale. Giusi sta meglio, gli sorride. Dopo i saluti, gli chiede subito: "Come vanno le indagini sulla morte di Mark Staub?"

"La polizia non ha scoperto nulla" la informa Silvi.

"E tu? Hai qualche idea?"

"Ho dei sospetti, ma mi mancano le prove."

"Forse posso darti un elemento utile. Non te ne ho parlato prima perché stavo troppo male."

"Cosa?"

"Apri quella borsa, per favore" dice Giusi, indicando il tavolino su cui si trova la borsa.

Silvi la apre e trova una spilla. È una spilla maschile, da giacca. La guarda sorpreso e chiede: "Chi te l'ha data?"

"Nessuno" risponde Giusi, e aggiunge: "L'ho trovata ai Fori Imperiali."

"Quando?" chiede il detective. ·

"Qualche attimo prima del crollo..."

Silvi è pensieroso.

"Sai, il crollo non è stato un incidente" osserva Giusi.

"Perché?" chiede l'investigatore.

"Perché ho sentito un rumore, forte. Sembravano colpi di martello, qualcuno che colpiva il muro. E il suono veniva dall'alto. Ho alzato lo sguardo e... il muro è venuto giù."

"Anche la polizia sospetta un agguato" commenta lui. "Questa spilla forse è di chi ha tentato di ucciderti. Può essergli caduta mentre era sul posto..."

Giusi lo guarda sorpresa. Lei non aveva mai pensato a quella possibilità.

"Questo è un ottimo indizio, cara Giusi" dice Silvi e l'abbraccia. "Sento di essere sulla strada giusta."

Intanto il professor Peltri sta parlando dei prossimi esami con gli studenti che erano presenti alla festa di Aussone. "Non ci sono problemi, ragazzi, per l'esame. Come vi ho promesso le domande saranno alla vostra portata[3]..."

Un ragazzo mormora: "Con il regalo che gli stiamo facendo..."

"Che regalo?" chiede il compagno.

"Be' gli stiamo dando un alibi."

In quel momento il detective Silvi bussa alla porta.

"Scusi professore, sono qui per farle ancora delle domande. La disturbo?" dice entrando.

"No, abbiamo finito. I ragazzi possono restare?"

"Certo, forse mi possono aiutare. Può dirmi se la sera del delitto è sceso nel parco della villa?"

Peltri guarda i ragazzi e risponde: "Potete dirglielo voi dove ero e se ho lasciato la sala..."

Gli studenti esitano. Nessuno parla.

"Allora, parlate!" ordina il professore, con i nervi a fior di pelle[4], ma il silenzio invade l'ufficio.

"Sono sempre stato con loro, alla festa, nella sala dove si ballava..." dice il professore, e aggiunge: "Non è vero, ragazzi?"

Un debole "sì" giunge dopo un lungo silenzio. Troppo lungo.

---

3. **alla vostra portata** : molto facili.
4. **con i nervi a fior di pelle** : sul punto di esplodere, al massimo della tensione.

Comprensione scritta e orale

1 Rileggi il capitolo e indica l'affermazione corretta.

1 Lucio trova l'ufficio
   a ☐ in ordine.
   b ☐ in disordine.
   c ☐ arredato con mobili nuovi.

2 L'investigatore
   a ☐ chiama un falegname.
   b ☐ bagna i fiori.
   c ☐ sistema la sedia e la scrivania.

3 Giusi chiede a Lucio
   a ☐ come vanno le indagini.
   b ☐ se ha deciso di cambiare lavoro.
   c ☐ cosa gli hanno detto i medici.

4 Nella borsa di Giusi c'è
   a ☐ una spilla.
   b ☐ una lettera.
   c ☐ un portafoglio.

5 Giusi racconta di aver raccolto la spilla e di aver visto
   a ☐ un aereo.
   b ☐ un corvo.
   c ☐ il muro che crollava.

Competenze linguistiche

1 Indica il significato delle seguenti parole e espressioni.

1 *A soqquadro*
   a ☐ Sporco
   b ☐ In disordine
   c ☐ Con molti quadri

2 *Con i nervi a fior di pelle*
   a ☐ Senza vestiti
   b ☐ Con grande rabbia
   c ☐ Al massimo della tensione, sul punto di esplodere

3 *Alzare lo sguardo*
   a ☐ Essere molto orgoglioso
   b ☐ Guardare verso l'alto
   c ☐ Avere una meta difficile da raggiungere

4 *Volerci un secolo*
   a ☐ Avere una grande importanza storica
   b ☐ Costare molto denaro
   c ☐ Richiedere moltissimo tempo

Grammatica

I pronomi interrogativi

I pronomi interrogativi introducono una domanda diretta o indiretta.
Sono: **chi, che cosa, quale, quanto**.
Il pronome interrogativo **chi** è invariabile.
Che e **(Che) cosa** si usano indifferentemente, anche se la forma
completa **che cosa** è più formale e adatta al linguaggio scritto.

Chi di voi, ragazze, ha preso la valigia?
Non so chi abbia potuto dire una simile stupidaggine.
Che cosa hai detto?   Cosa farai da grande?   Che significa questo?

1 Inserisci nelle seguenti frasi i pronomi interrogativi corretti.

1 .... altro dobbiamo aspettare?
2 .... vuoi fare questo pomeriggio?
3 .... ha preso i fogli che erano su questo tavolo?
4 .... delle due preferisci? La torta con la crema o
   quella con il cioccolato?
5 .... ha detto queste cose?
6 .... vuoi per cena?
7 .... spendi al mese?
8 .... manca per arrivare al mare?

Produzione scritta e orale

CELI 2

1 Immagina di essere uno scrittore. Descrivi un ambiente in una pagina, un ufficio ad esempio. Concentrati sugli oggetti presenti nella stanza e sulla loro condizione. Prova a spiegare come essi ci 'parlino' del loro proprietario e di quello che fa.

CELI 2

2 Cerca di entrare nei panni di Lucio nel momento in cui scopre che i ladri sono entrati nel suo ufficio. Racconta ad un compagno, che farà la parte di un amico, quello che è successo e come ti sei senti.

Prima di leggere

1 Troverai queste parole nel capitolo 9. Associa ogni parola all'immagine corrispondente.

a carrozzella	**c** moneta	**e** corridoio
b bancarella	**d** cassetto	**f** dipinto

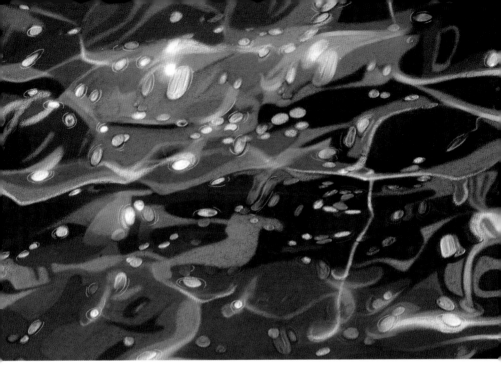

Ecco il movente!

I giorno seguente Lucio è alla Fontana di Trevi e la guarda incantato. L'acqua scorre ai piedi delle statue e alcune monete brillano sul fondo. Un gruppo di turisti si ferma ad ammirare e dei bambini giocano nella piazza. Una ragazza giapponese scatta delle foto a degli amici a bordo di una carrozzella a cavalli. In un angolo, alcune bancarelle vendono souvenirs della capitale, un'altra offre, invece, deliziosa frutta e verdura. C'è una grande allegria nell'aria: Roma è incantevole.

Lucio Silvi finge di essere un turista e butta una moneta nella fontana.

"Fammi trovare una prova" mormora. Poi va verso la Galleria d'arte di Dino Aussone, davanti alla piazza.

Il mercante è sorpreso. 'Quest'uomo inizia a essere un problema' pensa non appena lo vede.

"Caro Silvi, si accomodi" gli dice mostrandogli una comoda poltrona tra un antico dipinto e una statua di marmo. Gli sorride e intanto aspetta. 'Prima la polizia e ora questo ficcanaso[1]… Quando mai avrò un po' di pace?' riflette, inquieto.

Lucio gli chiede: "Può rispondere a qualche domanda, per favore?"

Nella sala vicina un telefono squilla. Aussone si alza per andare a rispondere. Anche Lucio si alza. A pochi passi ci sono una scrivania e un computer. Guardando il monitor l'investigatore legge un'email molto interessante… di cui memorizza subito il contenuto.

Sente dei passi nel corridoio e torna alla poltrona.

A Dino Aussone basta un'occhiata per capire di essere stato un ingenuo ad allontanarsi…

Qualche giorno dopo, una forte scampanellata fa correre alla porta il detective.

"Oh, commissario, che piacere vederla!" esclama Silvi, pensando che i poliziotti devono aver perso ogni speranza di catturare il colpevole.

Felisi sembra giù di morale. "Niente indizi, niente prove, brancoliamo nel buio[2]. Lei ha scoperto qualcosa?" chiede.

Lucio ha un'aria compiaciuta, perché il commissario è meno brusco del solito, e a quanto sembra ha davvero bisogno di lui. Però vuole togliersi la soddisfazione di farlo aspettare. Non risponde subito in maniera diretta alle domande sulle sue indagini, prende tempo.

---

1. **ficcanaso** : curioso, impiccione. Persona che si intromette nei fatti degli altri.
2. **brancoliamo nel buio** : ci muoviamo senza certezze e senza aver trovato nulla.

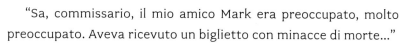

"Sa, commissario, il mio amico Mark era preoccupato, molto preoccupato. Aveva ricevuto un biglietto con minacce di morte..."

Alla fine il commissario perde la pazienza: "E lei cosa ha scoperto, oltre allo strano biglietto con minacce?" domanda.

L'altro apre un cassetto e gli mostra la spilla di Giusi.

"Ecco, la mia segretaria l'ha trovata ai Fori Imperiali, prima del crollo del muro."

Il commissario lo guarda stupito.

"Lo sa che questa è una grave negligenza[3] da parte sua? Doveva consegnarla subito alla polizia."

"Lo so, ma avevo bisogno di un po' di tempo per fare delle ricerche e scoprire il proprietario."

'Come, è anche riuscito a scoprire il proprietario della spilla? Ma chi è: Superman?' pensa tra sé Felisi.

"Vede, commissario" spiega il detective "queste sono spille speciali, sono onorificenze[4] date solo a illustri archeologi."

"Il professor Peltri!" esclama il commissario.

"Proprio lui!" ribatte Lucio. "E a questo punto, siccome ha un alibi, deve intervenire lei, commissario... Io non posso fare altro" conclude soddisfatto.

"Che genere di alibi?" chiede il commissario.

"I suoi studenti dichiarano di essere sempre stati con lui la notte in cui Mark Staub è stato ammazzato."

"Ah, un alibi inattaccabile" osserva il commissario.

"Sì, un alibi di ferro" dichiara il detective. "Mai io sospetto che il professore non sia molto onesto e che quell'alibi sia falso."

"Perché?" chiede l'altro.

---

3. **negligenza** : mancanza di attenzione; (qui) comportamento che va contro i propri doveri professionali.

4. **onorificenza** : riconoscimento, premio.

Ecco il movente!

"Il professore incontra ladri, delinquenti, persone note alla polizia... Non ha belle frequentazioni, insomma."

"I nomi, voglio i nomi!" urla il commissario.

"Fausto Giovannelli, per esempio. Ho trovato un messaggio nel computer di Aussone che lo collegava al professore..."

"Ah, Giovannelli, quel ladro!" commenta il commissario, e aggiunge: "Dove sono le prove?"

"Gliel'ho già detto: l'email è nel computer di Aussone, il mercante d'arte, il padrone della villa dove è avvenuto l'omicidio. Ho trovato nel messaggio notizie riguardanti Peltri, una statua d'oro, una vendita non avvenuta e infine un riferimento a molti soldi, una cifra notevole..."

"In conclusione, quindi" dice il commissario "Giovannelli ruba la statua, cerca di venderla a Mark Staub ma non ci riesce, la consegna ad Aussone. Anche lui cerca di venderla a Mark Staub, ma inutilmente. Poi Aussone cerca di venderla al professor Peltri, e anche lui rifiuta di comprare..."

"Sì, è così" afferma l'investigatore.

"Dunque, Mark Staub è stato ucciso dalla segretaria..." dice Felisi con una smorfia.

Silvi lo interrompe: "No, commissario. I camerieri mi hanno detto che la signorina Elisa non ha mai lasciato la sala quella sera."

"E l'orecchino?" chiede il commissario.

Silvi risponde pronto: "Qualcuno l'ha messo lì... Interroghi il professor Peltri. Le ripeto che secondo me ha un alibi falso. Uno studente mi ha detto che l'ha visto scendere nel parco, la sera del delitto. La spilla trovata ai Fori Imperiali è sua, e l'orecchino può averlo lasciato lui, vicino al corpo di Mark Staub."

CAPITOLO 9

Il commissario Felisi continua a non essere convinto. Tuttavia, ha cominciato a stimare molto il giovane collega e decide di tenere in considerazione i suoi suggerimenti e la sua ipotesi.

Qualche giorno dopo, Lucio Silvi cammina lungo Ponte Milvio. Le acque del Tevere, che scorre sotto il ponte, sono verde scuro. L'investigatore si sforza di ricordare qualche particolare importante. Ripensa ai protagonisti di quella storia e a come si sono svolti i fatti. Infine considera il professor Peltri.

'Non mi è mai piaciuto, fin dalla prima volta che l'ho incontrato. Ma quando è stata la prima volta?' si chiede.

All'improvviso gli tornano in mente le parole dell'amico Mark. Sì, Mark aveva litigato con l'archeologo qualche giorno prima di venire ucciso: l'aveva minacciato di rivelare da dove aveva copiato gli articoli. Questa minaccia doveva aver completamente sconvolto l'archeologo. In un ambiente come quello universitario, dove lui era da tanti anni una celebrità, un'accusa del genere avrebbe creato uno scandalo in grado di rovinare per sempre la sua carriera. E molto probabilmente anche la sua vita privata.

L'investigatore stringe i pugni e alza le braccia al cielo. È più che soddisfatto: ha trovato il movente e l'assassino.

Comprensione scritta e orale

1 **Rispondi alle seguenti domande.**

1 Che cosa ammira Lucio all'inizio del capitolo?
2 Chi c'è attorno a lui e com'è l'atmosfera?
3 Dove va Lucio, dopo essere stato alla Fontana di Trevi?
4 Cosa pensa Dino Aussone di Silvi?
5 Cosa vuol sapere Lucio da Dino Aussone?
6 Da chi riceve una visita Lucio e perché?
7 Cosa mostra Lucio al commissario Felisi?
8 Qual è la reazione del commissario?
9 Cosa pensa Lucio del professor Peltri?
10 Cosa succede alla fine del capitolo?

Competenze linguistiche

1 **Indica il significato delle seguenti parole ed espressioni.**

1 *Ficcanaso*
   a ☐ Curioso, invadente
   b ☐ Un oggetto per coprire il naso
   c ☐ Un giocattolo

2 *Scampanellata*
   a ☐ Suono di un campane
   b ☐ Suono di una sveglia
   c ☐ Suono di un campanello

3 *Brancolare nel buio*
   a ☐ Essere ciechi
   b ☐ Non avere una pista da seguire
   c ☐ Allungare le braccia

4   *Tornare in mente*

   a ☐ Tornare a casa

   b ☐ Tornare sui propri passi

   c ☐ Ricordare

5   *Compiaciuto*

   a ☐ Molto allegro, su di morale

   b ☐ Soddisfatto, contento di sé

   c ☐ Presuntuoso

Produzione scritta e orale

CELI 2

❶ **Immagina di avere un blog dove scrivi di viaggi. Intervista alcuni compagni su questo argomento. Poi scrivi un breve articolo.**

Tieni presenti i seguenti aspetti:

- mete preferite
- mezzi di trasporto
- lingue conosciute e interessi culturali
- sistemazioni prescelte (campeggio, hotel, ospitalità presso amici etc).

CELI 2

❷ **Visiterai Roma in estate. Cosa metti in valigia? Dove cercherai notizie sui monumenti e sui luoghi da vedere? Cosa ti interessa di più? Raccontalo per iscritto oppure parlane con un compagno.**

Puoi inoltre prendere in considerazione questi aspetti:

- cucina locale e ristoranti famosi
- parchi e ville degni di interesse
- eventi importanti che si svolgono a Roma nel periodo estivo
- località adatte a gite fuori porta.

Prima di leggere

1 Troverai queste parole nel capitolo 10. Associa ogni parola all'immagine corrispondente.

a trattoria

b busta

c patatine fritte

d medaglia

e pubblico

f assegno

Tradito da un biglietto

"La spilla, caro professore, ci dice che è stato lei a far crollare il muro ai Fori Imperiali..."

Sono le quattro del mattino, e da ore il commissario interroga il professor Peltri.

"L'avrò persa durante una delle mie tante visite ai Fori, in un giorno qualsiasi..." dice con voce debole il professore.

"No, non è così. C'è stata molta pioggia questo mese, ma la spilla non era nemmeno sporca di terra, quindi lei l'ha persa da poco. E ci risulta che ultimamente lei è stato ai Fori solo nel giorno in cui è crollato il muro che ha investito la signorina Rosso..."

Il commissario fissa il professore. 'Non confessa, è troppo furbo' pensa. Poi, ad un tratto ricorda: Mark Staub aveva trovato qualcosa e si era rivolto a Lucio Silvi. Ma cosa aveva trovato?

Appoggia la mano sulla scrivania e un foglio cade a terra. Il commissario lo guarda sorpreso, poi ha un'intuizione.

"Il biglietto! Il biglietto!" urla e continua: "Il biglietto di minacce ricevuto da Mark Staub ha la sua calligrafia [1], non può negarlo! E comunque ci aiuteranno le analisi sulle impronte digitali e gli accertamenti scientifici del caso, ne può star certo!"

Il professore, tradito da questa intuizione di Felisi, scoppia a piangere e confessa: "Sì, l'ho ucciso io, voleva rovinarmi, dire che avevo copiato gli articoli, che non valevo niente come studioso. Ero terrorizzato al pensiero del disonore, della perdita del lavoro, di mia moglie, dei miei figli... Dovevo farlo tacere per sempre..."

Una settimana dopo, in una trattoria di Trastevere, Felisi e Silvi gustano sereni un piatto di spaghetti. Dopo la soluzione del caso, sono passati al 'tu' e, a guardarli pranzare insieme, sembrano due vecchi amici.

"C'erano poche prove" dice il commissario.

"Poche, ma sufficienti ad arrivare alla soluzione" ribatte l'investigatore.

"È vero, però è stata la fortuna ad aiutarmi. Vedi, il professor Peltri è crollato quando gli ho detto che la calligrafia del biglietto con le minacce a Mark Staub era la sua. E non ne ero certo, ho solo provato a indovinare. Quel Peltri è davvero un uomo molto ambizioso e furbo" commenta il commissario.

"Certo, l'idea di usare l'orecchino di Elisa come una prova contro di lei dimostra quanto Peltri sia furbo" aggiunge Silvi.

"Un caso fatto di piccole cose: un biglietto, una spilla, un orecchino..." afferma il commissario.

"Dimentichi il mio ufficio messo a soqquadro, e questa non è

---

1. **calligrafia** : scrittura a mano.

una piccola cosa. Peltri deve aver cercato la spilla anche lì" osserva l'investigatore.

"Probabile. Penso che abbia capito di essere in trappola quando si è accorto di averla persa."

Dopo gli spaghetti il cameriere porta in tavola un meraviglioso abbacchio alla romana[2]. "Vi porto subito le patate fritte" annuncia.

"Bene, caro collega" aggiunge il detective.

Il commissario gli sorride.

"Avrai un premio" annuncia.

"Quale premio?" domanda Lucio, stupito.

"Non hai riconsegnato tu la statua del dio Apollo?"

"Be', certo. Ma non mi aspettavo un premio."

"Non fingere! Sai benissimo che c'è una grossa somma di denaro per chi la riconsegna. Ora mi vuoi dire da chi l'hai avuta?"

Silvi si riempie la bocca di patatine fritte. Non può fare nomi: questi sono i patti con Dino Aussone. Il mercante d'arte gli ha dato la statua, ma vuole essere dimenticato. Nessuno deve fare il suo nome. La statua è invendibile e lui non vuole guai. Quindi ha trovato chi la restituirà...

Qualche mese dopo Lucio Silvi stringe la mano alle autorità comunali, riceve una medaglia e una busta con un assegno davanti al pubblico riunito in una grande sala. Tutti applaudono.

"Questo è un premio a un uomo onesto, che ha ridato a Roma una bellissima statua, simbolo del suo passato" dice uno degli assessori. L'investigatore è emozionato, guarda soddisfatto la medaglia e sorride alla sua segretaria, in prima fila tra i presenti. Lei ricambia il sorriso e spera che Lucio finalmente...

---

2. **abbacchio alla romana** : tipico piatto romano, a base di carne d'agnello, che si prepara soprattutto a Pasqua.

Comprensione scritta e orale

1 **Metti in ordine gli avvenimenti.**

a ☐ Lucio Silvi pranza con il commissario Felisi.

b ☐ Il commissario Felisi interroga Peltri.

c ☐ Il padrone della trattoria porta in tavola le patatine fritte.

d ☐ Silvi riceve una medaglia e una busta dalle autorità cittadine.

e ☐ Il commissario Felisi dice a Peltri di avere un biglietto con la sua calligrafia.

f ☐ Giusi ricambia il sorriso di Lucio.

g ☐ Tutti applaudono.

2 **Indica l'alternativa corretta.**

1 Il commissario Felisi interroga

  a ☐ Giusi Rosso.

  b ☐ Fausto Giovannelli.

  c ☐ Francesco Peltri.

2 Lucio Silvi e il commissario Felisi pranzano

  a ☐ in un ristorante di via Condotti.

  b ☐ nel bar di una stazione.

  c ☐ in una trattoria di Trastevere.

3 Il commissario Felisi dice a Silvi

  a ☐ che dovrebbe prendersi una vacanza.

  b ☐ che ha fatto bene a cambiare ufficio.

  c ☐ che riceverà un premio.

4 Lucio Silvi

  a ☐ stringe la mano a chi gli dà il premio.

  b ☐ sale sul treno per Genova.

  c ☐ entra in un'agenzia di viaggi.

Grammatica

Le congiunzioni

Le congiunzioni servono ad unire tra loro parole e frasi. Possono essere semplici o composte. Quelle semplici sono formate da una sola parola: **e, né, o, ma, che, se, però, dunque, anzi, mentre.**

Le congiunzioni composte sono costituite da due o più parole unite. Le più comuni sono: **perché, finché, eppure, infatti.**

CELI 2

1 Completa le frasi con la congiunzione semplice opportuna.

1 Il commissario Felisi sorride a Silvi .... gli racconta dell'interrogatorio di Peltri.

2 "Non voleva confessare" gli dice Felisi "............. io l'ho costretto a farlo."

3 Il commissario continua a parlare: "............. è stato molto difficile."

4 "............. lo interrogavo, mi sono ricordato del biglietto ricevuto da Mark Staub."

5 "............. non confessa ora, non confesserà mai più, ho pensato" dichiara Felisi.

6 "Il professor Peltri non è stato .... furbo .... attento" commenta Silvi.

CELI 2

2 Completa le frasi con la congiunzione composta opportuna.

1 "Non è stato un caso semplice" commenta il commissario Felisi "............. c'erano solo indizi e poche prove."

2 "............." dice Silvi "Peltri ha fatto tanti errori."

3 "Hai ragione. .... solo uno sciocco poteva pensare di sfuggire alla giustizia" osserva il commissario.

4 "............. farò l'investigatore, darò importanza ai piccoli indizi."

Prima di leggere

1 Troverai queste parole nel capitolo 11. Associa ogni parola all'immagine corrispondente.

a torta nuziale   d foglie

b cornetta   e calice

c campagna   f pelle

Viva gli sposi!

opo un'estate molto calda è giunto un settembre fresco.
I parchi di Roma sono pieni di foglie gialle e rosse. Il
sole illumina il pavimento di marmo del nuovo ufficio di
Lucio Silvi, che ora siede su una poltrona di vera pelle. Le
librerie alle sue spalle sono di legno pregiato. Nell'ufficio
ci sono anche un divano, un tavolino e delle poltrone per i
clienti. Tutto è nuovo ed elegante. L'investigatore ha molti clienti.
Il telefono squilla in continuazione.

Lucio solleva la cornetta per fare una telefonata, ma la posa sulla
scrivania appena vede entrare Giusi. Le va incontro e l'abbraccia.

"Allora, cara, hai provato l'abito?" le chiede.

Un mese dopo, nel parco di un bel ristorante, gli invitati si
affollano attorno ai tavoli apparecchiati. Il pranzo per festeggiare
il matrimonio di Lucio e Giusi è ottimo. Tutti sono contenti e allegri.

Sono stati invitati anche alcuni studenti.

"Non potevamo non aiutarlo" dice un ragazzo a una biondina in un elegante vestito azzurro.

Lei ribatte: "Aiutarlo a fare cosa?"

"A indebolire l'alibi del professore."

"Ah! È vero. Lui ha capito che mentivamo."

"Sono andato dal detective e gli ho detto che il professore era sceso nel parco, verso le undici di sera…"

"Allora sei stato tu a far crollare il suo alibi?"

"Sì, sono stato io" ammette il ragazzo.

"Bravo, hai fatto bene!" esclama la ragazza, e lo trascina al tavolo dei dolci.

Intanto Lucio Silvi e la moglie tagliano la torta nuziale fra gli applausi dei presenti. I bicchieri tintinnano. "Viva gli sposi! Viva gli sposi!" gridano tutti.

La musica raggiunge i prati e i pini. Molti ballano.

Dino Aussone parla con il commissario.

"Ci sono stati altri furti di opere d'arte?" chiede il mercante.

"No, i furti sono finiti, per ora… Giovannelli, il più astuto ladro internazionale, è stato finalmente arrestato" risponde il commissario e aggiunge: "Grazie a Silvi abbiamo trovato un ladro e un assassino…"

"Davvero bravo il nostro Silvi!" commenta Aussone e pensa: 'Sono stato molto fortunato; è stato leale e non ha detto nulla su di me.'

"Bravo, onesto e intelligente!" aggiunge il commissario.

Lucio e Giusi sollevano i loro calici e sorridono. Poi guardano la via Appia antica, che si snoda fra il verde. La campagna romana splende in tutta la sua dolcezza.

Comprensione scritta e orale

1 Ascolta il capitolo e rispondi alle seguenti domande.

1 In che mese siamo?
2 Com'è il nuovo ufficio dell'investigatore Silvi?
3 Qual è l'evento più importante del capitolo?
4 Cosa ha fatto uno studente per indebolire l'alibi di Peltri?
5 Chi partecipa al ricevimento?
6 Cosa pensa ora Dino Aussone di Lucio Silvi?

Competenze linguistiche

1 Indica l'alternativa corretta.

1 Lucio è
   a ☐ bravo e onesto.
   b ☐ disattento.
   c ☐ furbo.
2 Giusi è
   a ☐ una sposa felice.
   b ☐ una brava madre.
   c ☐ una casalinga impegnata.
3 Il commissario Felisi è
   a ☐ contento.
   b ☐ arrabbiato.
   c ☐ infelice.
4 Gli studenti sono
   a ☐ allegri.
   b ☐ annoiati.
   c ☐ in preda alla paura per gli esami.
5 Il finale del giallo è
   a ☐ lieto.
   b ☐ tragico.
   c ☐ malinconico.

1 **Leggi queste frasi e scrivi sotto a ciascuna il nome del personaggio che secondo te può averla pronunciata.**

1   Ho problemi con i soldi. Non mi basta lo stipendio.

   ....

2   Sono molto disordinato, ma sono un bravo investigatore.

   ....

3   Sono innamorata di lui, ma non sembra accorgersi di me.

   ....

4   Roma mi ha portato tanta sfortuna.

   ....

5   Sono noto alla polizia per i miei furti.

   ....

6   La mia galleria d'arte è famosa.

   ....

7   Ho agito per paura di essere smascherato e ora sono nei guai.

   ....

8   Peltri ha confessato grazie al mio interrogatorio.

   ....

2 **Sei un blogger. Devi presentare *Mistero a Roma* a chi ti segue nel blog. Scrivi il tuo post in venti righe.**

Includi questi aspetti:

· presentazione dei personaggi

· riassunto della trama

· commenti e motivazioni che incoraggino alla lettura del testo.

3 **Indica cosa succede a questi personaggi nel corso della storia. Più di una risposta può essere possibile.**

1 Lucio Silvi
   a ☐ diventa ricco.
   b ☐ si sposa.
   c ☐ diventa povero.

2 Elisa
   a ☐ perde il suo datore di lavoro, Mark Staub.
   b ☐ si dispera perché viene accusata di omicidio.
   c ☐ fugge da Roma.

3 Mark Staub
   a ☐ viene ucciso.
   b ☐ acquista una statua romana.
   c ☐ torna negli Stati Uniti.

4 Giusi Rosso
   a ☐ si sposa con Lucio Silvi.
   b ☐ litiga con l'investigatore.
   c ☐ trova un altro lavoro.

5 Dino Aussone
   a ☐ fa buoni affari.
   b ☐ viene aiutato da Lucio Silvi.
   c ☐ riceve delle minacce.

6 Fausto Giovannelli
   a ☐ viene catturato dalla polizia.
   b ☐ fugge all'estero.
   c ☐ si nasconde a Roma.

7 Francesco Peltri
   a ☐ diventa un noto archeologo.
   b ☐ uccide il direttore di un museo.
   c ☐ finisce in prigione.

8 Il commissario Felisi
   a ☐ riceve un aumento di stipendio.
   b ☐ è contento perché l'assassino è in prigione.
   c ☐ collabora con Lucio Silvi.